ADVANCE PRAISE FOR

Justice in Search of Leaders

"*Justice in Search of Leaders: A Handbook for Equity-Driven School Leadership* should be required reading for every teacher, administrator, and psychologist, no matter how many degrees they possess. In a nutshell, this is what it's all about—that when we talk of ignorance about 'race', what we're actually talking about is skin color. I hope that this remarkable book will cause its readers to see the world in an entirely different way, and to appreciate their fellow human beings as they never have before. Until we rid ourselves of the belief in several different races, and begin to realize, recognize, and admit we are all members of the same race, the *human* race, we will continue to treat others in less than human ways. In denying the humanity of others, we dehumanize ourselves."

—Jane Elliott, Creator of the Blue Eyes–Brown Eyes Exercise;
Internationally-Known Teacher, Lecturer, and Diversity Trainer

"Gloria Graves Holmes provides a passionate and clearly reasoned case for placing racial equity and social justice at the heart of any school change efforts. She challenges school administrators and teacher leaders to a higher calling for our work—not merely closing gaps and moving data points, but deconstructing the arrangements of social dominance that are the deeper causes of racial disparities. Holmes' lifetime of research and activism shines through in every chapter."

—Gary R. Howard, Author of We Can't Teach What We Don't Know;
Founder, The REACH Center for Multicultural Education;
Civil Rights Activist and Tireless Advocate for Social Justice
and Educational Equity

Justice in Search
of Leaders

Dear Gary,

Your work has influenced me more than you'll ever know, and your collegiality and generosity of spirit is deeply moving —

Jorge

7/28/18

Studies in Criticality

Shirley R. Steinberg
General Editor

Vol. 516

The Counterpoints series is part of the Peter Lang Education list.
Every volume is peer reviewed and meets
the highest quality standards for content and production.

PETER LANG
New York • Bern • Berlin
Brussels • Vienna • Oxford • Warsaw

Gloria Graves Holmes

Justice in Search of Leaders

A Handbook for Equity-Driven School Leadership

PETER LANG
New York • Bern • Berlin
Brussels • Vienna • Oxford • Warsaw

Library of Congress Cataloging-in-Publication Data

Names: Holmes, Gloria Graves, author.
Title: Justice in search of leaders: a handbook for equity-driven
school leadership / Gloria Graves Holmes, Ph.D.
Description: New York: Peter Lang, 2018.
Series: Counterpoints: studies in criticality; v. 516 | ISSN 1058-1634
Includes bibliographical references and index.
Identifiers: LCCN 2017037207 | ISBN 978-1-4331-2721-2 (pbk.: alk. paper)
ISBN 978-1-4331-2722-9 (hardcover: alk. paper)
ISBN 978-1-4331-4860-6 (ebook pdf)
ISBN 978-1-4331-4861-3 (epub) | ISBN 978-1-4331-4862-0 (mobi)
Subjects: LCSH: Educational leadership—United States. |
Educational equalization—United States. | Discrimination
in education—United States.
Classification: LCC LB2805.H6244 2018 | DDC 371.2—dc23
LC record available at https://lccn.loc.gov/2017037207
DOI 10.3726/b11812

Bibliographic information published by **Die Deutsche Nationalbibliothek.**
Die Deutsche Nationalbibliothek lists this publication in the "Deutsche
Nationalbibliografie"; detailed bibliographic data are available
on the Internet at http://dnb.d-nb.de/.

The paper in this book meets the guidelines for permanence and durability
of the Committee on Production Guidelines for Book Longevity
of the Council of Library Resources.

© 2018 Peter Lang Publishing, Inc., New York
29 Broadway, 18th floor, New York, NY 10006
www.peterlang.com

Printed in the United States of America

CONTENTS

TABLES

ACKNOWLEDGEMENTS

We can never know where inspiration will come from; never know whether or not the next door we open will bring us into light or darkness, or into a space that will cause our spirits to grow, even flower, or shrivel and die slowly. My inspiration and support for this book came from many sources, and some I will forget to remember, so please forgive me if you played a role in either inspiring or supporting me, and I forget to acknowledge you formally. Just know that this journey has been an extraordinary one for me, and that my heart is filled with gratitude for all of you who have offered support in overt demonstrable ways, or who tacitly wished me well.

Even though I know that the impulse to address the issues I cover in the book were germinating since I was a small child, I know that I was inspired to make a formal commitment to write about leadership and social justice during the year I spent as a fellow in the Community Leadership Program in New Haven, CT. This program was the brainchild of Bill Graustein, who heads the William C. Graustein Memorial Fund, which serves as a think tank, funder, convener, and resource for anti-bias training, community leadership, and capacity building. The *heart* and *heatbeat* of all of this is Bill Graustein, who is my hero. Mine is only one of the countless lives he touched in profound, life-changing ways. Bill's generosity and commitment to social justice

X JUSTICE IN SEARCH OF LEADERS

and equity education is transforming the face of CT in ways that can never be quantified. Thank you Bill.

Once I knew that I would and could write a book, and that it would be a book about school leadership and social justice, I began to pay attention differently to the experienced leaders around me. Among other things, I realized how much I did not know. And, early in the process, I turned to my former colleague at Quinnipiac University, Gary Alger, who patiently read my first attempts at developing some coherence around these complex subjects. Using the lens of his deep experience as a professor and administrator, Gary helped me clarify and articulate what I was thinking. Thank you Gary.

Years into the process, after I had sifted through dozens of articles and books, I came across a small book, *Renewing Struggles for Social Justice, A Primer for Transformative Leaders* (2008), that helped me reframe my thinking about justice and leadership. Instead of thinking about justice as a static, lifeless thing as embodied in the *Statue of Liberty* and the blindfolded *Lady Justice*, this book helped me see justice as something that *just is*; animated, vibrant, engaged and regenerative. It informed how I conceptualized justice, and it inspired my title.

I would like to acknowledge and thank my colleagues at Quinnipiac University's School of Education. More than colleagues, they are part of my *family*, and they helped keep me sane. They put up with my eccentricities, and never stopped loving me or supporting me no matter how difficult I was. I arrived at the School of Education (formerly the Division of Education) as an only child, but left with two sisters, Susan Clarke, and Anne Dichele, and a brother, Mordechai Gordon. Together, we survived and stayed whole through many unnerving challenges, and we shaped a small world in which a belief in equity and justice prevailed over all of our differences because we knew they were more important that skin pigment or cultural, ethnic, or experiential differences. And, I must give a special thank you to Mordechai, the most prolific writer among us. His astounding generosity helped us all become better scholars.

Quinnipiac also gave me Marilyn Ford, a colleague, friend, advisor, role model, and sister. Described as a force of nature, Marilyn's energy and commitment to caring for, and serving others is uplifting, and I'm a much better person, because of her.

Thank you Becky Abbott for being my friend and confidante, for bringing light into the sometimes dark spaces that surrounded me, for always being a willing listener, and for your wise counsel.

I want to thank my unofficial readers, Thom Brown, Robert (Bob) Acevedo, and Claudette Parker. These are friends, whom I love, who had no professional obligation to help, but they always did, with sensitivity, intelligence and honesty. And, Claudette is a sister/friend whom I loved before we ever met; she gave me the comfort of knowing that she was always there for me, no matter what.

Edward Porter, a friend, and early contributor provided support, and the benefit of his vast knowledge and experience as an administrator and trainer, and he guided my thinking in the early stages of this project. Thank you Ed.

In ways that I could never have anticipated, moving to CT to join the faculty at Quinnipiac University, prepared me to write *this* book. In CT, I was welcomed into a vibrant community of diversity educators that expanded and deepened my understanding of how bias and discrimination were undermining equity in schools, and sharpened my commitment to being an advocate for social justice. In this regard, I would like to thank my colleagues and friends at the Anti-Defamation League, especially Marji Lipshez-Shapiro, whose lifelong fight for social justice was a model for me. This community also gave me mentors and friends like Bill Howe, Jack Hasegawa and Thom Brown.

There is a special thank you for Eugene Marsh, a tech genius, who generously provided tech support time and time again when my aging computer threatened to defeat me and destroy my sanity.

I also would like to remember, and thank those people who gave me support long before I began writing this book. They are no longer here in body but their spirits will always remain a part of my conscious being. My sister/friend Madeline did not survive to see this book completed, but her humor, and constant love and encouragement still feel like a warm embrace; she taught me that friendship has no season, and no beginning or end. Rose Zimbardo, my professor, mentor, friend and coach was the consummate teacher. She told me once that she would never stop teaching. Even if she 'retired,' she said, if necessary, she would stop people on the street and *teach* them. Rose was a role model for me, and she never stopped believing in me. How does one quantify that? *Saint Rose* was one of the smartest, most caring people I ever knew, and she changed my life. It saddens me that she won't get a chance to read and critique my book.

My friend and colleague, Kevin Basmadjian, is not here to read my book, but I smile when I remember his caring leadership, and his *light*, and his compassion, and his generous spirt, and his unfailing support for my work.

And what can I say about my family? We tend to think that they have to love and support us, but really, they don't, so I take neither their love nor support for granted. My mother, Thelma Hicks, will be 92 when this book is published, and it fills me with joy and gratitude to know that she will experience this with me. At 92, she is still the strongest, most generous person I know, and she has taught me the power and beauty of unconditional love. My oldest daughter, Lalise, did not live to share this moment with me, but her survival for many years against great odds was, and still is, an inspiration for me. She taught me many lessons about courage and strength. She always believed in me, as I believed in her.

My daughter Luana, has been a partner, a friend and a sister, and we have fought in many wars shoulder to shoulder. I used to say that in a fight, I wanted her in back of me. Now, I say, in a fight, I want her in front of me, because she's been my shield so often.

Support from my granddaughters, Brandi and Marjani means so much, and Jayda's silly humor and loving touch has lifted my spirit so many times, and kept me writing. My great grandson Javion is only seven, and he does not know that he reminds me why I must continue to care about the plight of black boys who are being forced to carry an intolerable weight in this society because they are Black.

My brilliant millennial granddaughter Jazmin is a kindred spirit, and she has often inspired me with her wit, and her wisdom that is far beyond her years. So often, she has read and critiqued my writing, and sometimes, with scathing honesty, she has shown me a different and important perspective that I would have missed. Jazmin, the image of you is forever inside me.

I would like to thank Michael Carr, my pastor at Central Church in Hilton Head, SC who has provided a religious lens for my scholarship, and has shown me how to bridge the sacred and the secular in ways that continue to inspire my writing.

I must also acknowledge those people, who at important transitional moments in my life intentionally tried to block my progress. Instead of encouraging me to soar, they tried to anchor me to the ground, even bury me. They did not succeed. They tried to discourage me from reaching my academic or career goals, and tried to undermine my self-esteem, and dis-empower me. They did not succeed. Their efforts had the reverse effect. Inadvertently, they motivated me to work harder, focus more, challenge myself, and never give up. In an odd way, the completion of this book is also a tribute to them.

Finally, I would like to thank God for making me, me.

PREFACE

I've been Black all of my life, and in some respects, this book is a substation in a long journey to interpret what that means. I'm Black *and* black, an American, an African American, a woman, a mother, and a teacher; a product of Harlem, a Long Island suburb, and a Pentecostal church; a former high school drop-out, and a PhD. All of these identities coalesced in the writing of this book.

Several months ago, when I began thinking about a preface and the strong impulses that drove me to write *this* book, I remembered two incidents in my life, separated by about three decades. And yet, despite the difference in time and place, these incidents seemed like mirror images. The first happened when I was a girl-child living in Harlem, and the second happened when I was a professional, home-owning woman living in a largely white Long Island suburb.

At the age of nine or ten, as I stood on a corner in NYC waiting for the stoplight to change, a white man in a car stopped in front of me. Unprovoked by anything that I had said or done, he began to yell angrily, "Why don't you go back to Africa!!!" He then drove off. It was a stunning and confusing moment that I've never forgotten. I didn't understand why this stranger was screaming angrily at me, or why my very existence seemed to infuriate him.

The second incident occurred about thirty years later, when I was a professional educator, and a well-established suburbanite shopping in my own Long Island neighborhood. I had parked my car on one side of the street, and decided to cross the street to shop in a store on the other side. Before I could cross, a white man driving-by pulled-up in front of me and asked, "Can I give you a ride to Wyandanch?" Wyandanch wasn't Africa, but it was a nearby city that had a population that was about 90% black.

The second time, I was slightly surprised, but I was not confused.

Reflecting on these two incidents brought other disturbing memories to the surface; memories that I've strung together over time; memories that form a pattern that has informed my experience as a Black, and as a woman living in the world's greatest democracy.

I was a thoughtful and precocious child, and I remember embracing, even internalizing the romanticization of the American past, and loving, and being inspired by, stories of the triumphs of hardy European pioneers trekking across the American plains to make new lives for themselves in someone else's home. To me, a little dark girl growing up in Harlem, they were all 'giants in the earth,' and their 'conquest' of the west seemed heroic and right. It never occurred to me that they were trekking over, and appropriating someone else's land, or that their history trampled mine. My schools and my teachers, most of whom were White, reinforced these ideas, and since I loved my schools and I loved my teachers (most of them), as a child, I instinctively believed and trusted them; they were among the most important and influential adults in my life. I was taught to respect them, so trust came naturally. I trusted them to tell me the truth about American history. I trusted them to explain where I, and my little black and brown classmates, fit into the American story.

And yet, I distinctly remember that there came a time when I began to question what Ron Takaki called the *master narrative* that was an integral part of my *daily bread*. On some subconscious level, I understood that I lived in what Toni Morrison has called a 'wholly racialized society' long before I had any clear idea what this meant or how it would shape my life. Race, and racism and the tension around blackness versus whiteness always swirled around me; it was like the *smog* Beverly Daniel Tatum described that had the effect of robbing her of her innocence as a child. I felt this, too. It was like a toxin that was diminishing me and the quality of my life with every breath I took.

I also remember that when I was in the fifth grade, I learned what it felt like to be invisible. Intuitively, I understood at that early age what Ellison was describing when he said, "*I am invisible, understand, simply because people refuse to see me … they see only my surroundings, themselves, or figments of their imagination—indeed, everything and anything except me."*

One day when my white social studies teacher spent an entire class period listing the accomplishments and contributions of *all* of the different cultural groups that made America a great nation, I learned a lesson that he never taught and I never forgot. Even though he was facing a room full of black fifth graders who were engaged and intent, he wasn't seeing us at all. He was oblivious to our reality, or our value and significance as part of the American story other than as the detritus left from America's dark slave past. This is what I now believe.

In this class, we learned of the exploits and accomplishments of Europeans who were becoming Americans. They were British and French, Dutch and Italian, and Norwegian and Spanish, and they all produced heroic and memorable people who were presented to us as larger than life. Seemingly, as an aside, we learned about George Washington Carver, a former slave, our *Black* hero, the *peanut man*. At the time, experimenting with peanuts didn't sound like much, and Carver wasn't presented as particularly significant or heroic like those who were discovering new land, finding gold, surviving blizzards, or winning battles in war.

Years later, when I became an educator, I learned that there is a distinct difference between what a teacher thinks she's teaching, and what students actually learn. I now understand that my fifth grade social studies teacher taught me lessons that continue to resonate, and in many ways, they serve as the foundation for this book.

* * *

Writing about race and racism, Blackness and Whiteness, oppression and power and privilege, advantage and disadvantage, and justice and injustice in the context of school leadership is difficult, especially when you want to leave readers feeling hopeful. Writing about these things reminds me of a line spoken by Marlon Brando in the movie, *Apocalypse Now*; it had something to do with trying to walk and balance yourself on the sharp edge of a razor blade.

It's difficult to convince readers that you are trying to sound hopeful when the subjects are bias, discrimination and prejudice. And even though the title, *Justice in Search of Leaders*, is explicitly about *justice*, which is *hopeful*, the title is also implicitly about *injustice*, which can trigger a sense of *hopelessness*.

And yet, when you think about it, democracy and hopelessness should never coexist because 'democracy' in its purest sense implies a relentless, unyielding challenge to hopelessness.

As I wrote the book, I began to realize how often I came back to the idea of the *promise* of American Democracy, and how this promise shapes American education; every day, American schoolchildren pledge to uphold this *promise*. The word 'promise' is future-oriented and this is a good thing, especially when we think of it in the context of the deeply embedded American values of fairness and fair-play. To me, the *promise* of Democracy means that our democratic nation is evolving, because it must, and that America is, and has always been, in the process of *becoming* America. Maxine Greene expressed this best when she said "... *democracy is, and has been, an open possibility, not a possession.*"

However, no matter where you are on the human spectrum of race, color or culture, you will likely respond viscerally to the subjects of discrimination and race. And when these subjects come up, most want to crawl out of the room through the back door, or shrink into their skin or do anything to get lost, as long as they don't have to confront these sensitive subjects, particularly in mixed-race settings.

And this is why courageous school leadership matters. Courageous leadership matters because it is courageous to talk about race. This is not a process meant to make people feel good, or placate one person's ego or rub another's the wrong way. It does take courage, and honesty and hopefulness, and more honesty, and more courage, and a great deal of honest self-reflection and self-awareness. Being a brave, self-critical truth-seeker is not easy because it means having a willingness to talk back to power. And, being a brave, self-critical truth-seeker is not easy when you are the power-broker, and are responsible for leading others. Being a brave, self-critical truth-seeker is not easy because it means being realistic, and patient, and persistent, and tough and tender. Being a brave, self-critical truth-seeker is not easy because it may mean developing the strength and courage to isolate yourself even from those you love, and who are connected to you by blood, or by class, or by culture; it means making a commitment to doing the right thing because it is the right thing even if you become a target, and because as Audre Lord reminded us, our evasion, or *silence will not protect us.*

I MUST HAVE BEEN MISTAKEN

Shaylah McQueen-Lee[1]

Is it just you or I that walks with two feet, that click and clack on the concrete?
Is it your kind—or my kind that gives off that beat—that beating sound that seems to
protrude through the very walls of our skin?
Well, I must have been mistaken ... because I thought we both had beating hearts,
I'm sorry

What can a fair toned figure and a colored skinned figure actually have in common?
You have blue eyes, I have brown eyes
I have black tears while you shed white cries
Really, I must have been mistaken ... I must have been color blind because I could
have sworn our tears shared the same color, same taste, same feeling

Is it just you or I who has been mistaken? Did you or did I ever face discrimination
or prejudice?
It is both of us—**US, WE** as humans have been ignorant of our total being- We went
looking for a beautiful and mysterious world without seeing

BECAUSE we grew up in a world that taught **US** to look at the wrong things—we
chose to complain and look with disgust at the mocking bird who chirped and choked
uncontrollably
instead of wondering why the poor bird could not sing

1. Shaylah McQueen-Lee is an educator, poet and social activist residing in New Haven, CT: shaylah-mcqueen.ydp@gmail.com

In fact, we knew why this poor creature could no longer possess the sweet sound of victory and harmonious integrity but we failed to put our pride and hatred aside
We failed to be the people that we said our country was made out to be: **The Land of The free, of Liberty, and of Justice for ALL.ALL.ALL**

Instead of allowing diversity to expand our love, cooperation, and inspiration for one another, we allowed it to let us as a whole, as a country, fall
Well I refuse to be mistaken any longer
Because I know that the very attributes that makes us different, though seen as weaknesses in some ways, can and will make us stronger

How, you say? Because we are people: we have arms; though yours-white, mine-brown
The minute we create links by locking our arms and holding our ground- **THEN BOOM!! <u>Our</u> true strength is found!**
Found in the very words we use-that may burn down the bridges we create between each other, yet can in turn be seen as tools, that is if we don't refuse
to mend any broken connection- despite the rejection- we are each other's protection
In order for you to see what I see, you must replace your pupils with chambers of your heart
Because once we are able to view each other as brethren and as re-united family members then

NO One-and-No Thing ...
can tear the love that we discover for one another apart

OUR LOVE
would be glowing out of the sockets embedded in the skin on our faces
The same skin that covers my body; my soul; my flaws-is the same skin that protects and covers you
Pigmentation is no indication that we are dissimilar, but that we are transparent once we view each other as **BOTH HUMANS** and **BOTH Beautifully, Intelligently, Equally, Similarly**
And **Uniquely made** ... on the inner.

PART ONE

· 1 ·

IF NOT *COURAGEOUS* *CONVERSATIONS*, THEN WHAT?

When leaders fail, people suffer.

—Michael Carr, Pastor Central Church

Where after all, do universal human rights begin? In small spaces, close to home—so close and so small that they cannot be seen on any map of the world. Yet they are the world of the individual person; the neighborhood he lives in; the school or college he attends; the factory, farm, or office where he works. Such are the places where every man, woman and child seeks justice, equal opportunity, equal dignity without discrimination. Unless these rights have meaning there, they have little meaning anywhere. Without concerted citizen action to uphold them close to home, we shall look in vain for progress in the larger world.

—Eleanor Roosevelt

I've asked myself many times why we need another book about social justice and multicultural education because the current market seems to be glutted with books on multiculturalism, human diversity, culturally responsive teaching, intercultural communication, cultural proficiency, etc. etc. etc. Since so much is already available, it becomes difficult to sift the wheat from the chaff, so to speak. Of greater concern is a fear that the value, essence, and raison d'être that initiated and drove the debate, generated the interest, formulated arguments, established a rationale, created a context, and a sound

philosophical foundation for multicultural education and culturally responsive practice, if not lost, are being diluted by the flurry of activity around
the broad concept of 'diversity' and how educators should respond to it in
their districts, schools, and classrooms. Practitioners and theorists, and aca-
demicians, and social scientists have posited endless ideas and approaches to
address the reality of human diversity and how it impacts *how*, and *what*, we
teach students in twenty-first-century America, an America that is still struggling to define itself in an attempt to address the dissonance between its past
and its present; between what it wants to believe it is, and the stark, and
sometimes painful, reality of persistent injustice that many have learned to
ignore or normalize. Ostensibly, *injustice* is *un-American* because it is diametri-
cally opposed to everything America traditionally stands for, and yet *injustice*
resides deep within America's moral cortex and has a vibrancy and regenerative power that is often frightening.

To be relevant, any discussion of multicultural education must include
an examination of justice. It must also include an open and direct examination of power, privilege, bias, and institutional discrimination, and their
causal relationship to the racialized 'achievement gap' in schools, because
the 'achievement gap' is symptomatic of other racialized gaps in housing,
health care, political access, etc. Approaching multicultural education without recognizing the intersectionality that exists between these and other
social issues undermines any well-meaning efforts to make constructive
change either in schools or in society.

These discussions are difficult because they challenge us to *see* ourselves,
the people around us, and the world we inhabit, differently. Moreover, they
challenge us to *act* on our new sense of the world that we are destined to share
with those we are culturally, socially, and racially compatible as well as with
those we are not. This process is implicitly and explicitly about school reform
and fundamental systemic change, because it means *re*forming education as
we know it; reconceptualizing our role as educators, and deconstructing existing institutional structures and traditional classroom practices. This kind of
comprehensive change means displacement, disruption, and loss; it means
moving away from the comfort of the solid ground of the *known*, and onto the
shifting sands of an often frightening unknown.

This is also a process that invariably invites significant subtle or overt
resistance, especially from those who are expected to lead change whether
it is leadership at the state, local, or building level. Some leaders actually
believe that they believe in justice and change, but are unwilling to access

their own internalized biases. Others are more overt, and are inclined to use what Maxine Greene (1976) calls *mystification*, a form of subterfuge or double-speak to make it *appear* that they support these changes when in actuality they want to cling to the present ways of doing things despite credible evidence of the harm that some of their policies cause traditionally marginalized groups. Researchers describe these as forms of *modern* prejudice, where bias and prejudice operate undercover; they are more elusive, and manifested in subtle ways, which makes members of dominant racial groups more "likely to express anti-Black prejudice [only] when it can plausibly be denied (both to themselves and to others)" (Plous, 2003, p. 18). In these instances, resistance may simply be saying or doing nothing to interrupt or avert worsening 'gaps,' and, doing nothing makes them complicit. Some of these leaders and policy-makers even resist facts because "[f]acts are insufficient when the person with whom you seek to share those facts is so dug in as to have a real and persistent *need* to ignore them ... [and] to revert back to their preconceived notions ..." (Wise, 2008, p. 110).

Paul Gorski captures the sense of this kind of hypocrisy and ambivalence in his poem *Reckoning*. He says "A time comes when we no longer can say Change takes time. A time for reckoning. Tears are not enough. Even if we collect them in buckets they are no mitigation for hunger, no cure for asthma ... [T]he half-crooked grins of good intentions ... we wear ... like badges, wave ... like banners [are merely] half-hearted protest[s] ... A time comes when slow and steady means when *I'm* ready ... [Slow and steady] emerges as polite inaction inaction inaction" (Gorski, 2013).

Complicating these issues is the fact that the concept of 'diversity' is both elusive and ever-expanding as society becomes aware of, and more sensitive to, all that 'diversity' encompasses, and slowly moves its thinking beyond the limiting and limited confines of 'race.' This is both appropriate and troubling. It's appropriate because too many equate diversity with 'race,' and, by extension, skin color only. In America, that has tended to be a deceptively simple black/white binary way of thinking which can "... conceal the checkerboard of racial progress and retrenchment and hide the way dominant society often casts minority groups against one another to the detriment of all" (Delgado & Stefancic, 2012, p. 79).

On the other hand, thinking of diversity more broadly in ways that embrace all aspects of human difference including diversity of language, religion, sexual preferences, etc., reflects progress in our thinking as a society. However, this also can be problematic because some use this broader understanding of diversity to shift focus *away* from race, undervalue its importance in these discussions, and delude themselves that we are now in a postracial society. We are not there yet.

In their book, *Courageous Conversations About Race*, Singleton and Linton (2006) argue that any discussion of diversity and multicultural education must begin with deeply personal, deeply invasive, and sometimes deeply painful courageous conversations about race before substantive progress can be made in closing the achievement gap. Describing their findings, they say that they "… have found that many prominent educational researchers and practitioners express solid understandings of other diversity topics but fail to explore or even recognize race as a viable factor affecting the school culture and student achievement … [and yet] race impacts 100% of our life experiences— … [however] popular educational research theory, and practice virtually ignore and sometimes explicitly reject any notion that race matters in schooling processes and outcomes" (Singleton & Linton, 2006, p. 89). They go on to point out that this does not mean that race is the *only* critical factor to be considered, and ask "… how can race at the very least not play a role in our cycle of inquiry regarding closing the racial achievement gap?" (Singleton & Linton, 2006, p. 89).

Whether or not we acknowledge it, race is always in the room, and we respond viscerally to its presence in conscious and subconscious ways. Moreover, avoidance of the presence of race is not really disengagement; it is actually a form of engagement that is either subversive or subconscious, or both. Ignoring the omnipresence of race in our lives amounts to denial, evasion, and even self-delusion, and this is not surprising, because as a country, race has always been a touchy, even frightening subject. To say it is controversial is a gross understatement. The election of an African-American president of the United States, although history-making, was a catalyst that brought race and racism to the surface of the American consciousness in contradictory ways. For example, we now talk about race more, and more openly in the public forum. Most public and private institutions and corporations are explicit in their attempts to diversify their faculty, staff, and general workforce, and being a 'diversity consultant' has become big business; everyone seems to be on the bandwagon. And yet, one prominent diversity educator has said that when a major corporation contracted him to train its staff on 'diversity,' he was explicitly told in advance that he could not mention 'race' as part of the training. The irony of this deepens as we anticipate the seismic demographic and cultural shifts that will make people of color the numerical majority and whites the numerical minority in the United States by 2050.

In the educational realm, accrediting bodies look for explicit, verifiable evidence of racial and other types of diversity as part of their institutional evaluations, and as one of the indicators of institutional excellence. And yet, significant ignorance persists regarding race and diversity even at very high academic levels. For example, I have recently encountered revered, highly degreed, senior university professors who simplistically believe that campus 'diversity' simply means that they have black, or brown, or red or yellow-skinned students sitting in their classes, and remain ignorant of the fact that even if every student in their rooms was white, male, blond, blue-eyed, and of the same height, the classroom would be a richly diverse environment. That this ignorance and/or denial can reside in educators at the highest levels supports the idea that educators and policy-makers across the spectrum from building level administrators and teachers through the university level as well as at state and national policy-making levels also can be "uncritical of deep-seated overt and covert racist values that shape who they are and how they teach or lead" (Young & Laible, 2000 cited in Brooks, 2012, p. 1). Therefore, it's not surprising that although American society has come a long way in terms of its social policies as they relate to race, we still have a very long way to go.

Miller Williams' (1999) eloquent poem *Of History and Hope* captures these uniquely American dilemmas so well when he says

We have memorized America,
how it was born and who we have been and where.
In ceremonies and silence we say the words,
telling the stories, singing the old songs.
We like the places they take us. Mostly we do.
The great and all the anonymous dead are there.
We know the sound of all the sounds we brought.
The rich taste of it is on our tongues.
But where are we going to be, and why, and who?
The disenfranchised dead want to know.
We mean to be the people we meant to be,
to keep on going where we meant to go.

But how do we fashion the future? Who can say how
except in the minds of those who will call it Now?
The children. The children. And how does our garden grow?
With waving hands—oh, rarely in a row—
and flowering faces. And brambles, that we can no longer allow.

Who were many people coming together
cannot become one people falling apart.
Who dreamed for every child an even chance
cannot let luck alone turn doorknobs or not.
Whose law was never so much of the hand as the head
cannot let chaos make its way to the heart.
Who have seen learning struggle from teacher to child
cannot let ignorance spread itself like rot.
We know what we have done and what we have said,
and how we have grown, degree by slow degree,
believing ourselves toward all we have tried to become—
just and compassionate, equal, able, and free.

All this in the hands of children, eyes already set
on a land we never can visit—it isn't there yet—
but looking through their eyes, we can see
what our long gift to them may come to be.
If we can truly remember, they will not forget. (Williams, 1999)

This book attempts to move the conversation about 'diversity' in another direction; a direction consistent with America's dream of itself to be a bastion of justice, equality, and equal access to prosperity; a place where *hope*, not *hopelessness* is the defining paradigm. Specifically, it examines diversity and race at the intersection of social justice and school leadership. It grows out of the inherent tension made fertile by this age of political correctness where, to use Lisa Delpit's phrase, 'silenced dialogues' can smother productive intercultural communication, and *color-blindness* and *color-muteness* can fracture or abort relationships between students and teachers and parents and administrators in irremediable ways. Not only can these fractures refortify and harden the areas of difference, they can widen and complicate the spaces between us, so that instead of being *many people coming together*, we are more like *one people falling apart*. All of this is happening in the present educational environment that is consumed by concerns with assessing and 'fixing' an *achievement gap* which is inflected by *race* and *class*, while simultaneously ignoring the deeper implications of *race* and *class*. Cornel West (1993) astutely addresses this paradox, and points out that our discussions about race in America tend to be 'truncated,' and that we "fail to confront the complexity of the issue in a candid and critical manner" (West, 1993, p. 4). He goes on to describe the 'paralyzing framework' that exists around discussions of race because we "confine discussions about race in America to the 'problems' Black people pose for Whites rather than consider what this way of viewing Black people reveals about us as a nation" (West, 1993, pp. 5–6). Looked at from this vantage point, the present that attempts to 'fix' the achievement gap through a relentless focus on accountability, data-driven assessments, and ongoing statistical analyses deserves another look. Among other things, these trends "which value technocratic and quantifiable aspects of education has led to the marginalization of the philosophy of education, social justice education, critical pedagogy and any other project that does not explicitly stay within the paradigm of NCLB" (Heybach, 2009, p. n.a.) trivialize and narrow the conversation and undermines true progress.

Although No Child Left Behind (NCLB) has been replaced by the 2015 Every Student Succeeds Act which promises to correct the weaknesses of NCLB, a cursory search of its focus areas shows some alarming omissions. For example, as was pointed out to me, key words like *social justice, racism, multicultural,* and *bilingual* are almost absent from this new education law. And yet, the disproportionate focus on *charter schools* is difficult to miss. Given what we know about recent history, similar attempts at school change have been disappointing in closing the 'gap' despite the grandiloquence of the plans, the flood of dollars spent, and the mandated data collection that threatened to smother entire school districts. Perhaps the 'paralyzing framework,' which characterizes America's handling of race and racial issues, provides a partial explanation of why those at the bottom end of the 'gap' seem to have taken up permanent residence there.

Further complicating our ability to effectively narrow or eliminate the 'achievement gap' is our tendency to conflate the concepts of *equity* and *equality*. Although America seems to have an unending love affair with the concept of equality, DeCuir and Dixson (2004) point out that "[i]n seeking *equality* rather than *equity* the processes, structures, and ideologies that justify inequity are not addressed or dismantled. Remedies based on equality assume that citizens have the same opportunities and experiences. Race and experiences based on race, are not equal. Thus, the experiences that people of color have with respect to race and racism create an unequal situation. *Equity*, however, recognizes that the playing field is *unequal* and attempts to address the inequality" (DeCuir and Dixson (2004) cited in Singleton and Linton, 2006, p. 29). Paul Gorski (2014) addresses the same problem from a different perspective in *Reaching and Teaching Students in Poverty: Strategies for Erasing the Opportunity Gap*, by arguing that educators must develop *equity literacy*. These are the skills and consciousness that will allow them to "recognize, respond to, and redress conditions that deny some students access to educational and other opportunities enjoyed by their peers" (Gorski, 2014, p. 6). As he sees it, some multicultural approaches that focus on developing *cultural competence* decenter equity, and this can "mask the inequities that plague schools" (Gorski, 2014, p. 1). Therefore, according to Gorski, educators must maintain their focus on the explicit needs of students, and develop *cultural competence* and *equity literacy* to eliminate the achievement gap and increase equitable opportunities for those being underserved by schools.

Almost forty years ago, Maxine Greene (1976) warned that education would be dominated by "the new cultists of efficiency, the scientific managers [who would attempt to] describe education as a technocratic operation, dependable because linked to what is most controllable and 'real'" (Greene, 1976, p. 19). She was anticipating the *scientification* of the teaching and learning experience, a sterile dehumanizing process, which is often far removed from abstractions like *social justice*. In many educational circles, there is strong support for this approach because data is hard to argue with; not impossible, but difficult to controvert. And yet, statistics, and scientific analyses also can offer a convenient subterfuge; they can mask important things that are not easily quantifiable because of an "impoverished interpretative framework ... used to find meaning in the data" (Whelan, 2013, p. 2). I argue that these interpretive frameworks are 'impoverished' by the absence of a sensitivity to, and an acknowledgement of, the fact that in the end, all of this activity should be focused on *human beings*, and the socially constructed power dynamics which complicate the perceived similarities and differences between them. Data points are not people. Assessment should not lose its focus on the needs of *people* because making a positive difference in the present and future lives of people, and by extension, society, is the only reason schools should exist, and ultimately, this is the most important thing we should be trying to assess.

Complicating the increasing reliance on scientific approaches to school assessment, and precise measurements for academic output, and academic success is the creeping infusion of a corporatist, performance-driven mindset which is also influencing how policy-makers think about teaching, learning, and leading. A corporatist perspective in education "requires benchmarking and innovative, but standardized nationally-set, and eventually computer-networked, assessment ... [In this model] (e)ducational leaders and teachers are team leaders and 'vendors of schooling as a client-driven, worklife derived commodity' [where] the crisis of education is recast as a 'design problem'" (Wexler, 1993, p. 124). Here, the goal is to "restructure public schools to be like restructured workplaces, so that they will be high-performance organisations producing measurably high-quality learning outcomes that will enable high-skill jobs to be competitively accomplished by new collar American workers in the global marketplace" (Wexler, 1993, p. 124). This corporatist agenda appears to be turning schools into "testing mills" (Whelan, 2013, p. 1) which further dehumanizes the problem of the 'achievement gap,' detaching it from other complex diversity issues that may remain unaddressed.

This book presents the argument that the confluence of science and corporatism and education is a virtual trifecta that in the end may not generate and promote socially just policies that help the neediest children that schools should be designed to serve. For one thing, facts can be separated from values, and decisions can be "made on grounds independent of moral propriety (for all the ostensible moralism in the schools) … [And the] … separation of facts from values … allows persons to claim that the knowledge they depend on is wholly neutral even when used to dominate" (Greene, 1976, p. 17), control, and oppress. Among other things, in this model as well, the *human* element is often missing, devalued, or derided. Whelan (2013) addresses these issues in his essay "Can Humanism Prevail Over the Technocracy?" He frames the present educational arena as a battleground between technocrats and humanists, and his argument is relevant here.

Humanists, according to Whelan, are concerned with the whole human being, and affirm "… the value and dignity of particular, individual human beings and their individual potential …" (Whelan, 2013, p. 1). In contrast, *technocrats* tend to "see humans as abstractions in the aggregate, as data points on a spread sheet" (Whelan, 2013, p. 1), and anything considered qualitative is "soft, unmeasurable, and thus trivial" (Whelan, 2013, p. 2). The reason that this is a problem, he argues, is not simply that a technocratic mindset is comfortable in bureaucratic settings, nor is it that it is "procedure oriented and lacks practical wisdom or adaptability to the unforeseen or the uncontrollable" (Whelan, 2013, p. 1). The problem is what he calls 'abstract and delusional' thinking; a "mentality obsessed with measurement: if it cannot be measured, it does not exist" (Whelan, 2013, p. 1). So, what does this mean in the context of a discussion about diversity, and race and the 'achievement gap,' and social justice? For one thing, it promotes a mindset that would lead us to think that

> … all kids who live in poverty can succeed academically if we improve their teachers without changing their life conditions outside of the school building. It's the McDonald's mentality that wants to standardize everything so the hamburger you get in Dayton, Ohio, is the same one you get in Anchorage, Alaska. But our kids are

not hamburgers or widgets or anything that should be treated in a standardized way. (Whelan, 2013, p. 3)

Conceptually, trying to standardize children and their lived experiences is counterintuitive especially in any conversation about multiculturalism, diversity, and social justice. For example, in this mindset, one erroneously could conclude that if pain cannot be accurately measured, it does not exist statistically speaking, and if it does not exist, it's outside of the scope of assessment metrics, and narrowly contrived curricular goals. A mentality driven by the idea that anything that cannot be measured does not exist, or has no statistical value, seriously problematizes any discussion of race and racism and bias, especially when we consider that the 'achievement gap' is perforated by race and racism and bias. Moreover, any attempt to deconstruct the effects of racism and bias requires honest introspection, and is therefore difficult to assess especially on institutional and systemic levels. This is an important point because, for example, "[a] White person can never 'own' the experience of a person of color, just as a person of color cannot 'own' the white experience. We are only experts in defining our own experiences and personal realities. Part of our struggle is rooted in our inability to search for meaning in the racial perspective of others ..." (Singleton & Linton, 2006, p. 63). However, if school leaders are incapable of *finding meaning* in the racial perspectives and lived realities of their students who are stuck in the 'achievement gap,' they are complicit in maintaining inequitable educational outcomes for those who have the greatest need.

In a sense, a *McDonald's* mindset, which validates and promotes standardization, is distantly related to the assimilationist mindset emblematized by the *melting pot* theory that gripped the collective imagination of the American populace in 1911 and continues to have resonance today. The *melting pot* theory established a culture-killing, cookie-cutter version of how a true *American* should look, think, speak, and act, and established a Euro-centric gold standard of social dominance that privileged those who were White, male, Christian, and English-speaking. Among other things, this Euro-centric gold standard of social dominance established a foundation for today's chronic 'achievement gap,' and although this standard was always challenged on some level, it took the implacable momentum of the 1960s civil rights movements to generate a new level of resistance, and defiance. Importantly, they provided a new energy, a new form of social activism, and significantly, a new vocabulary to counter the prevailing assimilationist orientation that traditionally inflected the social, political, and educational domains and institutionalized discriminatory practices. For one thing, racial issues became a matter of public debate in the aftermath of the 1954 Brown decision. It was also in the 1960s that the concepts of *multiculturalism* and *multicultural education* gained traction in the public forum. They provided a counternarrative to the entrenched culture-stripping melting pot idea that stands in direct opposition to the culture-affirming concept of *multiculturalism* which is always linked to social justice.

* * *

This book is not meant to offer a balanced critical analysis of scientific research-based interventions, instruction, or assessment, but instead to posit the idea that the present immersion in scientific process creates a climate in the educational realm which presents unique challenges for advancing *courageous conversations* about race in school settings, especially among policy-makers. A disproportionate immersion in scientific process has potentially deleterious effects on teaching, learning, and leading. I argue that *courageous conversations* about race, racism, and personal belief systems are antithetical to the data-driven, fact-based way educators are now being forced to view their practice. This has particular implications for school leaders because assessing human belief systems is inherently imprecise, especially as it refers to racial identity development, and how this factors into leadership decisions and policymaking. Moreover, the data-driven, fact-based way educators are now being forced to view their practice runs counter to the way humans develop racial identities and form judgments about human issues like *justice* and *fairness*. How, for example, can school leaders and policy-makers focus on social justice without having a very personal, a very human, understanding of who they themselves are in terms of their personal attitudes and biases, and how their deeply held beliefs impact the decisions they make on behalf of the schools and the children under their control? And can we ignore the complex, mutually reinforcing relationship between racial bias and the 'achievement gap?'

Discussions about the 'achievement gap' are implicitly or explicitly about justice (or the lack thereof), and they are always implicitly or explicitly about race. Yet, increasingly, we seem to be living in a social and political environment where 'justice' is becoming a dirty word especially when it is racialized. However, shouldn't we expect school leaders to function as the moral centers of their schools and districts? How can they do this without facilitating conversations about race? Shouldn't we expect school leaders to directly or indirectly link all efforts to close the 'achievement gap' to 'justice,' and to the needs and lived experiences of the schoolchildren most affected by unjust social policies (i.e., the ones who are putrefying in the 'gap')? Without this kind of focus, school leaders on every level risk foreclosing their own success in eliminating the 'gap'; they also risk foreclosing the possibility of institutionalizing social justice policies and pedagogies that have the potential to bring about sustainable school reform. However, what appears to be a wholesale commitment to technical process, scientific analysis, and data-driven assessments and outcomes provides a convenient way to dilute or undermine or delegitimize this focus. And, there is a historical context for this that needs to be recognized. Asa Hilliard (1995) framed it this way when he said: "The knowledge and skills to educate all children already exist. Because we have lived in a historically oppressive society, educational issues tend to be framed as technical issues which denies their political origin and meaning … (Hilliard cited in Singleton & Linton, 2006, p. 47). In other words, we cannot expect to achieve justice for underserved children until we confront the sociopolitical and historical contexts for the 'achievement gap' and other inequities in schools which cannot necessarily be quantified.

Einstein's wisdom seems appropriate here. He said "Everything that can be counted does not necessarily count; everything that counts cannot necessarily be counted." This is a lesson we have yet to learn.

References

Brooks, J. S. (2012). *Black school, white school racism and educational (mis)leadership*. New York, NY: Teachers College Press.

Carr, M. (2016). Excerpt from a sermon delivered at Central Church in Hilton Head, SC.

J. T., & Dixson, A. D. (2004). Cited in Singleton, G. E., & Linton, C. (2006). *Courageous conversations about race* (p. 29). Thousand Oaks, CA: Corwin Press.

Delgado, R., & Stefancic, J. (2012). *Critical race theory—An introduction*. New York, NY: New York University Press.

Gorski, P. (2014). *Equity literacy: An introduction* (p. 1). Retrieved July 11, 2014 from http://www.edchange.org/handouts/Equity-Literacy-Introduction.pdf

Gorski, P. C. (2013). *Reckoning*. Retrieved July 13, 2015 from http://edchange.org/publications/reckoning.html

Greene, M. (1976). Challenging mystification: Educational foundations in dark times. *Educational Studies, 7*(1), 9–29.

Heuberger, B. (2002). *Cultural diversity building skills for awareness, understanding and application*. Dubuque, IA: Kendall/Hunt Publishers.

Heybach, J. (2009). *Rescuing social justice in education: A critique of the NCATE controversy.* Ohio Valley Philosophy of Education Society. Retrieved July 23, 2012 from http://niu.academia.edu/JessicaHeybach/Papers22132/Rescuing_Social_Justice_in_Education_A_Critique_of_the_NCATE_Controversy

Hilliard, A. (1995). *Do we have the will to educate all children? In the maroon within us: Selected essays on African American community socialization.* Baltimore, MD: Black Classic Press. Cited in Singleton, G., & Linton, C. (2006). *Courageous conversations about race* (p. 47).

Plous, S. (2003). *Understanding prejudice and discrimination.* Boston, MA: McGraw-Hill.

Plous, S. (n.a.). *Understanding prejudice and discrimination* (p. 10). Retrieved July 11, 2016 from http://www.understandingprejudice.org/apa/english/page10.htm

Roosevelt, E. (1958). *Excerpt from a speech by Eleanor Roosevelt at the presentation of "In Your Hands: A Guide for Community Action for the Tenth Anniversary of the Universal Declaration of Human Rights."* Thursday, March 27, 1958. United Nations, New York.

Singleton, G. E., & Linton, C. (2006). *Courageous conversations about race.* Thousand Oaks, CA: Corwin Press.

West, C. (1993). *Race matters.* New York, NY: Vintage Books.

Wexler, P. (1993). *Educational corporatism and its counterposes.* Keynote address presented at the international conference: After competence: The future of post-compulsory education and training, Centre for Skill Formation Research and Development, Griffith University, Brisbane.

Whelan, J. (2013). *Can humanism triumph over technocracy?* Retrieved August 16, 2013 from http://blogs.edweek.org/teachers/living-in-dialogue/2013/04/jack_whelan_can_humanism_preva.html?print=1

Williams, M. (1999). *Of history and hope.* Poetry Foundation. Retrieved May 14, 2014 from https://www.poetryfoundation.org/poems-and-poets/poems/detail/47107

Wise, T. (2008). *White like me, reflections on race from a privileged son.* Brooklyn, NY: Soft Skull Press.

Young, M. D., & Laible, J. (2000). White racism, anti-racism and school leadership preparation. *Journal of School Leadership, 10*(5), 374–415. Cited in Brooks, J. S. (2012). *Black school, white school racism and educational (mis)leadership* (p. 1). New York, NY: Teachers College Press.

· 2 ·

CHALLENGING THE MYSTIFICATION
OF SOCIAL JUSTICE

We hold these truths to be self-evident, that all men are created equal, that they are endowed by their Creator with certain unalienable Rights …
—Declaration of Independence (July 4, 1776)

If you're going to hold someone down you're going to have to hold on by the other end of the chain. You are confined by your own repression.
—Toni Morrison

Although the *American Dream* that anyone who works hard enough and is resilient enough can succeed is seductive and greedily internalized by most Americans, it *is* a dream. And, it is a fallacy to assume that in America there is a rock-solid foundation of social justice that ensures that this dream can become a reality for these legions of hard-working American *dreamers*. It is a fallacy to assume that there is universal acceptance of the idea that social justice is guaranteed because it is the birthright of *every* American. It is also a fallacy to believe that there is even a common understanding of what social justice actually means even though it is implicit in America's constitutionally endorsed moral stance which states unequivocally that: "We hold these truths to be self-evident, that all men are created equal, that they are endowed by their Creator with certain unalienable Rights …" For many, the concept of social justice is like background music for the mythic American story; a mere commodity or bargaining chip; a strategy meant to confuse and conceal, to mystify.

However, one need look no further than the recent headlines in American newspapers to *know* with profound certainty that America's official stance on *social justice* is often a veneer or a rhetorical ploy that masks a deep, dark, well of injustice that hides residues of pain and human suffering that some prefer to ignore. For generations, we have ignored state-sanctioned abuses (including murders) of unarmed and defenseless people by rogue police officers, which is no less troubling than chronic inescapable poverty and the demonization of the poor, or the institutionalization of discrimination in American schools. As a nation, we often fail to see that we are all connected, bound together for good or ill; that the bonds are often invisible but forever unbreakable. We also fail to see that our destinies as a nation are inextricably woven together whether we like it or not. When Toni Morrison wisely said,

> If you're going to hold someone down you're going to have to hold on by the other end of the chain. You are confined by your own repression. (Morrison, n.a.)

she was making a statement about (in)justice, and reminding us of this basic truth: as a society, we are all confined, limited, and diminished by our own repressive behavior toward others. Further, it can be argued that, in general, Americans are victims of their own dream of themselves, and that the myth of America as a refuge for *outcasts* and *huddled masses*, and as the *land of the free* and the *home of the brave* has been so completely internalized that we believe the hype, especially when it benefits us, as individuals or groups, to do so. And when the response to cultural difference is catalyzed into hateful cries of '*Get out of my country,*' and the angry declaration that '*we have to take our country back!!!*' many choose to ignore the underlying xenophobic attitudes that these words imply.

And although some see social justice as a goal we've achieved, a shore that we have already reached, others (especially those with power) exploit the idea of social justice as an achievable ideal even as they undermine, or discredit it through political rhetoric or in their everyday business or professional practices. Consider, for example, that one mega-retail chain that represents itself as *Making Better Possible* (Walmart, 2014, p. n.a.) by opening doors to a better future for their legions of underpaid 'associates,' while profiting from, and feasting on their ignorance, undereducation, and failed ambitions. For such corporations, ignorance and miseducation are *good* things, because they ensure an endless supply of dreamless workers, with limited options and bleak futures, who are forced to accept low wages and subsistence as a way of life. For example, most of the Walmart corporation's workers are paid so little that American taxpayers end up supplementing these low salaries (and indirectly boosting Walmart's wealth), by paying as much as $6.2 billion dollars annually for needed services that these Walmart 'associates' cannot afford to pay for themselves. And fast food companies, like McDonald's, collectively cost taxpayers as much as $7 billion dollars annually for the same reason. By "quietly [outsourcing] a significant chunk of their labor costs to the taxpayer" (O'Connor, 2013, p. n.a.) these companies can boast of the fact that they employ millions of people (which ostensibly boosts the American economy) while sidestepping the fact that the low wages they pay force their 'associates' to rely on state and federal subsidies to supplement the cost of food, housing, health care, etc., which actually drains the American economy. This is a sophisticated, mystifying scam meant to trick the most vulnerable into thinking that they are the beneficiaries of corporate largess while they are actually being exploited by corporate greed. The mystification deepens when companies like Walmart simultaneously underpay their associates while they generously (and publicly) fund and disseminate formal research studies that examine the causes and effects of poverty and food insecurity even as their business model guarantees their continued existence. These business models mystify this process, making *social justice* a commodity, and a public relations strategy, while actual *justice* quietly succumbs to profit and self-interest.

The *mystification* of social justice in the world of education follows a similar pattern; it is a process that is complexly layered, sometimes sinister, and it has potentially life-crushing consequences for some children that are in place long before they enter elementary school.

This chapter is not about Walmart and McDonalds. It is about social (in)justice, and how as a society we've bruised, even shredded the concept of social justice, and why this should matter most to school teachers and leaders. It is about how some, with the power to do so, have distorted the meaning of social justice for self-serving purposes, and mystify this process to protect carefully constructed public images, and to keep hidden their 'private purposes.'

This chapter is also about challenging fixed patterns of social dominance in order to reclaim social justice for those whose lives are marinating in the pain of (in)justice daily. It argues that school teachers and leaders are essential to reclaiming social justice on behalf of those who are powerless to do so on their own—the children for whom they act in *loco parentis*. The chapter is also about professional responsibility, and argues that since educators act as surrogates for parents and represent themselves as the primary transmitters of democratic principles and ideals, they have a greater responsibility to be actively engaged in the process of social change and equity-driven practice. If not them, who should or will do this?

* * *

In fact, democracy is, and has been, an open possibility, not a possession.

—*Maxine Greene*

Decades ago, in his seminal work *Democracy and Education* (1963), John Dewey examined the explicit and implicit ideas and values that define a democratic society, and applied them to the challenges confronting public education. Considered by many the dean or 'Father' of American progressive education, Dewey saw democracy as the bedrock of American education, and in his view, democratic values provided the necessary philosophical underpinnings for how we, as a nation, should conceptualize education in American schools. He saw education as an essential social and social-izing function and, importantly, a way to develop and 'free' intelligence and 'emancipate' the mind. And yet, depending on how it was perceived, education could function either retrospectively or prospectively; as a way to accommodate the future to the past, or as a way to utilize the past as a resource in a developing future (Dewey, 1963, p. 79). This is another way of saying that the educative process conforms to prevailing social goals, and either embraces change or maintains the status quo depending on how the relationship with the past is perceived and valued. The relationship with the past also can predict the degree of interest in and commitment to social justice and the social changes needed to achieve it. Further, how we relate to the past informs how we relate to the future, and whether or not we have a vision that is looking forward or backward.

To some extent, how we think about the future is predicated on how we feel about risk-taking. For example, embracing future change usually involves courageously creeping toward a scary unknown that forces us out of our com-fort zones making us feel vulnerable. However, being wedded to the past is, in some ways, risk-free because it involves reconstructing, or reconstituting a 'known' series of practices and beliefs despite the fact that they may not have served all groups well. In the end, how society relates to the past informs how committed we are to 'freeing' intelligence and 'emancipating' the mind, and this can challenge and undermine social justice goals and ideologies.

Not surprisingly, in many ways, Dewey's body of work anticipated some of the contemporary debates and social policies that serve to weaken or problematize the relationship between social justice, democracy, and the formal educative process. In 1916 Dewey expressed a belief that

> ... every society which has ever existed, [is] full of inequity ... [therefore, progressive education should aim to correct] unfair privilege and unfair deprivation, not to perpetuate them. (Dewey, 1963, pp. 119–120)

What this means, among other things, is that education is of supreme importance as an organizing and socializing force. It neither exists, nor is developed, in a vacuum, and there is, or should be, a cause and effect relationship between what happens in society, and what happens in schools. What we don't want, according to Dewey, is to see education as an instrument that facilitates the "exploitation of one class by another" (Dewey, 1963, p. 98). What we don't want is the separation of people into privileged and subject classes, or education that "educate[s] some into masters, [and] educate[s] others into slaves" (Dewey, 1963, p. 84). Dewey insists that unless democratic ideals dominate the public education system, education is a farce and a tragic delusion.

Maxine Greene contemporizes some of the same concerns expressed by Dewey, but narrows her focus to teacher preparation programs, teacher candidates, and, by extension, to in-service teachers and school leaders. In her essay, *Challenging Mystification: Educational Foundations in Dark Times*, Maxine Greene (1976), like Dewey, expresses her concern with our relationship to the past, and shows that *how* we relate to the past can threaten the actualization of wide-scale social justice in society because of a general unwillingness to challenge social 'norms,' even when they are patently unjust. This threat, Greene argues, has particular significance for those in the field of education because of the preeminent role that schools play in shaping American society, defining American values, and establishing progressive goals for the future. According to Greene, teacher preparation is a special dimension within the larger educative process, and it has a unique function in the area of social justice. In an age focused on accountability and objective measurements of 'success' or 'failure,' Greene fears that teachers may be less reflectively self-critical in questioning whether or not the decisions they make are intrinsically *right*. She fears that "[f]acts have been easily separated off from values ... [and that] decisions have been made on grounds independent of moral propriety (for all the ostensible moralism in the schools)" (Greene, 1976, p. 16). Teacher preparation, she feels, should arm teacher candidates with the skills and tools they need as facilitators to overcome ignorance, ward off manipulations by special interest groups, and resist the cynicism and the sense of powerlessness that threatens to silence and paralyze them (Greene, 1976, p. 11).

Specifically addressing the preparation of teachers, Greene makes a strong case against the institutional discrimination that has taken root in some teacher preparation programs. She demonstrates that social justice is being weakened surreptitiously, because some preservice teachers are being programmed to support the status quo in society rather than try, through their teaching, to dismantle unjust social systems. In effect, they are being trained to *not notice* that social reality is a construct, and *not notice* the intentionality and design that maintains structural social inequities. Instead, they are being programmed to embrace rather than deconstruct institutional discrimination through an uncritical acceptance of what Greene calls an *unexamined surface reality*. This has demonstrable long-term consequences for teacher candidates and, by extension, for the future students whom they ostensibly will prepare to function as *upstanding* citizens in a presumably *just* democratic society. What that actually means has been, and continues to be, controversial especially now as issues of class, culture, race, and ethnicity have added more texture and substance to the debate about justice and injustice. However, the nexus between education and democracy is *not* controversial, and is generally accepted as 'truth,' even though *how* schools interpret and actualize this connection varies widely. Similarly, how schools respond to the democratic impulse toward 'justice' is also subject to interpretation.

Ironically, even though schools are society's preeminent sites for social engineering, they have functioned as everything from holding pens for some American youth, to intellectual filling stations, where children passively receive a fixed, basic knowledge of selected core subjects. And, paradoxically, schools are being expected to preserve, protect, and disseminate a fixed set of iconic American values and fundamental democratic ideals while they simultaneously provide a platform for new ideas some of which are contestatory, and challenge traditional ways of thinking about the connection between education and democracy. The resulting tension places teachers in a very precarious position because of a number of conflicts of interest.

A central conflict for practicing teachers is that they are integral parts of a system they should be prepared to critique even though it is the source of

their livelihood; the well-known adage *don't bite the hand that feeds you* resonates here. Another conflict is that teachers are expected to be future-oriented
while in many respects being chained to the past; they are expected to be
change agents while they are expected to embrace traditional ways of thinking
and teaching.

Greene (1976) points out that some teacher preparation programs are
complicit in complicating and deepening these conflicts. This, she says,
expands the breadth of the challenge to how social justice is perceived, and
to what degree it ultimately drives overall classroom practice, as well as policy
decisions on the leadership level. Greene argues that traditionally, teacher
education has been concerned with initiating teachers-to-be into some
authoritative knowledge of the "given"—a prepackaged, predetermined,
body of knowledge that is preapproved, vetted, traditional, and unquestionable. This has the effect of muzzling teachers, making them either unable or
unwilling to critique or interrogate the existing social order. This is especially
true when their critiques and interrogations can implicate entrenched power
structures that are sustained and propped up by policies and practices that
are patently unjust. (It's important to note that the teachers and their families are often beneficiaries of these same power structures.) Greene contends
that in teacher preparation programs there has been a tendency to present
an *"unexamined surface reality as 'natural,' and fundamentally unquestionable"*
(Greene, 1976, p. 10). In other words, teachers are being taught to overlook
the constructed character of social reality. This may put conversations about
social justice and injustice at risk of being silenced, or sidelined in school
settings, or teachers may inadvertently transmit 'benign' or 'neutral' versions
of social reality. This is dangerous because unlike beauty, justice should not
be in the eye of the beholder.

Greene uses Melville's Moby Dick, and the ill-fated Captain Ahab, as
metaphors to show how teacher preparation can be complicit in maintaining
the status quo in society by producing teacher candidates who demonstrate
"a more or less uncritical acceptance of meritocratic arrangements, of [social]
stratifications and hierarchies" (Greene, 1976, p. 12). The result is that they
pay minimal attention to "the insufficiencies of the culture—to inequity, racism" (Greene, 1976, p. 12) and greed rather than advocate for social change.
In some teacher preparation programs, according to Greene, social justice
succumbs to sociopolitical pressures designed to mute the debate about the
role of social justice in the educative process. She points out that there are
multiple levels of meaning and intent embedded in teacher training that are

disturbing because they obfuscate and mystify, making the foundational principles and goals of the program confusing and unclear. Greene calls this *mystification* because it amounts to dissembling. This *mystification*, she says, creates a surface reality that masks another controlling reality which is always powerfully present, but which exists on a deeper level, out of sight, and perhaps unacknowledged.

We contribute to this *mystification* when we operate under the assumption that education is politically neutral. We contribute to this *mystification* when we prefer to believe that education, whether it is taking place in public schools or in schools of education, has no political agenda. This has never been true; teaching itself and the policies that inform teaching on every academic level do not exist, and never have existed, in a vacuum.

In Moby Dick, the mystifier Captain Ahab was on what Greene calls a "manic quest" for the elusive, white, killer whale; he both exploited and deceived his own crew, and ultimately persuaded them to be complicit in their own destruction. Greene uses the captain to represent all of the "Captain Ahabs of the world," who have absolute control of a *ship* and a *crew*, but "… keep hidden a 'private purpose' that takes no account of the crew's desires and needs. [Their purpose] is to delude [the crew] and use them by appealing to what they are made to think is their true self-interest. They are demeaned in consequence: and in the end, they are destroyed" (Greene, 1976, p. 9). Although Greene is attempting to expose *mystification* as it applies to the role and function of social foundation courses in teacher preparation programs, her argument has far broader implications for in-service teaching, learning, and leading. Since mystification, according to Greene, obscures vision and a true sense of the world, and presents "an unexamined surface reality as 'natural' [and] fundamentally unquestionable" (Greene, 1976, p. 10) the implications are that there is a likely disconnect between what programs appear to be teaching and what candidates are actually learning.

Unfortunately, the parallels between what is happening in some teacher preparation programs and in public schools are hard to miss. In public schools too, there is a great deal of evidence that "unexamined surface realities are presented as 'natural,' fundamentally unquestionable" (Greene, 1976, p. 10) and are part and parcel of day-to-day operations.

For example, in a school setting, *mystification* can account for a number of things some choose to ignore or normalize such as an erroneous belief in the *special* innate value of some groups, some skin colors, some cultures, some languages, some religions, and some lifestyles. Mystification can encourage educators to overlook the "*constructed* character of social reality" (Greene, 1976, p. 10), particularly when it masks the causes and consequences of social ills like poverty, homelessness, the school-to-prison pipeline, racialized gaps in academic achievement, and economic opportunity. This is relevant in any discussion of social justice, and diversity and multiculturalism, and equity because these are social issues school teachers and leaders cannot keep at bay because they can, and do, infiltrate the walls of schools and classrooms every day. And, sadly, too often, the students themselves are the living embodiments of these social ills.

And yet, it is simplistic to say that "teachers consciously mystify or deliberately concoct the positive images that deflect critical thought" (Greene, 1976, p. 12) or that they are unwilling to transform social and academic conditions that are either deficient or inhumane. Because teachers represent a cross-section of society and, like many others, are sucked into the bureaucracies where they work, they are more likely to take for granted what everyone else takes for granted. This means that there is a greater likelihood that they will represent the world around them as a 'given', that is "probably unchangeable, predefined … [and they may] transmit, often tacitly, benign or neutral versions of the social reality" (Greene, 1976, p. 12). In the end, teachers not only become the most visible and accessible representatives of a flawed educational system, by default, they also can promote stasis and avoid interrogating or critiquing that system.

Greene (1976) argues that educators have a responsibility to not only be aware of the oppressive social constructs that they have absorbed and internalized through interactions with their families, schools, or society at large, they also should have the tools to critique, and perhaps reshape these constructs. Educators, according to Greene, must be prepared to interrogate oppression, and to "break with conceptions of the given, of the predefined" (Greene, 1976, p. 14). However, conceptions of the *given* or *predefined* often involve internalized beliefs that some groups *should be* privileged and *should* socially, culturally, economically, and, perhaps, intellectually dominate other groups.

One important precondition for a meaningful social critique is *understanding* the dynamics of social dominance and privilege, not merely on an abstract intellectual level, but on a personal level as well. This means not only understanding how dominant privilege informs self-perception, but also how it informs professional relationships that impact how one moves through the world on a daily basis. This is important because "[d]ominant] privilege is the umbrella concept that allows for oppression, inequality and other [forms of unfair] treatment of nondominant groups" (Heuberger, 2004, p. 20). And, according to Heuberger (2004), "[i]t is not possible to understand racism, sexism, ageism, ableism, homophobia and other types of discrimination without understanding dominant privilege" (p. 20). Heuberger's (2004) outline provides a useful framework for developing a deeper understanding of the interplay between dominant privilege and the ability to be self-critical, and why awareness of this is a necessary precursor to demystifying oppressive social constructs that undermine equity-driven teaching and leading:

> If you are in the dominant group, you can choose to be aware of difference or choose to not be aware of difference. *That choice is part of your privilege.*
>
> If you are in the dominant group, you can choose to understand difference or choose to not understand difference. *That choice is part of your privilege.*
>
> If you are in the dominant group, and you choose to be aware of and understand difference, *then you must also understand how your privilege is a barrier to doing so.*
>
> If you are in the dominant group, and you choose to be aware of and understand difference, *then you must take responsibility for your own learning. A person in the non-dominant group may choose to be a resource, but is not responsible for educating you or justifying his or her perspective.*
>
> If you are in the dominant group, your motivations for awareness and understanding may be different from those in the non-dominant group. *You will want to examine your personal motivations to determine how your privilege affects you.*
>
> If you are in the dominant group, developing an awareness of your privilege requires *consistent and conscious effort, may be uncomfortable at times, and will be an ongoing and challenging effort.* (Heuberger, 2004, p. 20)

It requires an intentional, ongoing effort to (de)mystify and diminish the effects of dominant privilege which are at work in school settings, and this should be an ongoing process that is reflective of, and consistent with, a school's culture. And it has to be a wholesale commitment which simultaneously takes place on individual and institutional levels. This means that individuals have a responsibility to address their own personal issues, and school leaders have a responsibility to create a fertile school environment where everyone is motivated and encouraged to address these issues in the classroom as well as in the overall school setting. School leaders must be prepared to acknowledge and critique the barriers to intergroup and intragroup understanding and communication, and consciously and conscientiously deconstruct barriers based on perceived differences in class, culture, ethnicity, and race that result from sociocultural or economic dominance and privilege. It also means opening doors to new and deeper kinds of communication and professional collaboration. This can create a culture in which teachers and school leaders help each other distance themselves from socially inscribed beliefs in hierarchies of power and privilege that function as inoculations against intercultural understanding. Ideally, this is a culture in which teachers and school leaders see themselves as part of a whole, as part of a larger human community. This frame of mind both enables and encourages individuals to reflect on their lived experience, and the "lives they lead in common with [others, and] not merely as professionals or professionals-to-be, but as human beings participating in a shared reality" (Greene, 1976, p. 10). Developing this type of mindset is difficult, and may represent a paradigm shift for some, but it is important and necessary; it is a way educators can consciously resist mystification, or the self-delusion that can simultaneously function on internal or external levels. By adopting this type of mindset, they will be able to resist the mystification that is manifested in *not* recognizing that we are all "participant[s] in a damaged culture" (McIntosh, 1988, p. n.a.) and damaged by it, and *not* recognizing that skin color can be a distinct social advantage or disadvantage, or *not* recognizing that many see class in hierarchical terms and as a predictor of human value. They will understand that mystification

> succeeds most dramatically when people believe that the expressed commitment to human freedom and human rights has been consistently acted upon throughout American history. Mystification succeeds when people take it for granted that democracy has been achieved. ... (Greene, 1976, p. 15)

Mystification succeeds when we confuse the *American Dream* with the American reality. Mystification succeeds when we normalize bigotry and poverty, and racism and institutionalized discrimination. Mystification succeeds when we forget that America is a *work in progress*; that America is still *becoming America*, as Miller Williams (1997) said, "degree by slow degree." Mystification tempts us to believe that the American journey is complete, and that as a country, we have already become "just and compassionate, equal, able, and free" (Williams, 1997) but we're not there yet.

Defining Social Justice

Dantley and Tillman's (2010) research on leadership and social justice makes clear that essentializing the definition of social justice would misrepresent and confine a concept that is complex, expansive, and multifaceted. Rather than try to contain, and therefore limit the frameworks and various interpretations being studied, they identified some pervasive themes and salient characteristics of social justice which are included below:

> First, social justice is about recognizing the multiple contexts within which education and educational leadership exist. Simply contemplating the concept of social justice in educational settings demands a more comprehensive perspective on the spaces within which education functions. Academic and intellectual work is located in a space that is affected by political, social, cultural, historical and economic realities. Social justice demands deconstructing those realities in order to disclose the multiple ways schools and their leadership reproduce marginalizing and inequitable treatment of individuals because their identities are outside of the celebrated dominant culture. A second theme in these articulated definitions is that social justice is to operate in a democratic environment because inherent in the fiber of democracy is the celebration of the multiple voices, identities, and perspectives of all those in the community. (p. 22)

A consistent thread that links all of the definitions Dantley and Tillman (2010) studied is that they focus on individuals and groups that have been subjected to various forms of social oppression and marginalization that contravene certain basic principles of democratic morality.

Dantley and Tillman (2010) also identify five characteristics that are applicable to the various definitions of social justice and educational leadership for social justice. They are:

1. A consciousness of the broader social, cultural and political contexts of schools.
2. The critique of the marginalizing behaviors and predispositions of schools and their leadership.
3. A commitment to the more genuine enactment of democratic principles in schools.
4. A moral obligation to articulate a counterhegemonic vision or narrative of hope regarding education.
5. A determination to move from rhetoric to civil rights activism. (p. 23)

Are Social Justice Initiatives Part of a *Radical Social Agenda*?

However it is defined or conceptualized, some respond to the term *social justice* as though it were an expletive, an idea that has no place in either the preparation of school educators or in-school practices, and they want to delete it from formal guidelines that shape objectives and goals, drive school policy, and inform classroom practice. They critique others for politicizing the concept, even as they themselves politicize it by equating social justice education with indoctrination, and social engineering of the meanest sort. They have labeled it a *radical social agenda* that is antithetical to American values, especially the right of free speech. Heybach (2009) counters this antisocial justice argument, by accusing the *detractors* themselves of having a *radical social agenda* that aims to "de-democratize the role of public education" (p. n.a.) which is radical indeed. Heybach sharpens her point by arguing that along with equality, social justice is a defining element of the American democratic tradition, and that removing social justice from educational discourse on any level would distort not only the meaning of democracy but also our understanding of the unfolding present as well as significant moments in America's past. According to Heybach, if we concede that the most democratic movements in U.S. history like the abolitionist movement, the suffragette movement, and the civil rights movement embodied values of social justice, "then it follows that American democracy is indebted to *radical social agendas* ... [Further, to] deny this element of the national tradition as somehow outside the knowledge base that teacher candidates should learn is to alienate them from what is most democratic in United States history" (Heybach, 2009, p. n.a.).

This contentious, mystifying debate played out very publicly on the national stage in 2006 when the National Council for the Accreditation of Teachers of Education (NCATE) was undergoing a recertification process by the U.S. Department of Education's National Advisory Committee on Institutional Quality and Integrity (NACIQI). The NCATE and its affiliates set the standards and guidelines for the preparation of school educators nationwide, and an endorsement by NCATE is rigorously sought and highly regarded by teacher and leadership preparation programs as a measure of excellence. This makes NCATE not only a powerful and influential entity that shapes how teachers teach, and how leaders lead in schools across the country, it also makes it an arbiter of values and moral predispositions. This is implicit in the standards regarding educator dispositions, which had up to that point included a commitment to social justice, as a preferred value and guiding principle for preservice and in-service professionals. However, in 2006 several organizations, including the Foundation for Individual Rights in Education (FIRE), the American Council of Trustees and Alumni (ACTA), and the National Association of Scholars (NAS), argued against the reaccreditation of NCATE and/or the removal of social justice as a dispositional goal in NCATE standards. The NAS even filed a formal inquiry with the U.S. Department of Education arguing that social justice "is a term necessarily fraught with contested ideological significance, [and that NCATE was] clearly encouraging and legitimating the adoption by teacher preparation programs of what appears to be a political viewpoint test" (cited in Butin, n.a., p. 3). Affirming this position, ACTA's president, Anne Neal, argued that NCATE be denied reaccreditation unless it stopped using *social justice* as a measure of educators' dispositions. Under the threat of losing its right to accredit teacher and leadership preparation programs, the NCATE's president Arthur Wise never argued in defense of social justice, but instead decided to remove all references to it from NCATE standards, and as a result of this strategic maneuver, NCATE was reaccredited. However, subsequent to its reaccreditation, and without engaging in further public debate on the matter, NCATE (now known as the Council for the Accreditation of Educator Preparation (CAEP)) restored the term *social justice*, as evidenced by the following description of Standard 5.0 in the 2011 Educational Leadership Program Standards which have been developed by the Educational Leadership Constituent Council (ELCC):

> **ELCC Standard 5.0**: A building-level education leader applies knowledge that promotes the success of every student by acting with integrity, fairness, and in an ethical manner to ensure a school system of accountability for every student's academic and social success by modeling school principles of self-awareness, reflective practice, transparency, and ethical behavior as related to their roles within the school; safeguarding the values of democracy, equity, and diversity within the school; evaluating the potential moral and legal consequences of decision making in the school; and promoting social justice within the school to ensure that individual student needs inform all aspects of schooling. (p. 18)

One of the most troubling things about this NCATE debacle is that the concept of social justice and social justice education was denigrated and bandied about during the reaccreditation process, and apparently was used as a bargaining chip for self-serving political purposes by the country's premier teacher accreditation body. However, one unexpected outcome of NCATE's contradictory positions was that they sparked a heated, but necessary, national debate among scholars and educational leaders about the meaning and importance of social justice in general, as well as in the context of American democracy. For example, Heybach (2009) and many others offered strong critiques of NCATE's weak stance and subsequent vacillation without engaging in what is now considered an important and necessary conversation about the nexus between social justice and democracy as it relates to teaching, learning, and leading. According to Heybach (2009), "... in the United States democratic education is, in crucial ways indebted to the very idea of social justice both historically and philosophically. [Moreover, the] removal of social justice from NCATE's vocabulary of concern could therefore be seen as a violation of the values and aims of democratic education" (p. n.a.). In his critique, Butin (n.d., p. n.a.) points out that during the reaccreditation process, no one defended the "ancient origins of, societal consensus around, and empirical evidence for, social justice as a cause for all individuals [especially future teachers] in a democratic and pluralistic society" (Butin, n.d., p. n.a.).

There are many lessons school teachers and leaders can learn from the NCATE controversy. One is that we cannot take for granted that every teacher and school leader is aware of the many ways to conceptualize social justice, or that everyone is philosophically attuned to the same definition and interpretation of social justice, or that social justice or equity is a common goal. Another lesson is that personal politics can inflect (or infect) professional practice and filter how one conceptualizes social justice. This presupposes that educators do not shed their political views and values when they walk through the doors of their schools, and that these values and beliefs shape their vision of how schools and society should operate, how policies are interpreted and implemented, and importantly how they relate to the children under their supervision and control. This raises the question of whether or not school teachers and leaders should have the power or privilege of interpreting social justice according to their personal tastes, attitudes, values, and political persuasions. If we concede that they do, given the perceived unbreachable connection between democracy and justice, doesn't this also mean that they have the power to redefine democracy to fit a prevailing political agenda? And, what if that political agenda is racist or homophobic or anti-Semitic? How would this impact the classroom practice or the school leadership of someone who harbors attitudes like these? Moreover, how do we reconcile any of this with an American's right to exercise his or her free speech under the First Amendment? Although there are no simple answers to any of these questions, these are issues that should not be ignored because doing so can intensify mystification, and condone stasis, or, worse, perpetuate injustice.

In the end, among other things, this entire debate highlights the role of politics in the educative process. It shows that sometimes those at very high levels who are neither teachers nor school leaders, and are therefore divorced from the day-to-day activities in schools, can mystify and hijack the agenda, and inform school policy and practice for purely political ends. This is reminiscent of Ahab's ill-fated *manic quest*. Apparently lost in this philosophical and rhetorical battleground are the children, especially the ones who ironically are waiting to be justly served by school systems that, at least rhetorically, revolve around the axis of *justice* daily.

How, When, and Why Did *Justice* Become a 'Dirty' Word, and What Does This Have to Do with Social Dominance?

How, when, and why did *justice* become a 'dirty' word, and why do some consider it inconsistent with the aims of democracy and a democratic education? Is this not mystification of another sort? If so, where is the underlying 'hidden purpose,' and who are the *captains* running this *ship*? What is the correlation between justice, personal politics, and social dominance? And, why should this debate be important to teachers and school leaders, especially those who are committed to equity-driven leadership, and to *safeguarding the values of democracy through integrity, fairness, ethical behavior, equity, moral decision-making,* and *social justice* as per NCATE leadership standards? Moreover, can *integrity, fairness, ethical behavior, equity, moral decision-making,* and *social justice* really be construed as *undemocratic* or freighted with ideology? Probably. But, isn't a reconciliation of these conflicts necessary if educators take seriously their commitment to prepare students to become upstanding citizens in a democracy?

Although there are no simple answers to these questions, one thing is clear: teachers and school leaders occupy a unique space in our social structure, have special responsibilities, and are held to different and higher moral, ethical, and behavioral standards than the average citizen because of the sacred cargo they are expected to carry—the nation's children—who for better or worse represent the nation's future.

Research suggests that the answers to these questions go far beyond surface politics and political persuasion (i.e., conservative, liberal, libertarian, or progressive ideologies). In subtler ways, this is also about perceptions of power, class, and the dynamics of sociopolitical and economic dominance, because what is *just* or *unjust* looks different if socially you're on the *top* of the social hierarchy than it does if you're on the *bottom*. This is partly because, as Tatum (1997) points out, "dominant groups generally do not like to be reminded of the existence of inequality" (p. 24), whereas those who are without social, economic, or political power wallow in injustice daily. If you're in a socially dominant group, you see the world from a different perch from those who are socially or economically *beneath* you. The irony is that being on top does not necessarily permit you to see or understand more; it may, in fact, result in you seeing or understanding less, much less, as did former President George W. Bush during his infamous flight high above New Orleans in Air Force One ostensibly surveying the post-Katrina storm devastation. The president had a panoramic view of the landscape, but he saw and understood very little about the suffering of people who were *beneath* him literally and figuratively. As a result, the overall governmental response to the suffering of those American citizens, most of whom were poor and Black, was woefully inadequate. This demonstrated how a dominant social orientation can be desensitizing, and can virtually make nondominant groups invisible, and their needs and demands irrelevant. On another level, the presidential response was a dramatic example of the institutionalization of social dominance. It was quite evident that in America, what constitutes social justice is not simply in the eye of the beholder, it is also under the control of the powerful which makes this an important diversity issue. Social justice may look different if you are White than it does if you are a person of color; similarly, it may look different if you are rich, than it does if you are poor; if you are heterosexual or homosexual; if you are Christian or Muslim; if you are male or female; the list can go on and on. The common denominator is power (who has it, and who doesn't), and the tension between the powerful and the powerless; between dominant and nondominant group membership, and the different values and perspectives that this tension generates.

What social justice is or is not and whose interpretation should be the predominant one is an important 'diversity' issue because one of the tenets of multicultural education is that multiple perspectives must be acknowledged, encouraged, and validated. Therefore, both 'liberal' and 'conservative' interpretations of social justice need to be not only heard and respected, but also critiqued. However, because most educators are conditioned to think about 'diversity' in terms of attitudes, values, and biases, in racial, cultural, or ethnic contexts, they rarely think of it in terms of diverse political beliefs and/or affiliations. In part, this is because as a nation, we've been taught that one's politics is a private matter. As a result, it is even more rare for educators to think of political bias as a factor in school leadership. And yet, attempting to excise "the political from the life of the mind" (Morrison, 1992, p. 12) is a costly erasure, what Toni Morrison (1992) calls "a kind of trembling hypochondria always curing itself with unnecessary surgery" (p. 12). For an educator, the costs of ignoring how personal political orientations inform thinking and decision-making are incalculable because there is clearly a nexus between personal politics, how one views democracy, and how one interprets the meaning of social justice.

The NCATE controversy demonstrates that it is naïve, and perhaps dangerous, to take for granted that social justice means the same thing to everyone. Given the strident arguments coming from both sides of the NCATE debate, it is possible to project that if these types of conflicting positions about social justice were held by two administrators responsible for two different schools, how they interpret social justice would have a distinctly different impact on the vision that guides their leadership of their individual schools. Similarly, how they rationalize the decisions they make would be informed by their personal political orientations (stated or unstated), dominant social status, and how they are conditioned to think about, and relate to, those in nondominant groups. In addition, their decisions about professional development for faculty, program design, classroom practice, and assessment, etc., may be very different, and come from very different places depending on how these school leaders define social justice. But again, the question is: Should the concept of *justice* be subject to arbitrary interpretations if you are a teacher or school leader who through training and personal conviction has accepted the charge of *safeguarding the values of democracy through integrity, fairness, ethical behavior, equity, moral decision-making, and social justice*? And, if educational leaders are permitted to act on their own personal interpretations of social justice, especially what this means in the context of democracy, what potential impact could this have on generations of students over time? For example, could these differences in leadership perspective be directly or indirectly linked to some of the abysmal racialized gaps in learning outcomes? Moreover, should students' lives and futures be controlled by the vagaries of shifting attitudes and times, and personal political agendas? Finally, is it morally defensible to use taxpayer money to support sociopolitical agendas that are inimical to social justice and basic democratic principles?

Some would argue that a protracted discourse about the nature of social justice is merely a time-consuming rhetorical exercise that is overly philosophical, and uselessly abstract when considered in the context of the range of challenges and decisions that confront a school leader every day. Some would question the need to engage in debates about the principles of democracy when democratic ideals and values are embedded in K–12 curricular materials, and taught to students every day, beginning with the (not so solemn and very controversial) pledge of allegiance. How, they might ask is a debate about social justice related to daunting challenges like the following:

- High rate of teacher absences → disproportionately high number of substitute teachers (especially long-term substitutes)
- High student/teacher ratios
- High percentage of inexperienced teachers and frequent teacher turnover
- Large class size
- Inadequate funding and inadequate classroom materials

How, some might ask, is a discussion of social justice, personal politics, and social dominance related to daily leadership decisions about how to track students, or whom to suspend, or who teaches lower level or advanced classes? Abstract questions about what social justice is or is not may seem irrelevant when decisions are being made about whether or not a child (especially a margin-dwelling child) takes high-level math or science, or takes a language, or is directed to college and a professional career, or to a permanent niche in the Walmart 'family' which dangles the dream of *Making Better Possible* (Walmart, 2014, p. n.a.) in front of its hapless 'associates.'

The answer is that social justice should-*not* and can-*not* be divorced from the everyday life of schooling, nor can it be absolved from indirect responsibility for acts of violence or hatred or unfairness that occur in schools (or in society) because either students have not been taught or, are not being taught, that there is a nexus between social justice, democracy, and American citizenship. This is especially important if *we hold these truths to be self-evident that all men are created equal, that they are endowed by their Creator with certain unalienable rights*. This includes the civil right to an equal and equitable education in American schools. Either we *do* democracy every day or we're doing the obverse: *de-democratizing* public education. We are either building it up or tearing it down because issues related to democracy and social justice are being played out every day, in every day acts of bias, or antibias, or compassion, or contempt (whether subtle or overt). The fact that in America, social justice *needs* advocates, and *needs* to be defended *every* day, or validated as having a legitimate place at the center of how we frame the educative process in American schools is itself a travesty, and according to Gordon (1999), "our nation cannot continue to function as a democracy in the absence of social justice" (p. xiii). And, it is likely that, despite the sometimes-showy displays of bombastic rhetoric and political gamesmanship, most Americans have internalized this idea. Like God, most expect American justice to be there to protect them when they need its protection.

This dichotomous thinking about America and democracy and freedom and justice, and the cluster of American ideals and values that are part of a sacred trust for most Americans, is nothing new. It has always been evident in the nation's display of cognitive dissonance that allowed a commitment to human slavery and human freedom to coexist in the same largely Christian country, or a belief in the inviolable rights of man and human dignity to coexist with the practice of defining some men and women as fractionally human. Historian David Brion Davis (2006) has argued fervently that not only did slavery and democracy coexist, "the ultimate contradiction [is] that our free and democratic society was made possible by slave labor" (p. n.a.). Looked at another way, this means that historically, a disturbing symbiotic relationship existed between democracy and slavery; justice and injustice; equality and inequality. Arguably, this disturbing symbiotic relationship continues to exist today, but it has been recast, contemporized, and *mystified*. However, if we look closely, we can see a disturbing symbiosis underlying a number of today's controversial social issues. Florida radio host Joyce Kaufman's bitter anti-immigrant sentiment is an appropriate example: .

> To "illegal immigrants": "If you commit a crime, while you're here, we should hang you and send your body back to where you came from, and your family should pay for it." (cited in Ho et al., 2012, p. 583)

Other social issues include the widening (some say chronic) gap between the rich and the poor, the school-to-prison pipeline which sweeps up some children as early as third grade, and the racialized achievement gap in schools which makes a mockery of Horace Mann's idea that school is the *great equalizer*.

Many years ago, in his study of the nature of prejudice, Gordon Allport (1979) offered an astute psychosocial analysis of this dichotomous thinking about America and democracy and freedom and justice which links it to stages of human development, how we learn prejudice, and perceptions of social dominance. Looking at in-groups and out-groups through a racial lens, he pointed out that even young American children have internalized the idea that there is a socially condoned, and therefore acceptable, difference between their *public* stance regarding justice and equality, and their *privately* held beliefs and attitudes toward individuals and groups that Toni Morrison calls the *not me*. According to Allport (1979), white American children learn very early that they live in a culture that encourages ethnocentrism, but

> ... [a]t the same time [they] must give lip service to democracy and equality, or at least ascribe some good qualities to ... minority group[s] and somehow plausibly justify the remaining disapproval that one expresses. It takes the child well into adolescence to learn the peculiar double-talk appropriate to prejudice in a democracy ... Now when the teaching of the schools takes effect, the child learns a new verbal norm: he must talk democratically. He must profess to regard all races and creeds as equal ... Prejudiced talk and democratic talk are reserved for appropriate occasions, and rationalizations are ready for whatever occasions require them. Even conduct is varied according to circumstances. ... Double-dealing, like double-talk is hard to learn. It takes the entire period of childhood and much of adolescence to master the art of ethnocentrism. (Allport, 1979, p. 310)

By adulthood, most have become masters of duplicity because these contradictory ways of thinking, speaking, and behaving have taken deep root. In a sense, as a society, we've normalized mystification through a pattern of socially condoned *double-dealing* and *double-talking* about personal biases and public positions on these same subjects. It's easy to imagine what this could look like on an individual or interpersonal level. For example, a white male could *worship* a black sports figure, but simultaneously could resist the idea of welcoming him into the family as a son-in-law, into the social circle as a friend or into the community as a neighbor.

Democracy and equality, and justice rest at the heart of what makes the American experiment unique; they are what distinguish America as a nation, and as a world state. However, do Americans merely give *lip service* to the ideals and values they say they cherish the most? Do school educators merely give *lip service* to the ideals and values that they are professionally obligated to promote? Can educators, especially school leaders, afford to ignore or dismiss these contradictions and inconsistencies as they are manifested in society, in their schools, and more importantly in themselves especially when the lives and futures of children are at stake?

Although it is clear that these are very complex questions with no simple answers, it is equally clear that these questions pose particular challenges for educators, especially school leaders, because among other things, they invite a reconsideration of the implications of ethical behavior and moral transformative leadership. Although Palmer's (1998) prescient statement, "*we* teach who *we* are" (p. 2) is undeniably true, it is also true that we *lead* where *we* want to go. And, where *we* want to go is informed by everything that shapes our thinking and our being. Despite what may appear to be insurmountable challenges, change, even transformation, is possible because we do have some control over who we are, what we believe, and the attitudes and beliefs that guide the decisions we make in both our personal and professional lives.

References

Allport, G. (1979). *The nature of prejudice*. Cambridge, MA: Perseus Books.

Butin, D. W. (n.a.). Dark times indeed: NCATE, social justice, and the marginalization of multicultural foundations. *Journal of Educational Controversy*. Western Washington University. Retrieved July 15, 2014 from http://www.wce.wwu.edu/Resources/CEP/eJournal/v002n002/a003.shtml

Council for the Accreditation of Educator Preparation (CAEP). Retrieved from http://caepnet.org/

Dantley, M., & Cambron-McCabe, N. (2001, April). *Administrative preparation and social justice concerns in Ohio*. Paper presented at AERA annual meeting, Seattle, WA.

Dantley, M. E., & Tillman, L. C. (2010). Social justice and moral transformative leadership, in Catherine Marshall & Maricela Oliva, *Leadership for social justice: Making revolutions in education*. Boston: Allyn and Bacon.

Davis, D. B. (2006). *Inhuman bondage: The rise and fall of slavery in the new world*. New York, NY: Oxford University Press. Retrieved October 2014 from http://www.goodreads.com/author/quotes/104072.David_Brion_Davis

Dewey, J. (1963). *Democracy and education an introduction to the philosophy of education*. New York, NY: The Macmillan Company.

Educational Leadership Constituent Council (ELCC). Retrieved from http://caepnet.org/accreditation/caep-accreditation/spa-standards-and-report-forms/elcc

Gordon, E. W. (1999). Education & justice: A view from the back of the bus. New York: Teachers College Press.

Greene, M. (1976). Challenging mystification: Educational foundations in dark times. *Educational Studies, 7*(1), 9–29.

Heybach, J. (2009). *Rescuing social justice in education: A critique of the NCATE controversy*. Ohio Valley Philosophy of Education Society. Retrieved July 23, 2012 from http://niu.academia.edu/JessicaHeybach/Papers22132/Rescuing_Social_Justice_in_Education_A_Critique_of_the_NCATE_Controversy

Ho, A. K., Sidanius, J., Pratto, F., Levin, S., Thomsen, L., Kteily, N., & Sheehy-Skeffington, J. (2012). Social dominance orientation: Revisiting the structure and function of a variable predicting social and political attitudes. *Personality and Social Psychology Bulletin, 38*(5), 583–606.

Hueberger, B. (2002). Cultural diversity: Building skills for awareness, understanding and application. Dubuque, Iowa: Kendall/Hunt Publishers.

Leadership for student learning: Redefining the teacher as leader: School leadership for the 21st century initiative.

McIntosh, P. (1988). *White privilege and male privilege.* This paper was presented at the Virginia Women's Studies Association conference in Richmond in April, 1986, and the American Educational Research Association conference in Boston in October, 1986, and discussed with two groups of participants in the Dodge seminars for Secondary School Teachers in New York and Boston in the spring of 1987.

Morrison, T. (n.a.). Retrieved August 12, 2014 from http://www.edchange.org/multicultural/language/quotes_alpha2.html#G

O'Conner, C. (2013). Report: Fast Food Companies Outsource $7 billion in Annual Labor Costs to Taxpayers. Retrieved 8/29/14 from http://www.forbes.com/sites/clareoconnor/2013/10/16/reports-fast-food-companies-outsource-7-billion-in-annual-labor-costs-to-taxpayers/

Palmer, P. J. (1998). *The courage to teach: Exploring the inner landscape of a teacher's life.* San Francisco, CA: Jossey-Bass.

Tatum, B. D. (1997). *Why are all of the black kids sitting together in the cafeteria? And other conversations about race.* New York, NY: Basic Books.

Teacher Leaders Network Forum. (n.a.). *Teacher leadership 3.0—An interview with Gayle Moller.* Retrieved March 2011 from http://www.teacherleaders.crg/node/3898

Walmart. (2014). *Walmart Home Page.* Retrieved August 29, 2014 from http://careers.walmart.com/

Williams, M. (1999) *Of History and Hope.* Poetry Foundation. Retrieved 5/14/14 from https://www.poetryfoundation.org/poems-and-poets/poems/detail/47107

· 3 ·

REENTERING THE RACIAL *SELF*

Examining and Deconstructing Personal Biases

There exists a dissonance between America's official identity as the definitive world *democracy* and its *de facto* reality as a country still struggling to acknowledge its racist substructure while simultaneously affirming its' multicultural past, present, and future. American schools reflect this tension, and this chapter examines what this looks like in terms of everyday biases that inflect and infect policies and practices in schools.

The chapter explores in some detail America's ambivalent response to race, racial identity development, the nature of prejudice, and how humans form values, and develop belief systems in terms of what this means for the educative process. And, there is a critique of *Whiteness* as a sociopolitical concept as it relates to power and privilege, and as a demographic reality as it relates to institutional discrimination in schools; it is not meant to be a critique of *white people,* and that is an important distinction. The goal of the chapter is to get educators to acknowledge, confront, and deconstruct personal biases that sustain institutional and systemic inequities in schools.

Keywords: personal biases, racism, white privilege, American exceptionalism, new Jim Crow, color blindness, school-to-prison pipeline, zero tolerance, race, institutional discrimination

Identity seems to be the garment with which one covers the nakedness of the self ...

                    —James Baldwin

... ignoring race is understood to be a graceful, even generous, liberal gesture.

                    —Toni Morrison

Prologue: Nakedness

For some of us, one of the most intimidating things we can do is stand before our naked reflections in a mirror. Among other things, nakedness reminds us of how imperfect we are; it exposes what we perceive to be the good, the bad, and the 'ugly' parts of ourselves. Nakedness can make us feel vulnerable and defenseless, insignificant and powerless, angry and depressed. Nakedness confronts us with stark realities about our physical being that we might prefer to keep hidden. Nakedness brings us face to face with our own humanness and our own mortality; our own truth. No matter what power and confidence we project to the world, in the end it's just skin that we see after all, and it's weak and penetrable. In private, we can choose to see ourselves truly or not; we can turn away, or cover ourselves, or adjust the lighting, because most of us have something that we prefer to hide from ourselves and from others. In most cases, we resist, sometimes vehemently, being exposed to critical public scrutiny or attack or derision, and we can exercise some control over our physical selves; we can use undergarments that restructure and reshape our bodies to produce a more desirable effect that we believe is fit for public consumption, even adulation. Rarely, would any of us voluntarily risk exposing our nakedness in public because it would likely bring deep humiliation, fear, shame, and even questions about our judgment, competence, and worthiness. I point this out, not because this chapter is meant to be a study in human prurience, but because in a sense, it is about nakedness of another sort; the nakedness we feel when we take a critical look *inside* ourselves and confront our own very personal biases.

* * *

People are trapped in history, and history is trapped in them.

                    —James Baldwin

Central to the meaning of whiteness is a broad, collective American silence. The denial of white as a racial identity, the denial that whiteness has a history, allows the quiet, the blankness to stand as the norm. This erasure enables many to fuse their absence of racial being with the nation, making whiteness their unspoken but deepest sense of what it means to be American.—Grace Elizabeth Hale

Being an 'American' places a heavy burden on white people, especially those with privilege, because of the dissonance between America's official identity as the definitive world *democracy* and its *de facto* reality as a country struggling to acknowledge its racist substructure. This 'burden' is complicated by America's deep-seated abhorrence for the concept of *racism*, which causes it to recoil from the *thought* of being called a *racist* country even while it desperately clings to a belief in *American exceptionalism* which is steeped in racism and white privilege ideologies. Akin to the medieval concept of 'divine right,' *American exceptionalism* can be traced to the Puritan John Winthrop, who drew his inspiration from a key concept in Jesus' *Sermon on the Mount* which states: You are the light of the world. A city that is set on a hill cannot be hidden (Matthew 5:14).

Winthrop believed that the new Massachusetts colony would become that "city that is set on a hill," and that its colonists, of European descent, were destined to be that powerful 'light of the world' about which Jesus spoke. This belief led to the perception of divine elevation for the people and the colony, and a Biblical endorsement of their *exceptionalism* in all the world. It also provided the sanction of 'divine right' to justify their ambitious empire-building plans that ultimately transformed the face of the American continent. What began in 1630 as religious inspiration for an American colony has evolved into political certitude for a country. Although no one mentions 'divine right' anymore in an increasingly secular sociopolitical environment, the concept of *American exceptionalism* has been internalized by a nation, and is deeply rooted in the fabric of the American consciousness, and the social, political, and educational implications are enormous.

Among other things, *American exceptionalism* provides validation for America's right to *lead* a world filled with people who stubbornly insist on being racially and ethnically diverse, and who are systematically the targets of American racism and ethnocentrism. This is tragically evident on the world stage in the endless insensitive and heavy-handed way that racial and cultural differences are handled in American diplomacy and political discourse, and it curdles American attempts at nation-building which have come in the aftermath of American war-making in places like Afghanistan and Iraq. On the world stage, *American exceptionalism* has become synonymous with Western, Eurocentric supremacy.

On the national stage, however, *American exceptionalism* has more subtle connotations, and has become synonymous with *white exceptionalism*, *white* privilege, and *white* social and political dominance. There are many salient examples of this which are embedded in social policies and within the national discourse: Florida's racialized school assessment plan which proposed to vary academic expectations and standards by race; social studies textbook revisions adopted in Texas which attempt to neutralize or ignore the horrors of American slavery; a variety of state and federal voter suppression policies which disproportionately disenfranchise people of color; assertions by *presidential* candidates that *Spanish is the language of the ghetto, not the language of prosperity*, and that Mexicans are rapists and murders; defamatory racist descriptions of the first African-American president in the media, and most notably, retrogressive patterns of racialized school segregation nationwide.

Another disturbing example, directly linked to everyday bias in schools, is what Michelle Alexander (2010) calls the 'New Jim Crow,' or the mass incarceration of African-American, Latino, and Native American males. She describes this as "a stunningly comprehensive and well-disguised system of racialized social control that functions in a manner strikingly similar to Jim Crow" (p. 4). In her social critique, Alexander connects several pertinent themes all of which are linked to race and racism: social stratification and caste, color blindness, and the school-to-prison pipeline.

In the era of color blindness, it is no longer socially permissible to use race, explicitly, as a justification for discrimination, exclusion, and social contempt. So we don't. Rather than rely on race, we use our criminal justice system to label people of color 'criminals' and then engage in all of the practices we supposedly left behind. Today it is perfectly legal to discriminate against criminals in nearly all the ways that it was once legal to discriminate against African-Americans. Once you're labeled a felon, the old forms of discrimination—employment discrimination, housing discrimination, denial of the right to vote, denial of educational opportunity, denial of food stamps, and other public benefits, and exclusion from jury service—are suddenly legal. As a criminal, you have scarcely more rights, and arguably less respect, than a black man living in Alabama at the height of Jim Crow. We have not ended racial caste in America; we have merely redesigned it (Alexander, 2010, p. 2).

One of the most astonishing aspects of Alexander's research is that increasingly, American schools are complicit in propping up the school-to-prison pipeline because of current policies that criminalize students for minor infractions using a 'zero tolerance' justification rather than providing in-school counseling or other remedial types of behavioral and academic support. Often ignored are the broader contexts which impact student behaviors such as poverty, learning disabilities, underachievement, miseducation, or a personal history of abuse or neglect. Here too, racial dynamics are evident because the students most affected are students of African-American, Latino, and Native American descent.

The fact is that racism and other forms of discrimination are "part of the structure of schools, the curriculum, the education most teachers receive, and the interactions among teachers, students and the community" (Nieto & Bode, 2012, p. 64). And, in American schools, there are many implicit and explicit examples of how racial politics are embedded in school policies that structure and sustain inequitable academic outcomes that can be disaggregated by race; tracking and the elimination of bilingual programs immediately come to mind, as well as the gaping racialized disparities in academic achievement that cast a pall over every conversation about school 'progress.' Collectively, these are forms of institutional bias which some have begun to call '*second-generation segregation*,' a "largely silent, but powerful form of institutional racism in American education" (Brooks, 2012, p. 73).

These examples suggest that the belief in American *exceptionalism* has become a convenient façade that masks America's chronic fixation with race, and white supremacy, which is balanced by its chronic denial of these same beliefs at a level that approximates a national paranoia. The tension is as intense and heated as tectonic plates colliding, and the social eruptions are seismic and ubiquitous. Clearly, racism is endemic in American life and history and culture and politics and it is pernicious and destructive on many levels. Like the discredited concept of the *melting pot*, American *exceptionalism* was, and is, directed at white-skinned Americans; it was never meant to include the black and brown citizens who were, and continue to be, relegated to the margins of the American social and political structure.

Not too long ago, Donald Sterling, the billionaire owner of a major basketball franchise, exposed a moment of cognitive dissonance, and shocked the nation and perhaps the world by stating openly (and vehemently) that he didn't want Black people to attend his team's basketball games; he was seemingly oblivious to the fact that the team, a major source of his income, is largely composed of Black men. Although his comments seem senseless, even lunatic on the surface, on some deeper levels, they make perfect sense. This chapter is not about Donald Sterling, but it is about why Donald Sterling's comments make sense in the context of social psychology, and the complex way humans develop attitudes and values and prejudices that shape how they view the world and relate to the people in it, especially those people they perceive as the 'other.' Although Sterling's comments are offensive, blatant, and public, they are also instructive. How likely or possible is it that a legislator, or an educator could have internalized similar attitudes but remain silent about them? For example, could an administrator of a school filled with black and brown children, who is charged with leading them to academic and social success, harbor a similarly contradictory set of biased feelings and beliefs? If so, why is this possible? And what would this mean for the children, for the school's climate and culture, and for the kind of teaching that goes on in that school? What impact would such deeply biased and contradictory feelings and beliefs have on curricular decisions and staff development, etc.? And what does it mean if we think of this in terms of the school community more broadly, and include secretaries, aides, bus drivers, and the facilities staff? The point is that Donald Sterling is *not* an anomaly; there exist many like him who have power and influence, and who often manage to conceal their attitudes because they have the *power* to control the narrative, or because discussing race is not *politically correct* in the present social climate where silence, evasion, and denial are the norm.

Using the complex American tapestry as a backdrop, this chapter offers a frank discussion of race and racism and prejudice and discrimination and bias, specifically as it relates to a black/white binary construction. This acknowledges the peculiarly American interracial dynamics which have their origins in American slavocracy. The goal of the chapter is to lift the veil of silence, which we've traditionally draped over these issues, and encourage both objective and subjective analyses of these difficult subjects that we've taught ourselves to ignore. It also explores in some detail America's ambivalent response to race, racial identity development, the nature of prejudice, and how humans form values and develop belief systems. And there is a critique of *Whiteness* as a sociopolitical concept as it relates to power and privilege, and as a demographic reality as it relates to institutional discrimination in schools; it is not a critique of *white people*, and it's important that readers make that distinction. This opens a discussion of the tricky and challenging process of *changing* beliefs and values, and attitudes as it relates to school leaders, and teachers, and students and parents and policymakers, and how all of this is connected to the social dynamics of power and powerlessness in schools and in society.

The goal of the chapter is to get readers to confront and deconstruct personal biases that may have professional consequences. It is a direct challenge to readers of all colors, races, ethnicities, and cultural affiliations to engage in self-reflection that acknowledges our individual racial selves and the socialization patterns that inform our thinking and behavior on personal and professional levels because they are related. The chapter challenges readers to think deeply about sensitive subjects which are socially abhorrent, which make us uncomfortable, and which sometimes cause us to retreat to the safety of our *comfort zones* because for most underserved students there is no retreat, there is no safety, and there are no comfort zones. It's important for readers to understand this because these issues, whether acknowledged or not, are always there; sometimes they pierce the surface, but they mainly exist at subterranean levels; like magma, always hot, and always potentially dangerous when ignored. These subjects, and the policies they influence, are universally impactful regardless of skin color, race, ethnicity, cultural affiliation, or class, and the chapter is designed to make this clear. Finally, this chapter is a pointed reminder that an educator's first responsibility is to the children she or he serves, and it further makes the case that when we remediate problems associated with race and bias on personal, social, and institutional levels, society at-large is enriched. Conversely, when we ignore or deny these problems, and allow them to fester, our personal humanity shrivels a bit, and society at-large is diminished, an affirmation of John Donne's profound wisdom that *no man is an island.*

Playing in the Dark ...

Prejudgments become prejudices only if they are not reversible when exposed to new knowledge. A prejudice, unlike a simple misconception is actively resistant to all evidence that would unseat it. We tend to grow emotional when a prejudice is threatened with contradiction. Thus, the difference between ordinary prejudgments and prejudice is that one can discuss and rectify a prejudgment without emotional resistance.

—Gordon Allport

In *Playing in the Dark—Whiteness and the Literary Imagination,* novelist and social critic Toni Morrison eloquently affirms the omnipresence of race and racism in American literature and, by extension, in the American character. Among other things, Morrison addresses what she calls the "racial disingenuousness and moral frailty at [America's] heart" (Morrison, 1992, p. 6). And, she argues that despite living in a "wholly racialized world" (Morrison, 1992, p. 4), Americans are often incoherent when they try to talk about race because ignoring race is understood to be a graceful, even generous, liberal gesture. To notice is to recognize an already discredited difference. To enforce its invisibility through silence is to allow the black body a shadowless participation in the dominant cultural body. According to this logic, every well-bred instinct argues *against noticing* and forecloses adult discourse (Morrison, 1992, pp. 9–10).

The obvious paradox is that although some believe that racism is pervasive, others vehemently deny that we, as Morrison has asserted, live in a "wholly racialized world" and have made an industry of this denial; denying that it has meaning in the context of culture; denying that it infects or inflects our thinking about, and behavior toward, people and cultures that are 'different' from the perceived 'norm'; denying that racism influences official policies and practices on the federal, state, and local levels. This denial has taken some peculiar forms as in the present fixation with 'political correctness.' And yet, it is counterintuitive to think that we can live in a "wholly racialized world" *without* the existence of racism in it. In *The Anti-Social Contract*, political theorist Y. N. Kly (1997) points out that from the very beginning of the American experiment, moral frailty subverted America's fundamental ideals and values. According to Kly, American colonists attempted to reconcile the philosophical ideal of human freedom, and what he called *anti-ideals*. Colonists wanted to continue to identify with the ideals of freedom and equality as basic human rights while they embraced *anti-ideals* which included their right to enslave Africans, dispossess Native Americans, promote their own self-interests at the expense of human rights, and profit from human devastation. "The result was the American 'trick': the surrender of morality and higher aspirations to self-interest ..." (Kly cited in Biven, 2005, p. 49). However, even though from the beginning, Americans internalized moral frailty and chose to live in a "wholly racialized world" America's democratic promise, though tarnished, still endured in part, because America's high *official morality* continues to make it unique among the countries of the world:

> No other country has such ringing expressions of the creed of equality in its historic papers of State. ... It would be impossible for any child in America to grow up without knowing, and in some degree respecting, this guideline for national conduct. In many countries of the world, by contrast, we find official discrimination against minority groups practiced by the government itself. But in the United States, discrimination is *unofficial*, illegal, and in a profound sense, regarded as un-American. And the founding fathers took a strong stand on the matter. And the common people, from the earliest days of the republic knew what that stand was. (Allport, 1979, pp. 330–331)

Moreover, America's heroic renunciation of the ruling English monarchy to begin a new nation guided by freedom and justice made a good *story*, one that the citizenry wanted to embrace, and wanted to believe. More than two hundred years later, it's still a good *story*, and the underlying *de facto* realities were always glaringly present; equality never reigned, not entirely, and America was never either willing or able to reconcile its ideals and *anti-ideals*; it was never either willing or able to reconcile privilege and caste, and race and equality. We know this because even though there was always a rhetorical reverence for 'diversity' and individual freedom at the heart of America's promise, America never embraced all of its people. *Moral frailty* was part of the American fabric. We know this because of the 'peculiarly' American institution of slavery, and the systematic extermination of Native Americans. We know this because the celebrated transcontinental railroad, which transformed the nation in progressive ways, was built over the backs of Chinese Americans. We know this because of contemporary images of African-Americans dying on rooftops, or their bodies putrefying in stagnant water in post-Katrina New Orleans. We know this because of the 'new Jim Crow.'

And yet, America's *promise* is a good one, even a great one, but it remains unfulfilled, in part, *because* too many American's *choose* to live in a "wholly racialized world," in which racism is pervasive. In America, racism is like an addiction. Sometimes secret, often unarticulated; individually and collectively, this addiction can distort our vision, blunt our senses, and sometimes force us to do and say crazy and contradictory things. Racism is corrupting America's vitals, and diminishing us as a nation; it is literally and figuratively a silent *killer*, and like any *addiction*, it can be accompanied by denial and dismissal. The national response to racism is complex, multilayered, and deeply rooted in world and American history, and yet, despite the implicit Constitutional denunciation of racism, it stubbornly persists in high and low places causing incalculable damage to generations of citizens, especially those with the least power. But the essential question remains: Whose job is it to "unravel belief systems that belittle any of our citizens" (Delpit, 2012 cited in Brooks, pp. xii–xiii)? Legislators? Educators? Religious leaders? Parents? Part of the challenge is to avoid insularity; to avoid thinking exclusively in terms of special interest groupings, and to begin acknowledging our common history, and our common destiny.

Cornel West (1993) addressed this point in *Race Matters* when he said that "our common destiny is more pronounced and imperiled precisely when our divisions are deeper" (p. 8). Although West made the statement more than twenty years ago, it is very relevant now in the prevailing racial climate that has made the discussion of race even more contentious now than it was then. West elaborates on this point when he says that "[t]here is no escape from our interracial interdependence, yet enforced racial hierarchy dooms us as a nation to collective paranoia and hysteria—the unmaking of any democratic order" (p. 8). And yet, even though racism is destined to be everyone's problem to some degree, everyone does not see bias reduction as part of her or his responsibility, or as a social problem that affects her or him personally.

Critical to making any progress is being able to define the problem accurately, and unfortunately, some continue to define entire racial groups as *the problem* rather than focus on the obvious flaws in American society that *cause* the complex social problems that are crushing entire groups of people. According to West, we err when we narrow our understanding of race in America to the 'problems' that black people presumably pose for white people, rather than being self-reflective and considering what this way of viewing black people can tell us about ourselves as a country. But many don't want to know what this reveals about us as a nation because it seems tantamount to self-flagellation. As a result, many have disengaged, or have internalized a sense of personal absolution, and therefore feel no obligation to be part of the official solution even when this is part of their 'official' responsibility as a leader; as a principal or superintendent, or board president. Sometimes, however, because of external pressures by accrediting bodies, or because of state or national policy guidelines, these tensions *are* addressed in schools, but often in superficial or simplistic ways. In the end, these one-dimensional 'solutions' may do more harm than good. For one thing, they can give the erroneous sense of a *mission accomplished*, and give people permission to stop working for change, and acquit themselves of the need to work on behalf of equity and social justice.

Educator Lisa Delpit comes to a similar conclusion about America's tortured response to race when she says

> I have come to believe that the real problem is not so much the culture of the students or the culture of the schools, but the culture of the larger American society. That is the culture that needs to be addressed. The larger society has consistently expressed a kind of cultural violence toward all things of African descent, and this national culture can crush children of color. We, as a country, desperately need to look at ourselves and use all of our collective energy to unravel belief systems that belittle any of our citizens. (Delpit, 2012, cited in Brooks, pp. xii–xiii)

Although I agree with Delpit's analysis, among other things, it confronts us with the chicken or the egg conundrum—What comes first, and whose job is it to *unravel belief systems that belittle any of our citizens*? Do we act as individuals to heal ourselves (and surely healing is needed), and how do we do this?

How do we know where to begin? Do we act as a nation, and redouble our efforts to strengthen existing laws, or do we make new ones? And can legislation change beliefs and attitudes? And who will facilitate this process? How do we move from a state of willful blindness and self-serving denial to a state of mind that allows us to be self-critical, as we undergo the often painful and deeply unsettling process of confronting our own biases both as individuals and as a nation?

If we accept the premise that we have a common destiny, in the end, it's everyone's problem (whether it is acknowledged or not), and it's everyone's responsibility to 'fix' the problem. This is part of the burden that *whiteness* confers on some Americans: being responsible for fixing a racial problem which they themselves co-create, perpetuate, and derive unearned benefit, but often ignore because of social conditioning, or because they prefer to maintain a racial hierarchy that gives them status and power. Whether individually or collectively, many of the citizens of a nation which defines itself by the concepts of equality, fairness, and justice, and who generally revere Martin Luther King's teachings, have not yet internalized his wisdom that "injustice anywhere is a threat to justice everywhere," and until they do, America will be incapable of much more than a rhetorical disavowal of racism.

The Nature of Prejudice: Why We Need to Talk About It

Prejudice is one of the inescapable consequences of living in a racist society. Cultural racism—the cultural images and messages that affirm the assumed superiority of Whites and the assumed inferiority of people of color—is like smog in the air. Sometimes it is so thick, it is visible, other times it is less apparent, but always day in and day out, we are breathing it in.
—Beverly Daniel Tatum

One must be careful not to take refuge in any delusion—and the value placed on the color of skin is always and everywhere and forever a delusion.
—James Baldwin

This extended passage from Gordon Allport's (1979) *The Nature of Prejudice* is illustrative of many of the issues that follow it. I've entitled the passage *On Being a Dwarf in a Land of Giants—A Parable.*

Ask yourself what would happen to your own personality if you heard it said over and over again that you were lazy, a simple child of nature, expected to steal, and had inferior blood. Suppose this opinion were [sic] forced on you by the majority of your fellow-citizens. And suppose nothing that you could do would change this opinion—because you happen to have black skin ... One's reputation, whether false or true, cannot be hammered, hammered, hammered, into one's head without doing something to one's character.

A child who finds himself rejected and attacked on all sides is not likely to develop dignity and poise as his outstanding traits. On the contrary, he develops defenses. Like a dwarf in a world of menacing giants, he cannot fight on equal terms. He is forced to listen to their derision and laughter and submit to their abuse.

There are a great many things such a dwarf-child may do, all of them serving his ego defenses. He may withdraw into himself, speaking little to the giants and never honestly. He may band together with other dwarfs, sticking close to them for comfort and self-respect. He may try to cheat the giants when he can and thus have a taste of sweet revenge. He may in desperation occasionally push some giant off the sidewalk or throw a rock at him when it is safe to do so. Or he may out of despair find himself acting the part that the giant expects, and gradually grow to share his master's own uncomplimentary view of dwarfs. His natural self-love may, under the persistent blows of contempt, turn his spirit to cringing and self-hate. ... (Allport, 1979, pp. 142–143)

In what many consider a definitive study, psychologist Gordon Allport (1979) affirms the complex nature of prejudice and, by extension, the necessity for complex multidimensional remedies. His research showed that the causes of prejudice are multifaceted, sometimes in conflict, and are intricately connected to almost all of the domains of human experience and human development. This means that challenging prejudice in any form will be a difficult, long-term process that will defy superficial responses (which is too often the norm), and this has significance for policymakers, and especially for educators who have the special task of shaping (or reshaping) young minds, hearts, and perspectives. Among other things, Allport's work deconstructs the many complex layers that connect human behavior, belief systems, and racial identity formation to patterns of individual and group response to individuals and groups classified as 'different' from the perceived social 'norm.' Here he addresses the inner conflict that can accompany prejudice. According to Allport

The course of prejudice in a life seldom runs smoothly. For prejudice attitudes are almost certain to collide with deep-seated values that are often equally or more central to the personality. The influence of the school may contradict the influence of the home. The teachings of religion may challenge social stratification. Integration of such opposing forces within a single life is hard to achieve. (1979, p. 326)

Prejudice is also fairly easy to rationalize, and it takes less effort to maintain a prejudice than to extirpate it. In addition, "we find our prejudgments approved and supported by our friends and associates [and] … [i]t is comforting to find that our [ways of thinking] are similar to those of our neighbors upon whose goodwill our own sense of status depends" (Allport, 1979, p. 24).

Allport cautions us to be aware that when it comes to the development of various prejudices, it's important to understand that home, school, social strata, religious affiliation, cultural patterns, peer pressure, etc., can all collide, disrupt, and undermine each other rather than affirm and complement the core values which they separately promote. Consequently, achieving integration and harmony of such opposing forces is no easy task either for an ordinary individual or for an educator who hopes to facilitate this process for himself or for those under his care and supervision. Achieving integration and harmony of such opposing forces will take self-awareness, a sophisticated understanding of the complex challenges involved, commitment, and above all, patience.

Adding to the complexity of this discussion and process is some confusion or even sloppiness about the meanings of, and distinctions between, the standard terms we use for the analysis of prejudice and related concepts, so it's important to begin with definitions of basic terms. Without a common vocabulary, we invite misunderstanding, misinterpretation, and miscommunication, all of which are counterproductive.

Definitions of Key Terms—*Prejudice, Racism, and Discrimination*

As a point of departure, it is important to distinguish between *prejudice, racism, and discrimination*. Allport (1979) wrote an entire book on the nature of prejudice, indicating how complex and nuanced the concept is, and the following excerpts describing prejudice are both instructive, and sobering:

- [Prejudice is] *a feeling favorable or unfavorable, toward a person or thing, prior to, or not based on, actual experience.* … *ethnic prejudice is mostly negative.* (p. 6)
- Here we have the test to help us distinguish between ordinary errors of prejudgment and prejudice. If a person is capable of rectifying his erroneous judgments in light of new evidence he is not prejudiced.

Prejudgments become prejudices only if they are not reversible when exposed to new knowledge. A prejudice, unlike a simple misconception is actively resistant to all evidence that would unseat it. We tend to grow emotional when a prejudice is threatened with contradiction. Thus, the difference between ordinary prejudgments and prejudice is that one can discuss and rectify a prejudgment without emotional resistance. (p. 9)

- Ethnic prejudice is an antipathy based upon a faulty and inflexible generalization. It may be felt or expressed. It may be directed toward a group as a whole, or toward an individual because he is a member of that group. (p. 9)
- Prejudice is the *moral evaluation* placed by a culture on some of its own practices. It is a designation of attitudes that are disapproved. (p. 11)
- Prejudice is a pattern of hostility in interpersonal relations which is directed against an entire group, or against individual members; it fulfills a specific irrational function for its bearer. (p. 12)
- Much prejudice is a matter of blind conformity with prevailing folkways. (p. 12)
- We have said that an adequate definition of prejudice contains two essential ingredients. There must be an *attitude* of favor or disfavor; and it must be related to an overgeneralized (and therefore erroneous) *belief.* Prejudiced statements sometimes express the attitudinal factor and sometimes the belief factor. (p. 13)
- Prejudice is an existing psychological fact, just as discrimination is an existing social fact. (p. 516)

Racism is a *form* of prejudice, and in the general population, there is a tendency to use the terms interchangeably, but many researchers and theorists have cautioned against thinking of *prejudice* and *racism* as synonymous. Doing so ignores the *systemic* nature of racism, and importantly, the *dynamics of power* which sustains it, and gives it traction. No more is racism simply about interpersonal hatred between individuals or groups, than rape is about love or desire between two people. Both are driven by the dynamics of power and control. Racism *is* about racial enmity, but "like other forms of oppression, [racism] is not only a personal ideology based on racial prejudice, but a *system* involving cultural messages and institutional policies and practices as well as beliefs and actions of individuals" (Tatum, 1997, p. 7). Not only does it understate the problem to think about racism simply as an antagonistic or contentious dynamic between individuals or between groups representing different races, rather, than as systematized advantage and disadvantage *based on* race, it causes us to misdirect our efforts to eradicate it. At its core, racism posits the belief that one group, by virtue of its race, is superior to other groups; entitled to power (earned or unearned), and justified in using its power to structure advantages for its group members and disadvantages for the 'other' groups. Morrison calls them the "not-me" (Morrison, p. 38).

These structured advantages and disadvantages are often deeply and intricately woven into the social fabric and

> [u]nfortunately, some definitions of racism and discrimination obscure the institutional nature of oppression. Although the beliefs and behaviors of individuals may be very hurtful and psychologically damaging, institutional discrimination—that is, the systematic use of economic and political power in institutions (such as schools) that leads to detrimental policies and practices—does far greater damage. These policies and practices have a destructive effect on groups that share a particular identity, be it racial, ethnic, gender, or other. The major difference between individual and institutional discrimination is the wielding of *power*. It is primarily through the power of the people who control institutions, such as schools, that oppressive policies and practices are reinforced and legitimized. (Nieto & Bode, 2012, p. 64)

This analysis shows that racism, prejudice, and discrimination are part of a continuum. However, discrimination has important dimensions that are sometimes missed or unacknowledged. According to Nieto and Bode (2012), as with racism, it is important to avoid thinking of discrimination narrowly in terms of biased interactions between individuals even though "[d]iscrimination is usually based on prejudice, that is, on the attitudes and beliefs of individuals about entire groups of people" (Nieto & Bode, 2012, p. 63). Like prejudice, discrimination can encompass many forms of bias, and racial discrimination is just one of the official categories that has been identified and prohibited by the federal government in the Civil Rights Act of 1964. This Act makes clear that discrimination is situated by federal law, in the discernible *damage* that discrimination can cause an individual, or group, at the *institutional level*. Below, Nieto and Bode (2012) further clarify the broader institutional dimensions of discrimination:

> Institutional discrimination generally refers to how people are excluded or deprived of rights or opportunities as a result of the normal operations of the institution. Although the individuals involved in the institution may not themselves be prejudiced or have any racist intentions, or even an awareness of how others may be harmed, the result may nevertheless be racist. Intentional and unintentional racism may differ but because they both result in negative outcomes, in the end it does

not really matter whether racism and other forms of discrimination are intentional. Rather than trying to figure out whether the intent of a discriminatory action was to do harm or not, educators' time would be better spent addressing the *effects* of racism. (Nieto & Bode, 2012, pp. 64–65).

The passage above raises some critical issues. There are strong arguments to be made that the significance of *intentionality* always needs to be acknowledged in any program or process designed to remediate discrimination at either the institutional or individual level. First, because it is connected to causality, and precipitates the undesirable *effects* we want to eradicate, intentionality needs to remain at the center of the process. Second, intentionality is intimately connected to personal attitudes, belief systems, and values, essential elements that shape individual and collective identity. Our personal attitudes, belief systems, and values guarantee that each of us has a partisan perspective on everything that we do. Therefore, it is impossible to ignore intentionality, because every individual is a partisan of his or her "own way of life, [and] we cannot help thinking in a partisan manner" (Allport, 1979, p. 25). This natural *partisanship* shapes our thinking, our behavior, and our intentions every day, and it is "obvious, then, that the very act of affirming our way of life often leads us to the brink of prejudice" in our day-to-day interactions with others as well as in our decision-making. Furthermore, we live by and for our values, seldom thinking about them or weighing them, and significantly, our personal values are so important "that evidence and reason are ordinarily forced to conform to them" (Allport, 1979, p. 25) rather than the reverse.

Moreover, understanding the *Why?* when we're dealing with discrimination (institutional or individual) is always important. *Why?* is a question that needs to be answered even when it is difficult and generates significant resistance. Simply put, if any of this were easy, and we could ignore the hard questions, we would not be facing the re-segregation of schools, the New Jim Crow, a widening achievement gap that continues to foreclose academic success for generations of Black and brown children, and other egregious problems in schools that have a disturbing racial underside. Intentionality matters because we have to understand *why* systems discriminate, and *who* makes the decisions to maintain the dysfunctionality that institutionalizes disadvantage for some groups, and bestows advantage on other groups that are considered superior, and more worthy. It's important to be able to interrogate institutional power structures, and get answers to these questions:

Who is controlling the system? *Why* are particular decisions being made? Are there hidden institutional or systemic inequities embedded in the process?

Is race or discrimination a factor, and if so what does it look like, and what resources do we need to deconstruct them?

Who stands to benefit from the decisions, and who stands to lose?

What are the expected outcomes, and are they being met?

What structures support the stated goals and which do not?

Is there a disconnect between the stated goals and what is actually being done?

Do unstated, personal biases impact decision-making, and *who* will interrogate this and *how* and *when* will it be done?

If school leaders and policymakers don't ask these questions, and demand answers to them, they may as well be the naïve, uncritical dwellers in the fictive land of Oz, blindly revering and propping up a hidden system of power and control that ostensibly serves the needs of the entire community, while counter-forces operate surreptitiously behind a curtain, in the dark *intentionally* working against the best interests of specific targeted groups.

Finally, it also can be argued that our present approach to deconstructing institutional discrimination is a *see no evil, hear no evil, speak no evil* approach designed to evade the deeper issues, causes, and *intentions* behind policies (which can sometimes be informal hidden agendas). This approach is consistent with society's controversial promotion of *political correctness* as the preferred strategy to strengthen intercultural communications and reduce bias. But, much of what we're presently doing isn't effectively changing the status quo, and the overall educational system risks being just one more case study proving Einstein's well-known definition of insanity which is: *doing the same thing in the same way and expecting a different result.*

Of course, while doing the important and difficult work of coming to terms with the racial contexts within which they operate, educators and policymakers also must invest much more time to come up with a variety of creative solutions to eliminate racism and discrimination in schools; this means systemic change; it means usurping vested interests in maintaining the status quo. Although not a solution in itself, more money and resources are needed to respond to the *effects* of individual and institutional discrimination as manifested in policies and practices in schools, and classrooms, assessment data, textbooks, teacher preparation, tracking, suspension policies, and even on school buses. But, in the end, a metaphorical *exorcism* is needed to eliminate racism and institutional discrimination in the educational system, and nothing less than a comprehensive approach will make a difference. The baseline question is: Do *we* as a society, and as a profession, have the will?

More Definitions—*Attitudes* and *Beliefs*

Two other terms that are important in the discussion of racism, prejudice, and discrimination are *attitudes* and *beliefs*, concepts that have become virtually synonymous in the public domain. We tend to conflate them, blurring their significant distinctions. However, it is important to differentiate them because they represent two essential ingredients of prejudice. For example, in order for prejudice to occur, "[t]here must be an *attitude* of favor or disfavor; and it must be related to an overgeneralized (and therefore erroneous) *belief*" (Allport, 1979, p. 13). According to Allport,

> ... it is useful to distinguish attitude from belief. For example ... certain programs designed to reduce prejudice succeed in altering beliefs but not in changing attitudes. Beliefs, to some extent, can be rationally attacked and altered. Usually, however, they have the slippery propensity of accommodating themselves somehow to the negative attitude which is much harder to change ... Thus the belief system has a way of slithering around to justify the more permanent attitude. The process is one of rationalization—of the accommodation of beliefs to attitudes. (pp. 13–14)

Allport (1979) provides a few examples to clarify the distinction between beliefs and attitudes which I have contemporized using some prevailing attitudes for groups that are presently marginalized in American society. In the following paired statements, the first expresses an *attitude*, the second, a *belief*:

> I can't stand Blacks.
> Blacks are lazy
> I wouldn't live in a neighborhood with Muslims.
> There are a few exceptions, but in general all Muslims are pretty much alike.
> I don't want homosexuals in my church.
> Homosexuals are perverts.
>
> (adapted from Allport, 1979, p. 13)

Attitudes and beliefs tend to function in tandem, and "[w]hen we find one, we usually find the other. Without some generalized beliefs concerning a group as a whole, a hostile attitude could not long be sustained. In modern researches it turns out that people who express a high degree of antagonistic attitudes on a test for prejudice, also show that they believe to a high degree that the groups they are prejudiced against have a large number of objectionable qualities" (Allport, 1979, p. 13).

And prejudice has many faces; it is slippery and not always easily recognized. It can masquerade as kindness, and solicitousness according to early research by Massey, Scott, and Dornbusch (1975). Their study, "Racism Without Racists: Institutional Racism in Urban Schools," shows that "oppression can arise out of warmth, friendliness and concern" (Massey et al., 1975, p. 18). Delpit's research affirms this, and in fact, she introduces what is being called the "modern" face of prejudice which is more subtle, more modulated, and often fraught with contradictions. Pettigrew and Martin's research on prejudice in the workplace affirms that

> ... because of their subtlety and indirectness, these modern forms of prejudice and avoidance are hard to eradicate. Often the black is the only person in a position to draw the conclusion that prejudice is operating in the work situation. Whites have usually observed only a subset of the incidents, any one of which can be explained away by a nonracial account. Consequently, many whites remain unconvinced of the reality of subtle prejudice and discrimination, and come to think of their black coworkers as "terribly touchy" and "overly sensitive" to the issue. For such reasons, the modern forms of prejudice frequently remain invisible even to its {sic} perpetrators. (Pettigrew & Martin, 1987, p. 50)

Perhaps it is a misnomer to call behaviors such as these the *modern face of prejudice* because prejudice has always had several faces: a public one, a private one, and possibly one that lurks beneath the surface of human consciousness. There are infinite historical and public referents for this, as well as a body of sociological and psychological research attempting to explain this perplexing psychic schism. One poignant historical example comes from the life of the emancipated slave, Frederic Douglass, in the person of his owner's wife, Mrs. Auld, who began to teach him to read. At first, Douglass describes her as "a woman of the kindest heart, and the finest feelings" (Douglass, 1986, p. 77). However, within a short time, another face emerged:

> The fatal poison of irresponsible power was already in her hands, and soon commenced its infernal work. The cheerful eye, under the influence of slavery, soon became red with rage; that voice, made all of sweet accord, changed to one of harsh discord; and that angelic face gave place to that of a demon. (Douglass, 1986, pp. 77–78)

Another fairly recent example played out in the public domain was the revelation by one of the most ardent bigots in the U.S. Senate, that he had fathered a black daughter, with whom he secretly had a loving, supportive relationship. And then there's billionaire Donald Sterling, who was scheduled to receive a public service award from the NAACP at the time he made his fateful racist remarks that demeaned his team of Black basketball players. There are countless everyday examples like this that don't receive national attention or spark public outrage and censure.

Some might argue that these analogies have limited application to schools or society at large because of their unique circumstances. However, when looked at in the broader context of the overall sociopolitical climate in which race is increasingly a subtext (the resegregation of schools, the racialized achievement gap, the New Jim Crow, etc.), the examples seem fitting.

Inner Conflicts

A double minded man is unstable in all his ways

—James 1:8

In some ways, this complex ambivalent stance in an individual regarding race replicates the confounding split in America's psyche, evidenced by the ongoing conflict between its ideals and *anti-ideals*, which allows a fervent national commitment to freedom, justice, and equality to coexist with discrimination, injustice, and inequality. And, the internalized belief in *American exceptionalism* adds another layer of complexity to this. Ironically, this duality is also reminiscent of the inner conflict implicit in W. E. B. DuBois' (1994) concept of *double consciousness*, originally addressed to African-Americans, which describes "two souls, two unreconciled strivings, two warring ideals" (DuBois, 1994, p. 2) in one body. However, educators cannot afford to be of two minds especially when it comes to anti-bias initiatives, and yet it is important to remember that privilege and self-interest are powerfully influential motivations for one to make professional decisions that pose no personal risk, no personal loss. Rarely does one choose to relinquish power and control especially if she or he feels a sense of entitlement by virtue of status, past practice, or prevailing social 'norms' which stratify individuals or groups according to race or culture or class. Those in power control the debate, influence or direct policy decisions, decide when to move forward, or to move back, or to stop a process completely. They decide which 'voices' and positions are valuable and will be heard, and which 'voices' and positions are inconsequential and will be silenced. Therefore, double-consciousness in a leader is a dangerous state of mind that can result in what Adrienne Rich called "psychic disequilibrium," a state of mind that is destabilizing, and potentially immobilizing, "as if you looked into a mirror and saw nothing" (Rich, cited in Maher & Tetreault, 2001, p. 201). In the case of social justice initiatives, for a school leader, it could mean looking into a mirror, and *doing* nothing.

Rich was describing this emotional state of "psychic disequilibrium" from the point of view of the 'victims,' the individuals who are made to feel invisible by unfair life-crushing policies that concretize racism, ableism, linguicism, and ageism. However, here, the concept of psychic disequilibrium is being applied to the 'perpetrators,' those leaders who, consciously or not, are responsible for *implementing* these discriminatory policies in schools. They are equally part of the *problem* and part of the *solution* because of the privilege and power invested in them simply by virtue of their leadership role. Although it may be an overstatement to call "psychic disequilibrium," a pathology in a clinical sense, it is undoubtedly an indicator of some psychic distress or damage.

Toni Morrison's (1995) powerful imagery of a fishbowl makes it easier to understand how one can experience *double-consciousness*, and simultaneously exist in two competing worlds: one inside the other

> It is as if I had been looking at a fishbowl—the glide and flick of the golden scales, the green tip, the bolt of white careening back from the gills; the castles at the bottom, surrounded by pebbles and tiny, intricate fronds of green; the barely disturbed water, the flecks of waste and food, the tranquil bubbles traveling to the surface— and *suddenly I saw the bowl, the structure that transparently (and invisibly) permits the ordered life it contains to exist in the larger world* [italics mine]. (Morrison, 1992, p. 17)

Morrison's elegant fishbowl metaphor can represent many things, and the perspective all depends on whether one is *inside* the fishbowl, or *outside* of it. The metaphor can represent double consciousness, or cognitive dissonance, or the isolation and self-delusion of privileged social status. It can also represent an outsider's view of a world that she or he cannot share. In all cases, it's important to understand that the fishbowl is a *construct* that permits an unreal, controlled environment to exist regardless of the chaos that might exist beyond the glass walls. It's also important to understand that both the fish and the bowl are vulnerable because self-delusion and denial are always risky, and an uncritical, *dysconscious* acceptance of a fictive world is always dangerous.

Joyce King's (1991) teaching and research brought the terms dysconsciousness and dysconscious racism to our attention, and her research advanced the conversation about the internal workings of bias, how it affects attitudes and belief systems, and importantly what this can mean for teachers and school leaders and, by extension, for the students they teach or supervise.

Similar to two concepts Freire (1973) called *naïve* and *magic* consciousness, dysconsciousness, according to King, is "an uncritical habit of mind (including perceptions, attitudes, assumptions and beliefs) that justifies inequity and exploitation by accepting the existing order of things as given ... [D]ysconsciousness accepts [the social order] uncritically ... it involves a subjective identification with an ideological viewpoint that admits no fundamentally alternative vision of society" (King, 1991, p. 135). Dysconsciousness is somewhat like living in a *fishbowl*, and accepting the ordered life within it as a true and complete representation of the world even if there is evidence that there are other realities. However, schools cannot be *fishbowls*; not for the students, not for the teachers and especially not for the schools' leaders. An *uncritical* acceptance of systemic or institutional discrimination is very dangerous, not only because it results in a severely limited mindset, but also because it is an impairment, and results in a myopic vision of the world. In a sense, dysconsciousness is what we expect from young children: a simplistic, uncritical acceptance of a construct of the world, and of 'truth,' as it's presented to them by their parents and elders. But teaching is not child's play, and an impaired vision in an educator can be life-crushing for some of their students, usually the ones that are most in need of support.

King's research on dysconsciousness grew out of her work with *pre*service teachers, most of whom were white, but it has far-reaching implications for *in*-service teachers and school leaders as well. Consider, for example, what a dysconscious mindset could mean in the context of projected future demographics which confirm that American teachers and school leaders are now, and will be, disproportionately white for the foreseeable future. Further, the well-established equation of Whiteness and social privilege is a reminder that race is not inconsequential in any of this, and it's a delusion to think otherwise. Even though there have been significant public initiatives to change the racial demographics in school staffing, the process is a protracted one, and overall, the results have been disappointing. Added to this, we know that teachers and school leaders represent a cross-section of American society; they are human incubators nurturing a wide range of attitudes, predispositions, biases, prejudices, and a variety of deeply held beliefs some of which are unacknowledged and/or unarticulated. King's research on dysconsciousness helps explain why some can successfully complete a teacher or leadership preparation program, take one or more 'diversity' courses, and continue to be uncritical of racial injustice and other forms of structural bias, as well as their own complicity in sustaining and supporting discriminatory policies and practices.

Veteran teachers and administrators are not exempt from a dysconscious mindset, and in fact may pose the greatest challenge when it comes to addressing these issues if they use their years of experience and ostensible classroom 'success' to rationalize their particular understanding of, and support for, existing social and institutional structures. Ironically, despite having this *impairment*, those with a dysconscious mindset may, in the context of school reform initiatives, be expected to become change agents, and advocates for social justice and equity-driven teaching and leadership. Even though they may harbor a mindset that can rationalize and *justify* a system that rationalizes and *justifies* inequity and exploitation, they have been socialized to do so, and it can be emotionally destabilizing. It is important to point out that this is a socialization process of which they are virtually unaware. The deeper conflict is that, because of professional commitments and pressure, they may be expected to be both integral parts of racialized systems which are designed to maintain the existing socially inscribed power structures from which they benefit, *and* to deconstruct those same systems. This presumes a kind of self-induced cognitive dissonance which simultaneously puts them in the position of being an active part of the problem *and* an active part of the solution.

In one sense, dysconscious racism can be seen as one significant effect of a general miseducation; specifically, the miseducation of white people.

Almost a century ago, Dr. Carter G. Woodson (1990) wrote a book called *The Mis-Education of the Negro*, and although his work was directed at a 'Negro' audience, when examined in a contemporary context, his words seem prescient and relevant to this discussion if we simultaneously apply his words to the 'Negro' and to the White person with the premise that both of them are being *miseducated in counterpoint to each other*. It's a bit like mirror images: what is right for one, is left for the other.

And it is clear that both sides are being damaged by this racially inscribed, socially constructed, *miseducation*; both sides are suffering an incalculable loss, and although the situations and consequences are vastly different, it's important to acknowledge both perspectives because both the *perpetrators* and the *victims* of prejudice have to be seen as part of the equation in any conversation about racism and discrimination; both have thoughts, feelings, and responses. Moreover,

[e]very human relationship is reciprocal. For every aggressor there is someone aggrieved; for every snob there is someone who resents his condescension; for every oppressor there is someone who strives against the oppression. Therefore, it is

reasonable to expect that certain traits may develop as a response to victimization. (Allport, 1979, p. 126)

And, I would argue that it is reasonable to expect that certain traits may develop as a response to being an oppressor. These too must be acknowledged.

The Double-Edged Blade—Racism Damages Everyone It Touches—Even White People

When we think about racism, and discrimination in the context of schools, we tend to think about how they affect the children, because there is no doubt that at the lower end of the institutional hierarchy children suffer the greatest losses because of institutional discrimination and unfair policies. Lowered self-esteem, racial isolation, underperformance, and diminished access to a good quality of life are among the chronic problems that have been documented, and there is no debate that this focus is important, and right, and necessary because children are the most vulnerable, and the least powerful members of the educational hierarchy. However, the almost single-minded focus on the damage done to the *victims* of racism, and the absence of analysis of the damage that accrues to the *perpetrators* of racism ignores the fact that racism is like a double-edged blade that wounds everyone it touches; in a figurative sense, there is comingled 'blood' everywhere. The point is that everyone suffers a loss on some level. Everyone is damaged by racial injustice even if they don't know it (or don't want to know it); victims and perpetrators are damaged; the privileged and the disprivileged are damaged; the virtual 'masters' and the virtual 'slaves' are damaged, and yet, it's a perspective we don't often consider because among other things, it's difficult to quantify diminished humanity.

In her treatise on whiteness and the literary imagination, Toni Morrison (1992) addresses this same pattern evidenced in American literature, of "always defining [racism] asymmetrically from the perspective of its impact on the subject of racist policy and attitudes." She points out that although "[a] good deal of time and intelligence has been invested in the exposure of racism and the horrific results on its objects, [we ignore] the impact of racism on those who perpetrate it" (p. 11) and she proposes that we "examine the impact of notions of racial hierarchy, racial exclusion, and racial vulnerability and availability on nonblacks. ..." Using historical referents, Morrison affirms that it is important that we study the affects of racism on both the victim and the perpetrator saying that

The scholarship that looks into the mind, imagination, and behavior of slaves is valu-able. But equally valuable is a serious intellectual effort to see what racial ideology does to the mind, imagination and behavior of masters. (Morrison, 1992, p. 11)

The essential questions for this analysis are, What does harboring a racial ideology do to the mind, imagination, and behavior of 'masters,' and What can be done about it?

McIntosh's (1988) groundbreaking article, *White Privilege and Male Privilege*, outlines her struggle with the social, emotional, cultural, and moral implica-tions of racism, and the difficulty of facing the meaning of her privilege and her Whiteness. She said

For me, white privilege has turned out to be an elusive and fugitive subject. The pressure to avoid it is great, for in facing it I must give up the myth meritocracy. If these things are true, this is not such a free country; one's life is not what ones makes it; many doors open for certain people through no virtues of their own. These perceptions mean also that my moral condition is not what I had been led to believe. The appearance of being a good citizen rather than a troublemaker comes in large part from having all sorts of doors open automatically because of my color. (McIntosh, 1988, p. 5)

Clearly this represents a deep, transformative, life-changing moment in her life that touched the core of her personal identity as well as her sense of the meaning of freedom in America. In this one moment, she exposed the *anti-ideals* from which she had been her cloistered by her privileged upbring-ing. Implicit in this statement are the emotional costs to learning that the world, as you knew it, was a construct.

Paul Kivel (2002), a White man, offers a similar perspective. According to him

... the costs of racism to white people are devastating. ... They are not the same costs as the day-to-day violence, discrimination, and harassment that people of color have to deal with. Nevertheless, they are significant costs that we have been trained to ignore, deny, or rationalize away. ... We have been given a distorted and inaccurate picture of history and politics because the truth about racism has been excluded, the contributions of people of color left out, and the role of white people cleaned up and modified. We also lose the presence and contributions of people of color to our neighborhoods, schools, and relationships. We are given a false sense of superiority, a belief that we should be in control and in authority, and that people of color should be maids, servants, and gardeners and do the less valued work of our society. Our experiences are distorted, limited, and less rich the more they are exclusively or pre-dominantly white. ... Racism distorts our sense of danger and safety. We are taught to live in fear of people of color. We are exploited economically by the upper class and unable to fight or even see this exploitation because we are taught to scapegoat people of color. ... There are also spiritual costs. ... Our moral integrity is damaged as we witness situations of discrimination and harassment and do not intervene. Our feelings of guilt, shame, embarrassment, or inadequacy about racism and about our responses to it lower our self-esteem. Because racism makes a mockery of our ideals of democracy, justice, and equality, it leads us to be cynical and pessimistic about human integrity and about our future, producing apathy, blame, despair, self-destructive behavior, and acts of violence, especially among our young people. (Kivel, 2002, p. n.a.)

Kivel's (2002) point is that historically White people have been miseducated through a distorted, self-serving, and sanitized view of the world, especially history and politics; a cluster of survival stratagems that include denial, rationalizations, and justifications for social inequities; a heightened and unrealistic sense of personal value in relation to those considered the 'other'; the normalization of *moral frailty* in relation to social justice and fairness for those who are considered *different*, and perceived as threats; the development of a bystander mentality and social disengagement; feelings of guilt, shame, embarrassment, or anger. One significant point is that Whites are *taught to live in fear of people of color*, and this alone has major implications on every level of social interaction between Whites and Blacks. This fear can be manifested on conscious or subconscious levels, and to greater or lesser degrees, and is related to the contexts in which interracial interactions occur. Fear alone can trigger a defensive posture, antagonistic relationships, an *us* vs. *them* interpersonal dynamic, an oppositional frame of reference, and an overarching sense of threat. These dynamics are evident in the workplace, and can stall progress and undermine healthy intercultural communication.

Talking About Racism in the Workplace: Patterns of Denial and How We Interrupt Progress

Playing the Race Card

It already has been established that prejudice, racism, and discrimination are complex and layered, and can damage individuals; however, it is equally important to acknowledge the structural damage that they can cause as well. For example, they can stifle intercultural communication which is especially problematic when schools and districts lack this awareness, or simply choose not to act on it, but attempt to promote dialogue between different cultural groups or engage in professional development aimed at bias reduction. Rather than improving communication, and reducing intercultural tension, schools may inadvertently stall progress. Delpit (1995) contends that the only way to effectively begin an intercultural dialogue is to learn to listen with "open hearts and minds," to those who have been silenced; otherwise, we risk calcifying the status quo which may ensure that negative biases and detrimental policies and practices stay firmly in place.

One very effective strategy for preserving the status quo is to explicitly or implicitly accuse anyone who brings up race in policy debates of *playing the race card*. The implication is that bringing up race shifts an argument in that person's favor, giving him or her an unfair advantage in any discussion or policymaking process probably because it ostensibly introduces historical elements connected to guilt and shame, and it's a not-so-subtle reminder of the *moral frailty* that continues to weaken America's *heart*. Talking about race makes people uncomfortable because metaphorically, it brings sound and light to dark places, and rattles the cage of denial; it does not allow them to *play in the dark* to paraphrase Morrison. Accusing someone of *playing the race card* is an accusation that invites tension into the space, heightens sensitivity to the subject, and increases the chances for miscommunication, and greater philosophical and emotional distance between the discussants. Moreover, introducing the subjects of race and racism is like putting a virtual hand grenade in the center of a table in a room full of people. The instinctive reaction is to duck and hide for self-protection, and get as far away from the concussive impact as possible. Thereafter, the protective shields are up, and there's a price to pay for the one who brought the *hand grenade*.

Since introducing the subject of race can be perceived as an attack, it can invite a counterattack. For example, the person accused of *playing the race card*, often a person of color, may be effectively silenced or muted by the counterattack, or become defensive because the accusation that one is *playing the race card* amounts to a countercharge of racism. In effect, *the one bringing up the subject of race is then charged with being a racist*. Not only does this counterattack negate and belittle the idea that race and racism should be part of the discussion, it can also reinforce the belief that race and racism have no discernible impact on present or future policy discussions. The irony is that the negation itself is a red flag, a signal that a thorny problem exists, and in the end, it can maintain and perhaps deepen the status quo. However, it is clear that the accusation and counterattack trivialize and dismiss the problem of race by putting it in the category of a 'game' or, at the very least, a mere stratagem.

And yet, the charge that one is *playing the race card* to gain a strategic advantage is flawed logic especially when you consider that the most obvious victims of racism are unwilling participants in a 'game' they neither created nor can 'win' because the ostensible 'winners' and 'losers' are preordained especially when Whiteness and privilege collude. This charge amounts to dissembling of the highest order, and it is a very effective strategy because it poisons the atmosphere, and effectively revictimizes the victim by implicitly (or explicitly) branding her or him as a *racist*.

In an ironic twist, one could accuse institutions of *playing the race card* when, for example, a school district hires a person of color for a high-level position as part of a veiled strategy to foreclose any future discussion about race, because that person would be expected to become the embodiment of that district's success in erasing the perceived *race* problem. This goes beyond *tokenism*, and the greater irony is that the person of color may be effectively muzzled on the subject of race, especially if the district is largely white. This is because a belief exists within some white faculty and staff that any time a person of color brings race into the picture, it represents a *natural* and therefore expected fixation with 'race'; in their minds, 'race' is something other people have. All too often, at this point, they can become dismissive and stop listening or minimize the racial implications of policy decisions. One salient example of this can be seen on the national level. For example, as soon as Barack Obama was elected President of the United States, some pundits pounced on the opportunity to tout America's racial progress, and claim that America was magically in a post-racial era. This was self-congratulatory nonsense; clearly they didn't factor in the racial markers that are evident in the *school-to-prison* pipeline, the high school dropout rates, the high incidence of unemployment among blacks and Latinos, academic underachievement, and *second-generation segregation* which is casting a darkening shadow over America's schools nationwide.

It is important for educators to be aware that racism is insidious, and that it is everyone's problem. It is "co-constructed by the oppressor and the oppressed, among oppressors and among the oppressed; and these relationships are mediated by a great many variables and factors that are constantly changing. So, in a way, no matter how hard we try, how thoughtful we may be, we are likely part of *both* the problem, *and* the solution at the same time" (Brooks, 2012, p. 2). This also means acknowledging and addressing the intentional or unintentional ways that everyone can be complicit in supporting systemic and institutional bias in schools before any real progress can be made. This is not easy.

The question is, How does any of this inform *individual behavior?* This is a critical question because in the end, *individuals* manage systems, and will have to be responsible for deconstructing systemic discrimination. This is a good question for all of us, but especially for educators and the institutions and organizational structures with which they are affiliated because "What people actually do in relation to groups they dislike [overtly or covertly] is not always directly related to what they think or feel about them" (Allport, 1979, p. 14) and, conversely, what people actually feel in relation to groups they dislike [overtly or covertly] is not always directly related to what they do. Therefore, even though discrimination, because of its power to corrupt entire institutions, has greater reach, it's important to remember that no matter how abstract they are, institutions are run by *individuals*.

Dancing on Hot Coals: The Problem of Deconstructing Whiteness

The human capacity to injure other people has always been much greater than its ability to imagine other people. Or perhaps we should say, the human capacity to injure other people is great precisely because our capacity to imagine other people is very small.

—Elaine Scarry

There is a pivotal (and painful) scene in Hurston's masterpiece, *Their Eyes Were Watching God* (1978), in which the main character, seven-year-old Janie, discovers that she is Black. This is a stunning moment for the character and for the reader because Janie has grown up in the 'Jim Crow' South in the early 1900s where racial apartheid was the social norm, and where Blacks were confronted daily by their racial selves. Theirs was a daily education about racial realities and how these realities structured and controlled their lives, and yet, Janie did not know, until she saw a group picture in which she stood among her White friends, that she was Black. At first, she rejected the idea, presumably because despite her dissociative response to this new identity, in her child's mind she had already internalized the idea that being Black meant something different from being White, something vaguely negative. Perhaps she had already understood that there were different values placed on white skin and black skin, and that these values translated into privileges that would either be granted to her or withheld from her because of structural racism. From a psychological perspective, this confusion about racial identity is a normal part of any child's racial identity development, and even though the developmental patterns sometimes overlap for Black and White children, there are distinctive differences that can be linked to America's unique response to race. Janie spends the rest of the novel on a journey to establish mature, healthy identities as a woman and as a Black. It's a journey that every person, regardless of race or gender, has to take, and this complex process is different for everyone because it involves many variables, and must be understood in the particularly 'American' sociopolitical and historical contexts. In Janie's case, the entire focus of the novel is on her literally and figuratively finding her own voice, and her self-definition. The reader follows along as Janie discovers the politics of race and gender, and learns that these powerful (sometimes destructive) outside forces exist, and that she has to develop strategies to resist them for her own personal survival. The reader watches as she learns that although "self-perceptions are shaped by the messages that we receive from those around us" (Tatum, 1997, pp. 53–54) she can *empower* herself and (re)define herself, *for* herself although the process can be perilous and painful.

Janie is a character in a novel, but her journey is instructive for educators and relevant to this discussion of prejudice and racism because among other things, it shows that racial identities evolve over time, and that they are informed by the social milieu, and co-constructed by the individual and those with whom she or he comes into contact. Hurston is dramatizing an early stage in the process of racial identity development, and this is relevant because the scene shows that the, sometimes nebulous, pressure of racial hatred from outside social forces can turn inward and be internalized even by a very young child. Overall, Janie's life journey is a reminder that in spite of the enormous power that can be exerted by a variety of outside forces, humans have the capacity to resist those forces that threaten to control and misdirect their lives, subvert their dreams, and distort an authentic sense of self. In other words, we have the power to define ourselves. This is as true for Janie, who is Black, as it is for her White friends. And yet, although Janie *must* come to grips with her Blackness for her own personal survival, as members of the dominant group, her friends can choose to ignore the socioeconomic and political implications of Whiteness; this is part of their privilege.

Deconstructing Whiteness

Discussing Whiteness is a bit like attempting to perform a graceful ballet on hot coals; it's not easy. This is especially true if the audience is largely

White, and unused to addressing the concept head on and in an open and honest way. Even though the advent of multicultural pedagogies and culturally responsive practice has resulted in the proliferation of research on Whiteness, and it has become commonplace to see interpretations of the concept of Whiteness that include White consciousness, White guilt, White privilege, White backlash, White denial, White supremacy, Whiteness studies, etc., it is still very difficult to have the conversations outside of the confines of a classroom or professional development setting, or a relatively small circle of multicultural educators and theorists; even then, it's a long, risky, slow, potentially painful, sometimes emotional, but often rewarding process. There are many reasons for this: the social *norming* of Whiteness, which makes it invisible to many; an unwillingness to connect white skin color to social privilege; the rejection of the idea that social status and economic success have anything to do with white skin, and everything to do with hard work. In general, Whites have a repugnance for the possibility that any group should receive unearned advantages in a democratic society because it contradicts their internalized belief that we live in a meritocracy, and yet, even when contrary evidence is presented, denial and repression become standard defense mechanisms. However, there are other reasons that many can't (or won't) talk about race and Whiteness that are complex and very personal as is evidenced by the following account by Christine Sleeter, a well-known multicultural educator and researcher who offers her perspective as a White woman. According to Sleeter:

> White adults generally feel threatened by adults of color because we are aware of contradictions in the broader society that we would prefer to deny. On the one hand, most of us don't want to be prejudiced, thought of as racist, or disliked personally, and don't approve of overt expressions of racial prejudice. We want to view racism as solved and ourselves personally as good people, as "good whites." We also want confirming evidence from people of color that we are not racist, and many of us are afraid of saying something wrong that might undermine our "nonracist" self-perception. At the same time we are aware that whites collectively are better off on many indices of social life than are people of color. Further, the great majority of us are doing little or nothing to change that. We may not have started racism personally, but aside from trying to be friendly and fair with individuals of color we may encounter, we aren't doing anything to change it. When forced to think about it, many of us are uncomfortable being white in a racially stratified society that espouses equality. When surrounded by only whites, we can ignore this contradiction; being around people of color causes us to focus on it, to at least some degree. (Sleeter, 1996, p. 23)

Sleeter's last point that being around people of color causes Whites to focus on inequalities also accounts for the tensions that can tinge the atmosphere in mixed-group settings when race, or diversity, or cultural differences enter the conversation. This is an atmosphere in which one could be accused of *playing the race card*, if race or prejudice is brought up, and as has been previously said, the accusation is itself a form of denial. But Sleeter's comment points to a deeper issue as well: Whites feel most *White* in a setting when juxtaposed against Blacks; similarly, most Blacks are more self-aware when juxtaposed against Whites. Sleeter's point is that being around people of color disrupts white denial, but it may also reinforce the perception that blacks themselves are the embodiment of racial problems, so just their presence may be perceived as a silent accusation; for Blacks, just being in the room with White people may be a physical (and discomforting) reminder to Whites of social inequities from which they benefit and may have repressed. Hence, a sense of unease, or caution may also permeate the room.

Tatum (1997) points out that Whites can reach their maturity without thinking much about the impact of Whiteness and collude in maintaining a cloak of silence around race even among themselves. This silence amounts to an unspoken acquiescence to the dominant paradigm which affirms their right to the privileges they have, as well as their place in the social hierarchy. This is a corrosive silence which allows Whites "… to think of racial identity as something that other people have, not something that is salient for them. But when, for whatever reason, the silence is broken, a process of racial identity development for Whites begins to unfold" (Tatum, 1997, p. 94).

In *Why Are All the Black Kids Sitting Together in the Cafeteria?* Tatum (1997) argues that we pay a high price for the shroud of silence that we impose around the subject of racism whether it is manifested on personal, cultural, or institutional levels. When racism on any level goes unchallenged, according to Tatum, society suffers a "loss of human potential, lowered productivity, and a rising tide of fear and violence …" (Tatum, 1997, p. 200). However, there are different costs for individuals. In addition to stifling personal growth and development, a "culture of silence [can cause some Whites] to disconnect from their own racial experiences" (Tatum, 1997, p. 201), and have a distorted sense of the racial experiences of others, a distorted sense of the world, and a distorted sense of their place in it.

Breaking the Silence—Step One Toward a Healthy White Racial Identity

... it is not difference which immobilizes us, but silence.
And there are so many silences to be broken.

—Audre Lorde

In 1964, Paul Simon stunned the world with his song, 'The Sound of Silence.' Its powerful lyrics created haunting images of human isolation and loneliness, and its transcendent message seems even more relevant to us with the passage of time. In the song, the narrator describes

... People talking without speaking
People hearing without listening. ... (Simon, 2011, p. 5)

There's no way to know for sure if Paul Simon was thinking about the ways racism and racial hatred separate people or about their power to corrupt the social order when he wrote this song, but his words are prophetic, and capture perfectly the racial dilemma educators face today. Simon's title is an elegant oxymoron which pairs *sound* and *silence* to remind us of the primal human need to be connected to others, and the unspeakable loss when we fail to do so. Simon gives us a glimpse of a world where people talk, but don't say anything. It is a world where people hear, but don't listen, and metaphorically, the *sound of silence* can be deafening, and discordant; it also can be deadly.

Silence about race and racism can be fear-filled complicity and denial. And, there are those who justify the silence. Some say that we spend too much time talking about race anyway, and then there are those who say that we don't spend enough time talking about it. Perhaps the perspective depends on whether or not you are the oppressor or the oppressed; the abuser or the abused. Perhaps it depends on whether or not you have the power to impose the silence as part of your privilege; to deny voice to those you can control; the power to disempower those you consider beneath you; to turn off their mics, so to speak. And yet, it's important to remember that those who are silenced still have voices (though unused or unheard); they still have points of view, and perspectives (though ignored or dismissed). Denying others the opportunity to speak and forcing them into *wells of silence* doesn't mean that they don't exist, or that you've managed to extinguish their humanity; their spirits; their inner being. They can and do survive in spite of the external pressures designed to silence them.

Perhaps much of the silence around race and racism is fear-induced, and paralyzing in ways that not only prevent some of us from *speaking out* against racism and bias, it prevents some of us from *acting* against them as well. Fear "… immobilizes, traps words in our throats, and stills our tongues. Like a deer on the highway, frozen in the panic induced by the lights of an oncoming car, when we are afraid it seems that we cannot think, we cannot speak, we cannot move" (Tatum, 1997, p. 194). We know that fear can sustain and deepen silence, yet how do we *break the silence*, as Tatum suggests, and unlearn the fear?

Often unasked or unanswered is the question: *What* do Whites fear when it comes to talking about race?

According to Tatum, some Whites fear "[i]solation from friends and family, ostracism for speaking of things that generate discomfort, rejection by those who may be offended by what we have to say, the loss of privilege or status for speaking in support of those who have been marginalized by society, physical harm caused by the irrational wrath of those who disagree …" (Tatum, 1997, p. 194) with your position. Silence is easier; it provides a bit of cover; a bit of safety because speaking out can be dangerous.

One way to begin to break the silence around race and racism is to become introspective; to become intentional about deconstructing personal biases, and to commit to developing healthy racial identities. And research suggests that in general, those who are self-aware and self-critical demonstrate a higher degree of tolerance for others, and a willingness to accept personal responsibility for their thoughts and behaviors (Allport, 1979, p. 436). However, although self-insight is an important and necessary first step toward breaking the silence, and achieving a healthy White racial identity, self-insight

> … does not automatically cure prejudice. At best it starts the individual wondering. And unless one questions the truth of his convictions, he certainly is unlikely to alter them. If he begins to suspect that they are not in conformity with facts, he may then enter a period of conflict. If the dissatisfaction is great enough, he may be driven to a reorganization of beliefs and attitudes, Self-insight is ordinarily the first, but not in itself a sufficient step. (Allport, 1979, pp. 328–329)

Yet, the possibility for developing a healthy White racial identity does exist, but it is a process that must begin with White people acknowledging that they too are racial beings, and that their racial identity "does not depend on the perceived superiority of one racial group over another …" (Helms 1993, p. 49). Developing a positive racial identity also means that White people must abandon racism in all of its manifestations, including individual, institutional, and cultural racism, and understand and accept the responsibility for ending racism (Helms, 1993). However, this, according to Helms, is a daunting task because the absence of a healthy White racial identity is just one of the harmful effects of racism that have to be addressed. Another harmful effect is the refusal by some Whites to either acknowledge that Whiteness has particular social meanings and power, or to self-identify as white, but instead identify with an ethnicity such as Polish, Irish, Italian, or a religious affiliation such as Catholic or Jewish, etc. She argues that this points to either an inability or unwillingness to acknowledge an identity connected to racial oppression, and unearned privilege, what McIntosh (1988) referred to as an "invisible knapsack." However, it also suggests that many Whites have internalized the idea that Whiteness is the *norm*, and therefore believe that it is not necessary to acknowledge it; like air, it just *is*. Another proposed reason for not acknowledging Whiteness, according to Helms, is that some "Whites may feel threatened by the actual or presupposed presence of racial consciousness in non-White racial groups" (Helms, 1993, p. 50) and find it safer to remain silent, and not mention race at all. This may, in part, account for the tension that can fill a space when racial issues are brought up in a mixed-race group, causing some to retreat to *political correctness* as a cloaking device.

Helms' Model of White Racial Identity Development

In her book, *Black and White Racial Identity—Theory, Research and Practice*, Janet Helms (1993) offers a research-based study of race from a psychological perspective in order to help us understand how racial identity informs Black *and* White behavior. Interestingly, Helms sees a correlation between racism and White identity, and argues that "[t]he development of White identity in the United States is closely intertwined with the development and progress of racism in this country. The greater the extent that racism exists and is denied, the less possible it is to develop a positive White identity" (p. 49). Consequently, according to Helms, eliminating racism hinges on the existence of positive White racial identities. She made it easier to understand these complex identity development processes by creating the *White Racial Identity* model and the *Black Racial Identity* model which outline the separate stages and phases of racial identity development for Whites and Blacks. Helms makes clear that these models describe processes which are different for each individual, and they progress at different rates. Furthermore, each stage has "its own unique effect on attitudes, behaviors, and emotions" (Helms, 1993, p. 66).

The abbreviated summary *Helms White Racial Identity Development* and the chart that follows it, *Stages and Phases of White Racial Identity Development,* are included because they are useful self-assessment tools for personal and group use.

Helms' Model of White Identity Development

Contact: Whites pay little attention to the significance of their racial identity; "I'm just normal"; perceive themselves as color-blind and completely free of prejudice.

Disintegration: Growing awareness of racism and White privilege as a result of personal encounters. This new awareness is characterized by discomfort.

Reintegration: Feelings of guilt or denial may be transformed into fear and anger directed toward people of color. Whites may be frustrated if seen as a group rather than as individuals.

Pseudo-Independent: The individual gains an intellectual understanding of racism as a system of advantage but doesn't quite know what to do about it.

Immersion/Emersion: Marked by a recognized need to find more positive self-definition. Whites need to seek new ways of thinking about Whiteness, ways that take them beyond the role of victimizer,

Autonomy: Represents the culmination of the White racial development process. A person incorporates the newly defined view of Whiteness as part of a personal identity. The process is marked by an increased effectiveness in multiracial settings.

(adapted from Singleton & Linton, 2006, p. 204)

Stages and Phases of White Racial Identity Development

Phase One: Abandonment of Racism
Contact $\mapsto$ Disintegration $\mapsto$ Reintegration $\mapsto$

Phase Two: Defining a Nonracist White Identity
Pseudo-Independence $\mapsto$ Immersion/Emersion $\mapsto$ Autonomy
(adapted from Helms, 1993, p. 56)

The Helms' models demonstrate that the racial identity development process is complex, sometimes confusing, nonlinear, individuated, and subject to a cluster of unpredictable variables. Moreover, it is a lifelong process unfolding over time, and it is informed by the various personal, professional, and social environments which constitute ordinary living. Racial identity development is an evolving socialization process of which we are often unaware. This means that whether one is White or Black, our self-definition is not fixed or immutable, and our attitudes and beliefs about race, and everything else for that matter, can change as circumstances change.

It is not an overstatement to say that the work of Janet Helms has helped to transform the way that multicultural educators, diversity trainers, and researchers think about race, racism, prejudice, and discrimination. Among other things, building on earlier research, Helms has helped change the trajectory of discussions and research aimed at prejudice reduction, and intercultural communication in ways that encourage more optimism about the future. Her focus on White racial identity development has become a mainstay in teacher and leadership preparation programs, and her research has shown that deconstructing Whiteness should be considered a necessary and pivotal part of present and future social justice initiatives. Gary Howard's (2006) personal experience as a White multicultural trainer and researcher affirms this. He says:

> [W]e cannot begin to dismantle the legacy of dominance without first engaging Whites in a deep analysis of our own role in perpetuating injustice. We need to decode White dominance and also provide ourselves and our White colleagues with positive visions for engaging in the process of change. (Howard, 2006, p. 99)

I would also argue that accompanying discussions about White racial identity development, there should be considerable attention placed on deconstructing dominant privilege, because along with *Whiteness* and *power*, dominant privilege is part of a triad and the three elements are complementary and mutually reinforcing. Yet it is important to understand that privilege can stand alone; it is not always connected to race or specifically to Whiteness. Given the multiple identities that all individuals have, anyone can, according to circumstances, be privileged or not. For example, having wealth, regardless of race, ethnicity, or culture, bestows privileges that the poor, regardless of race, ethnicity, or culture, do not have. Likewise, being heterosexual confers privileges that homosexuals do not have (i.e., marriage equality), and this tension between dominant privilege and subordination is evident in most interpersonal, intergroup, and intragroup relationships.

Like White racial identity, dominant privilege has implications for how we approach multiculturalism in schools. Presently, there appears to be a greater focus on the tangible aspects of privilege in terms of wealth, economic advantage, class status, etc., but there are psychological and behavioral dimensions of privilege, which complement discussions about White identity development, and these invite more attention because

> Regardless of which groups we're talking about, privilege generally allows people to assume a certain level of acceptance, inclusion and respect in the world, to operate within a relatively wide comfort zone. Privilege increases the odds of having things your own way, of being able to set the agenda in a social situation and determine the rules and standards and how they're applied. Privilege grants the cultural authority to make judgments about others and to have those judgments stick. It allows people to define reality and to have prevailing definitions of reality fit their experience. Privilege means being able to decide who gets taken seriously, who receives attention, who is accountable to whom and for what. And it grants a presumption of superiority and social permission to act on that presumption without having to worry about being challenged. (Allan G. Johnson cited in Paula S. Rothenberg, 2002, p. 103)

Sociologist David Wellman (1993) offers another, more insidious aspect of privilege by showing that not only do those with privilege have distinct social, economic, political, and educational advantages, they also benefit, in an almost parasitic way, from the *disadvantages* of those who are disprivileged. In other words, "[t]he disadvantages of race experienced by black Americans are often translated into advantages for whites" (Wellman, 1993, p. 21). For example, "White high school seniors using illicit drugs ... *benefit* when 40 percent of the drug arrests are made in Black communities" (Wellman, 1993, p. 21) because this means that a disproportionate amount of law enforcement resources are diverted to the Black community "regardless of the actual crime rate. This, of course, inadvertently provides white law violators with an advantage: It increases opportunities for practicing illegal activities relatively undetected" (Wellman, 1993, p. 21). Wellman goes on to point out other ways that Whites benefit from the structural disadvantages that accrue to Blacks including: disproportionately high loan-rejection rates for Blacks translates to disproportionately high percentages of loans given to Whites; salaries for Blacks and Whites with the same credentials and same job description can vary as much as 15% or more in favor of White workers; the lower pay for Black workers means more money available to pay their White counterparts. Perhaps the most tragic example is discrepancies in the level of medical care which can impact both the quality of life and life expectancy itself. In other words, "inadequate medical care for black Americans underwrites the health of whites" (Wellman, 1993, p. 22). This pattern is also evident in schools in terms of the disproportionately low placement of Black students in advanced classes which in effect leaves more seats available for White students.

Privilege, in all of its manifestations, whether it operates independently or in conjunction with Whiteness has important implications for educators because it influences attitudes and mindset, as well as the interactional patterns between individuals and groups. This matters in terms of how teachers teach, and how leaders lead, and why certain policy decisions are made. Moreover, the ability to *ignore* the *cultural authority* that privilege confers, or that privileged people can *define reality*, the way they want to define reality, or that they can do these things with the *presumption of superiority*, is itself a function of privilege.

There is a diversity training exercise in which a large group is divided into two smaller groups, and one group is labeled privileged/dominant and the other group is labeled disprivileged/subordinate. Each group is told to caucus among themselves and come up with persuasive arguments to join the opposite group. Invariably, the subordinate group gives up because no argument that they make is strong enough to persuade any member of the dominant group to switch sides. Appeals based on altruism, fairness, social justice, religion, democratic ideals are never strong enough to persuade any member of the opposite group to give up social and economic advantage; self-interest tends to trump everything. In contrast, everyone in the subordinate group gets up and moves into the dominant group. This is a simple exercise, and yet it is instructive in terms of how human nature operates. People rarely choose to give up advantage whether it is earned or not; fair or not. People rarely choose to give up advantage even when it contradicts deeply held values; their sense of ethics and their moral center. This was evident in the founding of America when colonists neatly planted democratic ideals alongside *anti-ideals*, and allowed them to grow together side by side. Like a weed wrapping itself around a rosebush, racism and discrimination are wrapping themselves around the American promise, smothering it. If the weed is not uprooted, eventually the rosebush will die; if racism and discrimination are not uprooted, what does our future hold?

References

Alexander, M. (2010). *The new Jim Crow mass incarceration in the age of colorblindness.* New York, NY: The New Press.
Allport, G. (1979). *The nature of prejudice.* Cambridge, MA: Perseus Books.

Baldwin, J. (1993). *The fire next time* (p. 104). New York, NY: Vintage Books.

Baldwin, J. (n.a.). Retrieved July 14, 2014 from http://thinkexist.com/quotes/with/keyword/nakedness/

Biven, D. K. (2005). What is internalized racism? In Maggie Potapchuk, Sally Leiderman, Donna Bivens, & Barbara Major (Eds.), *Flipping the script: White privilege and community building* (p. 49). Retrieved July 16, 2015 from www.capd.org. The article is also available on-line at www.racialequitytools.org/resourcefiles/What_is_Internalized_Racism.pdf.

Brooks, J. S. (2012). *Black school, white school racism and educational (mis)leadership.* New York, NY: Teachers College Press.

Delpit, L. (1995). *Other people's children.* New York, NY: New Press.

Douglass, F. (1986). *Narrative of the life of Frederick Douglass, an American slave.* New York, NY: Penguin Books USA.

DuBois, W. E. B. (1994). *The souls of black folk.* Mineola, NY: Dover Publications.

Freire, P. (1973). Education for critical consciousness. New York: Continuum.

Helms, J. (Ed.). (1993). *Black and white racial identity: Theory, research, and practice.* Westport, CT: Praeger Publishers.

Howard, G. (2006). *We can't teach what we don't know.* New York: Teachers College Press.

Hurston, Z. N. (1978). *Their eyes were watching God.* Urbana, IL: University of Illinois Press.

Johnson, A. G. (2005). Privilege as paradox. Cited in Rothenberg, P. S. (Ed.). (2002). *White privilege essential readings on the other side of racism* (p. 103). New York, NY: Worth Publishers.

King, J. E. (1991). Dysconscious racism. *The Journal of Negro Education, 60*(2), 133–146.

Kivel, P. (2002). *The costs of racism to white people.* Retrieved June 9, 2014 from http://www.paulkivel.com/issues/racial-justice/item/94-the-costs-of-racism-to-white-people

Kly, Y. N. (1997). *The anti-social contract.* Atlanta, GA: Clarity Press. Cited in Bivens, D. K. (2005). What is internalized racism? In Maggie Potapchuk, Sally Leiderman, Donna Bivens, & Barbara Major (Eds.), *Flipping the script: White privilege and community building* (p. 49). Retrieved July 16, 2015 from www.capd.org

Lorde, A. (1977). *The transformation of silence into language and action.* A speech by Audre Lorde originally delivered at the Lesbian and Literature panel of the Modern Language Association's December 28, 1977. Retrieved February 15, 2012 from http://shrinkingphallus.wordpress.com/the-transformation-of-silence-into-language-and-action-by-audre-lorde/

Massey, G. C., Scott, M. V., & Dornbusch, S. M. (1975). "Racism without racists: Institutional racism in urban schools," cited in Lisa Delpit, *Other people's children* (1995). New York: New Press.

McIntosh, P. (1988). *White privilege and male privilege.*This paper was presented at the Virginia Women's Studies Association conference in Richmond in April 1986 and the American Educational Research Association conference in Boston in October 1986 and discussed with two groups of participants in the Dodge seminars for Secondary School Teachers in New York and Boston in the spring of 1987.

Morrison, T. (1992). *Playing in the dark.* New York, NY: Vintage Books.

Morrison, T. (n.a.). Retrieved August 12, 2014 from http://www.edchange.org/multicultural/language/quotes_alpha2.html#G

Nieto, S., & Bode, P. (2012). *Affirming diversity: The sociopolitical context of multicultural education*. Boston, MA: Allyn & Bacon.

Pettigrew, T. F., & Martin, J. (1987). Shaping the organizational context. *Journal of Social Issues, 43*(1), 41–78.

Rich, A. (n.a.). Cited in Maher, F. A., & Tetreault, M. K. T. (2001). *The feminist classroom, dynamics of gender, race and privilege* (p. 201). Oxford: Rowman and Littlefield.

Rothenberg, P. S. (Ed.). (2002). *White privilege essential readings on the other side of racism*. New York, NY: Worth Publishers.

Scarry, E. (1996). The difficulty of imagining other people. In J. Cohen (Ed.), *For love of country: Debating the limits of patriotism* (p. 103). Boston, MA: Beacon.

Simon, P. (2011). *Paul Simon lyrics 1964–2011* (p. 5). New York, NY: Simon & Schuster Paperbacks.

Singleton, G. E., & Linton, C. (2006). *Courageous conversations about race*. Thousand Oaks, CA.: Corwin Press.

Sleeter, C. (1996). *Multicultural education as social activism*. Albany, NY: State University of New York Press.

Tatum, B. D. (1997). *Why are all of the black kids sitting together in the cafeteria? And other conversations about race*. New York, NY: Basic Books.

Wellman, D. (1993). *Portraits of white racism* (2nd ed.). Cambridge: Cambridge University Press.

West, C. (1993). Race matters. New York: Vintage Books

Woodson, C. G. (1990). *The mis-education of the Negro*. Trenton, NJ: Africa World Press.

· 4 ·

IMPLICIT BIAS AND THE BIAS AWARENESS GAP

Implications for Equity-Driven Teaching and School Leadership

This chapter looks beneath some of the typical factors used to explain racialized educational disparity. Typically, the data addresses academic gaps, funding gaps, opportunity gaps, college admission gaps, etc., which focus on tangible things that can be counted and tabulated. There are, however, important factors that cannot be counted and assessed through typical data collection methods, and the chapter focuses on two intangible factors implicated in the failure of American schools to equitably serve all of its children. They are: implicit (unconscious) bias and personal beliefs about social dominance. The chapter argues that there is a significant cause and effect relationship between racialized underachievement and latent biases in educators that can be connected to their attitudes toward social dominance. Using research on social dominance, the chapter examines how *beliefs* or *predispositions* toward social dominance and social equality or inequality can be translated into *oppressive* behaviors and *oppressive* school policies *even when these beliefs* or *predispositions are unintentional, and individuals are unaware of them.* This chapter encourages practitioners and policymakers to *look* at themselves and their own attitudes and beliefs, and consider if, and how, they are accomplices helping to sustain and reinforce inequitable outcomes for some children.

Keywords: social dominance, achievement gap, equity, explicit bias, implicit (unconscious) bias, school-to-prison pipeline, diversity, culture, minority, majority, race, privilege

How we do race will be consequential to the kind of society we have in the future. Our racing will be impacted by our history, our experience, as well as our imagined future. Our future will be impacted by the way the conscious and unconscious make meaning of our new social constructions. We must intertwine race with the other urgent issues we must confront including extreme inequality, mass incarceration, full participation in our political and cultural structures, and—perhaps most critically—with our most fundamental questions about who we are.

—john a. powell

There have been significant academic gains for Black and brown students over the last decade, but despite the many and various efforts to address the issue of educational disparity, they continue to lag behind White students in reading and math proficiency, as well as high school and college completion. For decades now, there has been a great deal of data collection, discussion, analysis, policy proposals, and hand-wringing. It is commonplace for analysts to point to a variety of contributing factors for why schools continue to underserve students for whom race, color, ethnicity, socioeconomic position, and other categories of difference are markers for their subordinate status in American society. The irony is that the data generally addresses academic gaps, funding gaps, opportunity gaps, college admission gaps, etc. Typically, it focuses on tangible things; things that can be counted. But, according to the wisdom attributed to Albert Einstein, "everything that can be counted does not necessarily count [and] everything that counts cannot necessarily be counted." In other words, some things do not lend themselves to data collection, some important things will be overlooked, and some important questions will remain unasked.

This chapter and the one that follows focuses on two of the intangible factors implicated in the egregious failure of American schools to equitably serve all of its children: implicit (unconscious) bias, and personal beliefs about social dominance. The chapters ask a question that usually goes unasked (and therefore unanswered): Is it possible to connect the persistent, life-altering achievement and proficiency 'gaps' to latent biases in educators (and others), and to their attitudes toward social dominance? They argue that *beliefs* or *predispositions* toward social dominance and social equality or inequality can be translated into *oppressive* behaviors and *oppressive* school policies *even when these beliefs* or *predispositions are unintentional, and individuals are unaware of them.* Significantly, whether or not there is intentionality, these attitudes and predispositions can promote and sustain the various 'gaps' which arguably form the bedrock upon which educational and social inequality rests.

Researchers regularly point to a variety of obvious causes for the failure of American schools to achieve their stated goals, and many of them impinge on the educative process from the outside. These include endemic poverty, extreme socioeconomic disparities, displacement, national origin, unstable family arrangements, a pervasive culture of violence, and personal trauma which could include: physical or sexual abuse, hunger, or intermittent home-lessness. "Such factors can lead to behaviors in school that reflect a perva-sive form of childhood post-traumatic stress disorder" (Ireland, 2016, p. n.a.). When combined, these can create a toxic mix of seemingly insurmountable social problems and challenges that serve to further marginalize those already marginalized by race and ethnicity, anchoring them to school failure. These become the gap-dwelling children, the ones who slip through the cracks in the 'systems' into dim or hopeless futures. For many of them, the ideal of equity or 'equality' merely mocks the reality of their lives.

The ideal of 'equality' has mocked the reality of Black lives for a very long time especially when it came to equal access to a good education. American history confirms this. History tells us that even enslaved African-Americans placed a high value on literacy, and many actually risked life and limb to become literate because they knew it was literally and figuratively, a door-way to 'freedom.' Young Frederick Douglass learned this the day he heard his owner say

> A nigger should know nothing but to obey his master—to do as he is told to do. Learning would ~spoil~ the best nigger in the world. "Now … if you teach that nigger (speaking to myself) how to read, there would be no keeping him. It would forever unfit him to be a slave. He would at once become unmanageable, and of no value to his master."

Hearing this, Frederick understood something he would never forget. He expressed it this way:

> I now understood what had been to me a most perplexing difficulty … the white man's power to enslave the black man. … From that moment, I understood the path-way to freedom. It was just what I wanted, and I got it at a time when I least expected it. … I set out with high hope and a fixed purpose, at whatever cost of trouble, to learn how to read. … (Douglass, 1986, pp. 78–79)

Literacy and race were intertwined during Douglass' day, and ironically, liter-acy and race are still intertwined, and remain at the center of a sociopolitical firestorm. Today, many Black (and brown) lives are still *at risk*, not because it is illegal to learn to read, but because of miseducation and undereducation that result from a constellation of individual, systemic, social, and institutional failures, and because of unaddressed *latent* biases and attitudes toward social dominance. Presently, the problems of educating students marginalized by race, color, and ethnicity are so severe that even the highly esteemed Frederick Douglass could be a casualty of the education gap or the school-to-prison pipeline. In an odd way, this possibility was recently dramatized by a thirteen-year-old girl.

In 2012, an 8th grader inadvertently brought racial disparity to the nation's attention after reading, analyzing, and writing about the *Narrative of the Life of Frederick Douglass, an American Slave*. Inspired by the challenges Douglass faced as he fought for literacy, the student, Jada Williams, wrote an essay in which she boldly compared the quality of the schooling she and her African-American schoolmates were receiving in Rochester, New York, to modern-day slavery. Despite a campaign of harassment from both teachers and administrators that led to her being home-schooled, Jada is being hailed as a modern-day abolitionist because she forced the entire educational hierarchy to hear her *voice*, and take her critique seriously. "In her essay, Williams argued that a parallel existed between the way slave masters used illiteracy and ignorance to maintain oppression and the current situation in her illiteracy-ridden school district. The charges of illiteracy in Rochester are completely justified as 75% of the district's students cannot read at the appropriate grade-level. An analysis by the New York Times last year identified the district to be among the lowest performing in the state" (Lawrence, 2012, p. n.a.). Williams described

- Teachers who had the "… power to dictate what I can, cannot, and will learn, only desiring that I may get bored because of the inconsistency and the mismanagement of the classroom."
- Teachers who merely "pass out pamphlets and packets" instead of teaching
- Students who were expected to read and compete the work independently even though most of her classmates "… cannot read and or comprehend the material that has been provided." (Dwyer, 2012, p. n.a.)

In a district in which the teachers and administrators were predominantly White, Williams ascribed these problems to racial oppression akin to what Frederick Douglass faced in the nineteenth century. She argued that very little had changed in almost two hundred years. Her conclusion was that very little had changed from Douglass' time to hers because "the same old discrimination still resides in the hearts of the white man" (Dwyer, 2012, p. n.a.). In the end, she called for activism from her classmates, and urged them to "start making these white teachers accountable for instructing you" (Dwyer, 2012, p. n.a.), but her strongest critique was for teachers who were not willing to share their knowledge "because of the color of my skin" (from Dwyer, 2012, p. n.a.).

Even though in today's sociopolitical discourse, education, excellence, and equity are commonly linked, these education failures like those described by an 8th grader persist and have become more complex. For example, even though the subjects of *diversity* and *culture* seem to be on everyone's agenda, and demographic data shows that a significant population shift is resulting in the *browning* of America, schools are still underserving its Black and brown students. More important than the fact that Hispanics are the fastest growing ethnic group, or that by 2050 Whites of European descent will no longer be the numerical majority, is the paradigm shift marked by the psychic changes that this entails. It seems like the nation cannot fathom the unfathomable; that the White, largely Anglo-Saxon, majority is losing numerical advantage. The resulting psychic dilemma is evidenced by the nation's difficulty in even finding the words to describe this new paradigm. Consider, for example, the embedded meanings in the words *minority* and *majority* which are commonly used to distinguish population groups in America.

Although we don't tend to think about their usage too much, the terms have distinct connotative and denotative meanings that have special significance in American sociopolitical and historical contexts. Both words have multiple meanings, but when we think about American populations, we instinctively think in numerical terms, that is, majority means greater numbers or more than 50%; minority means lesser numbers or less than 50%. However, if we apply other connotative and imagistic associations, different meanings emerge. Consider, for example, the visual significance of the following: Major. minor. Consider, too, the following definitions in terms of their connotative meanings:

Major
a. one of superior rank, ability, etc., in a specified class
b. **legal definition:** a person with the full legal rights of an adult

Minor
a. lesser, as in size, extent, or importance, or being or noting the lesser of two
b. minor share
c. not serious, important, etc.
d. a minor role

e. having low rank, status, position, etc.

f. **legal definition:** under the legal age of full responsibility

Minority

a. group in society distinguished from, and less dominant than, the more numerous majority

b. racial, ethnic, religious, or social subdivision of a society that is subordinate to the dominant group in political, financial, or *social power without regard to the size of these groups*

(from Dictionary.com)

In America, these terms have always been racial cues, and therefore represent value judgments connected to social dominance and privilege, and social subordination and disadvantage. In America, major(ity) has always referred to white populations, and minor(ity) has always referred to black/Hispanic/Asian/Native American populations. However, these meanings continue to resonate *in spite of the demographic changes underway and in spite of the size of these groups*. Hence, even as the white population sinks below 50%, in American society it is not (and perhaps never will be) referred to as a *minority* group because it would give voice (and substance) to this significant paradigm shift that is underway. Instead, the term *minority–majority* is now being used to accommodate this new numerical reality, a new numerical *majority* comprised of people of color. The long-term significance of this is uncertain, but the usage of the term is clearly linked to long-standing internalized attitudes toward social dominance and race that are uniquely American.

Since the 1960s educators have been anticipating these demographic shifts, and have been proactively developing programs, workshops, and curricular materials that explicitly address this new reality, and the needs and concerns of a conspicuously multicultural populace. Simultaneously, these educators have redefined and expanded the concepts of *diversity* and *culture*, making them more inclusive and more representative of the real world. Of course, this does not mean that this was not a diverse and multicultural country before the 1960s, because as Gary Howard (2006) has wisely said, diversity is not, and never was, a *choice*. The only *choice* was (is) how America *chose* to deal with it.

This chapter is not designed to review, reexamine, evaluate, or critique already established facts and conclusions, especially when the existing statistical data is indisputable and perhaps already overanalyzed. Instead, rather than look at the *external* challenges to the educative process, this chapter looks at *internal* challenges that emerge from a completely different domain, one that is often overlooked, ignored, or dismissed as inconsequential. These include *attitudes* and *beliefs* about social dominance, race, privilege, and power as factors that impact how teachers teach, how guidance counselors guide, and how and where leaders lead. What is most troubling is that although a growing body of research is telling us that we all are blind to the deeper unconscious beliefs that influence the decisions we make, we're just beginning to use this information as a lens to look at society as a whole, and particularly at what this means to educators and the education community. And, it is worth noting that most of the individuals and institutions conducting general educational research reflect a dominant perspective to some degree, and therefore the research domain itself may replicate some of the same racialized power dynamics that exists in society because researchers are also products of, and shaped by, the same societies they put under scrutiny. Although this is mere speculation, it means that the choice of whether or not to conduct research on belief systems means that they must be objective, and investigate the behaviors of others, but it also means that they *should be subjective, and look at themselves and their own attitudes and beliefs, and consider how they impact the choices that they make as researchers.* This is a reflexive process that could open doors to a level of self-examination some researchers may not want to enter. This also may be a partial answer to the questions of why there isn't a greater focus on attitudes and beliefs in a country that has struggled with its probias and antibias instincts from its inception, and why it's taken so long to get to where we are today in terms of evaluating how these issues impact the educative process. It is also worth noting that a significant amount of the research on implicit bias and social dominance is happening *outside* of the United States and focuses on groups that have emigrated from the Middle East, Africa, and Asia to European countries like England, Germany, Denmark, etc. However, it is also interesting that many of the European researchers are using the United States as a case study, and are applying their findings to the racial and cultural dynamics in American schools and society. Among other things this points to the universal acceptance and validation of the concept of implicit bias which is now considered "a new diversity paradigm—one that recognizes the role that bias plays in the day-to-day functioning of all human beings" (Hassouneh, cited in Staats, 2014b, p. 24).

In everyday bias, Howard Ross (2008, 2014) underscores the significance of implicit bias saying that "[o]ur minds automatically justify our decisions, blinding us to the true source, or beliefs, behind our decisions. Ultimately, we believe our decisions are consistent with our conscious beliefs, when in fact, our unconscious is running the show" (Ross, 2008, p. 11). This tension between our implicit and explicit beliefs can create a dissonance between the conscious and unconscious sides of ourselves, so

> [w]e live with this inherent dichotomy between the rational decisions we think we are supposed to be making, and the real impact of our unconscious processing and our emotional reactions, which can remain under the surface, unobserved and, often, discounted. We want to think of ourselves as good people, but we still have these emotional impulses. This can create an enormous dissonance between what we think we see and evaluate and what's actually going on. ... We know for example, that we are 'not supposed to be biased,' and so we convince ourselves that we are not, even sometimes in the face of evidence to the contrary. (Ross, 2014, p. 15)

No one is exempt from this, not researchers, not teachers, not school principals and superintendents, not guidance counselors, not school board members, and it's important to remember that when, for example, the data affirms the sobering fact that if black students were a *country*, they would rank in last place behind Mexico (Fryer, cited in Ireland, 2016, p. n.a.). Even if this is *not* partially the result of conscious, intentional bias on the part of educators and policymakers, it would be egregiously negligent to continue to discount or underestimate the significance of bias that is implicit: unconscious and hidden.

* * *

In 2016, the National Education Association (NEA), considered by many to be both the 'voice' of American education professionals and their leading advocacy group, reaffirmed its Vision, Mission, and Values which state in part

Our Vision
Our vision is a great public school for every student.

Our Mission
Our mission is to advocate for education professionals and to unite our members and the nation to fulfill the promise of public education to prepare every student to succeed in a diverse and interdependent world.

Our Core Values
These principles guide our work and define our mission:

Equal Opportunity. We believe public education is the gateway to opportunity. All students have the human and civil right to a quality public education that develops their potential, independence, and character.

A Just Society. We believe public education is vital to building respect for the worth, dignity, and equality of every individual in our diverse society.

Democracy. We believe public education is the cornerstone of our republic. Public education provides individuals with the skills to be involved, informed, and engaged in our representative democracy …
NEA also believes every student in America, regardless of family income or place of residence, deserves a quality education.

> (National Education Association [NEA], 2016, p. n.a.)

These admirable goals are unimpeachable, and although the specific wording may differ, the NEA's vision, mission, and values are consistent with those adopted by state departments of education nationwide, as well as with the mission of the U.S. Department of Education which is: "to promote student achievement and preparation for global competitiveness by fostering educational excellence and ensuring equal access." Collectively, they express a belief in *equality* of opportunity, a *just* society, and the obligation of schools to live up to the principles of *democracy*, and prepare all American students to do so as well. Unfortunately, we know that none of this has been universally achieved. In fact, equality, justice, and democracy itself are merely *open possibilities, not possessions* (Greene, 1976, p. 15).

Despite the accretion of evidence from so many credible sources that race and underachievement are strongly linked, there is rarely more than a passing reference to belief systems, which may include bias and prejudicial attitudes based on race, ethnicity, and class (or any combination of these factors) that can profoundly impact how schools are run; how and why policies are created, how and why students are sorted and tracked, and, significantly, how and what students are taught. Addressing belief systems alone will not solve the problem, but neither will any other single-pronged approach. In fact, it disrespects the enormous complexity of the problem to think that any one solution will fix the gaping gaps in achievement, opportunity, and social access that create and sustain a steely caste system within schools as well as within the larger society.

Missing in most discussions of educational inequity and 'achievement gaps' is what I call the *Bias Awareness Gap* which is informed by the concepts of Implicit Racial Bias and Social Dominance Orientation. I define the *Bias*

Awareness Gap as the failure by most educators, researchers, and policymakers to look beneath the statistics to see a profoundly important subtext: **belief systems and how they are informed by unconscious biases and predispositions toward social dominance**; a failure to adequately address the relationship between an educator's personal beliefs about herself and the actualization of *equality* of opportunity, a *just* society, and the promise of *democracy*. If we acknowledge that there is a *Bias Awareness Gap*, it is easier to see the persistent, sometimes dysconscious, bias that is manifested in various ways at all levels in the educative process. This bias is deep-seated, and is socially constructed and validated; it resides in individuals and in groups, and it continues to corrupt and disrupt our attempts to make systemic changes that would enable us to teach all children well. It is an acknowledgement that since American society is constructed around race, it must be assumed that American schools are constructed around race as well, and there is ample evidence to support this.

The reality is that regardless of race or ethnicity, everyone carries the 'baggage' of racialized predispositions, stereotypes, and prejudices; family background, acculturation patterns, political affiliations, etc., make this 'baggage' heavier for some than others. So, whether one is creating policy on the state level, or designing curricular materials for a school, or teaching in a classroom, or leading a school or district, our complex, often contradictory attitudes about social dominance affect the decisions we make, and the feelings we feel about ourselves and others. This is a subtext underlying the test data, and it must be addressed openly, systematically, even clinically, if we are ever to close the achievement gap and make academic excellence a reality for all children.

Implicit Bias—An Overview

Having biases doesn't make you a bad person—it only makes you human.
                                                            —Cheryl Staats et al.

You can be a nice person, and still be a racist ...

                                                            —Anonymous

In America, we know what *explicit* bias looks like even when we choose not to name it.

We knew it in 1781 when Thomas Jefferson compared Black slaves to orangutans even as he copulated with his teenaged slave, Sally Hemings, and fathered her six children; we knew it in 1852 when the U.S. Bureau of Indian Affairs was driven by the ideas that *the only good Indian is a dead Indian,* and that physical and/or cultural extermination was a viable solution to the *Indian problem*; we knew it when the 1882 Chinese Exclusion Act excluded new Chinese immigrants, even though the Transcontinental Railroad was built over the backs of their forbears; we knew it post-WWII when returning African-American soldiers were steered away from the suburbs, funneled into urban ghettoes, and denied home mortgages with the complicity of the federal government; we knew it post-Katrina when we saw African-American citizens dying on rooftops and their putrefying bodies lay in stagnant water, or on the streets of New Orleans for days. We also knew what *explicit* bias looked like when we saw a major American textbook company collude with the nation's largest state to produce whitewashed American history books producing headlines like the following:

How Texas' School Board Tried to Pretend Slavery Never Happened and Why Your Kid's School May Be Next
by Bryan Monroe 05/24/2010

New history books in Texas downplay slavery's role in Civil War, omit KKK and Jim Crow laws
by Jim Young 7 Jul, 2015

Company Apologizes for Texas Textbook Calling Slaves 'Workers': 'We Made a Mistake'
by Zoë Schlanger on 10/5/15

Texas school board approves controversial textbook changes
by Need to Know Editor May 23, 2010

Texas officials: Schools should teach that slavery was 'side issue' to Civil War
by Emma Brown July 5, 2015

Even the hate-filled pronouncements of white supremacists and racial separatists, although scary, is *explicit* and open; we know where it's coming from, and we know it's coming.

In many ways, *explicit*, intentional, blatant bias is as intricately woven into the American experience as the Constitutional guarantees of justice and freedom. "Implicit biases come from the culture ... [they function like a] thumbprint of the culture on our minds" (Banaji, cited in Staats, 2014b, p. 14). Ironically, it is the *explicitness*, the openness, the blatancy that has allowed America and Americans to challenge, uproot, and *try* to extirpate racial, and other forms of bias through the power of legislation as emblematized by the Fourteenth Amendment and the thousands of laws that followed it. The combination of a Judeo-Christian worldview and a Puritan inflected value system has given Americans a strong moral center that unashamedly embraces the idea that individuals have both a responsibility and an obligation to work hard, strive to be honorable and just, and seek *rightness*, if not righteousness. Therefore, if we look back over the last fifty years, the country can be somewhat self-congratulatory about its overall efforts to undo racial and other destructive forms of bias, because there have been tangible, organized efforts that reflect a myriad of initiatives to *debias* itself that crisscrosses every level of American society. Ross (2014) catalogs these efforts, and points out that there have been unprecedented efforts worldwide to address human rights and socioeconomic inequality. And, in the United States

> we have seen the civil rights movement, the women's movement, and the expansion of acceptance of and equal rights for lesbian, gay, bisexual, and transgender (LGBT) people. The public discourse has changed so dramatically during these past fifty years that in a great many social and professional circles, it is now completely unacceptable to voice openly bigoted statements … We have established laws that limit people's biased behavior and hold them accountable for discriminatory behavior. We have hired chief diversity officers who have instituted diversity and inclusion guidelines and training programs for millions of people in schools, major corporations, small businesses, governmental agencies, not-for-profit institutions, and the military to teach us to be more "tolerant" of each other. We have established special holidays to recognize and honor the contributions made by previously unheralded individuals and movements. Large-scale summits and conferences meant to address equity issues take place [in the United States and] around the world on an almost daily basis. We have written thousands of books … made numerous movies, developed social movements, organized protest marches, and produced countless *Oprah* shows, all in an attempt to try to understand the problem and then try to fix it. There is no question that, at least on a conscious level, the standard we set for our behavior has changed. (Ross, 2014, p. xii)

All of this and much more can be used to affirm that as a society, there are significant ongoing attempts to redefine ourselves as a country, and rise above the sordid elements of an American past in which explicit racism and bigotry were normalized. While we can see significant progress in addressing attitudes and beliefs that reflect *explicit* bias, the bigger story is that *implicit* bias is more dangerous and sinister, because on a subterranean level, it impacts attitudes, behaviors, and decisions we make *without* our being consciously aware of its influence. For example, on a conscious level, we don't have to really believe that the negative associations that come to mind for certain individuals and groups are true or even defensible. In fact, if we fully understood the complex workings underlying implicit bias and the influences on, and causes of, these negative associations and the decisions they inspire, "we would probably reject them" (Payne, cited in Staats, Capatosto, Wright, & Contractor, 2015, p. 44). The challenge for researchers is that implicit bias functions like "an 'equal opportunity virus' that everyone possesses, regardless of his/her own group membership" (Dasgupta, cited in Staats, 2014, p. 16). This recognition has caused researchers to shift their focus from observations of, and research on, *explicit* forms of bias to observations of and research on *implicit* forms of bias. This movement from "explicit to implicit attitude measurement is one of the most significant changes to occur in the attitude literature in the last 20 years" (Blanton & Jaccard, 2015, p. 53). The question is, once you acknowledge it, observe, research, and define it, how do you treat this *virus*?

How do you legislate against *implicit*, unconscious, bias that is hidden and intangible, but very real, very damaging, and is operating on another plane? How do you make the invisible visible? How do you confront the hiddenness of it? How do you confront the stealth, the obfuscation, the amorphousness? The deniability?

These are not, or at least should not be, considered academic questions because at the nation's highest levels, we are being reminded that hurtful bias is un-American, and that it still exists; we are being reminded that being *America* demands that we *be* America, and at least strive to achieve our own ideals since they are unalterably inscribed deep in this country's heart. In a 2003 decision, Supreme Court Justice Ruth Bader Ginsburg reminded us that explicit and implicit racial bias are serious problems that have not gone away, and that they continue to undermine American principles when she said "It is well documented that conscious and unconscious race bias, even rank discrimination based on race, remain alive in our land, impeding realization of our highest values and ideals" (Ginsberg, cited in Staats, 2013, p. 65). In the same vein, john a. powell gets to the heart of the serious challenges we still face when he cautioned: "How we do race will be consequential to the kind of society we have in the future … We must intertwine race with the other urgent issues … and—perhaps most critically—with our most fundamental questions about who we are" (powell & Menendian, 2016, p. n.a.). In more clinical ways, social scientists are telling us the same thing, and there is a growing body of research that shows that the study of implicit (unconscious) bias not only is having a dynamic impact on social science research, it is changing the conversations about diversity.

Since the early work of psychologist Gordon Allport, psychologists and social scientists have affirmed that bias is a natural human function; it is part of the human process of categorization. And, according to Allport, "[t]he human mind must think with the aid of categories ... Once formed, categories are the basis for normal prejudgment. We cannot possibly avoid this process. Orderly living depends on it" (Allport, 1979, p. 20). This human process is a way to understand the world; a way to categorize our experiences; a way to protect ourselves; to identify where and when we are safe, and where and when we are in danger; it's a way to determine what things we can eat, and what things could kill us. "To manage and negotiate an extremely complex and busy world, we have developed the capacity to compartmentalize things and people we are exposed to on a regular basis. We put them in observable categories so we can quickly determine how they fit into our background of experience and then determine what we can expect from them in the future. Gender, race, sexual orientation, age and so on, are all such categories" (Ross, 2014, p. 6). The point is that "[h]aving biases doesn't make you a bad person—it only makes you human" (Staats, Capatosto, Wright, & Jackson, 2016, p. 15).

The groundwork for the present research on *implicit bias* was laid by the work of Gaertner and McLaughlin (1983) whose seminal article, *Racial Stereotypes: Associations and Ascriptions of Positive and Negative Characteristics*, opened a new line of inquiry in brain research. While this article is regarded as the first to introduce the world to implicit stereotyping, the 1989 article by Patricia G. Devine was considered the first to argue that "stereotypes and personal beliefs are conceptually distinct cognitive structures" (cited in Staats, 2013, p. 12). Building on this foundation, scientists Greenwald, Banaji, and Nosek (2003) have perhaps done the most to disseminate the idea of implicit bias to a broader audience. In 1998, they founded Project Implicit which produced the Implicit Bias Association Test (IAT), one of the best known and most widely used measures of implicit bias. Their stated goal, to "educate the public about hidden biases and to provide a 'virtual laboratory' for collecting data on the Internet," has allowed millions across the globe to participate in their research.

The IAT does not simply provide a way to measure implicit bias, it has brought the conversations about implicit bias out of university laboratories into the public domain by providing a lens for individuals to reflect on themselves in terms of their attitudes and behaviors, in their personal and professional lives. Importantly, it can bring to the surface disparities between how people think and feel on a conscious level as opposed to how people think and feel on an unconscious level. "The striking aspect of this test is that this bias pattern exists both among those who express explicit prejudices and those who deny them" (Wald, 2014, p. 21). Results from the IAT also provide a way for institutions to self-evaluate, and uncover and measure entrenched patterns of discrimination against particular members/groups within the organization.

Impressive work on implicit bias is also being done by the Kirwan Institute for the Study of Race and Ethnicity at Ohio State University. Each year since 2013 the Institute has produced a document, *State of the Science: Implicit Bias Review*, which "works to deepen understanding of the causes of—and solutions to—racial and ethnic disparities worldwide and to bring about a society that is fair and just for all people … [Their] research is designed to be actively used to solve problems in society" (Staats et al., 2016, p. 3). Each year they review the latest research, and share their work and expertise with a "network of colleagues and partners, ranging from other researchers, grassroots social justice advocates, policymakers, and community leaders nationally and globally, who can quickly put ideas into action" (Staats et al., 2016, p. 3). Overall, the increasing focus on implicit bias has caused people to look at themselves and society differently. Racial and cultural disparities that influence housing patterns, medical access and treatment, incarceration rates, and inequities in the judicial system are now being subjected to a different type of scrutiny because of the research on implicit bias.

Recently, the U.S. Supreme Court acknowledged the existence of "unconscious prejudice" as a factor in the ruling against the Texas Department of Housing and Community Affairs. The court decided that whether or not an existing policy demonstrated *intent* to discriminate, if it can be shown that the policy had "disparate impact," a plaintiff could win a legal challenge even in the absence of discriminatory intent. Expressing the majority opinion of the court, Justice Anthony Kennedy wrote, "Recognition of disparate-impact liability under the FHA also plays a role in uncovering discriminatory intent: It permits plaintiffs to counteract the unconscious prejudices and disguised animus that escape easy classification as disparate treatment" (Kennedy, cited in Yoshino, 2015, p. n.a.). Court watchers see this as something of a watershed moment because "the idea that disparate impact can be used to get at 'unconscious prejudices' is … an idea new to a Supreme Court majority opinion" (Yoshino, 2015, p. n.a.). If nothing else, this means that the idea of unconscious prejudice, or implicit bias again has been acknowledged and validated at the highest level of jurisprudence in the country, and it offers both a sharp rebuke to institutional discrimination and significant support for equity-driven social initiatives on every level.

This ruling, and the growing body of available research on implicit bias, is forcing us to recognize that all by itself, implicit bias plays an important part in subverting our efforts to become a nation where the phrase *freedom and justice for all* is not a mere rhetorical flourish.

When looked at in its entirety, it is significant that the compilation of research on implicit bias provided by the Kirwan Reviews shows that over the course of the last four years, only limited attention has been focused on the specific implications this research has for educators. However, it is promising that the National Education Association (NEA) and the American Federation of Teachers (AFT) have put implicit bias on their agendas, have published important research on it, and are sponsoring teacher trainings designed to transform thinking about the deep, hidden causes of racialized achievement gaps. All of this is increasing the pressure on building level educators to learn from the research and to acknowledge that: (a) implicit bias exists; (b) implicit bias is relevant to their daily practice; (c) implicit bias can have deleterious affects on already marginalized groups of students, and (d) implicit bias is malleable and can be controlled through training. Although "[t]raining teachers to understand bias will not eliminate it ... it could create an institutional environment in which it is clear that understanding bias and its effects is critically important. The long-term return on investment is inestimable" (Chemaly, cited in Staats et al., 2016, p. 34). In other words, human lives depend on what educators know and believe.

Even though the information about implicit bias is becoming increasingly available to those in the real world outside of the closed circles of research communities, *schools are not quickly putting these ideas into action and large groups of American children are continuing to fail.*

Implicit Bias—Quick Facts

Where Our Biases Originate

Our implicit biases are the result of mental associations that have formed by the direct and indirect messaging we receive, often about different groups of people. When we are constantly exposed to certain identity groups being paired with certain characteristics, we can begin to automatically and unconsciously associate the identity with the characteristics, whether or not that association aligns with reality.
—Staats et al. (2016, p. 14)

The Kirwan Institute's Reviews research on implicit bias is gathered from the areas of neuro-, social, and cognitive science. The following *Implicit*

Bias—Quick Facts is abstracted from the Kirwan Institute's Reviews from 2013 to 2016. This list gives an overview of the concept of *explicit* bias, and shows how it can inform attitudes and behaviors in individuals and institutions in every sector of society.

- Implicit bias refers to the attitudes or stereotypes that affect our understanding, actions, and decisions in an unconscious manner.
- Implicit biases are activated involuntarily, unconsciously, and without one's awareness or intentional control (see, e.g., Greenwald & Krieger, 2006; Kang et al., 2012; Nier, 2005; Rudman, 2004a)
- Our unconscious minds handle a tremendous amount of our cognition, even though we are completely unaware of it (Mlodinow, 2012). Some data indicates that the brain can process roughly 11 million bits of information every second. The conscious mind handles no more than 40–50 of these information bits, with one estimate as low as a mere 16 bits (Kozak; Lewis, 2011; H. Ross, 2008).
- Implicit biases are robust and pervasive (Greenwald et al., 1998; Kang & Lane, 2010; Nosek Smyth et al., 2007). Everyone is susceptible to them, even people who believe themselves to be impartial or objective, such as judges. Implicit biases have even been documented in children (Baron & Banaji, 2006; Newheiser & Olson, 2012; Rutland et al., 2005).
- Implicit biases and explicit biases are related yet distinct concepts; they are not mutually exclusive and may even reinforce each other (Kang, 2009; Kang et al., 2012; Wilson et al., 2000).
- Because implicit associations arise outside of conscious awareness, these associations do not necessarily align with individuals' openly-held beliefs or even reflect stances one would explicitly endorse (Graham & Lowery, 2004; Nosek et al., 2002; Reskin, 2005) ... [This disconnect between implicit and explicit biases is known as *dissociation*.]
- A 2012 study showed that as pediatricians' pro-White implicit biases increased, they were more likely to prescribe painkillers for vignette patients who were White as opposed to Black. This is just one example of how understanding implicit racial biases may help explain differential health care treatment, even for youth (Sabin & Greenwald, 2012).
- Most Americans, regardless of race, display a pro-White/anti-Black bias on the Implicit Association Test (Dovidio et al., 2002; Greenwald et al., 1998, 2009; McConnell & Liebold, 2001; Nosek et al., 2002) ...

- In the hiring process and other decision-making occasions, allowing adequate time to make decisions is vital. Research has demonstrated that time pressures create an environment in which unconscious biases can flourish (Bertrand et al., 2005).
- Once an implicit association is activated, it is difficult to inhibit (Dasgupta, 2013). Despite what may feel like a natural inclination, attempts to debias by repressing biased thoughts are ineffective. Due to rebound effects, suppressing these automatic associations does not reduce them and may actually amplify them by making them hyper-accessible (Galinsky & Moskowitz, 2000, 2007; Macrae et al., 1994). A great way to debias is to openly acknowledge biases and then directly challenge or refute them.
- Our implicit biases are not permanent; they are malleable and can be changed by devoting intention, attention, and time to developing new associations (Blair, 2002; Dasgupta, 2013; Devine, 1989).

(Staats, 2014b.)

The above facts on implicit bias are sobering reminders of how complex we are as human beings, how complex human interactions are, and how much work there is to be done if we actually believe in our own *exceptionalism*, and want to become an equity-driven society that actually is *the light of the world*; that *city … set on a hill [that] cannot be hidden* (Matthew 5:14). Addressing harmful implicit bias has to begin with nothing less than a wholesale commitment to social change, it has to begin with an honest self-assessment of who we *are*, who we *think* we are, and who we hope to *become* as a nation; we need to understand that these are not the same thing. We must acknowledge that implicit bias exists in all of us, and when it impacts us in our professional roles in ways that damage, denigrate, or deny basic human rights and privileges to other fellow Americans, we have a different responsibility to acknowledge the good, bad, and ugly sides of it, and try to fix it. The research on implicit bias is helping us "to better understand the disconnect between our society's ideal of fairness for all people and the continued reality of its absence" (powell, cited in Staats et al., 2016, p. 19). For example, when we learn that a considerable amount of credible research is now linking implicit bias to racial disparities in criminal justice, medical access and care, employment and other domains, it is important to avoid looking at the social manifestations of implicit and explicit bias as though they are completely distinct from one another, because social oppression doesn't shut down when life's necessities take you from one domain to another. In fact, social oppression magnifies and replicates itself because the resulting issues and problems overlap, intersect, and reinforce each other, and this deepens and complicates both the effects and affects of oppression. These interrelationships are referred to as *intersectionality*.

In its Primer on Intersectionality, the African American Policy Forum defines intersectionality, and explains that adopting the concept requires a paradigm shift for social justice advocates who have traditionally approached social oppression in more granular ways. Instead of thinking in terms of the interrelatedness of oppression, their approach had been to disaggregate social problems into discrete challenges facing specific groups, define them in mutually exclusive ways, and generate artificial distinctions between them (African American Policy Fourm, 2011, p. 2). Looking at problems through the lens of intersectionality is counter to that approach. Proponents of intersectionality believe that the traditional approach is less efficient and less effective because it can lead to conflicting agendas for social change which can potentially undermine each other. Accordingly, "it is essential that social justice interventions be grounded in an understanding of how these factors operate together ... [and intersectionality] can provide that grounding" (African American Policy Fourm, 2011, p. 2). This means that if one is subjected to implicit or explicit bias in the classroom, it can overlap and inform what happens in the courtroom. A considerable amount of research indicates that a racialized response to student discipline is fairly widespread and often has dire consequences for students of color.

> [T]here is clear evidence that children of color are punished more severely than White children for relatively minor, subjective offenses in schools ... There is also research that illustrates how the implicit biases or assumptions held by adults with decision-making authority lead to harsher treatment of Blacks than Whites for similar behaviors ... two sets of studies strongly suggest that implicit racial bias contributes to the differential treatment of children of color particularly Black boys in school settings. (Wald, 2014, p. 21)

Disproportional disciplinary practices that target students of color provide a clear example of the way intersectionality works: a zero tolerance policy in schools → school suspension → excessive school absences → academic underperformance → school dropout → limited employment prospects → antisocial behavior → criminal justice system → courtroom → racialized treatment, harsh sentencing → incarceration.

Understanding intersectionality is important because it "enables us to recognize the fact that perceived group membership can make people vulnerable to various forms of bias, yet because we are simultaneously members of many groups, our complex identities can shape the specific way we each experience that bias. For example, men and women can often experience racism differently, just as women of different races can experience sexism differently, and so on" (African American Policy Fourm, 2011, p. 3). This becomes even more important when we are attempting to find solutions to bias and social inequity. This approach helps us understand the multidimensional nature of most problems, and encourages us to avoid what is called a single-axis analysis or a silo-oriented structure of problem-solving. With this in mind, consider the implications of intersectionality as it relates to the research on implicit bias in the following social domains:

Criminal Justice—Key Issues
Discussing Race and Implicit Bias in Court
Implicit Bias can inform jury selection, and jurors' interpretation of evidence

Implicit Bias can inform judgments of guilt or innocence and types and lengths of sentences
Implicit Bias and Judges
Implicit Bias can inform judges' ability to listen openly and judge fairly
Attorney Interactions
Implicit Bias can inform attorney-client relationships and quality of representation
Shooter Bias—The Decision to Shoot
Implicit Bias can inform whether or not a law officer displays "shooter bias" (implicit associations connecting Blackness and weapons), the speed and accuracy of shooting decisions, and the decision to use lethal force
[A recent incident in Georgia deserves some attention here. It highlights the complex and dangerous intersection of implicit and explicit racial bias and documented police practices.
On August 31, 2017, the nation was stunned by the headline: *"We Only Kill Black People," Police Officer Says During Traffic Stop*. The news story detailed a 2016 traffic stop during which a white woman was pulled over by a white Georgia police officer because he suspected that she was driving under the influence of alcohol. Terrified by memories of many videotaped police shootings that she had seen, the woman refused to move her hands from the steering wheel. In an attempt to ease her fears, the white police officer said: "But you're not black ... Remember, we only kill black people. Yeah, we only kill black people, right? All the videos you've seen, have you seen any white people get killed?" (Bever & deGrandpre, 2017, p. n.a.)]
Health and Health Care—Key Issues
Differential Treatment
Implicit Bias can inform health care providers in terms of treatment decisions, and the quality of care given

Employment—Key Issues
>   Accent Bias
>   Implicit Bias can inform response to a person's accent or dialect (e.g. African American vernacular English or foreign accents), and potentially influence hiring decisions
>   Implicit Bias can inform how an accent or dialect is used for assessments of job qualifications, employability, promotion, and evaluations of job performance (Staats et al., 2016, pp. 32–34)

Education—Key Issues
>   Perceptions of Behavior and Related Disciplinary Situations
>   Implicit Bias can inform how student behavior is perceived and addressed, and kind and severity of discipline measures
>   Pre-Service Teachers
>   Implicit Bias can inform attitudes toward racial minority students that reflect a pro-majority bias

Implicit Bias—In-service Teachers
>   Implicit Bias can inform a preference for White over non-White students
>   Implicit Bias can inform the belief that they are unbiased and therefore play no role in contributing to, or perpetuating racism. (Staats et al., 2016, pp. 37–38)

Implicit Bias—Perceptions of Leadership
>   Implicit Bias can inform beliefs and expectations that school leaders should be White
>   Implicit Bias can inform decisions not to promote non-Whites to leadership positions because of the implicit association of Whites with valued leadership traits. (Staats et al., 2015, p. 29)

Despite the growing pillars of evidence that show that *implicit* biases prop up *explicit* biases and prejudices, and stereotypes as well as virulent forms of institutional discrimination, there are some who will choose to deny or ignore the problem(s). And they will find plausible reasons for their decision. The following reflection is meant to provide some *food for thought* for those people. This is inspired by religious philosopher Michael Carr, who based a recent sermon on the 40% Rule attributed to the indomitable Navy Seals. Talking about how difficult it is to change our ways and embody Biblical guidelines of moral behavior, Carr said: *Most people utilize only 40% of the effort needed to make real change. They expend up to 40% of the energy needed and nothing more.* The message from the Seals is that we only can achieve success if we push ourselves beyond what we perceive to be, and accept as, our physical and mental limits. Looking at the 40% Rule in the broader context of implicit bias and social dominance, the 40% Rule can be seen as a metaphor for stasis, and as a way to mask passive-aggressive behaviors that maintain existing patterns of individual and institutional social dominance and privilege. Since passive-aggressive behavior is characterized by indirection, passive resistance, and *malicious compliance*, or "veiling one's intent to not do something …" (Wikipedia.com, p. n.a.), it is aligned with the spirit and intent of the 40% Rule, or what amounts to a *40% (Dis)solution.*

Reasons to Ignore Implicit Bias

Michael Carr's Theory of Change— The *40% (Dis)solution*

If it is true that most people make only 40% of the *effort* needed to accomplish change, it also means that we accomplish only 40% of the *change* we need to make. Consequently, we achieve only 40% of the success (and 60% of the failure), 40% of the satisfaction of achieving something (and 60% of the dissatisfaction), and we stop trying less than half-way toward achieving our goal(s); 60% remains unfinished; 60% of the problem remains unfixed.

When our efforts dry up 40% of the way to completion, we can rationalize that change was a bad idea in the first place, or that we were going in the wrong direction, because we were going against established protocols and practices that are safe and predictable; or that the problem we were trying to fix wasn't really that bad, and we can live with it; *or that change is scary*; or that the status quo is what we know best and we've become experts in maintaining it; or the existing structures are natural and reliable; *or that change is scary*; or that colleagues may not accept us or the new ideas; or that the new ideas will make us part of a permanent outgroup; or that we should stop trying because the effort seems too great, or unproductive; or that others are not carrying their weight; or that we are not getting the results we expected; *or that change is scary*; or that we haven't fully assessed the problems, or what we need to correct them; or that it's a waste of time and resources, and the final outcomes may not satisfy our needs anyway; *or that change is scary*; or that the longer it takes to change things, the bigger the problem gets, putting us further away from a solution; or our efforts are doomed before we begin; *or that change is scary*; or that we're just not smart enough, or strong enough to make a difference.

These are some of the reasons we can give ourselves for embracing stasis.

But What Does This Have to Do with *Equity* and *Bias* in a School Setting?

Let's apply *the 40% (dis)solution* to a common diversity challenge related to cultural competence that confronts educators everyday nationwide: the *cultural mismatch* between some teachers and some of their students. This mismatch can cause cultural clashes that build walls of separation between White teachers and their students of color because of either an inability or unwillingness on the part of teachers to adequately learn about, and respect the cultural differences of their students, and use that knowledge to enhance classroom practice. A cultural mismatch can establish an 'us' vs. 'them' dynamic between teacher and student which can foment misunderstanding and miscommunication, and hinder the development of cultural competence. Research suggests that both implicit and explicit biases promote and sustain cultural mismatching.

The intersection of race, culture, and student discipline is one example of the affects of a cultural mismatch in schools between teachers and some of their students. This issue comes up again and again in the research on implicit bias. Among other things, the research shows that students of color get harsher, more sustained punishments for in-school offences than white students (approximately 3.5 times more suspensions and expulsions than White students). This often leads to either unnecessary or premature contacts with the criminal justice system. The research also shows that inequitable practices are often caused by a lack of cultural competency among the teachers and administrators. "In short, increasing teachers' cultural competency can help counter cultural misunderstandings that can lead to unnecessary disciplinary action. By better understanding and responding to students' cultures, teachers are better-positioned to interpret potential disciplinary situations in light of students' cultural orientations, as opposed to relying on implicit biases" (Staats, 2014a, p. 14).

Consider the implications of attempting to remedy a cultural mismatch between *White teachers and their students of color* if we apply the 40% dissolution hypothesis to the problem of unfair disciplinary practices, and the process of mitigating the underlying biases that these practices expose.

The *40% (Dis)solution*

If educators make only 40% of the *effort* needed to develop cultural competence, it means that professed equity-driven school leaders will expend only

40% of the effort needed to understand their own biases, and how their biases impact their decision making. Consequently, they will expend only 40% of the effort needed to make their schools culturally competent, and they will lead their schools only 40% of the way to transforming their school's culture. Professed equity-driven school leaders will lead their teachers only 40% of the way to developing the diversity skills they need to deconstruct their own biases, and 40% of the way to mastering the level of cultural competence they need to enthusiastically embrace all of their students, and transform classroom practice.

If educators succeed by 40%, they fail by 60%, which means that they stop trying less than half-way toward achieving their goal(s); 60% is left unachieved; 60% is left unfinished; 60% is left unchanged. Cultural incompetence leads to miscommunication and misunderstanding on so many levels, and can create a healthy environment for racial and ethnic bias to grow and prosper.

If educators expend only 40% of the effort needed, and accomplish only 40% of the change they say they want, it also means that they've accepted failure, and turned it into the new normal; 60% of what they say they want, or think they need, may be loss to them forever; 60% of the change that children will never see; 60% of their goals will never be met; 60% of their accomplishment will never be felt; never be celebrated; never be experienced.

Change is always inconvenient, and hard, and scary, but if we look at this more broadly in societal terms, 40% is a chilling number because it's a deep concession to failure. It means conceding that 40% is all that we ever hope to achieve as a society, and conceding that we can, and will, live with less. If we frame this around justice and equality, and fairness, ideals that embody America's core values, 40% is counter to almost everything that America stands for. It means that if we just fix 40% of what's wrong with our society, 60% will remain broken, and we accept that that is OK. If we fix 40% of the country's prejudice, it means that 60% remains firmly in place; this means that if people are suffering under oppression, we will expect to alleviate only 40% of their suffering, but 60% of their oppression will continue to eat away at them and diminish the quality of their lives in what many consider the greatest country in the world. If we frame this around schools and children, it is difficult to rationalize failure as an option; however, it is important to remember that we have already accepted the existence of 'dropout factories,' schools that institutionalize failure for thousands of American children every year because they graduate *less than* 60% of the students who enter the school as freshmen. This appears to be another shameful example of *the 40% (dis)solution*.

America's marginalized children cannot afford to wait for change, or to accept the derailment of their pursuit of happiness and prosperity. Their lives and futures are depending on more than a 40% *(dis)solution.*

References

African American Policy Forum. (2011). *A primer on intersectionality*. African American Policy Forum. Retrieved August 30, 2016 from http://www.aapf.org/2013/2013/01/intersectionality-primer

Allport, G. (1979). *The nature of prejudice*. Cambridge, MA: Perseus Books.

Banaji, M. R. (2010), cited in Hill, C., Corbett, C. & St. Rose, A. (2010), *Why so few? Women in science, technology, engineering, and mathematics*. Washington, D.C.: AAUW.

Bever, L., & deGrandpre, A. (2017). "We only kill black people," a cop told a woman—on camera. Now he'll lose his job. *The Washington Post*, August 31, 2017. https://www.washingtonpost.com/news/post-nation/wp/2017/08/31/remember-we-only-shoot-black-people-georgia-police-officer-told-a-woman-on-camera/?utm_term=.78a7b86c6d0b

Blanton, H., & Jaccard, J. (2015). Not so fast: Ten challenges to importing implicit attitude measures to media psychology. *Media Psychology*, 18(3), 338–369. http://dx.doi.org/10.1080/15213269.2015.1008102

Brown, E. (2015). *Texas officials: Schools should teach that slavery was "side issue" to Civil War*. July 5, 2015. Retrieved August 31, 2016 from https://www.washingtonpost.com/local/education/150-years-later-schools-are-still-a-battlefield-for-interpreting-civil-war/2015/07/05/e8fb-d57e-2001-11e5-bf41-c23f5d3face1_story.html?utm_term=.5bb1ed252218

Chemaly, S. (2016). Cited in Staats, C., Capatosto, K., Wright, R. A., & Jackson, V. W. (2016). *State of the science—Implicit bias review 2016*. Kirwan Institute. Retrieved from http://kirwaninstitute.osu.edu/wp-content/uploads/2016/07/implicit-bias-2016.pdf

Dasgupta, N. (2014). Cited in Staats, C. (2014). *State of the science—Implicit bias review 2014*. Kirwan Institute. Retrieved August 2, 2016 from http://www.kirwaninstitute.osu.edu/wp-content/uploads/2014/03/2014-implicit-bias.pdf

Devine, P. (2013). Cited in Staats, C. (2013). *State of the science—Implicit bias review 2013*. Kirwan Institute. Retrieved August 2, 2016 from http://kirwaninstitute.osu.edu/docs/SOTS-Implicit_Bias.pdf

Douglass, F. (1986). *Narrative of the life of Frederick Douglass, an American slave*. New York, NY: Penguin Books USA.

Dwyer, L. (2012). A 13-year-old's slavery analogy raises some uncomfortable truths in school education. *Democratic Underground*. May 7, 2012. https://www.democraticunderground.com/1002656867

Fryer, R. G. (2016). In the costs of inequality: Education's the one key that rules them all. Croydon Ireland. *The Harvard Gazette*, February 15, 2016. Retrieved July 17, 2016 from http://news.harvard.edu/gazette/story/2016/02/the-costs-of-inequality-educations-the-one-key-that-rules-them-all/

Gaertner, S. L., & McLaughlin, J. P. (1983). Racial stereotypes: Associations and ascriptions of positive and negative characteristics. *Social Psychology Quarterly, 46*(1), 23–30.

Ginsberg, R. B. (2003). Opinion rendered in "Grutter v. Bollinger." Cited in Staats, C. (2013). *State of the science—Implicit bias review 2013.* Kirwan Institute. Retrieved August 2, 2016 from https://search.yahoo.com/yhs/search?p=KIRWAN++INSTITUTE+IMPLICIT+BIAS+REVIEW+2013&ei=UTF-8&hspart=mozilla&hsimp=yhs-002

Greene, M. (1976). Challenging mystification: Educational foundations in dark times. *Educational Studies, 7*(1), 9–29.

Greenwald, A. G., Banaji, M. R., & Nosek, B. A. (2003). Understanding and using the implicit association test: I. An improved scoring algorithm. *Journal of Personality and Social Psychology, 85*(2), 197–216.

Hassouneh, D. (2013). Unconscious racist bias: Barrier to a diverse nursing faculty. *Journal of Nursing Education, 52*(4), 183–184. Cited in Staats, C. (2013). *State of the science—Implicit bias review 2014 edition* (p. 29). Kirwan Institute. Retrieved August 2, 2016 from http://kirwaninstitute.osu.edu/docs/SOTS-Implicit_Bias.pdf

Howard, G. (2006). *We can't teach what we don't know.* New York, NY: Teachers College Press.

Ireland, C. (2016). The costs of inequality: Education's the one key that rules them all. *The Harvard Gazette,* February 15, 2016. Retrieved July 17, 2016 from http://news.harvard.edu/gazette/story/2016/02/the-costs-of-inequality-educations-the-one-key-that-rules-them-all/

Lawrence, S. D. (2012). Racially-charged essay forces 13yr old to leave NY school. *Education Action Group Foundation.* March 13, 2012. Retrieved from http://www.educationnews.org/k-12-schools/racially-charged-essay-forces-13yr-old-to-leave-ny-school/

Monroe, B. (2010). How Texas' School Board tried to pretend slavery never happened and why your kid's school may be next. *The Huffington Post,* May 24, 2010. Retrieved from http://www.huffingtonpost.com/bryan-monroe/how-texas-school-board-tr_b_586633.html

National Education Association (NEA). (2016). Retrieved from http://www.nea.org/assets/docs/Vision_Mission_Values_2016_NEA_Handbook.pdf

Need to Know Editor. (2010). Texas school board approves controversial textbook changes. *PBS,* May 23, 2010. Retrieved August 6, 2015 from http://www.pbs.org/wnet/need-to-know/culture/texas-school-board-approves-controversial-textbook-changes/954/

Payne, B. K. (2015). Cited in Staats, C., Capatosto, K., Wright, R. A., & Contractor, D. (2015). *State of the science—Implicit bias review 2015.* Kirwan Institute. Retrieved August 2, 2016 from http://kirwaninstitute.osu.edu/wp-content/uploads/2016/07/implicit-bias-2016.pdf

powell, j. a. (n. a.). Retrieved August 7, 2016 from http://haasinstitute.berkeley.edu/johnpowell

powell, j. a., & Menendian, S. (2016). Segregation in the 21st century. *Poverty & Race Research Action Council, 25*(1), 1–2. Retrieved August 1, 2016 from http://prrac.org/newsletters/janfebmar2016.pdf

Project Implicit. Implicit Association Test (IAT). Retrieved from https://implicit.harvard.edu/implicit/

Ross, H. J. (2008). *Everyday bias. Identifying and navigating unconscious judgments in our daily lives.* Lanham, MD: Rowman and Littlefield.

Ross, H. J. (2014). *Everyday bias. Identifying and navigating unconscious judgments in our daily lives.* Lanham, MD: Rowman and Littlefield.

Schlanger, Z. (2015). Company apologizes for Texas textbook calling slaves "workers": "We made a mistake." *Newsweek*, October 5, 2015. Retrieved August 31, 2015 from http://www.newsweek.com/company-behind texas-textbook-calling-slaves-workers-apologizes-we-made-380168

Staats, C. (2013). *State of the science—Implicit bias review 2013 edition.* Kirwan Institute. Retrieved August 2, 2016 from http://kirwaninstitute.osu.edu/docs/SOTS-Implicit_Bias.pdf

Staats, C. (2014a). *Implicit racial bias and school discipline disparities exploring the connection.* Kirwan Institute. May 2014. Retrieved July 27, 2016 from http://kirwaninstitute.osu.edu/wp-content/uploads/2014/05/ki-ib-argument-piece03.pdf

Staats, C. (2014b). *State of the science—Implicit bias review 2014 edition.* Kirwan Institute. Retrieved August 2, 2016 from http://www.kirwaninstitute.osu.edu/wp-content/uploads/2014/03/2014-implicit-bias.pdf

Staats, C. (2015). *Understanding implicit bias what educators should know.* Retrieved September 27, 2016 from http://www.aft.org/ae/winter2015-2016/staats

Staats, C., Capatosto, K., Wright, R. A., & Contractor, D. (2015). *State of the science—implicit bias review 2015 edition.* Kirwan Institute. Retrieved August 2, 2016 from http://kirwaninstitute.osu.edu/wp-content/uploads/2016/07/implicit-bias-2016.pdf

Staats, C., Capatosto, K., Wright, R. A., & Jackson, V. W. (2016). *State of the science—Implicit bias review 2016 edition.* Kirwan Institute. Retrieved August 2, 2016 from http://kirwaninstitute.osu.edu/wp-content/uploads/2016/07/implicit-bias-2016.pdf

U. S. Department of Education. (2014). *Guiding principles—A resource guide for improving school climate and discipline.* U.S. Department of Education.

Wald, J. (2014). *Can "Debiasing Strategies Help to Reduce Racial Disparities in School Discipline? Summary of the Literature."* March 2014. Retrieved August 20, 2016 from http://www.indiana.edu/~atlantic/wp-content/uploads/2014/03/Implicit-Bias_031214.pdf

Yoshino, K. (2015). Supreme court breakfast table: The court acknowledges "unconscious prejudice." *Slate.* Retrieved August 27, 2016 from http://www.slate.com/articles/news_and_politics/the_breakfast_table/features/2015/scotus_roundup/supreme_court_2015_the_court_acknowledges_unconscious_prejudice.html

Young, J. (2015). *New history books in Texas downplay slavery's role in Civil War, omit KKK and Jim Crow laws.* July 7, 2015. Retrieved March 4, 2016 from www.rt.com/usa/272293-texas-history-slavery-kkk/

· 5 ·

SOCIAL DOMINANCE ORIENTATION (SDO)

Implications for Equity-Driven Teaching and School Leadership

Like implicit bias, the concept of Social Dominance Orientation (SDO) focuses on social inequities and biases, and this chapter explores the impact of SDO in schools. Understanding both concepts, and how they can complement, reinforce, and sustain each other, is important because teaching and school leadership that is uninformed by a comprehensive understanding of the dynamics of social dominance and implicit bias is complicit in maintaining unequal academic and social outcomes for students who are already chronically underserved by society. In addition to an examination of basic SDO theory and research, the chapter shows how understanding SDO can help educators understand the intersectionality of the attitudes, beliefs, and behaviors of *individuals*, *social groups*, and *institutions* in terms of how they interact to establish, entrench, and maintain systemic inequality in schools and in the overall educative process.

Keywords: social dominance orientation, implicit bias, institutional discrimination, systemic inequities, prejudice, oppression, legitimizing myths, busing

All animals are equal, but some animals are more equal than others.
—George Orwell, Animal Farm

We wear the mask that grins and lies,
It hides our cheeks and shades our eyes …
We wear the mask.
—Paul Lawrence Dunbar

Human beings are consistently, routinely, and profoundly biased. We not only are
profoundly biased, but we also almost never know we are being biased.
—Howard Ross

Like implicit bias, the concept of Social Dominance Orientation (SDO) focuses on social inequities and biases. However, whereas implicit bias exposes hidden, unconscious biases in individuals, SDO is primarily linked to an individual's conscious identification with a social group. While implicit bias focuses on hidden attitudes in individuals, the concept of SDO focuses on social groups and their attitudes, beliefs, and behaviors relative to privilege, power, and control. The concept of SDO is relevant to educators because it enhances understanding of the intersectionality of the attitudes, beliefs, and behaviors of *individuals, social groups,* and *institutions* in terms of how they interact to establish, entrench, and maintain systemic inequality in schools and in the overall educative process. Understanding both concepts, and how they can complement, reinforce, and sustain each other is important because teaching and school leadership that is uninformed by a comprehensive understanding of the dynamics of social dominance and implicit bias is complicit in maintaining unequal academic and social outcomes for students who are already chronically underserved by society.

The theory of SDO forces us to look at *achievement gaps* (as well as other socioeconomic gaps) through a different prism, and rethink what we mean by school reform and social transformation. It represents and clarifies some of the complex broad-based challenges that confront an equity-driven school leader. These are challenges that come from: personal biases and dispositions that may reside within administrators, students, faculty, and staff; institutionalized discrimination that can surreptitiously infect school systems; general socialization patterns linked to race, power, privilege, socioeconomic background, and political affiliation, etc. Looking at these complex issues from a social dominance perspective will expand our understanding of the problems, amplify discussion, and stimulate reflection on the issues of social justice, ethical decision-making, and equity-driven school leadership, all of which are precursors to closing the persistent education *gaps.*

The groundbreaking research by Pratto, Sidanius, Stallworth, and Malle (1994) sheds light on the complex nature of social dominance, and deepens the conversation about equality, social justice, and democracy as vital elements of the educative process. Their work shows the basis for attitudes and beliefs about social hierarchies, group preferences for social dominance, and how some types of dichotomous thinking and behaving on these issues evolve.

They link all of this to what they call social dominance orientation. Although their work explores the far-reaching implications of social dominance over a broad socioeconomic and political spectrum, it has particular relevance to the field of education, because it provides some important insights about how social dominance can operate in school settings, to either promote or hinder the presence of socially just beliefs and behaviors that inform the teaching/ learning process, policy development, and the overall culture of schools.

In *Social Dominance Orientation: A Personality Variable Predicting Social and Political Attitudes*, Pratto et al. (1994) study personality orientations and the origins of, and the interplay between, social dominance, power, privilege, and social and political attitudes in and among social groups. This research is distinct in the field because rather than look for one specific cause of prejudice and discrimination, using one type of analysis, they explore the interactions between "several levels of analysis—that is, the manner in which psychological, socio-structural, ideological, and institutional forces jointly contribute to the production and reproduction of social oppression" (Sidanius, Pratto, van Laar, & Levin, 2004, p. 846). The early and subsequent work on SDO is groundbreaking because it does not look only for individual or group motivations for discrimination and prejudice such as: why some individuals/groups have internalized negative or positive stereotypes about other individuals or groups; why some individuals/groups maintain prejudiced attitudes and or behaviors against other individuals/groups; why some individuals/groups believe in social equality, and why others do not. Significantly, the researchers also address the *consequences* and *contexts* of prejudice, discrimination, and group oppression as manifested by individuals and groups, and connect them to the power differentials that distinguish various social groups. Overall, the applications for this research are limitless because they inform many disciplines, subject areas, and social structures. For example, the research addresses wide-ranging subjects and issues from the inter- and intragroup dynamics affecting different sects of Israeli Jews, to the inherent basis for gender discrimination, to the root causes for political conservatism.

Although the implications for this work are global, transcending socioeconomic, ethnic, racial, and transnational boundaries, for the purpose of this discussion, the focus of the chapter will be the impact that SDO has on education in terms of teaching, learning, and school leadership.

Although the research on SDO is particularly relevant for educators and policymakers who are equity-driven and who are committed to being agents of social change, understanding the concept of SDO and applying it to the entirety of the educative process is a massive and complex undertaking that requires intentionality, collaboration, and commitment. Not only does it require engagement on many different levels, it requires a major paradigm shift which is difficult. It is difficult because, among other things, it forces people to confront issues they would prefer to ignore, and it draws people into uncomfortable conversations about things that usually remain unsaid in professional settings. For one thing, it is likely to reveal how educators (especially well-meaning ones) can be accomplices to *oppression*; how they may intentionally or inadvertently prop up and sustain inequities in their schools and districts.

Understanding SDO helps us identify, and address, group-based, de facto, *oppression* that is manifested in the way public schools are structured; *oppression* that is manifested in policies that intentionally or unintentionally cause and maintain structural inequities; *oppression* that is the outcome of conscious and/or unconscious biases and beliefs of individual teachers and leaders and policymakers (on the local, state, and national levels); *oppression* that is often ignored or overlooked and seems impossible to change.

Understanding SDO helps us understand the group dynamics of social power and status. It gives us a deeper understanding of what it means to be power*ful* or power*less*. It shows that those who have high levels of SDO are predisposed to behave in ways that can subjugate others. This behavior, to a large extent, reflects self-interest because it is self-protective and self-serving. The research shows that high status groups work harder to preserve and protect its group's integrity than do low status groups, because they have more to lose—power. In contrast, low status groups which are overtly or covertly maligned by society have less motivation to support and defend their group's lower status. For example, it makes no sense for those who are poor to defend their status as *poor* people especially when legitimizing myths that aggressively stigmatize them are harmful and pervasive. Instead, members of low status groups are more inclined to resist and denounce their status, and decry the institutional inequities that block their social progress. The problem is that they often do not have much power, or a platform from which to speak, and institutional constraints can make them virtually *voiceless*. Moreover, members of low status groups, like the economically disadvantaged, are likely to spend more time focusing on survival or subsistence than protesting systems and institutions that appear too big and too inaccessible to change. For example, poor individuals may recognize that schools are failing their children because they also may know that the same schools and the same systems failed them as well. They likely understand that this is a generational problem, even if they are unable to articulate it, or change the trajectory of failure for their own children. They know this because of the lives they lead, and the jobs they hold, and the places they live, and the food that they eat. They know this because often they have been socially immobilized, and they know that their opportunities for social and economic success have been, and are being proscribed.

This is one reason that often those from low status groups who *have* managed to rise above the oppression, leave their communities and low status, achieve a quality education, earn social and economic success, and higher levels of social acceptance, can then return to their neighborhoods, and find people they have known all of their lives, who are still there: *left back* by school; *left back* by time; *left back* by circumstances; *left back* by systems that are designed to oppress them.

Despite the constellation of problems and setbacks that they face every day, and the social stigmas that demean them because of their status, research shows that members of low status groups are motivated to maintain a positive identity. Unfortunately, this can be expressed in self-destructive ways. One pertinent example is evidenced in how some students from low status groups can respond to academic pursuit.

Social identity theory theorizes that there are at least three types of reactions to low status. One is to choose a different domain, a new playing field, as a reference to compare the in-group (White students) to the out-group (African-American students). In other words, it's a way to *flip the script*, and at least one study hypothesized that this is one reason that some African-American students both devalue, and seem chronically disengaged from, academic pursuits. The speculation is that if these students devalued academic success, it would no longer be valid as a source of their self-esteem. In essence, academic failure would no longer be a way to devalue and demean them, at least in their own minds (Van Laar & Sidanius, 2001, p. 247).

Understanding SDO helps us see relationships and causality that make social inequities seem *normal* or part of the natural order of things. For educators, SDO can provide a lens through which they can begin to see some of the deeper, underlying causes of inequities in schools that are documented by a variety of indicators. These include the chronic academic underachievement of some subordinated groups linked to race, class, ethnicity, and other out-group categories. Moreover, the concept of SDO can provide an important template for educators who are committed to implementing social justice strategies designed to change the culture of their schools, and to challenging individual and institutional discrimination wherever and however they are manifested. This includes rethinking hiring practices, teacher training, curricular decisions, student tracking, and the creation of a school culture that continuously interrupts and interrogates bias.

The pertinent questions that this research helps to address are: What does SDO look like in a school or district? How does SDO impact the makeup of faculty and staff? To what degree does SDO influence an individual's choice to enter the field of education or instead choose another career such as law enforcement or military service? How does SDO impact the personality orientations of school leaders and how might this be connected to the decisions they make on behalf of their students? How does one's SDO affect policy decisions on the local, state, and federal levels? Finally, can an understanding of SDO help us become more authentically democratic?

There are no easy answers to any of these questions, but understanding the theoretical basis for SDO makes it easier to understand the implications it has for teaching and learning, and equity-driven school leadership.

The Theoretical Basis for
Social Dominance Orientation

Pratto et al. (1994) developed the concept of SDO to explain a

> general attitudinal orientation toward intergroup relations [which reflects] whether one generally prefers such relations to be equal, versus hierarchical, that is, ordered along a superior-inferior dimension. [Their] theory postulates that people who are more social dominance oriented will tend to favor hierarchy-enhancing ideologies and policies, whereas those lower on SDO will tend to favor hierarchy-attenuating ideologies and policies. (p. 742)

Since its publication, this construct has attracted national and international attention and support, and is widely used by social scientists to understand sociopolitical ideologies, the nature of individual and group prejudice, and how all of this informs social policy and institutionalized discrimination. This concept establishes a research-based nexus between individual and group-relevant prejudice, the endorsement of group-relevant ideologies, and the development of, and support for, group-relevant social policies. "For example, SDO has been found to be a powerful predictor of generalized prejudice against, and persecution of, a wide array of denigrated groups such as poor people, Latinos, Asians, foreigners, gays, women, Arabs, Muslims, Blacks, Jews, immigrants and refugees ..." (Ho et al., p. 584). A cluster of ideologies can be linked to these prejudices including: political conservatism, nationalism, militarism, the demonization of the poor (as opposed to poverty), homophobia, sexism, linguicism, and significantly, a racialized blame-the-victim rationalization for academic underachievement. These ideologies then serve as the foundation for social policies including the school-to-prison pipeline, exclusionary immigration laws, "punitive criminal justice policies ... and opposition to humanitarian practices, social welfare and affirmative action ..." (Ho et al., 2012, p. 584).

At the basis of this research is the assumption that "[g]roup conflict and group-based inequality are pervasive in human existence" (Pratto et al., 1994, p. 741) and for their survival and well-being, social groups want to mediate and minimize intergroup conflict. They do this by establishing what Pratto et al. call *legitimizing myths*, a set of group norms and ideologies that protect the group's unity, cohesiveness, and status. To mitigate group conflict, all legitimizing myths require group consensus and must appear as "self-evident truths" (p. 741).

The researchers have identified two categories of *legitimizing myths*: *hierarchy-enhancing* legitimizing myths and *hierarchy-attenuating* legitimizing myths. Hierarchy-enhancing legitimizing myths are those that reflect a *preference* for social inequality, and promote the idea that one group is superior to another group; they are "the tools that legitimize discrimination" (p. 741). Social Darwinism and meritocracy are hierarchy-enhancing legitimizing myths that argue that hierarchies are part of the natural order, and that some individuals/groups have more social value than others. The following are examples of social attitudes and personal preferences that underlie *hierarchy-enhancing* legitimizing myths. These are taken from the SDO Scale created by Pratto et al. (1994):

- Some groups of people are simply inferior to other groups.
- It's OK if some groups have more of a chance in life than others.
- To get ahead in life, it is sometimes necessary to step on other groups.
- If certain groups stayed in their place, we would have fewer problems.
- It's probably a good thing that certain groups are at the top and other groups are at the bottom.

(Pratto et al., 1994, p. 763)

Hierarchy-attenuating legitimizing myths are those that reflect *opposition* to structures of social dominance and inequality in and among social groups.

They are ideologies that promote inclusiveness, and challenge inequality by promoting ideals like the *universality* of human rights and the belief in 'equal justice for all.'

The following are examples of social attitudes and personal preferences that underlie *hierarchy-attenuating* legitimizing myths taken from the SDO Scale created by Pratto et al. (1994):

> Group equality should be our ideal.
> - All groups should be given an equal chance in life.
> - We should do what we can to equalize conditions for different groups.
> - We would have fewer problems if we treated people more equally.
> - We should strive to make incomes as equal as possible.
> - No one group should dominate in society.
>
> (Pratto et al., 1994, p. 763)

Despite the inherent opposition between *hierarchy-enhancing legitimizing myths* and *hierarchy-attenuating legitimizing myths*, the tension between them serves a social purpose by providing a sinister kind of balance in the social order. Ironically, because they are consensual, *hierarchy-legitimizing myths* help to *stabilize* social oppression and *minimize* intergroup conflict by establishing "how individuals and social institutions should allocate things of positive or negative social value ..." (p. 741). This can include everything from jobs, to bank loans, government appointments, or the length and severity of prison sentences. Anti-Black racism is one pernicious example of a tenacious hierarchy-enhancing legitimizing myth, and Pratto et al. (1994) point out that

> ... the ideology of anti-Black racism has been instantiated in personal acts of discrimination, but also in institutional discrimination against African-Americans by banks, public transit authorities, schools, churches, marriage laws, and the penal system. (p. 741)

Clearly, individual and group acceptance of either hierarchy-enhancing legitimizing myths or hierarchy-attenuating legitimizing myths is directly linked to the development of social policies that actualize and institutionalize these internalized beliefs, and the implications for schools and the educative process are enormous.

The early and much of the subsequent research on SDO (Pratto et al. (1994); Van Laar and Sidanius (2001); Sidanius, van Laar, Levin, and Sinclair (2003); Sidanius et al. (2004); Pratto, Sidanius, and Levin (2006); Ho et al.

(2012, 2015); Sidanius, Cotterill, Sheehy-Skeffington, Kteily, and Carvacho [in press]) demonstrates that SDO is measurable and, to some extent, predictable given the number of variables that impact personality and group identity. The research shows that whether a person has a greater or lesser propensity toward social dominance not only can predict attitudes toward, and support for, group dominance and equality or inequality among groups, it also can predict the type of social roles, career choices, and institutions to which one is attracted. Moreover, based on the research, we learn that "those who are higher on SDO will become members of institutions and choose roles that maintain or increase social inequality, whereas those who are lower on SDO will belong to institutions and choose roles that reduce inequality" (Pratto et al., 1994, p. 742). For example, in the original research, *hierarchy-enhancing* careers included:

- finance and business
- law enforcement officers (i.e. police, corrections, sheriffs etc.)
- military personnel
- members of the criminal justice system (i.e. judges, lawyers, prosecutors)
- politics

In contrast, *hierarchy-attenuating* careers included:

- social scientists (including social science professors)
- social workers or counselors
- sociology teachers
- artists (painters, poets, actors, directors)
- public intellectuals (writers, editors, journalists)
- special education teachers.

(taken from Pratto et al., 1994, p. 742, 747)

The research shows that people choose careers and institutions of employment that are congruent with their values, attitudes, and social preferences, and the better the match between people and where they work, the greater the job satisfaction, and the greater the 'rewards' they accrue in the form of promotions, raises, positive job evaluations, acceptance by colleagues and supervisors, etc. In other words, "… person-organization congruence fuels successful and effective work relations, at least in part because those who most strongly identify with an organization are also those most likely to take on an organization's perspective and act in its best interests" (Haley & Sidanius, 2005, p. 192).

The research raises a number of relevant questions for those who play a role in shaping, directing, and educating children because we know that those who choose to teach, or lead, or develop school policy do not live in a vacuum, or assume their roles as *blank slates*. We know that everyone is a product of their social milieu, and everyone brings a cluster of personal attitudes and predispositions into their classrooms and schools, as well as into the inner sanctums where they discuss issues and make school and district policy. This means that one's SDO informs who we are, and what we do, and understanding and addressing this is a necessary prelude to changing the trajectory of academic outcomes for students who have been, and are, chronically underserved by today's schools.

Basically, since the research on SDO is about attitudes and predispositions toward equality and inequality, by extension it is also about justice and injustice. If we demand of American democracy that it live up to its highest values and principles, then public education *should be* equity-driven, not tinged with sexism, or heterosexism, or linguicism or racism, and yet, these and other forms of discrimination are endemic in how many American schools are run. The data on school failure keeps coming back to this, so perhaps those who declare a commitment to improving academic outcomes for chronically underserved students are not asking the right questions, or looking in the right places for solutions.

Seen through the lens of the educative process, some pertinent questions about SDO do emerge. For example: Is SDO relevant to educators as a way to understand an individual's (teachers, leaders, board members, etc.) preferences for group dominance, and attitudes about social equality or inequality? If so, how can this information be used to help us understand how attitudes and predispositions can inform school policies and practices (including who is hired and who is promoted; who is expelled or 'left back'; who is slotted for AP placement and who is not)? Are predispositions regarding social dominance and social equality or inequality related to whether or not pedagogy is mired in racism or classism that ends up providing excellence for some students, and what Martin Haberman (1991) called a *pedagogy of poverty* for others? Do predispositions regarding social dominance and social inequality impact the degree of equity-driven school leadership? If so, in what ways does it do this?

Arguably these are important questions because in America there is a strong correlation between access to a quality education, academic success, economic success, and upward social mobility. And, there is an equally strong correlation between those who languish at the bottom of the social hierarchy and subsist on its fringes, and those who languish on the bottom of the educational hierarchy and subsist on the fringes of academic excellence.

Connecting Social Dominance Orientation to the Educative Process: 15 Critical Elements of SDO

Although research on SDO continues to expand, and become more and more complex, for the purposes of this research, it is important to narrow the focus to better understand the concept itself, and the particular impact it has on how, and what, teachers teach; how, and what, students learn; how, and where, leaders lead, and how all of this is connected to support for social justice in school settings.

The following list of 15 Critical Elements of SDO and the companion chart that follows are abstracted from Social Dominance Theory and the Dynamics of Intergroup Relations: Taking Stock and Looking Forward by Pratto et al. (2006) to clarify the concept, and highlight important points, especially those that show the nexus between SDO and the educative process. The ultimate goal is to demonstrate that there is a triangular relationship between SDO, the educative process, and social justice.

A careful study of SDO research, and these intimate relationships, also reveals that the research findings are consistent with observations and critiques from a variety of well-known educational theorists made over the last century. These social critics and educators anticipated some of the challenges that still need to be addressed in schools today, and it is significant that then, as now, the binary racial opposition between Blacks and Whites continues unabated, and is the locus of much of the tension and conflict that characterizes discussions about academic success and failure, school improvement, and school reform. However, today the challenges are more complex, because racism is stratified by sexism, heterosexism, ageism, classism, and many other indicators of SDO that infect, and inflect, school policies and practices. Relevant quotes have been paired with the 15 Critical Elements in order to expand our understanding of the concepts, and frame them around specific challenges to equity-driven educational practice.

15 Critical Elements of SDO

1. **Social dominance systems serve dominant groups more than subordinate groups.** (Pratto et al., 2006).
   Carter G. Woodson—The Mis-Education of the Negro (1926)

The so-called modern education, with all its defects, however, does others so much more good than it does the Negro, because it has been worked out in conformity to the needs of those who have enslaved and oppressed weaker peoples. (Woodson, 1990, p. xii)

2. **Members of dominant social groups** have a disproportionate share of *positive social values* and desirable material and symbolic resources (i.e. political power, wealth, access to good housing, health care, leisure, and education). (Pratto et al., 2006)
Peggy McIntosh—White Privilege and Male Privilege (1988)

> I have come to see white privilege as an invisible package of unearned assets that I can count on cashing in each day, but about which I was 'meant' to remain oblivious. White privilege is like an invisible weightless knapsack of special provisions, assurances, tools, maps, guides, codebooks, passports, visas, clothes, compass, emergency gear, and blank checks. (McIntosh, 1988, p. n.a.)

3. **Members of subordinate groups** have a disproportionate share of *negative social value* and receive an unequal share of desirable material and symbolic resources (i.e. substandard housing, access to quality medical care leading to higher rate of preventable disease, underemployment, disproportionate punishment in the criminal justice system, stigmatization, and vilification in news media). (Pratto et al., 2006)
William Watkins—1998

> I want my students to become critical social scientists. I want them to question the arrangements of power, authority, wealth and control. I want them to believe that we little people can make a difference. We can create a new society without prejudice and want but only if we are armed with the knowledge and ideas to do so. (William Watkins cited in Ayers, Hunt, & Quinn, 1998, p. 188)

4. **Group-based social hierarchy** is produced by the *net effects* of discrimination across multiple levels: institutions, individuals, and collaborative intergroup processes. (Pratto et al., 2006)
Jonathan Kozol—Savage Inequalities 1991

> There is a deep-seated reverence for fair play in the United States, and in many areas of life we see the consequences in a genuine distaste for loaded dice, but this is not the case in education, health care, or inheritance of wealth. In these elemental areas we want the game to be unfair, and we have made it so; and it will likely so remain. (Jonathan Kozol cited in Ayers et al., p. xxxii)

5. **Hierarchy-enhancing legitimising myths** inform individual, group, and institutional *behavior and sustains dominance*. (Pratto et al., 2006)
   Anonymous White Female Teacher Referring to Black students

   > ...'they don't care. They have a culture that doesn't value education. They don't have books at home and their parents didn't graduate from high school, so they don't care if their kids do.' (cited in Brooks, 2012, p. 45)

6. **Hierarchy-enhancing legitimising myths** often leads *subordinates* to *collaborate* with dominants to maintain oppression (i.e. dominants and subordinates will agree with respect to these legitimising myths more than they will disagree). (Pratto et al., 2006).
   Kenji Yoshino—Covering 2007

   > I doubt any of these people covered willingly. I suspect they were all bowing to an unjust reality that required them to tone down their stigmatized identities to get along in life. (Yoshino, 2007, p. x)

7. **Hierarchy-enhancing (HE) institutions** promote and sustain *inequality* by allocating disproportionately *more positive* social value or *less negative* social value to dominant groups than to subordinate groups. (Pratto et al., 2006)
   John Dewey—Democracy and Education (1963)

   > ... it is the office of the school environment to balance the various elements in the social environment, and to see to it that each individual gets an opportunity to escape from the limitations of the social group in which he was born, and to come into living contact with a broader environment. (Dewey, 1963, p. 20)

8. **Hierarchy-enhancing (HE) institutions** *resist change*, and when individuals or groups try to challenge discriminatory practices, *institutions defend their discriminatory practices as part of defending the institution itself*. (Pratto et al., 2006)
   Jeffrey S. Brooks—Black School White School 2012

   > Teachers and educational administrators are among the nation's best and brightest public intellectuals ... but many of these people are also uncritical of deep-seated overt and covert racist values that shape who they are and how they teach or lead ... (cited in Brooks, 2012, p. 1)

9. **Legitimising myths are powerful and can induce self-debilitating or self-destructive behaviour by subordinate group members** (i.e. prevailing stereotypes of group inferiority may lead members of subordinate groups to behave in ways that reinforce these stereotypes and under-perform on intellectual tasks, have higher levels of school truancy, and higher school drop-out rates etc.) (Pratto et al., 2006)
Carter G. Woodson—The Mis-Education of the Negro (1926)

> ... the Negro's mind has been brought under the control of his oppressor. The problem of holding the Negro down, therefore, is easily solved. When you control a man's thinking you do not have to worry about his actions. You do not have to tell him not to stand here or go yonder. He will find his 'proper place' and will stay in it. You do not need to send him to the back door. He will go without being told. In fact, if there is no back door, he will cut one for his special benefit. His education makes it necessary. (Woodson, 1926, p. xiii)

10. **Legitimising myths (and stereotypes) that can induce self-debilitating** behaviors in members of subordinate groups can give members of dominant groups a "stereotype lift" i.e. better performance etc. (Pratto et al., 2006).
Carter G. Woodson—The Mis-Education of the Negro (1926)

> The same educational process which inspires and stimulates the oppressor with the thought that he is everything and has accomplished everything worthwhile, depresses and crushes at the same time the spark of genius in the Negro by making him feel that his race doesn't amount to much and will never measure up to the standards of other peoples. (Woodson, 1926, p. xiii)

11. **Individuals high in SDO justify their discriminatory actions** by supporting a wide variety of legitimising myths that have in common *the notion that dominant and subordinate groups deserve their relative positions of superiority and inferiority in the social hierarchy.* (Pratto et al., 2006)
Jeffrey S. Brooks—Black School White School 2012

> One of the things I saw over and over, especially talking to White teachers, was an uncritical sense of White privilege. It came out especially in their teaching. There was a lot of culturally irrelevant pedagogy. There was a lot of flat-out cultural abuse. There was no conversation about race going on in the school. There was nothing to prompt these teachers and administrators to question their assumptions ... (Brooks, 2012, p. 130)

12. **High-SDO individuals show more support for hierarchy-enhancing legitimising myths, less support for hierarchy-attenuating legitimising**

myths, and **more support for hierarchy-enhancing social policies** (e.g. restrictive immigration policies) and less support for hierarchy-attenuating social policies that maintain group dominance (e.g. affirmative action). (Pratto et al., 2006).
Peggy McIntosh—White Privilege and Male Privilege (1988)

> Whether through the curriculum or in the newspaper, the television, the economic system, or the general look of people in the streets, I received daily signals and indications that my people counted and that others either didn't exist or must be trying not very successfully, to be like people of my race. (McIntosh, 1988, p. n.a.)

13. **Much of the power of legitimising myths is that they provide rationales for institutional discrimination.** (Pratto et al. 2006).
Jeffrey S. Brooks—Black School White School 2012

> White school leaders tended to dismiss issues of race as issues of class … White school leaders' strategy of shifting the topic from race to class enabled them to avoid uncomfortable conversations with one another … (Brooks, 2012, p. 46)

14. **Social dominance theory helps us understand why people in different groups lack consensus on the existence of group inequality.** European-Americans and African-Americans use different reference points in deciding whether enough racial equality has been achieved. *European-Americans see challenges to dominance as a loss and unfair; African Americans see change as just.* (Pratto et al., 2006)
Malcolm X—

> You will never get the American white man to accept the so-called Negro as an integrated part of his society until the image of the Negro the white man has is changed, and until the image the Negro has of himself is also changed. (Malcolm X cited in Mazel, 1962, p. 105)

15. **Social dominance theory establishes a relationship between individuals and the social institutions in which they work in terms of basic values, orientations, and behavioural predispositions.** Social dominance theory argues that for hierarchy-enhancing and hierarchy-attenuating institutions to maintain their hierarchical posture, and function well, *the psychological character of individuals, especially their levels of SDO and their endorsement of legitimising myths, should match the hierarchical character of the institutions in which they work.* In

a hierarchy-enhancing institution, *individuals are rewarded* for holding institutionally congruent attitudes (Pratto et al., 2006).
William Ayers—2012

> This is a very complicated question and a very complicated issue ... Race and class intermingle in our culture ... It is the confusing of racism, the ideology, the idea, and the prejudice of White supremacy, the structure, the deep question of privilege and oppression ... Yet, it is not about their personal prejudice. It's actually about a system that you benefit from as a White person or you suffer from as a Black person without you personally doing anything. You don't have to do anything, because the thing bubbles along. (Ayers cited in Brooks, 2012, p. 130)

Using the 15 Critical Elements of SDO above, the following chart shows the intersection of SDO, Social Justice, and the educative process. The chart is not meant to be definitive or exhaustive, but is meant to establish a baseline for further discussion.

If, as they are presently structured, American schools are *hierarchy-enhancing* institutions, existing in contradistinction to basic democratic principles of equality and fairness and justice, then it means that we have to reexamine what we are meaning and what we are doing when we say we are *educating* America's children, and preparing them to become informed and engaged citizens in a democratic society. Henry Giroux implicitly voiced this concern when he said "[H]ow we experience democracy in the future will depend on how we name, think about, and transform the interrelated modalities of race, racism and social justice" (cited in Nieto & Bode, 2012, p. 82). And, social transformation is connected in large part to what schools are educating children for.

Schools are responsible for protecting, nurturing, and educating *all* of America's children because they were designed to function *in loco parentis*. In Latin, this means that they become, for part of every day, surrogate parents to *all* of the children that enter their doors. And yet, in light of the interminable, racialized gaps in academic outcomes, are they not abusive *parents?*; parents that favor and reward some of their children, while demonizing and punishing others?; parents whose loving care flows freely to some of their children but who intentionally withhold it from others?

Yes, schools are responsible for educating *all* of America's children. However, if they are educating *some* children to support, and be parties to, social hierarchies that give *some* of them unearned advantages and privileges, while 'other' children are being disadvantaged and dis-privileged, then they are

Table 5.1: The Relationship Between SDO, Schools, and Social Justice.

SDO Concept	Implications for Social Justice	Potential Impact(s) in Schools
1. Social dominance systems serve dominant groups more than subordinate groups	• Sustains institutional and systemic discrimination in schools and school systems • Underserves specific groups of students • Undermines democratic principles of fairness/equality	• Limited hiring/promotion of members of subordinate group for faculty/administrative/leadership positions • Potential for biased curricular decisions • Unequal access to high quality education resources • Less access to quality teachers and teaching • Policy decisions favor dominant groups
2. **Members of dominant social groups** have a disproportionate share of *positive social values* and desirable material and symbolic resources (i.e., political power, wealth, access to good housing, health care, leisure, and education)	• Dominants get more; subordinates get less • Equality is suborned in most areas of society • Dominants are privileged and have a strong sense of entitlement to superior social status • Subordinates are disprivileged and marginalized • Subordinates can engage in self-damaging behaviors and/or internalize self-hatred • Social categories are relatively fixed for both dominants and subordinates	• Members of dominant group are in power and control • Members of dominant group control hiring/promotion—can limit subordinate group access to faculty and administrative and leadership positions • Curricular decisions likely reflect bias toward dominant group attitudes, behaviors • Schools populated with children from dominant group tend to have better quality education, better teacher credentials, better educational resources, etc. • Children from dominant groups enter school more prepared to succeed

(Continued)

Table 5.1: (Continued)

SDO Concept	Implications for Social Justice	Potential Impact(s) in Schools
3. **Members of subordinate groups** have a disproportionate share of *negative social value* and receive an unequal share of desirable material and symbolic resources	• Subordinates are placed at a disadvantage and have difficulty competing • Subordinates get fewer opportunities for success (i.e. jobs, education, economic status) • Subordinates have higher incidence of substandard housing, medical care, disproportionate punishment in criminal justice system, vilification in the news media	• Less access to power/leadership positions in schools • Curricular decisions likely reflect bias toward dominant group attitudes, behaviors • Subordinate group's perspectives and culture are undervalued or absent from curricular materials • Higher incidence of poor teacher quality, higher teacher turnover, higher teacher absenteeism • Children from subordinate groups less likely to enter school prepared to succeed • Zero tolerance policies criminalize disproportionally high % of students of color
4. **Group-based social hierarchy** is produced by the **net effects** of discrimination across multiple levels: institutions, individuals, and collaborative intergroup processes	• Individuals, groups, and institutions work together to reinforce social inequities that undermine equal access	• Inequities in schools are systemic, entrenched, and sometimes invisible
5. **Hierarchy-enhancing legitimising myths** inform individual, group, and institutional *behavior and sustain dominance*	• Dominant and subordinate group's ideas about equality and inequality are entrenched • Inter- and intragroup stereotypes remain intact and undermine social change	• School reform/transformation is difficult • Individuals at all levels of the system are more likely to embrace or be resigned to the *status quo* • Children from both dominant and subordinate groups internalize misinformation about each other which affects how they relate to each other • Faculty and staff from both dominant and subordinate groups internalize misinformation about each other which affects how they relate to each other

6. **Hierarchy-enhancing legitimising myths** often lead *subordinates* to *collaborate* with dominants to maintain oppression (i.e., dominants and subordinates will agree with respect to these legitimising myths more than they will disagree)	• Individuals in subordinate groups can help to support and maintain social inequity • Individuals in subordinate groups can undermine their own progress toward success • Individuals in subordinate groups may ignore or support policies and/or practices that harm members of their own group	• Internalized self-hatred leads to low academic expectations and academic underperformance • Individuals in subordinate groups can engage in self-sabotage that widens the 'gaps' • School can become a hostile environment for students in subordinate groups
7. **Hierarchy-enhancing (HE) institutions** promote and sustain *inequality* by allocating disproportionately ***more positive*** social value or ***less negative*** social value to dominant groups than to subordinate groups	• Public institutions that are ostensibly neutral and fair actually support social inequity • Public institutions maintain the status quo • Members of non-dominant groups have limited chances for success	• Schools and school systems stratify inequities and perpetuate dominant privilege • Students from subordinate groups are generally underserved and underperform academically
8. **Hierarchy-enhancing (HE) institutions resist change**, and when individuals or groups try to challenge discriminatory practices, *institutions defend their discriminatory practices as part of defending the institution itself*	• Social progress is at risk • Prejudice reduction is at risk • Social inequality becomes the 'norm' • Institutions use their leverage as employers to challenge institutionalized inequities • Institution's support for inequity is self-serving	• Schools and school systems rationalize 'business as usual' • Schools and school systems deny/ignore inequities • Schools and school systems give little or no support to reform ideas • Schools and school systems give little or no support to anti-bias advocates/advocacy

(Continued)

Table 5.1: (Continued)

SDO Concept	Implications for Social Justice	Potential Impact(s) in Schools
9. **Legitimising myths are powerful and can induce self-debilitating or self-destructive behaviour by subordinate group members**	• Social inequality is supported by many of those who are the victims of oppression	• Internalized self-hatred leads to low academic expectations and academic underperformance • Individuals in subordinate groups can engage in self-sabotage • School can become a hostile environment for students in subordinate groups • Students from subordinated groups embody self-demeaning stereotypes • Students from subordinated groups demonstrate a higher incidence of truancy, school-drop rates, criminal behavior • Students from subordinated groups can be less motivated to perform academically
10. **Legitimizing myths (and stereo-types) that can induce self-debilitating** behaviors in members of subordinate groups can give members of dominant groups a **"stereotype lift,"** i.e., better performance, etc.	• Acceptance of negative stereotypes against out-groups motivates members of dominant groups to perform better • Social inequities remain in place	• Students from dominant groups who already benefit from systemic and institutional inequities in the ways schools operate also benefit from belief in their own group's superiority in terms of higher self-expectations

11. Individuals high in SDO justify their discriminatory actions by supporting a wide variety of legitimising myths that have in common *the notion that dominant and subordinate groups deserve their relative positions of superiority and inferiority in the social hierarchy*	• Entrenched power structures and social inequities remain in place because dominant and subordinate groups believe their relative positions as 'normal' and just	• Students in advanced classes (usually from dominant groups) and students in average or lower tracked classes (usually from subordinate groups) see their relative positions as 'normal' and just • Teachers who are dominant group members see inequitable racialized tracking practices 'normal' and justified • School leaders who are dominant group members see inequitable racialized tracking practices as 'normal' and justified
12. High-SDO individuals show more support for hierarchy-enhancing legitimising myths, less support for hierarchy-attenuating legitimising myths, and *more support for hierarchy-enhancing social policies* (e.g., restrictive immigration policies) and less support for hierarchy-attenuating social policies that maintain group dominance (e.g., affirmative action)	• Individuals in dominant groups support inequitable social arrangements that benefit themselves and create corresponding self-serving social policies that ensure advantages for them and disadvantages for those in subordinate groups	• Faculty and administrators who are members of dominant groups develop and/or support school policies that sustain inequity among students who are members of dominant and subordinate student groups
13. Much of the power of legitimising myths is that *they provide rationales for institutional discrimination*	• Internalized myths about social superiority and social inferiority provide justification and support for institutional discrimination	• Faculty and administrators who are members of dominant groups have internalized myths about dominant and subordinate groups and support the school and the school systems that maintain inequity

(Continued)

Table 5.1: (Continued)

SDO Concept	Implications for Social Justice	Potential Impact(s) in Schools
14. **Social dominance theory helps us understand why people in different groups lack consensus on the existence of group inequality.** European-Americans and African-Americans use different reference points in deciding whether enough racial equality has been achieved. *European-Americans see challenges to dominance as a loss and unfair; African-Americans see change as just*	• Membership in either a dominant or subordinate group presupposes conflicting perspectives about social inequality which advantages those who already have social power and privilege • Those in dominant and subordinate groups have different perspectives of social change • Dominants see threats to dominance as unjust and unfair • Subordinates see threats to dominance as fair and just	• Faculty and administrators who are members of either dominant or subordinate groups will be challenged to reach consensus on policies and practices as they relate to the presence of inequities in the educative process because their interests and perspectives are different • Faculty and staff in dominant groups tend to protect existing inequitable school structures because it's in their best interests to do so • Faculty and staff with high SDO see threats to school structure as unjust and unfair • Faculty and staff with low SDO see threats to dominance as fair, just, and progressive

15. Social dominance theory establishes a relationship between individuals and the social institutions in which they work in terms of basic values, orientations, and behavioural predispositions. Social dominance theory argues that for hierarchy-enhancing and hierarchy-attenuating institutions to maintain their hierarchical posture, and function well, *the psychological character of individuals, especially their levels of SDO and their endorsement of legitimising myths, should match the hierarchical character of the institutions in which they work.* In a hierarchy-enhancing institution, *individuals are rewarded for* holding institutionally congruent attitudes	• Individuals choose to work in institutions whose orientation to structures of social dominance match their own • Institutions that support structures of social dominance that may support social inequalities reward individuals who support them which sustains patterns of social inequality	• A symbiotic relationship must exist between faculty and staff who work in schools and systems and they are rewarded for their support of structures that sustain dominance • Faculty and staff support schools, districts, etc. because it is in their self-interest to do so • Faculty and staff support schools, districts even when policies and practices are inequitable to some groups

(taken from Pratto, Sidanius, and Levin pp. 271–320)

succeeding admirably. If schools are educating children to ensure that *some* internalize the idea that they are valued and valuable, while *'others'* internalize the idea that they are valueless, and should have limited opportunities, and few options to prosper, then they are succeeding. If schools are educating children with the goal of maintaining existing patterns of institutional discrimination, then they are succeeding. If schools are teaching some students to accept marginalization and social stigmatization, and embrace their own ignorance, then they are succeeding. If schools are focused on paying lip-service to democratic principles, while trampling on the ideal of America as a 'just' society, then they are succeeding. If schools are educating *some* children to be virtual 'masters,' and *'others'* to be virtual 'slaves,' they are succeeding quite well. Of course, this means that we need to redefine what we mean by *success*, and what we mean by *failure*.

As early as 1926, social scientist Carter G. Woodson predicted that education for Blacks would be a critical problem for decades to come in much the same way that in 1903 W. E. B. Dubois predicted that race, or the *color-line* would be the primary problem of the twentieth century. (Unfortunately, Dubois underestimated the weight of the problem since even as we approach the second decade of the twenty-first century, race seems to matter more than ever, and sometimes in deadly ways.) The irony is that they were both right because race and education are wedded, and the dynamic between them is almost parasitic for certain groups of students. Woodson's prescient critique identified a tragic flaw in the education of Black students (he called them 'colored') when he said, "… to handicap a student by teaching him that his black face is a curse and that his struggle to change his condition is hopeless (sic) is the worst sort of lynching. It kills one's aspirations and dooms him to vagabondage and crime … there would be no lynching if it did not start in the classroom. Why not exploit, enslave, or exterminate a class that everybody is taught to regard as inferior?" (Woodson, 1990, p. 3). And if a child is taught that he is inferior, and he internalizes that idea, why not act as an accomplice to his own exploitation, enslavement, and extermination?

Although it may seem excessively harsh and unnecessarily provocative to equate the education of American Blacks to *lynching*, most of the elements that contribute to school failure for many Black and Brown students are the same today as they were in 1926 when Woodson made this analogy. And, unfortunately, it can still be argued that the *lynching* starts when we teach a child that his black face is a *curse* and that his struggle to change his condition is *hopeless*, *or* that when he strives for academic excellence, he is criticized for *acting white* (Fordham & Ogbu, 1986). Maya Angelou (1991) expressed similar feelings about the plight of young Black men when she said: "In these bloody days and frightful nights when an urban warrior can find no face more despicable than his own, no ammunition more deadly than self-hate and no target more deserving of his true aim than his brother, we must wonder how we came so late and lonely to this place" (p. n.a.).

Implicitly, racism and discrimination are embedded in the educative process, so metaphorically speaking, and in insidious ways, on some level, it can be argued that *lynching* is taking place in American schools every day. And this has a great deal to do with *social dominance orientation* as it is manifested in individuals and institutions. The data speaks for itself.

Consider that in the 2010–2011 report, *Building a Grad Nation: Progress and Challenge in Ending the High School Dropout Epidemic* (Balfanz, Bridgeland, Moore, & Fox, 2010) which is produced by Civic Enterprises, America's Promise and the Everyone Graduates Center at Johns Hopkins University, that one of the key drivers of the high national dropout rate continues to be 'minority' status in American schools. Significantly, the research which began in 2010 urges educators and stakeholders on the local, state, and national levels to attack the unacceptably high national dropout problem with the same intensity that America brought to rebuilding a devastated Europe in the aftermath of WWII. The report suggests that a "Civic Marshall Plan" is needed to end the dropout *epidemic*, and ensure that by 2020 at least 90% of *all* American students, regardless of race, ethnicity, class, or handicapping condition, are on track to graduate and be prepared for college, work, and future success. However, in 2010, 2.1 million students were still attending *dropout factories* which are schools that graduate 60% or less of the students who enter as freshmen: most of the students in *dropout factories* are either Black or Hispanic.

Five years later, in the 2015 edition of the report, authored by DePaoli, Fox, Ingram, Maushard, Bridgeland, and Balfanz (2016) showed that although there was progress in reducing the dropout rate, it was uneven; three states, Georgia, New York, and Ohio, even experienced an *increase* in the number of *dropout factories*. In 2015, it was estimated that there were at least 1200 *dropout factories* in America placing at least 1.5 million students in substandard, racially segregated schools and in great jeopardy of becoming permanently marginalized by career-killing academic failure, socioeconomic underperformance, institutional discrimination, and racism. According to the report, some of the predictable barriers to academic success for these students are "discipline disparities that push them off track for graduation, language barriers, and lack of access to rigorous coursework that will enable them to be successful in college and career" (p. 6). And, the trends that show that white enrollment in schools is decreasing, while minority enrollment (especially among Hispanics) is increasing, also show one stable element: white teachers continue to dominate the teaching force, filling more than 80% of the teaching positions nationwide. Among other things, this means that for the foreseeable future, students in public schools will be disproportionately Black and brown, and teachers will be disproportionately white, so ignoring the implications of race and culture will always undermine even the most thoughtful, intelligent, and well-funded plans to equalize educational outcomes for all of America's children. It's important to remember that over generations, accents may fade, but skin color is permanent, and America's problem with skin color will not go away by itself. The data is suggestive.

Consider the following from the Education Trust on the State of Education for Native Students in 2013:

> In recent years, we as a nation have taken the critical step of acknowledging the gaps in opportunity and achievement that have for far too long consigned too many young people—particularly low-income students and students of color—to lives on the margins of the American mainstream. (p. 2)

Consider the following from the Education Trust on the State of Education for Latino Students in 2014:

> In 2013, 19 percent of Latino fourth-graders read at a proficient or advanced level on NAEP, compared with 45 percent of white fourth-graders.

> And in eighth-grade math, trends were similar. White eighth-graders were over twice as likely as Latino students to be proficient or advanced in math. (p. 6)

In answer to its own question, "Are school preparing Latino students for college and careers?" the disturbing answer is

> … far too few Latino high schoolers are being adequately prepared—despite … impressive gains. Among Latino students with high potential for success in AP math, just 3 out of 10 took any such course. Only 4 out of 10 Latino students with high potential for AP science took an AP science course.

> … fewer than half of Latino graduates who took the ACT met any of its college-readiness benchmarks, which are intended to show whether students have a good chance of succeeding in first-year college courses. Only 1 in 7 met all four—compared with 1 in 3 white graduates who took the ACT. (p. 7)

Consider the following from the Education Trust on the State of Education for African American Students (2014):

> ... too many African American students still are not getting the quality educa-
> tion they need and deserve, and the performance of African American students
> lags far behind that of white students. These gaps in achievement are driven
> by gaps in opportunity—African American students receive fewer of the with-
> in-school resources and experiences that are known to contribute to academic
> achievement. (p. 1)

In answer to its own question, "Are schools performing well enough for African American students?" the disturbing answer is:

> ... improvements are encouraging. However, too few African American students
> demonstrate the knowledge and skills they need to be successful in school and in
> life. And despite gap-narrowing, African American students still lag far behind their
> white peers on NAEP. In both fourth-grade reading and eighth grade math, African
> American students are about two and a half times as likely as white students to lack
> basic skills and only about one-third as likely to be proficient or advanced ... Just 1 in
> 20 African American graduates met all four college-readiness benchmarks, compared
> with 1 in 3 white graduates who did so. (p. 4)

In answer to its own question, "Are African American students graduating ready for the next step?" the disturbing answer is:

> Far too many African American students leave high school without a diploma.
> Nationwide, just over 2 in 3 African American students graduated from high school
> on time in 2012. That's compared with 86 percent of white students. (p. 8)

The accretion of data over time tells an alarming story: the slow pace of improvement is at the expense of generations of students who are slipping into social and economic oblivion. And, if we look beneath the bloodless anonymity of numbers, there are personal stories and anecdotes that dramatize the problems and make them more impactful and troubling. Consider the underlying significance of the following *real-life* school-related situations:

1. Joke told by a white, male, middle school, reading teacher to an 8th grade African American male:
   Question: Why do pimps wear wide-brimmed hats?
   Answer: To keep the pigeon shit off of their lips

2. Math Problems on a Worksheet for 3rd Graders in Norcross, Georgia … (2012)

> "Each tree had 56 oranges. If 8 slaves pick them equally, then how much would each slave pick?"

> "If Frederick got two beatings per day, how many beatings did he get in 1 week?"

3. Advice from a white male high school assistant principal to an African American male student (school has a 65% population of non-white, middle to low-income students):
   Why are you here? Why don't you drop out?
4. Ghetto Day.
   Students at a predominantly White suburban high school decide to generate excitement prior to a football game with a traditional rival. In addition to the usual pep rally, students get permission from school administration to declare the Friday before the big game "Ghetto Day." Most of the students wear baggy pants and gold jewelry.
5. Low expectations for African American students. A white teacher instructs class about a writing assignment. Afterwards, when an African American girl asks about the required length of the paper, the teacher responds: "the assignment is 8–10 pages, but you give me what you can."
6. Speak for the "race."
   During a history lesson on Reconstruction, the 8th grade class came across the unfamiliar word, *pickinniny* in the textbook. Instead of defining the word, the white male teacher called on the only black child in the room, and said, "You can define the word for the class, can't you?"
7. Mock Slave Auction—Black 5th Grader for Sale
   A mock slave auction was held in a 5th grade class in a New Jersey school (2017) during which a black child was auctioned off to a white child. In the same school district, students completed an assignment to make posters for slave auctions which depicted the faces of imaginary black "slaves" who were for sale to the highest bidder.

Research by Ron Ferguson, director of Harvard University's Achievement Gap Initiative, provides insights about other dimensions of the problem of inequity in schools. He calls the education gap the "root of inequality," because it is connected to other persistent societal inequities. According to Ferguson, the education gap that underserves children who are already marginalized by race or poverty limits their access to future career opportunities, wealth, and political participation. In contrast, closing the education gap empowers students, and gives them a sense of agency; it has the potential to change negative dispositions and self-sabotaging frames of mind (Ferguson, cited in Ireland 2016, p. n.a.).

Ferguson's body of research provides a clearer understanding of how SDO, and the presence of both conscious and unconscious racial bias, can look in the classroom when some teachers help White students more than Black students. In his article, Can Schools Narrow the Test Score Gap?, Ferguson describes patterns of teacher behavior that show how teachers treat students perceived to be low achievers:

- low achievers get wait less time for them to answer
- teachers are inclined to give low achievers the answers or call on someone else instead of trying to improve their responses by offering clues or repeating or rephrasing questions
- teachers are inclined to accept inappropriate behavior or incorrect answers
- teachers are inclined to criticize them more often for failure
- teachers are inclined to praise them less for success
- teachers are inclined to call on them less often with questions
- teachers are inclined to seat them further away from themselves
- teachers are inclined to demand less from low achievers
- teachers are inclined to have less friendly interactions—including less smiling and fewer other nonverbal indicators of support, attention and responsiveness (such as eye contact)
- teachers are un-inclined to accept and use their ideas
  (Ferguson, 1998, in The Black White Test Score Gap. Christopher Jencks & Meredith Phillips, pp. 341–342)

What hierarchy-enhancing behaviors are on display here? What messages do these teacher behaviors send to students? If this is a racially mixed class, what messages does this send to students who are high-achieving members of a dominant group with hierarchy-enhancing beliefs that are already in place? What messages do these teacher behaviors send to other teachers and to school administrators? And what does it mean if these teacher behaviors are considered acceptable and *normal*?

Although it is not the voice of any teacher that Ferguson used in his research, the following comment from a White teacher captures the spirit and tone of one who has internalized hierarchy-enhancing legitimizing myths that predispose her to marginalize rather than teach Black children under her care:

...'they don't care. They have a culture that doesn't value education. They don't have books at home and their parents didn't graduate from high school, so they don't care if their kids do.' (cited in Brooks, 2012, p. 45)

Testimonies from students describe how this kind of teacher behavior *feels*:

- The following is from a black eleven-year-old student who had been recently assigned to the low track at his school:

The only thing that matters in my life is school, and there they think I'm dumb and always will be. I'm starting to think they're right. Hell, I know they put all the Black kids together in one group if they can, but that doesn't make any difference either. I'm still dumb ... Upper tracks: "Man when do you think I see *those* kids"... If I ever walked into one of their rooms, they'd throw me out before the teacher ever came in. They'd say I'm holding them back from their learning. (cited in Ferguson in Jencks & Philips, 1998, p. 340)

- The following is from an anonymous non-white, male, high school student in Oakland, California.

The teachers that I have, they're not dedicated to helping out the students, especially most of the math teachers. You know, I sit there. I have problems with math. I usually get B's and C's, only a few A's. ... I ask questions to my geometry teacher, and he's like, "read the book." I've read the book about 15 times. He's like, "read the book." And I've read it. And he just can't explain it to me, and I'm not learning. (cited in Olsen, 2003, pp. 9–10)

The examples above expose the problem of bias through the eyes and sensibilities of individuals, and merely hint at the broader institutional issues that nurture, sustain, and in a real sense, condone discrimination. And, it would be counterproductive to allow the emotional impact of the way *individuals* experience bias to become a distraction from the larger, more damaging issue of *institutionalized discrimination* which is like the engine powering the train. It is important to remember that racialized policies and practices begin at the top and *trickle down* because the power that matters is invested in the people who *shape* and *control* the institutions, the development and implementation of policies, and funding allocations. The *trickle-down* effect of institutional discrimination is experienced and expressed by *individuals*. A good example of this comes from the story of METCO, a large-scale busing program in Boston, MA, that celebrated its fiftieth year of operation in 2016.

The METCO Program: Busing in Boston, or What It Feels Like to Be Treated Like a 'Guest' in Your Own School

After fifty years of trying to integrate Boston schools, the reviews of the METCO program are mixed; there are equal parts of pride and success and disappointment, exasperation and dismay. The METCO program is a reminder that even when major municipalities make a long-term public commitment to *de-bias* public schooling, serious issues persist despite reform efforts that involve social engineering on a massive scale, the consumption of millions of dollars, and decades of hard work and sacrifice.

In 1966 when the Civil rights movement was in its prime, the METCO program seemed like a rare beacon of hope for social justice and racial harmony in a town that had known decades of violent racial discord connected to schooling. It was a unique initiative because it began as a voluntary collaboration between Black urban parents and teachers from Boston, and White suburban school district leaders. The goal was to begin a process of desegregating Boston schools by busing Black children out of failing, mediocre urban schools into White suburban schools with a history of academic excellence. It was a 1960's version of racial uplift. Black parents were willing to remove their children from neighborhood schools, put them on school buses to take an hour-long bus-ride away from the safety of their homes, and into, sometimes hostile, White neighborhoods to give their children equal access to academic success and a chance to achieve the elusive *American Dream*. These parents were also willing to risk the family's estrangement from their own friends and communities, and the charge that by leaving their home community, they were abandoning their culture and *acting white* (Cornish, 2016a, p. n.a.). This charge, which has been internalized by some Blacks and Whites, is fed by the stereotype that equates Blacks with mediocrity and failure rather than with high academic achievement and social success.

In the aftermath of the controversial 1954 *Brown* decision, the founders of the METCO program didn't even want to use the term *busing* to describe the obvious. However, this is a one-way busing program that has been operating for five decades, and its supporters believe that it allows a small number of students to escape from virtual lockdown in some of the *poorest*, most racially segregated schools in the United States, to some of the *wealthiest* racially segregated schools in the United States.

There is much to celebrate on the fiftieth anniversary: METCO is now an eighteen million-dollar state-funded program; nearly 3,300 students participated in 2016; participating suburban school districts receive $5,000 dollars for each child in the program (Cornish, 2016b, p. n.a.); African-American and Hispanic students score higher on state proficiency exams than their counterparts in Boston schools, and have higher rates of high school graduation and college attendance (Lazar, 2017, p. n.a.).

In contrast, critics argue that "the yawning social disparities and tensions the plan aimed to ease remain—and painful incidents persist" (Lazar, 2017, p. n. a.). In part, this is because while busing brings some level of racial and cultural diversity to largely monocultural schools, and superficial compliance with the overarching goals of school integration, it presents significant racial challenges that are not being addressed adequately by physically transporting children from one place to another. Neither the state nor the municipalities are doing enough to confront and deconstruct bias despite an increase in bigoted incidents in, and around, these suburban schools. In 2016 alone, these incidents included white students posing with a Confederate flag, and "white pride" stickers placed in a boy's locker room, "emblazoned with information about a neo-Nazi website" (Lazar, 2017, p. n.a).

After fifty years, the program has not come to grips with the reality that children have to safely cross *more* than district boundaries; *they also must cross boundaries of race, culture, and class,* and according to both the program administrators and some of the children in the program, many of these goals are unrealized. For example, diversifying faculty, administrators, and staff is not mandated, nor is it a requirement for districts to provide training in cultural competence. Some METCO students say that they don't feel comfortable and *at home* in these schools. It feels "like this is not their community" (Caraballo, cited in Lazar, 2017, p. n.a.). The students feel like *outcasts* even though many of them have been in the district for years. One recent METCO graduate, who described a toxic environment in his high school, expressed his sense of racial isolation publically and permanently by writing under his yearbook picture: "I do not feel safe at this school" (Day cited in Lazar, 2017, p. n.a).

The METCO program leaves one wondering whether or not *any* American students should have to pay such a high price for a good education in American schools.

* * *

Together, the statistics, real-life situations, and testimonies paint a striking and disturbing picture of what is happening in some American schools. They take us back to Woodson's (1926) provocative equation of 'lynching' and the education of 'colored' students. The data and the incidents previously cited force us to ask whether or not the analogy is as valid today as it was in 1926 given the experiential realities of some students who have been overtly or covertly labeled *subordinate* because of race or color.

'Lynching' *is* a reprehensible term that conjures up painful images and moments in American history that most want to forget, and yet, when the definition is applied to what is happening in some American schools, the term seems more and more relevant. For example, 'lynching' is defined as:

- ... an *extrajudicial punishment* ... public execution
- ... [designed]to intimidate a minority group ...
- ... an extreme form of informal group social control
- ... more frequent in times of social and economic tension
- ... a means for a dominant group to suppress challengers
- ... it has also resulted from long-held prejudices and practices of discrimination that have conditioned societies to accept this type of violence as normal practices of popular justice.

(Wikipedia)

With this definition in mind, it is even possible to extrapolate it to describe some racialized policies that have been developed on the state level that appear to be blatantly discriminatory, and seem to reflect the influence of a SDO. For example, to meet national proficiency standards, several states explicitly set standards for academic proficiency by race. In Florida, it was proposed that the following standards for proficiency in reading and math be met by 2018: 90% for Asian students, 88% for white students, 81% for Hispanic students, and 74% for black students. Virginia went even further proposing that just 57% of black students needed to be proficient in math by 2017. Critiquing these proposals, Andy Rotherman (2012) pointed out that rather than working to improve opportunities for low-income students of color, Virginia was sending a "debilitating message" to students, parents, and educators about institutional discrimination and social inequality (Rotherman, cited in Richmond, 2012, p. n.a.).

The question remains: How does one describe or rationalize these types of punishing educational policies and practices that are part of a pattern of everyday bias practiced in American classrooms, schools, and even among state policymakers? In what context does any of this make sense other than a recognition that individuals and groups are predisposed to have certain attitudes about social hierarchies, which they do not shed in their professional settings?

Woodson's (1926) provocative critique of the education of Blacks (coloreds) anticipated some of the racial dynamics of inter- and intragroup dominance and subordination long before the concept of hierarchy-legitimizing myths was formulated, and yet, there is a conceptual continuity that is hard to ignore. Woodson's charge of *lynching* is a far cry from Horace Mann's idealistic description of education as *the great equalizer* because Mann was articulating a *hierarchy-attenuating* legitimizing myth. For Mann, education was an *inclusive* socializing process that challenged social inequality among groups, and neutralized structures of social dominance. Like Mann, John Dewey (1903, 1963) held the same Utopian ideals about the leveling effects of education, but saw them as self-evident *rights* guaranteed by a democratic system of government. Unfortunately, today, despite slow progress, an abundant amount of research tends to validate Woodson's perspective, because in general, American public schools actually function as *hierarchy-enhancing institutions*. Despite any claims to the contrary, or any lofty declarations that American education unifies rather than stratifies social, economic, racial, and ethnic groups, the data is unimpeachable, and the impact of racial stratification is undeniable. Bill Ayers (2012) did not overstate the complex American dilemma when he said

> Our country was built on White supremacy and it's flourished on White supremacy. White supremacy is absolutely one of the most entrenched but durable features in our national identity. Even as it changes colors somewhat and even as it changes meaning through the centuries, White supremacy finds a way to reassert itself as a dominant cornerstone of what our society looks like. (Bill Ayres cited in Brooks, 2012, p. 125)

Given the broad historical realities of White supremacy, especially its enduring impact on American values, attitudes, and cultural mores, it would be short-sighted to ignore the implications it has for the educative process in American schools, or the ways in which it informs *hierarchy-enhancing legitimizing myths* about race. However, despite what appears to be painfully slow progress, it is possible to transcend and/or diminish these toxic retrogressive attitudes.

Transforming Social Dominance Orientation and Deconstructing Bias in Schools or How to Stop Viewing the World as a 'Competitive Jungle'

With this bill, we reaffirm that fundamentally American ideal—that every child, regardless of race, income, background, the zip code where they live, deserves the chance to make of their lives what they will.
—President Barack Obama at signing of ESSA Bill

The mere imparting of information is not education. Above all things, the effort must result in making a man think and do for himself ...
—Carter G. Woodson, The Mis-Education of the Negro

Research should have more than probative value. If the information research provides has no social purpose, and does not move us forward as a society, then it presents the same age-old conundrum as *art for art's sake*. Hence, the research on SDO, which seemingly grows deeper and wider every day, is useful only to the degree that it can be used to affect positive social change. *Prejudice* is far more than a theoretical problem to be studied, discussed, and dissected in elite academic circles because prejudice hurts, and in its most extreme forms, it can cause people to die. Understanding why some groups nurture toxic attitudes, and harbor deep-seated prejudices, and intentionally and systematically dominate and oppress other groups, should be a prelude to praxis; *action* that leads to meaningful social change. This is applicable broadly on a societal level, but it has particular urgency and significance for schools and schooling because of the power schools have to transform the way we think about ourselves, the world, and our relationship to the other people in it. Schools have both the burden and the responsibility to create both the context and the environment for transformative social change because schools help shape the attitudes and dispositions of future generations; schools reflect society, and society reflects schools. Ultimately, this means placing the burden and responsibility for transformative social change on the shoulders of our children, some of whom have yet to be born.

As Miller Williams points out in his inaugural poem, in the end, *everything* is in the hands of our children, because as a country, our desire to be "just and compassionate, equal, able, and free" (Williams, 1998, p. n.a.) will resonate only as a hollow vestige of the *American Dream* until we stop allowing the *dream* of America to mask the *reality* of America. The dream of America *is* a beautiful one. We are a country that "dreamed for every child an even chance," but when we made concrete laws to enforce social equality, it was, "never so much of the hand as the head" (Williams, 1998, p. n.a.). In other words, as a country, we spend a great deal of time mythologizing the idea of America, or intellectualizing the concept of democracy, and too little time on the very hard work of actualizing democracy; too little time on the very hard work of actualizing equality, and freedom and justice, especially when it means uncovering painful or shame-inducing truths about ourselves as individuals, or about America as a nation.

References

Angelou, M. (1991). I dare to hope. *New York Times*, August 25, 1991.

Ayers, W., Hunt, J. A., & Quinn, T. (Eds.). (1998). *Teaching for social justice*. New York, NY: The New Press.

Balfanz, R., Bridgeland, J. M., Moore, L. A., & Honig Fox, J. (2010, November). *Building a grad nation progress and challenge in ending the high school dropout epidemic*. A Report by Civic Enterprises, America's Promise and the Everyone Graduates Center at Johns Hopkins University.

Brooks, J. S. (2012). *Black school, white school racism and educational (mis)leadership*. New York, NY: Teachers College Press.

Caraballo, I. (2017). In 50 years later, Metco's dream is still unanswered by Kay Lazar. *Boston Globe*. July 23, 2017. https://www.bostonglobe.com/metro/2017/07/23/half-century-later-diversity-still-eludes-school-desegregation-initiative/JWNkxX4angrq4OiID84y9N/story.html

Cornish, A. (2016a). Looking back on 50 years of busing in Boston. *National Public Broadcasting and Georgia Public Radio*. October 6, 2016. http://www.npr.org/sections/ed/2016/10/05/495504360/looking-back-on-50-years-of-busing-in-boston

Cornish, A. (2016b). Why busing didn't end school segregation. *National Public Broadcasting and Georgia Public Radio*. October 6, 2016. http://www.npr.org/sections/ed/2016/10/06/496411024/why-busing-didnt-end-school-segregation

DePaoli, J., Fox, J. H., Ingram, E. S., Maushard, M., Bridgeland, J. M., & Balfanz, R., (2016, November). *Building a grad nation progress and challenge in raising graduation rates*. A Report by Civic Enterprises and the Everyone Graduates Center at Johns Hopkins University. Retrieved June 11, 2016 from http://www.gradnation.org/report/2016-building-grad-nation-report

Dewey, J. (1903). Democracy in education. *The Elementary School Teacher*, 4(4), 193–204. Retrieved December 3, 2015 from http://www.jstor.org/stable/992653

Dewey, J. (1963). *Democracy and education—An introduction to the philosophy of education*. New York, NY: The Macmillan Company.

DuBois, W. E. B. (1994). *The souls of black folk*. Mineola, NY: Dover Publications, Inc.

Dunbar, P. L. (n.a.). We wear the mask. In Ruth Miller (Ed.), *Black American Literature 1760-Present*. Beverly Hills, CA: Glencoe Press.

Education Trust. (2013). The State of Education for Native American Students. *Education Trust.* Washington, DC. August 13, 2013. Retrieved June 13, 2016 from http://edtrust.org/wp-content/uploads/2013/10/NativeStudentBrief_0.pdf

Education Trust. (2014a). The State of Education for African American Students. *Education Trust.* Washington, DC. July 1, 2014. Retrieved June 15, 2016 from http://edtrust.org/wp-content/uploads/2013/10/TheStateofEducationforAfricanAmericanStudents_EdTrust_June2014.pdf

Education Trust. (2014b). The State of Education for Latino Students. *Education Trust.* Washington, DC. June 23, 2014. Retrieved June 13, 2016 from http://edtrust.org/wp-content/uploads/2013/10/TheStateofEducationforLatinoStudents_EdTrust_June2014.pdf

Ferguson, R. (2016). Teachers' perceptions and expectations and the black-white test score gap. In Christopher Jencks & Meredith Phillips (Eds.), *The black white test score gap* (pp. 273–317). Washington, DC: Brookings Institution Press.

Fordham, S., & Ogbu, J. (1986). Black students' success: Coping with the "burden of 'acting white.'" *The Urban Review, 18*(3), 176–206.

Haberman, M. (1991, December). The pedagogy of poverty versus good teaching. *Phi Delta Kappan,* pp. 290–294.

Haley, H., & Sidanius, J. (2005). Person-organization congruence and the maintenance of group-based social hierarchy: A social dominance perspective. *Group Processes and Intergroup Relations, 8*(2), 187–203.

Ho, A. K., Sidanius, J., Kteily, N., Levin, S., Thomsen, L., Kteily, N., … Stewart, A. L. (2015). The nature of social dominance orientation: Theorizing and measuring preferences for intergroup inequality using the new SDO 7 scale. *Journal of Personality and Social Psychology, 109*(6), 1003–1028. http://dx.doi.org/10.1037/pspi0000033

Ho, A. K., Sidanius, J., Pratto, F., Levin, S., Thomsen, L., Kteily, N., & Sheehy-Skeffington, J. (2012). Social dominance orientation: Revisiting the structure and function of a variable predicting social and political attitudes. *Personality and Social Psychology Bulletin, 38*(5), 583–606.

Jencks, C., & Phillips, M. (Eds.). (1998). *The black white test score gap* (pp. 273–317). Washington, DC: Brookings Institution Press.

Kozol, J. (1991). Savage inequalities. In William Ayers, Jean Ann Hunt, & T. Quinn (Eds.), *Teaching for social justice.* New York, NY: The New Press.

Lazar, K. (2017). 50 years later, Metco's dream is still unanswered. *Boston Globe,* July 23, 2017. https://www.bostonglobe.com/metro/2017/07/23/half-century-later-diversity-still-eludes-school-desegregation-initiative/JWNkxX4angrq4OiID84y9N/story.html

Malcolm, X. (1962). Cited in Mazel, E. (1998). *And don't call me a racist!* (p. 105).

McIntosh, P. (1988). *White privilege and male privilege.*[1] This paper was presented at the Virginia Women's Studies Association conference in Richmond in April 1986 and the American Educational Research Association conference in Boston in October 1986 and discussed with two groups of participants in the Dodge seminars for Secondary School Teachers in New York and Boston in the spring of 1987.

Nieto, S., & Bode, P. (2012). *Affirming diversity—The sociopolitical context of multicultural education.* Boston, MA: Allyn & Bacon.

Olsen, L. (2003). Quality counts 2003: The great divide. *Education Week*, January 9, 2003. Retrieved May 23, 2013 from 2003.www.edcounts.org/.../qc03/templates/article.cfm@slug=17divide.h22.html

Orwell, G. (1946). *Animal farm* (p. 123). New York, NY: The New American Library.

Pratto, F., Sidanius, J., & Levin, S. (2006). Social dominance theory and the dynamics of intergroup relations: Taking stock and looking forward. *European Review of Social Psychology*, *17*, 271–320. Retrieved February 12, 2016 from http://www.google.com/url?sa=t&rct=j&q=&esrc=s&source=web&cd=1&ved=0ahUKEwjc2bOd25PMAhXGDj4KHS-DrDFUQFgggMAA&url=http

Pratto, F., Sidanius, J., Stallworth, L., & Malle, B. F. (1994). Social dominance orientation: A personality variable predicting social and political attitudes. *Journal of Personality and Social Psychology*, *67*(4), 741–763.

Ross, H. J. (2008). *Everyday bias. Identifying and navigating unconscious judgments in our daily lives.* Lanham, MD: Rowman and Littlefield.

Rotherman, A. (2012). Virginia's "together and unequal" school standards. *The Washington Post*, August 24, 2012.

Sidanius, J., Pratto, F., van Laar, C., & Levin, S. (2004). Social dominance theory: Its agenda and method. *Political Psychology*, *25*(6), 845–880. Symposium: Social Dominance and Intergroup Relations. Retrieved December 15, 2015 from http://www.jstor.org/stable/3792281?seq=1#page_scan_tab_contents

Sidanius, J., van Laar, C., Levin, S., & Sinclair, S. (2003). Social hierarchy maintenance and assortment into social roles: A social dominance perspective. *Group Processes Intergroup Relations*, 6, 333. doi:10.1177/13684302030064002. Downloaded April 2015.

Van Laar, C., & Sidanius, J. (2001). Social status and the academic achievement gap: A social dominance perspective. *Social Psychology of Education*, *4*, 235–258. Retrieved April 2015 from http://link.springer.com/article/10.1023%2FA%3A1011302418327#page-1

Williams, M. (1999). Of history and hope. Poetry Foundation. Retrieved May 14, 2014 from https://www.poetryfoundation.org/poems-and-poets/poems/detail/47107

Woodson, C. G. (1990). *The mis-education of the Negro.* Trenton, NJ: Africa World Press, Inc.

Yoshino, K. (2007). *Covering the hidden assault on our civil rights.* New York, NY: Random House.

· 6 ·

MOVING FORWARD

Biasing, (De)biasing, and Strategies for Change

This chapter is about the importance of acknowledging implicit and explicit bias, and learning strategies for *(de)biasing*. In addition to deconstructing the concepts of color blindness and color muteness, the chapter looks at other subtle forms of bias, including *microaggression*, and form of *modern* racism. The chapter will conclude with research-based strategies for change.

Keywords: implicit bias, explicit bias, color blindness, color muteness, micro-aggression, race, modern racism diversity, prejudice, discrimination, subtle racism, symbolic, ambivalent, modern, aversive, discipline disparities, racial socialization, dysconsciousness, Implicit Association Test

> *It is easier to act yourself into a new way of thinking, than it is to think yourself into a new way of acting.*
> —Millard Fuller, The Theology of the Hammer

While driving down a flat, level road, have you ever noticed a sudden bump in the road that causes drivers to instinctively adjust their speed, and slow down, as they approach it because they know that going too fast over the bump could risk serious damage to the undercarriage of their cars, or even personal injury to the car's occupants? Have you ever noticed that sometimes there is a permanent road sign preceding one of these potentially dangerous bumps that says something like, *Caution, Bump Ahead*, to warn you of the upcoming road hazard? Have you ever asked yourself why those who have the power to do so develop policies and practices that essentially normalize the hazard to such a degree that drivers and pedestrians alike accept it as part of the landscape of their daily experience if they plan to drive or walk down that road? Knowing that the bump will be there, they also know that they will have to take appropriate precautions to avoid or circumvent it.

Have you ever asked yourself why those who have the power to do so would choose to invest municipal money to pay for a permanent road sign to warn you of the upcoming road hazard, instead of addressing the problem directly by digging up the road, evaluating the cause of the problem, and fixing the subterranean issues that caused the bump in the first place? Of course, this could mean redirecting underground pipes or removing overgrown or rotted tree roots, etc., and the likelihood is that it would not be easy, and potentially, it would be costly. However, the question is: Why leave a problem in place if you *know* that it exists, that it may impede progress, or signal danger to members of the community? And why leave a problem in place if there are viable solutions available to correct it? In other words, why make a *hazard* a permanent part of the landscape?

It can be argued that this *bump in the road* is a useful metaphor for a mindset that undermines the implementation of anti-bias strategies in schools and school districts; one that sees the problem of bias, but instead of attempting to 'fix' it, creates strategies to navigate over or around it, making it a permanent part of the *landscape* of schools. When we're dealing with racial bias, this mindset is tantamount to pretending to be *color blind* and *color mute* which are often misguidedly presented as remedies for racism. But, this is faulty logic.

This chapter is not about road bumps, and street repair. It is about acknowledging implicit and explicit bias, and addressing the complex and tricky process of *(de)biasing. (De)biasing* is tricky, and difficult, not simply because bias can be subtle, and can wear so many different faces; it is tricky and difficult because it often operates on subterranean levels, which make it virtually invisible. In addition to an overview of the problem of color blindness and color muteness which some misguidedly consider useful strategies for undermining or neutralizing bias and racism, the chapter will look at subtle forms of bias, including *microaggression*, and *modern* racism because they further complicate the (de)biasing process, and it is important to be aware of them. The chapter will conclude with research-based strategies for change.

The Problem with Color Blindness as a Response to Bias in Schools

Color blindness is offered as a remedy to racial bias usually only by Caucasians, and only when Caucasians are speaking to, or about, people of color. It is presented as a good thing, as one means to interrupt racism and bias, and to create interracial environments that are safe and comfortable for everyone. However, a *color blind* perspective ends up being an unspoken and often unintentional tribute to those who say they are *color blind* because they presume that it demonstrates their ability to be unbiased, inclusive and accepting of 'others.' This is ironic since the idea of 'blindness' of any sort is considered a defect; metaphorically, it conjures up images of denial and self-delusion. In our society, a *color blind* perspective is meant to honor, and show respect for, 'others,' but the unspoken underlying and implied sentiments are: *It's OK that you look different from me. I'll accept you anyway.* This implied meaning presupposes that the skin 'color' is really a problem, but we won't *talk* about it; it is a problem that can be overlooked, tolerated, or even *forgiven*.

A *color blind* perspective also presupposes that the person who claims to be *color blind* and the person of color see things the same way, and wordlessly agree that the darker skin color is problematic, reprehensible or detestable, or embarrassing, or shame-inducing. In other words, it is a problem, but we will agree to ignore it.

When one adopts a *color blind* perspective, it introduces a power dynamic into the situation because the one who *says* he or she is *color blind* is exercising *power* over the person of color: the power to choose to see that person, or not; to acknowledge that person's reality, or not; to acknowledge that person's value, or not; to accept that person's identity as it is, or not. In the end, a *color blind* perspective says: *I* have control over *your* identity; *I* will see you the way *I* want to see *you*; not the way *you* are or the way *you* want to be seen.

In contrast, people of color rarely (probably never) use the term 'color blind' or validate the concept because they live in their skins every day; their *colored* skins. This is their reality, a reality reflected in the faces of their children and families and friends. And the skin color is linked to culture, and traditions and values and history, and pride. So, if a Caucasian looks at a person of color and claims to be color blind, it is both a critique and a form of denial; it implies that the person of color is really defective and 'less than me,' but I'll pretend that it doesn't matter; that it doesn't influence social relations or how well we can communicate with each other. But, this too is faulty logic.

The concept of color blindness makes it harder to address racial issues in constructive ways, and begin the process of (de)biasing. It shuts down open, honest conversations between people who want to, and need to, communicate with each other. Color or race doesn't go away simply because we say we don't see it, or refuse to acknowledge it. Human nature tells us that people are more likely to notice the very thing that you tell them to ignore.

The concept of color blindness not only defies logic and human nature; it defies the uniquely American response to race and skin color that is deeply rooted in American history and fraught with human suffering. Similarly illogical, *color muteness* means consciously refusing to *talk* about people in racial terms as a way to defuse or neutralize racism. Neither strategy works; the pretense of refusing to *see* what is right there before our eyes, or refusing to *talk* about what we *see* right there before our eyes, is equivalent to the three monkeys who *see no evil, speak no evil,* and *hear no evil.*

Mica Pollock (2004) explains the complexity of color muteness, and offers a strong critique in Colormute Race Talk Dilemmas in an American School when she says:

> All Americans, every day, *are* reinforcing racial distinctions, and racialized thinking by using race labels; but we are also reinforcing racial inequality by refusing to use them. By using race words carelessly and particularly by *deleting* race words, I am convinced, both policymakers and laypeople in America help reproduce the very racial inequalities that plague us. It is crucial that we learn to navigate together the American dilemmas of race talk and colormuteness rather than be at their mercy. ... (Pollock, 2004, p. 4)

In the end, pretending to be *color blind* or choosing to be *color mute* causes us to ignore bias, and continue to walk over *bumps in the road* and through racial minefields.

"Bias Is Not a Choice, but Our Responses to It Certainly Are"

Diversity educator Gary Howard once said "Diversity is not a choice, but our responses to it certainly are" (Howard, 2006, p. 4). However, in light of the research on cognition which confirms that *implicit bias* is a normal, natural cognitive function in humans, Howard's wisdom can be expanded to also mean: '*bias is not a choice, but our responses to it certainly are.*' If we return to the *bump in the road* metaphor and mindset, it suggests that bias, the kind that is harmful, and poses some danger or threat, is always lurking beneath the surface of our professional experiences as educators; when it erupts, slows us down, or causes us to *fall*, too often, we move around it delicately, uncomfortably, or angrily, or simply pretend that the bump isn't there at all. Perhaps we just tell ourselves that the *road* is supposed to be *bumpy*, and *embrace the bump*. Even when we acknowledge that bias exists, and is surreptitiously corrupting everything from personal attitudes and interpersonal relationships, to institutional practices, often, rather than address it directly, we circumvent it, and delude ourselves into thinking that it doesn't matter; that it is not an impediment to progress; that it will fix itself over time, or we simply adjust our relationship to the problem. By doing this, we can then develop policies that accept bias as a natural part of the professional landscape. Figuratively, this amounts to putting up signs that say: *Caution, Bump Ahead*. Either way, we proceed down the road knowing that there will be other *bumps* ahead, and metaphorically we continue to stumble, or perhaps fall.

Research confirms and reconfirms that although the word *bias* preconditions us to recoil because of the socially inscribed negative connotations that connect it to racial (and other forms of) hatred, it is important to remember that implicit bias is not always a bad thing, and everyone is predisposed to be biased. However, for the purpose of this chapter's focus on *debiasing, and strategies for change*, let's put aside the neutral or harmless ways that humans express implicit biases, and look instead at the harmful effects of both implicit and explicit bias, especially as they impact educators and other policy-makers involved in the educative process. This also includes school board members and local and state policy-makers who are often left out of the discussion when we talk about anti-bias initiatives and cultural competence, etc.

"You Can't Handle the Truth!"

In the movie, *A Few Good Men*, Jack Nicholson's menacing, in your face charge, "*You can't handle the truth!*" made everyone cringe, because it was provocative, harsh, and deeply cutting. "*You can't handle the truth!*" resonates in so many areas, and on so many levels of our lives, and also could be used as a flashing, cautionary billboard on the road to (de)biasing schools: "*You can't handle the truth!*" "*You can't handle the truth!*" "*You can't handle the truth!*" Accepting that we all have biases that can be harmful to others is difficult for anyone to face.

For decades, psychologists and other social scientists have identified, and conducted research on *overt* racism, and as individuals, groups, communities, and as a country, we are still struggling to *handle the truth*; to face the depth and breadth of overt bias in our personal and professional lives. However, perhaps an even greater challenge comes from the subtler forms of racism and bias that have been identified by researchers. In the early 1980s, social scientists began to identify several interrelated forms of racism and bias that are complex and difficult to detect. These subtle forms of racism and bias make (de)biasing more challenging, because they are harder to pin down and address.

The research on forms of subtle racism is based on white prejudice against black people, and "even though each form of subtle racism has distinct features, the results have consistently pointed in the same direction: White people are most likely to express anti-Black prejudice when it can plausibly be denied (both to themselves and to others)" (Plous, 2003, p. 18).

The following list taken from Understanding Prejudice and Discrimination by Plous (2003) identifies and describes four distinct types of subtle racism: *symbolic, ambivalent, modern,* and *aversive.*

Forms of Subtle Racism

Symbolic Racism—Symbolic racists rejects old style racism but still express prejudice indirectly (e.g. opposition to policies that help racial minorities)—Primary Citations—Kinder and Sears (1981); McConahay and Hough (1976); Sears (1988)

Ambivalent Racism—Ambivalent Racists experience an emotional conflict between positive and negative feelings against stigmatized racial groups. Primary Citations—Katz (1981)

Modern Racism—Modern Racists view racism as wrong but view racial minorities as making unfair demands or receiving too many resources. Primary Citations—McConahay (1986)

Aversive Racism—Aversive Racists believe in egalitarian principles such as racial equality but have a personal aversion toward racial minorities. Primary Citations—Gaertner and Dovidio (1986)
(From Understanding Prejudice and Discrimination, Plous, 2003, p. 19)

These subtle forms of racial bias mask deep-seated prejudices, and present unique challenges because they allow people to normalize denial, and *appear* unprejudiced to themselves and others, even while the destructive effects of their biases and prejudices are on public display every day.

Microaggressions

Microaggressions are veiled insults that diminish, demean, and devalue individuals or groups in subtle or indirect ways. Psychologist Derald Wing Sue, author of *Micro-Aggressions in Everyday Life*, affirms that microaggressions can target any marginalized group, and are expressed in a wide spectrum of social situations, and *isms* (including class*ism*, ethnocentr*ism*, heterosex*ism*, sex*ism*, age*ism*, etc.). According to him, microaggressions are the

> everyday verbal, nonverbal, and environmental slights, snubs, or insults, whether intentional or unintentional, which communicate hostile, derogatory, or negative messages to target persons based solely upon their marginalized group membership. (Wing Sue, 2010, p. n.a.)

Although the concept of microaggression is new to many, it dates back to the 1970s when psychiatrist Chester Pierce coined the term.

Many microaggressions have racial undertones, but microaggressions are *not always about race*; they come in all *shapes* and *sizes* and anyone can be a target. And, it's important to note that microaggressions can happen any day and anywhere. They generally catch the targets off-guard. Ironically, the perpetrators, the microaggressors, often do not know that what they are saying is offensive, hurtful, or biased because microaggressions usually reflect deeply held internalized beliefs or attitudes that can hide beneath the surface of our consciousness reflecting implicit biases.

Heben Nigatu (2013) provided some graphic examples of common microaggressions when she posted her online story, *21 Racial Microaggressions You Hear On A Daily Basis*. She told of a photographer at Fordham University who decided to illustrate the presence of microaggressions in everyday life by asking her peers to write down the microaggressions that, like a stiletto, could pierce their spirits on any given day. She then photographed her colleagues holding the derogatory statements in front of them. The following list is adapted from that story which now has been viewed by over three million people:

- Statement made to a Black male: *"You don't look like a normal Black person ya' know."*

- Statement made to an Asian female: "*Can you see as much as White people? You know, because of your eyes.*"
- Statement made to a Black female: "*You're really pretty for a dark-skinned girl.*"
- Statement made about a Hispanic female by someone who chose not to sit next to her on a public train: "*She smells like rice.*"
- Statement made to a Black female: "*Why do you sound White?*"

(Nigatu, 2013, p. n.a.)

Microaggressions are tricky because they may seem insignificant, and inconsequential to the microaggressors, but they do hurt even though they may not elicit a response from the object of the aggression. It is likely, however, that the greater pain comes from the cumulative effect of a lifetime of absorbing the low voltage shocks of microaggressions in social settings, especially those social settings that should pose no threat, like schools. However, over time, being subjected to a pattern of microaggression can feel something like *death from a thousand cuts*. And, it is important to note that microaggression intersects other kinds of *isms*, which magnifies the effect of this kind of subtle bias. For example, if one is black, female, and homosexual, one is subject to being the target of microaggressions that reflect *sexism, racism, and heterosexism*. Similarly, if one is poor, elderly, and Jewish, one is subject to being the target of *classism, ageism,* and *antisemitism*.

According to Dr. Wing Sue, "Microaggressions reflect the active manifestation of oppressive worldviews that create, foster, and enforce marginalization" (Wing Sue, 2010, p. n.a.); therefore, it is a mistake to assume that the damage they cause is limited to one-to-one verbal interactions between individuals (i.e., teachers and students). In fact, because microaggressions reflect an array of deeply held individual biases, we carry them with us into the institutional settings to which we are connected. Therefore, these biases can infect policies, procedures, and decision making on many different levels. And the more power we have, the more impact our attitudes and beliefs have on the decisions we make. Decisions about hiring or promotion can be shaped by these deep feelings. Decisions about who gets a bank loan and who does not, or who goes to prison and who does not, or who is elected to public office and who is not, or who is suspended from school and who is not, are all possible consequences of hidden biases or prejudices that have not been acknowledged or overcome.

Although microaggression describes a form of generalized bias, research conducted at Columbia University's Teachers College has led to the classification of three distinct types microaggression that are racially coded, and these have implications for how educators relate to, and interact with, students. They are

- **Microassaults:** Conscious and intentional discriminatory actions ...
- **Microinsults:** Verbal, nonverbal, and environmental communications that subtly convey rudeness and insensitivity that demean a person's racial heritage or *identity* ...
- **Microinvalidations:** Communications that subtly exclude negate or nullify the thoughts, feelings or experiential reality of a person of color. (Wing Sue, 2010, p. n.a.)

Research by Portman, Bui, Ogaz, and Treviño (p. n.a.) specifically focuses on the manifestation of *microaggressions in the classroom*, and they used actual cases that were reported at the University of Denver. Some of the following examples are racial, others are not, but all are as relevant in public school settings as they are at the university level.

Table 6.1: Examples of Microaggressions in a Classroom Setting.

• Continuing to mispronounce the names of students after they have corrected you time and time again ... • Setting low expectations for students from particular groups ... • Expressing racially charged political opinions in class assuming that the targets of those opinions do not exist in class ... • Denying the experiences of students by questioning the credibility and validity of their stories ... • Assigning projects that ignore differences in socioeconomic class status ... • Singling students out in class because of their backgrounds ...	• Ignoring student to student microaggressions, even when the interaction is not course related ... • Making assumptions about students and their backgrounds ... • Assuming that all Latino students speak Spanish ... or all Asians are good at math ... that all African Americans know about poverty and the "Ghetto ..." • Assuming all students fit the traditional student profile and are proficient in the use of computers ... • Disregarding religious traditions or their details ...

(From Microaggressions in the Classroom, Portman et al., n.d., pp. 3–6)

Keeping It Real—Connecting Implicit Racial Bias to School Discipline Disparities

In 2014 and 2015, several important documents were published that reconfirmed the role of implicit bias as a significant factor in schooling, and specifically linked it to school discipline disparities that are inflected by race. Two of the documents were produced by the U.S. Department of Education: *Guiding Principles—A Resource Guide for Improving School Climate and Discipline*, and the *Office for Civil Rights Civil Rights Data Snapshot: School Discipline Issue Brief No. 1*. Cheryl Staats, a senior researcher at the Kirwan Institute, and the principal author of the Institute's Implicit Bias Reviews (2013, 2014a, 2014b, 2015; Staats, Capatosto, Wright, & Jackson, 2016), produced two documents that summarized the available research and provided a primer for educators on the connection between implicit bias and schooling. *Understanding Implicit Bias What Educators Should Know* (2015) published by the American Federation of Teachers, and her special report for the Kirwan Institute, *Implicit Racial Bias and School Discipline Disparities Exploring the Connection* (2014) both linked implicit racial bias to school discipline disparities, and provided specific examples of what this looks like in an average school.

Collectively, these documents crystallize the problem of implicit bias in school settings by focusing on specific concrete challenges that confront teachers and administrators every day in terms of what unconscious triggers motivate teachers and administrators to make disciplinary decisions that may disproportionately impact students of color. Every day they are forced to deal with inappropriate student behavior. Every day, they are forced to make countless decisions about how to respond to infractions of school or classroom policy. And if, as the research suggests, implicit bias plays a role in the disproportionate numbers of in- and out-of-school suspensions and expulsions for students of color compared to White students, understanding the connection between bias and race should be considered a priority for all educators especially since these decisions could have life-altering consequences for some students.

A review of these documents, and other available research, reveals that overall, there is consensus about the most effective generic *debiasing* strategies, and these will be outlined in the final section of this chapter. It is important to note, however, that there are some techniques that have greater relevance for educators, and this becomes very apparent from research that connects implicit bias to racialized disparities in school disciplinary policies and practices. This research points to the increasing likelihood that implicit bias plays a role in decisions about who is suspended and who is not, the degree and severity of punitive measures taken against certain groups of students, and the rationales given for these decisions.

This section will explore the symbiotic relationship that appears to exist between implicit bias and disciplinary practice. How, and to what degree, students are disciplined, and whether or not there is a racial subtext, is a virtual minefield because these issues exhume, and are connected to, other larger challenges that plague schools and society. For example, there appear to be links between the high rate of in- and out-of-school suspensions and expulsions for students of color, the academic achievement gap, and the school-to-prison pipeline. Although those suspected links are not new, the research on the possible role of implicit bias adds serious and troubling dimensions that must be considered if we are committed to the success of all students and changing the trajectory of this trend.

When the 2012 report by the Center for Civil Rights Remedies at The Civil Rights Project at UCLA stated that "Well over three million children are estimated to have lost instructional 'seat time' and to have been suspended from school, often with no guarantee of adult supervision, in 2009–2010 … [which is] about the number of individual children it would take to fill every seat in every major league baseball park and every NFL stadium in America, combined" (Losen & Gillespie, cited in Staats, 2014a, p. 4) they painted a devastatingly real picture of the problem that exists at the intersection of race and school discipline because the majority of those faces would be Black or brown.

The following highlights are taken from the reports to provide some context, and show the nexus between implicit bias and school disciplinary policies and practices.

A Brief Look at the Disaggregated Data on School Discipline by Race and Gender
(Source—Data Snapshot: School Discipline Issue Brief No. 1 March 2014)

Suspension of preschool children, by race/ethnicity and gender

- Black children represent 18% of preschool enrollment, but 48% of preschool children receiving more than one out-of-school suspension …
- white students represent 43% of preschool enrollment but 26% of preschool children receiving more than one out of school suspension.

Disproportionately high suspension/expulsion rates for students of color:

- Black students are suspended and expelled at a rate three times greater than white students.
- On average, 5% of white students are suspended, compared to 16% of black students …

Disproportionate suspensions of girls of color:

- boys receive more than two out of three suspensions …
- Black girls are suspended at higher rates (12%) than girls of any other race or ethnicity … [white] girls (2%).

Arrests and referrals to law enforcement, by race and disability status:
- Black students represent 16% of student enrollment ... 27% of students referred to law enforcement and 31% of students subjected to a school-related arrest ...
- [W]hite students represent 51% of enrollment ... 41% of students referred to law enforcement, and 39% of those arrested ...

Suspension of preschool children, by race/ethnicity and gender ...
- Black children represent 18% of preschool enrollment, but 48% of preschool children receiving more than one out-of-school suspension ...
- [W]hite students represent 43% of preschool enrollment but 26% of preschool children receiving more than one out of school suspension.

Disproportionately high suspension/expulsion rates for students of color ...
- Black students are suspended and expelled at a rate three times greater than white students ...
- 5% of white students are suspended, compared to 16% of black students ...
- Twenty percent (20%) of black boys and more than 12% of black girls receive an out-of-school suspension.

Disproportionate suspensions of girls of color ...
- [B]lack girls are suspended at higher rates (12%) than girls of any other [race or ethnicity

Arrests and referrals to law enforcement, by race ...
- [B]lack students represent 16% of student enrollment ... 27% of students referred to law enforcement and 31% of students subjected to a school-related arrest.
- [W]hite students represent 51% of enrollment ... 41% of students referred to law enforcement, and 39% of those arrested.

(U. S. Department of Education, 2014, p. 1)

One of the most troubling findings is that racialized discipline disparities begin in preschool, which means that a significant number of students of color may be academically crippled even before they enter public school. According to the data, almost half of African-American children receive more than one suspension from preschool. In addition to compromising them developmentally, these suspensions may undermine positive attitudes toward school and learning in the future. Research from a unique 2015 Yale study affirms that racialized discipline disparities begin in preschool, and that implicit bias may be implicated. One of the researchers, Walter S. Gilliam, director of the Edward Zigler Center in Child Development and Social Policy, and associate professor of child psychiatry and psychology at the Yale Child Study Center, creates a context for this study when he points out that "Implicit bias is like the wind. You can't see it but you can sure see its effect. It does not begin with black men and police; it begins with preschool" (Gilliam cited in Downey, 2016, p. n.a.).

Using a unique methodology that allowed the researchers to track the classroom observation patterns of preschool teachers, Gilliam and his team concluded that the participating preschool teachers and staff displayed signs of implicit bias in their disciplinary practices. The sophisticated eye-tracking technology that was used found that the teachers "show[ed] a tendency to more closely observe blacks and especially black boys when challenging behaviors are expected." Among other things, these conclusions underscore the significance of teacher expectations. Most of the time, teacher expectations are discussed in the context of academic outcomes. However, this research shows that they are also implicated in racialized discipline disparities that are evident as early as preschool. This is significant for a number of reasons, but foremost among them according to Gilliam, who has produced highly regarded work on preschool expulsions, is that "preschool is the best early frontline defense against the negative impacts of implicit bias" (Downey, 2016, p. n.a.), and by extension, the presence or absence of implicit bias in the teachers themselves determines whether they are *defenders against* the damaging effects of implicit bias, or *purveyors of* harmful race-based classroom practices.

The bottom line is if *"preschool is the best early frontline defense against the negative impacts of implicit bias,"* and if, preschool teachers themselves display bias toward certain groups of students, then the frontline is not a defense *against* implicit bias, but an incubator that nurtures and deepens it.

Table 6.2: Prevailing Research-Based Explanations for Disproportionate Discipline Policies and Practices.

• race contributes to discipline disproportionality independent of socioeconomic factors (R. J. Skiba et al., 2011; Wallace, Goodkind, Wallace, & Bachman, 2008; Wu, Pink, Crain, & Moles, 1982).
• [theories of cultural deficiency as a reason for discipline disparities] "... are grossly inaccurate" (Monroe, 2006, p. 104).
• [theories that culturally influenced behavioral style differences contribute to discipline disparities are not supported by the research]
• non-Whites' higher rate of suspension cannot be explained on the basis of more frequent misbehavior (Wu et al., 1982).
• no evidence ... supports the notion that there are concurrently higher levels of disruption among African American students
• [researchers found no] evidence that the higher rates of discipline for African American students could be attributed to behavior that was either more serious or disruptive (R. J. Skiba et al., 2002).

(Staats, 2014a, pp. 6–7)

Cheryl Staats' 2014 article, *Implicit Racial Bias and School Discipline Disparities Exploring the Connection*, provides a useful overview of current research on implicit racial bias and school discipline disparities. However, before focusing on implicit bias as a significant factor in the racialized discipline gap, the researchers used a process of elimination, in which they ruled out socioeconomic status (i.e., poverty), culturally influenced behavioral mismatches, as well as discredited ideas of cultural deficit. Overall, the research shows that African-American students are *not* more likely to violate school policy, or display behaviors that warrant punishment than any other racial group. This includes behaviors that lead to suspension and expulsion. In fact, White and Hispanic students are *more* likely than African American students to violate school policy and commit infractions that warrant expulsion from school. After eliminating other factors, the research suggests that *subjectivity* and *ambiguity* may play an important role in the disciplinary decisions that teachers and administrators make, and this opens the door to the possibility that in many instances, decision making may be influenced by unconscious, implicit bias. This can happen because "... many of the infractions for which students are disciplined have a subjective component, meaning that the school employees' interpretation of the situation plays a role in judging whether (and to what extent) discipline is merited. Some infractions such as 'disruptive behavior' are ambiguous and highly contextualized (Vavrus & Cole, 2002)" (cited in Staats, 2014a, p. 8). Therefore, even in a situation where a disciplinary response is appropriate, an educators' "'background experiences and automatic associations shape his or her interpretation of the scene'" (Ogletree, Smith, & Wald, 2012, p. 53) (cited in Staats, 2014a, p. 8) and this can lead to racialized discipline disparities. Studies also show that office referrals for students of color "tend to rely heavily on subjective interpretations of infractions such as 'disrespect' or 'excessive noise' whereas White students' office referrals are more frequently the result of an objective event, such as smoking or vandalism (R. J. Skiba et al., 2002, p. 332)" (cited in Staats, 2014a, p. 8).

The following data tells one side of the story, but it is almost useless without an understanding of how implicit bias, subjectivity, and situational ambiguity can collude to undermine fairness and racially neutral disciplinary decision making in schools:

Table 6.3: Complex Factors That Interact to Produce Race-Neutral or Race-Biased Disciplinary Decisions.

- African American students were not any more likely than students of other races to commit infractions that prompt removal from school ...

- White and Hispanic students were actually more likely than African Americans to engage in behaviors that merit mandatory expulsions ...

- the disconnect may be due to adult subjectivity: "High rates of disciplinary involvement among African-American students were driven chiefly by violations that are subject to the **discretion of school employees** ... (Fabelo et al., 2011, p. 46) ...

- punishment [of African American students] appears overly punitive for the severity of the infraction ... "the vast majority of suspensions are for minor infractions of school rules, such as disrupting class, tardiness, and dress code violations, rather than for serious violent or criminal behavior" (Losen & Martinez, 2013, p. 1) ...

(Staats, 2014a, pp. 4–5)

In the end, although there is still a great deal of research yet to be conducted, the consensus is that implicit bias may play a significant role in causing and maintaining the racialized discipline gap, and if educators ignore it, or trivialize its role, they wittingly or unwittingly perpetuate the problem.

(De)biasing and Strategies for Change (Part 1)— Rethinking White Racial Socialization

The key isn't to feel guilty about our [implicit] biases—guilt tends toward inaction. It's to become consciously aware of them, minimize them to the greatest extent possible, and constantly check in with ourselves to ensure we are acting based on a rational assessment of the situation rather than on stereotypes and prejudice.

—Neill Franklin

During a recent workshop on race, after being divided into small racially mixed groups, we were asked to think about, and then discuss, our first awareness of race. One of the White participants shared the following story during the small group discussion about her early experience of race as a preteen. There was a deep, nagging pain behind her eyes as she told her story which is paraphrased below.

Wendell's Story

I was born and grew up in the suburban Midwest, and was from a very affluent family. Race was never discussed, because it didn't have to be. The town was virtually all white, with one exception. A Black man named Wendell lived in the town. I never met Wendell, but be was the only Wendell in the town. No one ever said his last name; maybe no one knew it; he was just Wendell. Everyone knew him because he was a handyman, who did odd jobs and carpentry throughout the community. Wendell was respectful and polite, and as far as I could tell, he lived on the periphery of the town's life, and was nearly invisible. On the occasions that I did see him, he seemed to move through the town, quiet as a shadow, with his head tucked down toward his chest, and it seemed that although he was a tall willowy man, he was trying to make himself smaller so he would take up less space. He didn't bother anyone, and they didn't bother him. One day, a man in the town decided to *honor* Wendell by naming his black dog *Wendell*. This became a source of amusement for the man and others in the town. Soon after, others followed that man's lead, and eventually *every black dog in the town was named Wendell*. Thereafter, when the name Wendell was called aloud, it was difficult to know if it was for the man or a dog.

Among other things, Wendell's story is an example of how not just one child, but an entire town was socialized to think about race. Although dehumanizing Wendell became a town sport over the course of years, perhaps even decades, there is no way to know the long-term impact this had on individuals, especially children and young people, as they moved through their lives, entered professions, moved to other places, and started families of their own. There is also no way to know whether or not this painfully slow symbolic *lynching* of the town's only black man was ever addressed in social gatherings, or in the schools, and whether or not some of the participating townspeople were school board members, school administrators, teachers, or other school staff members. If so, given what research tells us about white racial identity development, and white racial socialization patterns, it is not inconceivable that a discussion that linked Wendell to *race and racism* never came up in the schools in formal ways. But this did not mean that what was happening to Wendell had no emotional impact on some of those who either witnessed or perpetrated this public emasculation. My colleague who shared this story indicated that then, as now, the memory of Wendell caused her sadness, confusion, and shame which is consistent with what we are learning from some of the emerging research on white racial socialization.

As part of a research study on white racial socialization, educator Ali Michael (Michael & Bartoli, 2014) used her own personal story to shed light on the emotional impact of being white, living and growing up in an all-white community, in a country constructed around racial divisions, and among people who spent their lives trying to erase race. Daily, she watched her people try to sanitize their lives and *bleach* out those '*damned spots*' from their racially segregated worlds while simultaneously wrapping themselves in Christian morality and democratic justice. However, although it was a long and difficult process, she learned that you can't erase 'race,' and you can't erase racism by pretending that they don't exist. In *What White Children Need to Know About Race* (Michael & Bartoli, 2014) Michael says

> Growing up in the suburban Midwest, I (Ali Michael) never talked about race with my family. We were white, all of our neighbors were white, and it never occurred to us that there was anything to say about that. As a result, in later years, I developed a deep sense of shame whenever I talked about race—particularly in college, where I was expected to make mature personal and academic contributions to race dialogues.
>
> At a certain point, I realized that this shame came from the silence about race in my childhood. The silence had two functions. It was at the root of my lack of competency to even participate in conversations on race. But it had also inadvertently sent me the message that race was on a very short list of topics that *polite people do not discuss*. My parents did not intend for me to receive this message, but because we never talked about race, I learned to feel embarrassed whenever it came up. And so even when I wanted to participate in the conversation, I had to contend with deep feelings of shame and inadequacy first. (Michael & Bartoli, 2014)

The research by Michael and Bartoli (2014) on white racial socialization expands and deepens the conversations about race, racism, explicit bias and implicit bias, and suggests that Michael's experience is not unique. Among other things, it reconfirms the complexity of the problem, and the multi-dimensional challenges that face equity-driven teachers and school leaders because white youth are being socialized to *believe* that whiteness has more social value than blackness. They also are being socialized to believe they *deserve* the disproportionate benefits they receive because of the social and economic value placed on white skin color. In contrast, Michael and Bartoli point out that the racial socialization of people of color is markedly different from that of white people, consequently the emotional, material, and experiential realities of the two groups are strikingly different, and these differences have been reflected in the disproportionate research focused on the racial socialization of families of color. Until recently, according to Bartoli et al. (2014), the presumption had been that because historically Americans of African descent had been the victims of racialized and racist social policies, there was a greater need for these parents to explicitly teach their children how to navigate their environment for their own safety. In contrast, there was a presumption among researchers that since historically white families were able to translate their 'race' into social power and privilege, it was unnecessary, even *superfluous* for them to engage in the racial socialization of their children. Consequently, until now, most research ignored racial socialization practices in white families, and perhaps this disparity of focus among researchers deserves further analysis.

Using a series of interviews from White children and their parents, Bartoli and Michael et al. (2014) uncover the tension and confusion that White parents and their children feel about the subject of race, and their presumed role in either mitigating or perpetuating racism. Well-meaning parents, often unknowingly, perpetuate racial *mis*understandings and tension even though they *believe* that they are contributing to racial harmony. The research suggests that for most White people, it would be reprehensible to be seen as a racist. However, they lack the skills, motivation, and willingness to address the subject with their children in consistent or substantive ways partly because of ignorance, a lack of awareness, feelings of guilt and shame, and significantly, fear of losing their privileged social and economic status. As a result, their approach to talking about race often amounts to a self-serving, self-protective panacea which masks and complicates the problem of acknowledging and confronting racism in schools and social settings. In general, for many white parents there is never a *right* time to initiate a conversation about race, and they default to addressing it reactively rather than proactively. In these circumstances, the conversations can be prompted by negative incidents (i.e., Black on White crime as in the Willie Horton rape of a White woman, or White on Black crime such as the murder of Trayvon Martin, or the recent rash of police shootings of Black men). In some ways, this reluctance to talk about race is comparable to the reluctance some parents have about discussing sex with their children. In both cases, this can lead to an unhealthy response to, and unhealthy tensions around, the subject. When for example, White parents tell children to ignore race because they think *people are all the same*, and 'race' is irrelevant, it makes racial issues *invisible*, sets up a pattern of denial, and neutralizes a child's response to the pervasive racism in society. When parents tell their children that they should not *see* race, they are making their children complicit in invalidating entire groups of people by ignoring their experiential realities. And, there is often a deep chasm between what parents *think* they are teaching their children, and what children are actually *learning*. As has already been discussed, implicit biases are always at work, therefore, even though on a conscious level, parents attempt to "convey to their children the belief that race *shouldn't* matter, the [actual] message their children receive is that race, in fact, *doesn't* matter" (Michael & Bartoli, 2014, p. n.a.).

Differentiating Between Active and Passive Racial Socialization

The prevailing racial socialization patterns for white and black children form the bedrock for implicit and explicit bias; therefore, in order for debiasing to be effective, it is necessary to differentiate between *active* and *passive* socialization, as well as *proactive* and *reactive* socialization. Active racial socialization is intentional and direct, and is considered an essential part of teaching children to coexist with others who are racially (and ethnically) different from them. It is designed to give children the "ability to effectively navigate their world" (Michael & Bartoli, 2014, p. n.a.). It means teaching children that the world is a complex place, and in age-appropriate ways, address and deconstruct the construct of 'race,' and racial bias, with the same intentionality and purpose that children are taught moral behaviors in both religious and secular contexts. Michael and Bartoli (2014) point out that "[b]ecause many white families generally do not consider racial competencies among the skills their children will need when they grow up, they tend to socialize passively and reactively … [this] strategy leads to silence about race in many white households" (p. n.a.). When it comes to racism and bias, silence is a sinister socialization strategy that can be deadly, because it "leaves unchallenged the many racial messages children receive from a number of socializing agents" (Michael & Bartoli, 2014, p. n.a.), especially the media. And, silence leaves unchallenged the structural and institutional inequities that undermine and degrade social justice.

The original 2014 study of white socialization by Bartoli et al. which consists of interviews of white parents and their children (aged 12–18) is revealing and instructive. The researchers

> found that most of the white families opted to socialize their children by telling them not to be racist, not to talk about race, not to use the word "black," and not to notice racial differences. They wanted their children to believe that all people are the same and that racism is bad. They defined racism as overt, violent, and, for the most part,

anachronistic. They felt that, if they emphasize these messages, they will impart to
their children messages of racial equality. (Michael & Bartoli, 2014, p. n.a.)

Interestingly, the interviews showed that the parents themselves had a deep-
seated ambivalence about race, and their ambivalence is reflected in the
mixed messages they were transmitting to their children. This means that that
even well-meaning parents can be complicit in keeping racism and bias alive.
By problematizing *blackness*, and *difference*, these parental practices serve to
expand the *us* vs. *them* dynamic that separates their white children from people who are racially or ethnically different. This ensures that there *will be*
distance between the races, and distance means misunderstanding, miscommunication, confusion, awkwardness, and fear in social and professional interactions. This also ensures that in interracial interactions, there will always be
the *unsaid*.

These parents were teaching their children what *not to do* and what *not
to talk about*, which is actually crippling their children, because it leaves them
unprepared to see or respond appropriately to the larger racial contexts that
frame their lives. This approach makes race a taboo subject; a *bogeyman* of
sorts, and ensures that 'race' becomes a scary subject for children. It also
negates and problematizes race and skin color, which infinitely complicates
any attempts to mitigate implicit and explicit bias. Whether they acknowledge it or not, White parents feel entitled to control the conversation, and
establish the self-serving protocols around racial socialization because they
have the power to do so. They are *burdened* with what McIntosh (1988) calls
the invisible *knapsack of unearned privileges* which they enthusiastically pass
on to their children. This is translated into entrenched, disproportionate
social power and access which they protect at all costs even while they insist
that *everyone is the same*. Moreover, on one level, these parents are displaying
what Joyce King (1991) calls dysconsciousness, "an uncritical habit of mind
(including perceptions, attitudes, assumptions and beliefs) that justifies inequity and exploitation by accepting the existing order of things as given ..."
(King, 1991, p. 135). Dysconsciousness is what we expect from young children: a simplistic, uncritical acceptance of a construct of the world, and of
'truth,' as it's presented to them by their parents and elders. However, dysconsciousness in adults is a very dangerous thing. A *dysconscious* mindset made
it easier for these parents to tell their children "not to talk about race, not to
use the word 'black,' and not to notice racial differences" (Michael & Bartoli,
2014, p. n.a.). Clearly, if you don't notice things, you don't have to critique

them, and an *uncritical habit of mind* when it comes to race can be *deadly* on so many different levels.

The research showed that by the time children become teens and young adults, racial socialization patterns become more subtle and complex. For one thing, older children have had more years to internalize attitudes and behaviors that they've learned and practiced all of their lives. Bartoli et al. (2014) also showed that the messages white teens received regarding race were contradictory and incomplete. While they *believed* they *believed* in equality, and that in a democracy everyone is the same,

> ... and that race is superfluous, and that hard work determines where one gets in life, they also professed beliefs about differences among racial groups, including that black people are lazy or poor, that poor black neighborhoods are dangerous, and that black people are physically stronger than whites. Because these white teens lacked a systemic analysis of racism, they had no way of understanding the impact of the structural racism they observed around them, such as the de facto segregation through academic tracking in their schools or in the geography of their cities. (Michael & Bartoli, 2014, p. n.a.)

Unfortunately, this shows that in spite of growing up with messages from their parents that race is irrelevant, in the end, implicit biases supplant their conscious statements and attitudes about race, and they were unable "to differentiate between what is racist and what is, simply, racial. They tended to classify any mention of race as racist" (Michael & Bartoli, 2014, p. n.a.).

White Racial Socialization: What Role Should Schools Play?

Perhaps the most pivotal role that schools can, and should, play is to first acknowledge the impossibility of maintaining racial neutrality in schools while operating in a society that is *wholly racialized*. Schools need to acknowledge how important racial socialization is, and how schools, as they are presently structured, may impede or undermine the process for white and nonwhite students. Schools also must be intentional, committed, and consistent about addressing racial socialization as a curricular goal to counteract the mixed messages and confusion students have about race. Finally, schools should "reflect an awareness of the need to teach racial skills and competencies in order to foster healthy racially diverse communities" (Michael & Bartoli, 2014, p. n.a.) for everyone.

Although the researchers concede that the home is the primary source of racial socialization for children, they are equally certain that racial socialization is a multidirectional process, and schools have to work hard to counter misguided messages students receive from home, the media, peer influences, and popular culture. Although many White parents in the Bartoli et al. study "used school as one of their only conscious racial socialization strategies" (Michael & Bartoli, 2014, p. n.a.), and some sent their children to racially diverse schools in the hope that they would become culturally competent, the researchers found that "… few schools currently engage in conscious policies to support the development of positive racial identity" (Michael & Bartoli, 2014, p. n.a.). This is further evidence of the breadth and depth of White parents' denial about the broader implications of race, and their "inevitable fear of stepping outside the boundary of [their collective] ignorance" (Howard, 2006, p. 15). Like parents, schools are also afraid to step *outside the boundary of ignorance* although this contradicts the primary reason they exist, but for this, there is a high price to pay.

Schools Are the Missing Link in the Racial Socialization Process

Schools are the *missing link* in the racial socialization process, because if we look at the big picture, to some extent, what parents do, or do not do, in terms of racial socialization is irrelevant. This is arguably true because parents, and society at large, expect schools to *complete* the education process; to be the *finishers*, so to speak; to refine the raw unfinished *products* that parents send them, and transform them into good, moral, character-driven citizens. This is evident in the increased focus on *character education* in schools. For many, *character education* is synonymous with democratic ideals and the presumption that justice and fair play are the guideposts for social interactions. And yet, as Bartoli et al. point out, "… few schools currently engage in conscious policies to support the development of positive racial identity" (Michael & Bartoli, 2014, p. n.a.); therefore, in general, schools are complicit in sustaining the gaping racial divide. Instead of countering the flawed approach to racial socialization that children experience at home, schools often replicate it. In a real sense, they may be doing the same thing that parents are doing in the home. Often, they are telling students not to say *bad*, racially derogatory words, and to ignore the implications of "race."

It is likely that teachers are doing this partly because they are products of the same society, and the same racial socialization processes that they are now being asked to challenge. However, because they have a different level of socially validated authority, teachers operate on a different plane from parents. Being educators gives them a different level of social power and influence. To some extent, being an educator confers a kind of *immunity* from critique because they are presumed to be trained specialists when it comes to the needs of children. This *immunity* is transferred to the policies and practices they endorse and promote. And yet, it is faulty logic to ignore the fact that, like the parents in the study, some white teachers have been socialized to be race-deniers or worse.

It's important to remember that teachers represent a cross-section of society, and some of them are also parents who have been subjected to the same kind of racial socialization patterns as the parents in the study. Therefore, teachers should not get a "pass" simply because they are teachers both because they may have been miseducated about their own racial identity, and because there are extreme cases where in-service teachers have been found to be active members of hate groups of the most virulent kind. Further, it would be foolish to presume that *veteran* teachers are exempt from a dysconscious mindset. If we default to relying on their years of experience and ostensible classroom 'success' to rationalize their particular understanding of racial socialization, we ignore the possibility that they may harbor a mindset that can rationalize and *justify* the status quo because they have been socialized to do so. Moreover, it is possible (and likely) that this is a socialization process of which they are unaware.

* * *

In *What White Children Need to Know About Race*, Michael and Bartoli (2014) provide a useful framework that includes strategies for schools to actively work to help white children develop a positive racial identity. They begin by offering a counternarrative about racial socialization through a set of debiasing messages. This is followed by suggestions for specific ways to address content knowledge, and suggestions for skill development that "would empower students to become proactive in their engagement with racial issues and conversations" (Michael & Bartoli, 2014, p. n.a.). The following is adapted from their framework.

Table 6.4: Messages About Race.

Messages About Race: List of some of the messages schools can offer.
Talking about race is not racist. It's OK—and important. [The idea of color-blindness leads students to believe that] merely talking about race is racist ... Students need to learn that ... *talking* about race [is not] and *being* racist. Racial talk leads to greater racial understanding and helps undermine the power of racist laws, structures, and traditions ... Avoiding race talk makes race itself unspeakable ...
Race is an essential part of one's identity ... Schools can help foster awareness about the meaning of whiteness by helping white students develop a positive racial identity, which requires an understanding of systemic racism ... [Students should know that] ... unearned privileges [are ascribed] to their whiteness ... [and] ... understand how they can work to change racism—and change what it means to be white.
Create a positive white identity that allows white students to move toward it. [Students need to develop an] antiracist white identity. Schools need to create spaces in which students can identify as white and simultaneously work against racism ...

Content Knowledge
... [Schools] that believe in equity and justice and want their students to be future leaders need to help students—especially white students—understand the history of race and racism and how both play out in contemporary society. This racial content knowledge constitutes a basic social literacy that all students should have. Students must develop a sense of how systemic racism works on an individual, community and institutional level.
Be clear about the meaning of "race." Race is a social construct, not a biological fact ... So schools first need to clarify our biological sameness and explore the implications of race as a social construct ... Studying how whiteness was constructed historically ... helps students see how whiteness began to be associated with certain social patterns and realities.
Understand systemic racism. Understanding systemic racism helps change the conversation ... It helps students ... see how racism shapes the wider landscape of their lives ... Students must develop a sense of how systemic racism works on an individual, community, and institutional level.
Learn how antiracist action is relevant to all. ... [The] history of antiracist struggles in the United States involved white people. The stories of these antiracists throughout history should be taught so that white students can envision possible ways to be white and antiracist.
Understand stereotypes and their counternarratives. Students are exposed to numerous stereotypes of people of color. It's essential for students to be able to recognize these, understand how they might have developed, analyze the function they play to maintain social hierarchies, and learn accurate information that counters the stereotypes. They need to hear counternarratives—stories of people whose lives do not conform to the stereotypes ...

Skills
Part of the work of supporting an antiracist identity for white students involves teaching them skills to be proactive in discussing race, confronting racism, building interracial friendships, and acknowledging racism.

Develop self-awareness about racist beliefs. Building a positive racial identity requires one to recognize and counter one's inaccurate beliefs about race. We routinely learn stereotypical and incorrect information from the world around us. Students should be encouraged to realize that no one is free of racist beliefs; therefore, the aim is *not* to not have them, but rather to recognize them and access the content knowledge needed to refute them. Self-awareness about race is a lifelong practice that asks us to notice race and racial bias consistently and critically.

Analyze media critically. Learning to filter and evaluate the racial messages students receive from media can help students apply their knowledge about race and recognize its impact in the world around them. This skill also helps them begin to realize the ways in which racist messages are delivered and reinforced. Such analytical skills will then provide them with further knowledge and language to resist and counter those messages in conscious and proactive ways.

Learn how to intervene. White youth (and many white adults) … need skills to recognize, name, intervene in, and/or reach out for assistance in racist incidents. Such skills might include recognizing relevant situations, identifying one's own sphere of influence, and accessing resources to respond either in the moment or afterward … [this] can be an empowering act for the student and, in itself, promote social change.

Manage racial stress. It is essential to provide students with tools to be able to understand their emotional reactions and learn to manage them. Strategies include identifying the sources of anxiety, normalizing them, and accessing relevant support in allies. Over time, the very process of confronting racism and withstanding the relevant anxiety makes the practice easier to navigate.

Honor and respect racial affinity spaces for students of color. Many schools now recognize the efficacy of creating racial affinity spaces for students of color, particularly with regard to countering the effects of stereotype threat[7] and creating a sense of safety and camaraderie within predominantly white spaces … Racially competent white students would understand such a gathering of students of color as ultimately supportive of interracial relationships, rather than in opposition to them …

Develop authentic relationships with peers of color and other white students. This skill involves learning to connect with peers of all different races with an understanding of the racialized context within which those relationships take place. In this context, the ability to name and discuss race in all of its facets (both enriching and problematic) is essential, so that everyone's reality can be accounted for, engaged with, and affirmed. This, in turn, will lead to more authentic interracial relationships.

Recognize one's racist and antiracist identities. Students must be able to acknowledge the "both/and" possibility of simultaneously being racist and antiracist …

(From *What White Children Need to Know About Race.* Michael & Bartoli, 2014)

(De)biasing and Strategies for Change (Part 2)

Despite the increasingly intense focus on unconscious or implicit bias, and (de)biasing, antibias or antiprejudice initiatives are not new. Social scientists have been confronting and consciously attempting to counteract prejudice since the 1940s. Today, schools, corporations, and public institutions continue to conduct what was, and is, sometimes called *sensitivity training*. The main goal of this type of training is to create harmony in the workplace by creating work environments that are characterized by professionalism and respectful interpersonal relationships, because disharmony in the workplace disrupts or undermines efficiency, productivity, and profit. Essentially, this type of training focused on how people *behaved* toward each other with little or no introspection about the root causes for behavior patterns, or the underlying attitudes that motivated them. However, beginning in the 1960s, spurred by the Civil Rights movement, a greater focus on human rights, ethnicity, culture, and the multiple ways that humans can be diverse began to change both the approach to prejudice reduction and the desired outcomes. Among other things, these trainings began to connect personal behaviors in the workplace to social issues like racism, and sexism, and homophobia. But, these trainings tended to focus on explicit, observable manifestations of bias, and behavioral changes rather than on reflection, introspection, and self-analysis that could transform personal attitudes about bias and prejudice. Today's focus on implicit bias is a logical progression from the early trainings, and the research shows that bias and (de)biasing are infinitely more complex than was once thought. Significantly, the research also makes clear that it is no longer defensible to simply focus on the ways that implicit bias is manifested in individuals while ignoring its social, institutional, and structural manifestations. Moreover, the research makes clear that conducting antibias training or education does not appear to be an effective "debiasing" strategy by itself unless the mechanisms of implicit bias are addressed in direct ways. Correll and Bernard (2006) go even further. According to them, a powerful debiasing strategy is the research itself. When, according to them, decision-makers are exposed to systematic, well-designed research that documents the existence of biased processes "... individuals tend to be more careful in scrutinizing their own decisions, thereby avoiding the cognitive shortcuts that lead to biased decisions" (Correll & Bernard, 2006 cited in Quintero, 2014b, p. n.a.).

Understanding should precede action; therefore, before presenting debiasing strategies, it is important to have some background on the nature of implicit biases. Although researchers may disagree about the best approaches to debiasing, there is basic consensus about how bias operates. The following list provides some background.

> [B]iases are malleable and can be unlearned ... Debiasing is a challenging task that relies on the construction of new mental associations, requiring "intention, attention, and time ..." the analogy of a stretched rubber band [shows] how debiasing interventions must be consistently reinforced ...
>   [D]ebiasing is not simply a matter of repressing biased thoughts ... [S]uppressing automatic stereotypes can actually amplify these stereotypes by making them hyper-accessible rather than reducing them ... (Staats, 2014b, pp. 20–21)

Successful Research-Based (De)biasing Interventions

So far, the most exhaustive and user-friendly analysis of the collective research on implicit bias and research-based suggestions for (de)biasing comes from the Kirwan Institute for the Study of Race and Ethnicity at Ohio State University. Beginning in 2013, and every year since, the Institute has published a report, *Implicit Bias, State of the Science: Implicit Bias Review*. The following is an abbreviated (and annotated) compilation of the information that they have published on *debiasing* since 2013. The information will be presented by year. Information that is duplicative, as well as specific details about the individual research projects and the researchers, has been removed. These details will be included in the Appendices, and I urge a fuller reading of the individual reports because they cover the impact of implicit bias in many fields beyond education, including the fields of: medicine, health care, criminal justice, employment, and housing.

The Kirwan Reviews show that research on implicit bias is expanding exponentially on both national and international levels, and covers many different social domains. This reaffirms the omnipresence of implicit bias, and validates the heightened sense of its importance in everyday life. Among other things, the broad range of the research underscores the intersectionality of the problem of bias, and makes clear that it is a complex and widespread problem that requires complex and widespread solutions.

Foremost among the recommendations regarding debiasing is that an individual must begin by acknowledging that implicit bias exists, not simply in a general sense, but on a personal level as well, and that implicit bias is something that everyone struggles with in one way or another. Most, if not all, of the available research recommends the use of the *Implicit Association Test (IAT)*, developed by Project Implicit at Harvard University, because it has been shown to be one of the most effective and widely used measures of implicit bias.

The IAT, which is taken online, either in a group setting, like a classroom, or in the privacy of one's home, allows individuals to reflect on how implicit bias inflects personal attitudes and behaviors that influence interpersonal relationships and professional duties. Importantly, this test can bring to the surface disparities between how people think and feel on a conscious level as opposed to how people think and feel on an unconscious level. "The striking aspect of this test is that this bias pattern exists both among those who express explicit prejudices and those who deny them" (Wald, 2014, p. 21). Results from the IAT also provide a way for institutions to self-evaluate, and uncover and measure entrenched patterns of discrimination against particular members or groups within the organization.

The 2016 Implicit Bias Review introduced another promising debiasing strategy: *mindfulness meditation*. Mindfulness meditation is described as a way to objectify thoughts and feelings, view them *nonjudgmentally* as part of mental processing, as opposed to shame-inducing self-deprecation, or personal indictments. "The social benefits of mindfulness meditation are based on the idea that nonjudgmental reflection has the potential to reduce cognitive biases" (Staats et al., 2016, p. 45). Research on mindfulness meditation, like all debiasing strategies, requires thoughtful planning, and skilled facilitation.

The following excerpts from *Implicit Bias, State of the Science: Implicit Bias Review 2014* (pp. 20–21) summarize other effective research-based strategies for debiasing. What becomes clear from the research is that: (a) there is no single *cure* for implicit bias, and (b) regardless of the strategy employed, the degree and permanence of *debiasing* cannot be accurately determined. In other words, the effectiveness of any strategy depends on many different variables including individual background and motivation, type and demands of one's profession, institutional climate, and above all, a commitment to social justice.

Other successful debiasing strategies include:

Table 6.5: (De)biasing Interventions for Teachers and Administrators (Part 1).

• **Counter-stereotypic training** in which efforts focus on training individuals to develop new associations that contrast with the associations they already hold through visual or verbal cues
• **[E]xpose people to counter-stereotypic individuals.** Much like debiasing agents, these counterstereotypic exemplars possess traits that contrast with the stereotypes typically associated with particular categories, such as male nurses, elderly athletes, or female scientists

- **Intergroup contact** generally reduces intergroup prejudice ... [S]everal key conditions are necessary for positive effects to emerge from intergroup contact, including individuals *sharing equal status* and *common goals,* a *cooperative* rather than *competitive* environment, and the *presence of support from authority figures,* laws, or customs

- **Education** efforts aimed at raising awareness about implicit bias can help debias individuals.

- **Having a sense of accountability,** that is, "the implicit or explicit expectation that one may be called on to justify one's beliefs, feelings, and actions to others," can decrease the influence of bias

- **Taking the perspective of others** has shown promise as a debiasing strategy, because considering contrasting viewpoints and recognizing multiple perspectives can reduce automatic biases

- **Engaging in deliberative processing** can help counter implicit biases, particularly during situations in which decision-makers may face time constraints or a weighty cognitive load ... [C]onstantly self-monitor in an effort to offset implicit biases and stereotypes

(Staats, 2014, pp. 20–21)

Writing for the Albert Shanker Institute, Esther Quintero (2014b) wrote a three-part series entitled *What Is Implicit Bias, and How Might It Affect Teachers and Students?* The series is useful here because unlike most of the available research on implicit bias which addresses the problem broadly, this series narrows its focus to the field of teaching. The following list of strategies is adapted from Part II—Solutions.

Table 6.6: (De)biasing Interventions for Teachers and Administrators (Part 2).

- "Individuating" (gathering very specific information about a person's background, tastes etc.) When you get to know somebody, you are more likely to base your judgments on the particulars of that person than on blanket characteristics, such as the person's age, race, or gender ... [this is] a potential intervention aimed at breaking stereotypic associations

- disrupt classroom (status) hierarchies which can emerge among students based on characteristics such as race, gender, academic ability. For example, by (authentically) praising a low status student on something specific that the student did well, the teacher can effectively raise the social standing of that student in the classroom. This, in turn, can elevate both the student's confidence and self-assessment (i.e., what the student thinks he/she is capable of accomplishing) as well as his/her peers' expectations (i.e., what other classmates think she/he is capable of). This is a powerful way of breaking stereotypic associations and equalizing learning conditions in the classroom.

(Quintero 2014b, p. n.a.)

All of the research tells us that implicit bias is malleable, and that it is possible to reduce, if not, eliminate. The hard question is: Given the unquantifiable damage that explicit and implicit biases can cause, as educators, do we *want* to acknowledge, confront, and overcome our biases? Research tells us that we have the resources. The real question is: Do we have the will?

* * *

Acknowledging both the existence and the '*naturalness*' of implicit bias is hard for Americans because it corrupts what we would like to think of as *Democracy*. In its purest sense, democracy is demanding because it imposes values that we feel compelled to live up to, and impose on others. In that context, having to acknowledge both our conscious and unconscious biases creates inner conflicts between what and who we *think* we are, what and who we *really* are, and what and who we *want to be* as citizens who fervently embrace democratic values. For example, Americans can both love *and* resent the pressure to be *Americans* in the truest sense of what that means: lovers and champions of *freedom, justice,* and *equality for all.* And, the belief in *freedom, justice,* and *equality for all* can weigh heavily on us, because as concepts, unlike in practice, they are unambiguous; one is either free, or not; being treated justly, or not; considered equal, or not.

In America, we live, as Toni Morrison has astutely pointed out, in a "wholly racialized world," and have made an industry of denying, or diminishing the idea that there is a relationship between implicit and explicit racial biases and racism. We deny that bias infects or inflects our thinking about, and behavior toward, people and cultures that are 'different' from the socially validated 'norm.' We also deny that racial bias influences official policies and practices on the federal, state, and local levels, as well as sustains institutional and systemic discrimination. And yet, it is counterintuitive to think that we can live in a "wholly racialized world" *without* the existence of racism in it.

The tensions and complex conflicts triggered by acknowledging both our conscious and unconscious biases supersede race. Therefore, skin color is neither a defense nor a shield against them. As one researcher has said, implicit bias is an 'equal opportunity virus,' so being Black does not give you immunity any more than being White make you the embodiment of bigotry. The reality is that whether one's skin is *white, black, brown,* or any shade in between, these tensions and conflicts coexist, and can take a toll on our psyches, but in different ways because of the experiential distance between the 'races.' For the most part, *distance* equates to *perspective* in terms of where you stand in the social, political, and economic order (i.e., whether you are among the powerful or the powerless). Clearly, oppressors and oppressed see the world differently.

And, here are two hypothetical questions: What if educators are the oppressors, by directly or indirectly contributing to the oppression of already marginalized social and racial groups who are under their supervision and care? What if educators are complicit in allowing personal bias to become a weapon that can pierce and eviscerate their own students' lives and futures?

These are important questions since educators are expected to be moral authorities, ethical role models, arbiters of justice, purveyors of history, and interpreters of the social milieu for their students. It is likely that they will fail in all of these roles unless they understand the subtle ways that bias is manifested in schools and society, and work aggressively to mitigate implicit and other biases, and (de)bias themselves, their practice, and their schools. Moreover, because teachers and school leaders inhabit public and private spheres, they also have a responsibility to model good citizenship in the sociopolitical domains that they inhabit outside of the school. A final irony is that the universality of implicit bias can be a 'good' thing because it is a kind of connective tissue linking disparate groups; we all have biases, so in a strange way, they provide common ground, and a place to begin the difficult but necessary work of debiasing ourselves and our schools.

References

Bartoli, E., Michael, A., Bentley-Edwards, K. L., Stevenson, H. C., Shor, R. F., & McClain, S. E. (2014). *Chasing colorblindness: White family racial socialization.* Manuscript submitted for publication.

Correll, S. J., & Bernard, S. (2006). *Gender and racial bias in hiring.* March 21, 2006. Retrieved from http://diversity.illinois.edu/SupportingDocs/DRIVE/Gender%20and%20Racial%20Bias%20in%20Hiring-1.pdf

Downey, M. (2016). *Does implicit bias begin in preschool? Yes, says new study.* September 28, 2016. Retrieved October 31, 2016 from http://getschooled.blog.myajc.com/2016/09/28/does-implicit-bias-begin-in-preschool-yes-says-new-study/

Fabelo, T., Thompson, M. D., Plotkin, M., Carmichael, D., III, M. P. M., & Booth, E. A. (2011). *Breaking schools' rules: A statewide study of how school discipline relates to students' success and juvenile justice involvement.* Council of State Governments Justice Center and The Public Policy Research Institute, Texas A&M University.

Howard, G. (2006). *We can't teach what we don't know.* New York, NY: Teachers College Press.

King, J. E. (1991). Dysconscious racism. *The Journal of Negro Education, 60*(2), 133–146.

Losen, D. J., & Gillespie, J. (2012). *Opportunities suspended: Disparate impact of disciplinary exclusion from school:* Center for Civil Rights Remedies at the Civil Rights Project. Cited in Staats, C. (2014). *Implicit racial bias and school discipline disparities exploring the connection* (p. 4). Kirwan Institute. May 2014. Retrieved July 27, 2016 from http://kirwaninstitute. osu.edu/wp-content/uploads/2014/05/ki-ib-argument-piece03.pdf

Losen, D. J., & Martinez, T. E. (2013). *Out of school and off track: The overuse of suspensions in American middle and high schools.* The Center for Civil Rights Remedies at the The Civil Rights Project (UCLA).

McIntosh, P. (1988). *White privilege and male privilege.* This paper was presented at the Virginia Women's Studies Association conference in Richmond in April, 1986, and the American Educational Research Association conference in Boston in October, 1986, and discussed with two groups of participants in the Dodge seminars for Secondary School Teachers in New York and Boston in the spring of 1987.

Michael, A., & Bartoli, E. (2014). What white children need to know about race. *Independent School Magazine,* Summer 2014. Retrieved January 16, 2017 from http://www.nais.org/ Magazines-Newsletters/ISMagazine/Pages/What-White-Children-Need-to-Know-About-Race.aspx

Monroe, C. R. (2006). African American boys and the discipline gap: Balancing educators' uneven hand. *Educational Horizons,* 84(2), 102–111.

Nigatu, H. (2013). 21 Racial microaggressions you hear on a daily basis. Retrieved September 9, 2013 from https://www.buzzfeed.com/hnigatu/racial-microaggressions-you-hear-on-a-daily-basis?utm_term=.byxxGVmy03" \l ".ugR4XD9WPM"

Ogletree, C., Smith, R. J., & Wald, J. (2012). Criminal law – coloring punishment: Implicit social cognition and criminal justice, in Levinson, J. D., & Smith, R. J. (Eds.), *Implicit racial bias across the law.* Cambridge, MA: Cambridge University Press.

Plous, S. (Ed.). (2003). *Understanding prejudice and discrimination.* Boston, MA: McGraw-Hill.

Pollock, M. (2004). *Colormute race talk dilemmas in an American School.* Princeton, NJ: Princeton University Press.

Portman, J., Bui, T. T., Ogaz, J., & Treviño, J. (n.d.). *Microaggressions in the classroom.* A report for the University of Denver Center for Multicultural Excellence, Denver, CO. Retrieved from http://otl.du.edu/teaching-resources/creating-an-inclusive-classroom

Quintero, E. (2014b). *What is implicit bias, and how might it affect teachers and students? (Part II—Solutions).* April 17, 2014. Retrieved September 27, 2016 from http://www.shankerinstitute. org/blog/what-implicit-bias-and-how-might-it-affect-teachers-and-students-part-ii-solutions

Skiba, R. J., Horner, R. H., Chung, C.-G., Rausch, M. K., May, S. L., & Tobin, T. (2011). Race is not neutral: A national investigation of African American and Latino disproportionality in school discipline. *School Psychology Review,* 40(1), 85–107.

Staats, C. (2013). *State of the science—Implicit bias review 2013 edition.* Kirwan Institute. Retrieved August 2, 2016 from http://kirwaninstitute.osu.edu/docs/SOTS-Implicit_Bias.pdf

Staats, C. (2014a). *Implicit racial bias and school discipline disparities exploring the connection.* Kirwan Institute. May 2014. Retrieved July 27, 2016 from http://kirwaninstitute.osu.edu/ wp-content/uploads/2014/05/ki-ib-argument-piece03.pdf

Staats, C. (2014b). *State of the science—Implicit bias review 2014 edition*. Kirwan Institute. Retrieved August 2, 2016 from http://www.kirwaninstitute.osu.edu/wp-content/uploads/2014/03/2014-implicit-bias.pdf

Staats, C. (2015). *Understanding implicit bias what educators should know*. Retrieved September 27, 2016 from http://www.aft.org/ae/winter2015-2016/staats

Staats, C., Capatosto, K., Wright, R. A., & Jackson, V. W. (2016). *State of the science—Implicit bias review 2016 edition*. Kirwan Institute. Retrieved August 2, 2016 from http://kirwaninstitute.osu.edu/wp-content/uploads/2016/07/implicit-bias-2016.pdf

U.S. Department of Education. (2014). *Guiding principles—A resource guide for improving school climate and discipline*. U.S. Department of Education.

Vavrus, F., & Cole, K. (2002). "I didn't do nothin'": Discursive construction of school suspension. *Urban Review, 34*(2), 87–111. Cited in Staats, C. (2014). *Implicit racial bias and school discipline disparities exploring the connection* (p. 8). Kirwan Institute. May 2014. Retrieved July 27, 2016 from http://kirwaninstitute.osu.edu/wp-content/uploads/2014/05/ki-ib-argument-piece03.pdf

Wald, J. (2014). Can "*debiasing strategies help to reduce racial disparities in school discipline? Summary of the literature.*" March 2014. Retrieved August 20, 2016 from http://www.indiana.edu/~atlantic/wp-content/uploads/2014/03/Implicit-Bias_031214.pdf

Wallace Jr., J. M., Goodkind, S., Wallace, C. M., & Bachman, J. G. (2008). Racial, ethnic, and gender differences in school discipline among U.S. high school students: 1991–2005. *Negro Educational Review, 59*(1/2), 47–62.

Wing Sue, D. (2010). Racial *micro-aggressions in everyday life—Is subtle bias harmless? Psychology Today*, October 6, 2010. Retrieved May 7, 2014 from https://www.psychologytoday.com/blog/microaggressions-in-everyday-life/201010/racial-microaggressions-in-everyday-life

Wu, S.-C., Pink, W., Crain, R., & Moles, O. (1982). Student suspension: A critical reappraisal. *The Urban Review, 14*(4), 245–303.

PART TWO

THE PARADOX OF POWER, JUSTICE, AND SCHOOL LEADERSHIP

Facing Diversity—Leading Change

We take the students who have less to begin with and then systematically give them less in school. In fact, we give these students less of everything that we believe makes a difference.

We do this in hundreds of different ways.

—Katie Haycock

In America, we presume to know what justice *is* and *is* not. And, we presume to be a *just* nation. Words like equality, equity, and justice are key values embedded in the cherished *American Dream*, and for most Americans, these ideas are neither ambiguous nor elusive, because they are cloaked over us like heavy garments, and have always been part of the country's DNA. *Justice* and its companions, *freedom and liberty*, are ingrained in our children as soon as they enter our public education systems. And yet, we've always had to use qualifiers when we refer to 'justice' because too often, justice, like beauty, was in the eye of the beholder, and under the control of the privileged and the powerful who dispensed it if, and when, it served their best interests to do so. And, in many ways, it seems paradoxical to speak of justice, power, and privilege in the same sentence because too often in American society, justice, power, and privilege are non sequiturs.

Even a superficial look at American history shows that it is replete with evidence of the unevenness of American justice. It was evident in the attempts to dehumanize entire groups of people; it was evident in the systematic attempts to deny certain groups equal access to the Constitutionally guaranteed *pursuit of happiness*, and it was evident in the attempts to fortify the caste-iron economic system that stratified poverty and wealth. And, there are many contemporary examples which show an unfortunate continuity with the past. In *American Apartheid*, for example, Sheryl Cashin points out that

> Fifty years after Brown v. Board, we now profess to believe that the United States should be an integrated society and that people of all races are inherently equal and entitled to the full privileges of citizenship. Here is the reality: while we accept these values in the abstract, we are mostly pretending that they are true. At the dawn of the twenty-first century, the ideals of integration and equality of opportunity still elude us, and we are not being honest or forthcoming about it. (Cashin, 2004, p. x)

Most disturbing perhaps is the pretense, the self-perpetuating myth that ignores generational poverty, pain, and exclusion. However, we can point to progress. In the sociopolitical realm, we can point to the recent two-term election of an African-American President of the United States. In the educational realm, we can point to a cluster of new pedagogies and approaches which aggressively confront injustice, explicitly foreground equity and equality, challenge institutional discrimination, and lead the way to promising school reforms.

Although controversial, multicultural social justice education is one of the most aggressive and comprehensive school reform movements designed to interrupt bias, and institutionalize justice in the overall educative process.

This chapter examines the rationale for multicultural social justice education in the context of the growing body of research on the role that social dominance orientation and implicit bias play in schooling. Research shows that dominant privilege props up, and helps to sustain denial and self-delusion around issues of institutional discrimination, bias, and unfair school practices. Therefore, the chapter also explores the paradoxes and challenges that underlie school leadership that is equity-driven in a world that is increasingly diverse and increasingly complex. The chapter questions how personal belief systems, tainted by racial, cultural, and socioeconomic biases, can coexist with democratic values that insist on equity, equality, and justice. Whether or not school leaders acknowledge the intersectionality of belief systems, and equity-driven school leadership, is correlated with whether or not they facilitate or hinder transformational school change.

The chapter will also show that multicultural education, in all of its iterations, has a fairly amorphous shape, which complicates the discourse about what multicultural education is, and is not, and potentially undermines the process of transformational school change. It is therefore important to identify the variety of overlapping and countervailing definitions for multicultural education, and to debunk the idea that multicultural education is a fixed set of homogeneous practices which are subscribed to by all of its advocates. Sleeter (1996) points out the danger of treating the field as if it were "static and homogeneous rather than dynamic and growing with its own internal debates" (p. 4). For example, it is important to clarify the distinction between multicultural education and multicultural social justice education, which are closely allied, because both are centered on issues of diversity, and challenge established power structures. Using the work of Sleeter and others, I will examine both the origins of these two concepts, and the sociohistorical contexts which continue to shape and reshape them in dynamic ways.

Moreover, I will examine multicultural education through the lens of critical race theorists, who have long argued that multicultural education has been usurped by the very systems it hopes to transform. These theorists assert that multicultural education has been emasculated, and deveined, and is now mostly a frail vestige of what its proponents originally designed it to be. They point out that too often, multicultural education has devolved into a formalized or stylized set of annual (or one-time) activities that look great on paper, but which are either superficial or ineffective or both. For example, Jay (2003) argues that although multicultural education purportedly provides a pluralist education that paves the way to equal opportunity, equal access, and an equitable distribution of power among all groups, these goals will be thwarted until a "thorough interrogation of the hidden curriculum in educational institutions is brought to the fore ..." as proposed by Critical Race Theorists. Jay (2003) also points out that "as a hegemonic device, the hidden curriculum helps keep current multicultural paradigms functioning in a manner that causes multicultural reforms to be 'sucked back into the system'" (Jay, 2003, p. 4) instead of transforming the way schools actually do business.

The chapter argues that educational leaders can use the concept of Critical Race Theory (CRT) as an effective tool to analyze, discuss, design, and implement strategies that ultimately eliminate the chronic racialized achievement gaps. In order to accomplish this, school leaders would have to interrupt/disrupt traditional business-as-usual practices that are more or less resigned to, or accepting of, the predictable disparity in academic achievement based on race, class, and culture. Leaders and policymakers would have to begin to question some of their basic assumptions including *colorblindness, equal vs. equitable* allocation of resources, the concept of *race-neutrality*, and the normalization of *white privilege*.

This examination will provide a context for the strategies that will be offered in later chapters to counterbalance the power structures that perpetuate institutional racism and discrimination in schools, and by extension in the larger society.

Finally, the chapter will consider some of the relevant research on effective leadership, and change theory, and how they support leadership for social justice. In addition to exploring the links between emotional intelligence and equity leadership, this chapter will show the nexus between multicultural social justice education, equity leadership, and school change. I argue, for example, that a commitment to multicultural social justice education is implicitly a commitment to *changing the status quo* in schools and society, and if effectively done, it is a commitment to major school reform as well. As such, it should be considered an essential dimension of the preparation of pre-service and in-service teachers and pre-service and in-service school leaders because it has the potential to be an effective weapon against social injustice and institutional discrimination, as well as one of the strongest supports for the American democratic ideal of *freedom and justice for all.* Furthermore, although the tenets of multicultural social justice education are consistent with education for citizenship in a democratic society, and are aligned with many of the basic goals we espouse in schools and more broadly in society, the fear of, and resistance to, change is one of its greatest obstacles. Therefore, the chapter will provide an overview of the dynamics of change, showing that personal change and transformation are important elements of, and precursors to, institutional change.

* * *

Proponents of multicultural social justice education say it is promising because it is aligned with social reconstructionist pedagogies and social advocacy to a high degree, and it demands a reconsideration of the role and organization of schools, how teachers teach, and how leaders lead. Opponents fear it for the very same reasons. According to Grant and Sleeter (2007) "Multicultural social justice education is based on the premise that political participatory consciousness should be learned in school … [because the] school is the primary social institution, outside the immediate family and perhaps religious institutions, in which young people spend much of their time. As such, the school is an ideal place for young people to learn collectively how to make an impact on social institutions" (pp. 258–259).

Grant and Sleeter (2007) go on to point out that in general, because schools are acutely aware of the sociopolitical and economic contexts in which they operate, they generally avoid controversial issues, and simultaneously "teach the young to revere rather than critique the nation's political and economic institutions, and to view society as fair and just, even with its flaws. One can argue that much of schooling helps to foster acquiescence and political apathy" (Grant & Sleeter, 2007, p. 259). This rings a sharply dissonant chord when we realize that for decades, *critical thinking*, one of the least controversial and most widely supported learning objectives across all grade levels, stands in stark opposition to the idea of uncritical acquiescence as a measure of learning outcomes, and teacher efficacy. This is even more striking when we realize that critical thinking is aligned with, and a precursor to, the development of critical consciousness and critical pedagogy, all of which are essential elements in social justice frameworks. In addition, it can be argued that there is an intellectual disconnect, whether conscious or unconscious, that allows some educators to segment and unhinge these mutually reinforcing concepts, and create unnatural boundaries between critical thinking, critical consciousness, critical pedagogy, and social justice.

In his book, *Lies My Teacher Told Me—Everything Your American History Textbook Got Wrong* (1995), James Loewen offers dramatic and disturbing examples of what this *intellectual disconnect* can look like in history classrooms. By analyzing a wide range of American history textbooks in use in American classrooms, Loewen concluded that American history is presented as what Ron Takaki (1993) called a 'master narrative,' a 'construct,' which like an ordinary novel, has a hero, a villain, and a plot. In this 'story' America itself is 'heroified.' This means that "textbook authors treat America itself as a hero, indeed as the hero of their books, so they remove its warts" (Loewen, 1995, p. 212). Loewen places responsibility for this on teachers, as well as publishers and those who influence them who

> have evidently concluded that what American society needs to stay strong is citizens who assent to its social structure and economic system without thought. As a consequence, today's textbooks defend our economic system mindlessly, with unsupportable pieties about its unique lack of stratification; thus they produce alumni of American history courses unable to criticize or defend our system of social stratification knowledgeably. (p. 212)

Loewen's analysis points to a powerful and frightening example of institutional discrimination in which schools are complicit in institutionalizing social *injustice* by cultivating in students an uncritical acceptance of a *constructed* version of American history, and by extension, an uncritical acceptance of unfair social policies that are unfair to large segments of the American populace. Furthermore, when schools systematically foster acquiescence to a whitewashed, sanitized, version of 'history,' they undermine and perhaps erode the same democratic principles that are being taught in their classrooms which privilege 'free' speech, and invite and encourage full participation of the American citizenry in the sociopolitical process. The *heroification* of America is also evident in English and other subjects, and this is evidenced either by the texts chosen or ignored, what groups are included in classroom discussions and what groups are left out, or general curricular decisions that guide pedagogy.

A multicultural social justice approach to teaching privileges critical thinking; it is an antidote to a mindless, uncritical, acceptance of the status quo. More advocacy-oriented, and social-reconstructionist than multicultural education, a multicultural social justice approach "holds that the school should consciously and actively teach and model participatory democratic living and that the entire school experience should be reoriented to address difference and justice based on race, social class, language, disability, sexual orientation, religion, and gender, both locally and globally" (Grant & Sleeter, 2007, p. 259). Ultimately, a multicultural social justice education approach challenges, and works to eradicate, various intersecting forms of social oppression, and research shows that even young children can learn these lessons. According to Tatum (1997), "We are better able to resist the negative impact of oppressive messages when we see them coming than when they are invisible to us. While some may think it is a burden to children to encourage this critical consciousness, I consider it a gift" (p. 47). A young child can be taught to recognize that when they are targets of discrimination, according to Derman-Sparks and the A. B. C. Task Force (1989), children have the right to say "That's not fair, "or I don't like that ..." (p. 77). And for children to develop empathy and respect for diversity, they need to be able to say,

> "I don't like what you're doing" to a child who is abusing another child. If we teach children to recognize injustice, then we must also teach them that people can create positive change by working together. ... Through activism activities children build the confidence and skills for becoming adults who assert, in the face of injustice, "I have the responsibility to deal with it, I know how to deal with it, I will deal with it." (Derman-Sparks & the A. B. C. Task Force, 1989, p. 77)

Although it is unambiguously aligned with the basic democratic principles of fairness and equality, multicultural social justice education is controversial. An outgrowth of the civil rights era, multicultural social justice education is controversial not only because it proposes to deconstruct traditional classroom practice, or that it deconstructs how we conceptualize education; it is controversial because it challenges us to see America and ourselves differently, and be transformed by what we *see*. Significantly, multicultural social justice education forces us to interrogate systems of power, and confront social injustice in the form of racism, sexism, classism, and institutional discrimination. It challenges and deconstructs existing curricula that present myopic Anglocentric world views, and traditional views of power and privilege which marginalize or demonize anyone who is different from the perceived *norm*. Multicultural social justice education embodies *change* on both the personal and institutional levels, and although most educators and theorists tend to begin with, and focus on, transforming organizational policies and practices, I argue that transformational teaching and transformational leadership must begin on a more personal level by reentering the *self*.

Socrates' ancient dictum, "Know thyself" anticipated the research of contemporary social scientists who have validated self-knowledge, and 'emotional intelligence' as key components in overall human intelligence and human behavior. The concept of emotional intelligence, as identified by Salovey and Mayer (1990), is "a subset of social intelligence that involves the ability to monitor one's own and others' feelings and emotions, to discriminate among them, and to use this information to guide one's thinking and action" (p. 189). Work (1995, 2000, 2002) expands the concept by connecting emotional intelligence to the leadership domain. Although much of the research linking emotional intelligence to leadership has emerged from organizations in the private sector, both an analysis of the research and the implementation of the assessments make clear that emotional intelligence is relevant to the public sector and to education specifically. For example, Cherniss, Goleman, and Bennis (2001) state that, "... emotional intelligence at the most general level, refers to the abilities to recognize and regulate emotions in ourselves and others" (p. 14). They also make an important distinction between emotional *intelligence* and emotional *competencies*, and go on to state that, "... emotional intelligence provides the bedrock for the development of a large number of competencies that help people perform more effectively" (Cherniss et al., 2001, p. 10). A review of the extensive work that has been done in this field reveals a common theme: honest self-awareness/

appraisal and rigorous self-management/control are consistent with effective leadership. Effective leaders must develop a number of proficiencies. They must

- look at themselves objectively and with rigor
- acknowledge troubling faults with courage
- maintain a healthy level of self-regard despite their flaws
- manage the difficult and often painful process of self-change
- build emotional intelligence competencies

When leaders allow themselves to go through this rigorous process they can *begin* to uproot stereotypes, biases, myths, and prejudices that are preventing them from seeing how, when, and where social injustice is operative in their schools, and they can begin to confront some of the fundamental causes of the pernicious achievement gaps which continue to undermine academic excellence for some students.

Multicultural Education and Multicultural Social Justice Education Defined

The dizzying plethora of terms and concepts which are considered synonyms for multicultural education makes it necessary to begin with a definition of terms. For example, anti-bias education, cultural proficiency, culturally relevant teaching, and culturally responsive teaching are often used interchangeably with multicultural education, but they can mean vastly different things in terms of school policies and practices. Even the word diversity is slippery. For some, diversity is simply a code word for race or ethnicity, but for most experts on the subject, it is all-encompassing, and represents all forms of human difference. Perhaps, the most unambiguous definition of multicultural education comes from the Dictionary of Multicultural Education (Grant & Ladson-Billlings, 1997):

> Multicultural education is a philosophical concept and an educational process. It is a concept built upon the philosophical ideals of freedom, justice, equality, equity, and human dignity contained in the U.S. Constitution and the Declaration of Independence. It recognizes however, that equality and equity are not the same thing; that is, equal access does not necessarily guarantee fairness. (p. 170)

Multicultural social justice education can be seen as an outgrowth or expansion of multicultural education. Perhaps one way to peel it away from multicultural education is its insistence that *equality and equity are not the same things*, and that *equal access does not necessarily guarantee fairness*. Multicultural social justice education involves advocacy to a high degree, is issue oriented, and is explicitly focused on social problems such as poverty, discrimination in housing, the legal system, etc., and how they impinge on the teaching/learning process. This focus is action-oriented, and tends to be skewed toward the systemic injustice at the core of American society and schooling and is guided by what people must *do* to make systemic changes. Ayers, Hunt, and Quinn (1998) put it this way:

> Teaching for social justice is teaching that arouses students, engages them in a quest to identify obstacles to their full humanity, to their freedom, and then to drive, to move against those obstacles. And so the fundamental message of the teacher for social justice is: You can change the world. (p. xvii)

In contrast, multicultural education has a greater focus on curricular changes that can engage the intellect, transform personal belief systems, and address institutional discrimination in schools. While 'culture' is a centerpiece in multicultural education, it can be somewhat sidelined or marginalized in discussions of multicultural social justice education in favor of action-oriented initiatives. Yet, multicultural education and social justice education are mutually reinforcing, and are sometimes difficult to distinguish. One way to view the difference is to consider multicultural social justice education as strategy, advocacy, and action, and multicultural education as content.

Blackmore's (2002) analysis brings some clarity to the concept of multicultural social justice education. For example, she offers a critical policy approach to the preparation of school administrators based on social justice principles, and questions to what extent educational policies support, disrupt, or subvert existing social structures. According to Blackmore,

> A socially just education requires educational leaders to practice moral outrage at the persistence, if not worsening of homelessness, hunger, poverty, which are not going away but worsening. It requires educational communities to defend and extend principles of human dignity, community, and realization of democratic process; to reinvent a sense of commitment to the public as a social good. And to restructure market models to limited spheres, which improve social relations and conditions of learning. (Blackmore, cited in Marshall and Oliva, 2010, p. 23)

It is noteworthy that Blackmore refers to the *moral outrage* educational leaders are expected to *feel* in the presence of social injustice. This raises the question of whether or not educational leaders have lost their focus on the relationship between schooling, the inculcation of democratic principles, and the role schools should play in preparing citizens to participate fully in the American democratic system which is driven by the concepts of justice and equality. Moreover, it's important to ask: Have educational leaders been swallowed up by self-serving political concerns and as a result abrogated their responsibility to help improve the society into which their students are delivered? Also, shouldn't leadership, education, and social change be mutually reinforcing?

Culture: *'Borders'* and *'Boundaries'*

It is important to begin by taking a brief look at what we mean by 'culture' because it is so central to the discussion of education, equity, and social justice. Therefore, in order to provide a nuanced view of culture, it is useful to see how culture is defined in introductory anthropology and sociology texts, as well as how it is defined in the realm of educational anthropology.

Primitive Culture (1871), by Sir Edward Burnett Tylor considered the founder of cultural anthropology, established the anthropological significance of culture. Since then, the concept of culture has become more and more complex. By 1952, Alfred Kroeber and Clyde Kluckhohn had cataloged over 100 different definitions of the word *culture* (Kroeber & Kluckhohn, 1952, p. 119). Today, common themes and common elements of *culture* are generally accepted by anthropologists, sociologists, and cultural observers.

T. S. Eliot (1949) problematized the concept of culture in an essay entitled, "Notes Toward the Definition of Culture" reflecting that many use the word culture, but have not, "pondered deeply on the meaning of the word before employing it ..." (p. 21). Culture is often looked at superficially, focusing on visible aspects such as food, dress, dance, holidays, celebrations, etc. However, there are deeper, invisible aspects of culture which are often ignored or misunderstood, and if we ignore the deeper aspects of culture—such as the conception of justice, attitudes toward elders, rules for judging right and wrong, patterns of social interaction, status and relationships, conception of self, and one's group—we undermine our ability to have a true understanding of a group's culture on the deepest, most meaningful levels. Eliot underscores this when he says:

> The term culture has different associations according to whether we have in mind
> the development of an individual, of a group or class, or of a whole society ... Culture
> of the individual is dependent upon the culture of a group or class, and the culture of

the group or class is dependent upon the culture of the whole society to which that group or class belongs. Therefore, it is the culture of the society that is fundamental, and it is the meaning of the word *culture* in relation to the whole society that should be examined first. (p. 21)

This is important to educators, because, "[i]n a sense, everything we do in education relates to culture—to its acquisition, its transmission, and its invention. Culture is in us and all around us, just as is the air we breathe. In its scope and distribution, it is personal, familial, communal institutional, societal, and global. Yet culture as a notion is often difficult to grasp" (Erickson, 2010, p. 35). This becomes infinitely more complex, according to educational anthropologist Frederick Erickson, because culture is both visible and invisible; it is not static, and it "shifts inside and outside our reflective awareness" (Erickson, 2010, p. 35). Everybody is cultural, everybody is multicultural, and, there is no evidence that one culture is intrinsically more valuable than another. At least, this last point is true if we are using objective measures. However, the *de facto* reality is "*that not all cultural practices are equal in power and prestige in the United States or any other country*" [italics mine] (Erickson, 2010, p. 36).

In a real sense, educators need to function like cultural anthropologists and sociologists, and constantly question whether they are really seeing the nature of other cultures, or simply filtering information through their own cultural lenses. Educators need to voluntarily submit to this type of self-examination when encountering and interacting with other cultures, because they are important lesson generators whether the curricular vehicle is formal, informal, or *hidden*. This is very difficult, because it means suspending *judgment* based on our initial (and superficial) understanding of what we see, hear, and feel, so that the cultural practices of others are then viewed as simply *different* rather than *good* or *bad*; *weird* or *exotic*. Such judgments impose a hierarchal value system which can be patronizing, self-serving, implicitly unfair, and can introduce high levels of cultural conflict into the classroom. Erickson's (2010) discussion of cultural boundaries and borders offers important insights about cultural conflict and is instructive for teachers and leaders.

According to Erickson (2010), there are two ways we can respond to culture: as a *boundary* or a *border*. He defines a cultural boundary as the discernible presence of some form of cultural difference. In contrast, a cultural *border* "is the treatment of a particular feature of cultural difference as grounds for differing rights—privilege or dis-privilege, favorable or unfavorable regard. Treating a cultural difference as a border matter politicizes that difference, while treating that same cultural difference as a boundary matter, depoliticizes that difference" (Erickson, 2010, p. 40). In a school or classroom, the implications can be significant especially if the construction of cultural borders leads to the marginalization of certain cultural groups, creating an 'us' vs. 'them' dynamic in the classroom or the school. This can set up a destructive two-way process "of mutual border framing" (Erickson, 2010, p. 43) during which each group engages in "projective 'othering,' [using] negative cultural stereotypes [and] making the fostering of intercultural and multicultural awareness a tricky business indeed" (Erickson, 2010, p. 43).

What teachers and leaders must be aware of and guided by is that everyone and every group has *culture*: teaching is culture-based; learning occurs in the context of *culture*, and curriculum transmits *culture*. Therefore, the effectiveness of instructional practices and academic outcomes is diminished when they *do not* have a broad-based understanding of culture in general, as well as an understanding of the specific *culture(s)* of their students. Conversely, the effectiveness of instructional practices and academic outcomes is enhanced when teachers and leaders *have* a broad-based understanding of culture in general, and the specific *culture(s)* of their students. All of this reintroduces the concepts of equity and justice, and validates the need for multicultural social justice education, not as a choice, but as a necessity for excellence in teaching, learning, and leading.

Multicultural Social Justice Leadership

Children don't get to choose to no longer experience inequity.
—Scheurich and Skrla

Multicultural social justice leadership is firmly situated within sociopolitical, and socioeconomic contexts, as well as in a social reconstructionist framework. It is consistent with, and a logical outcome of, our decades-long focus on critical thinking as a foundation for all learning. "Leadership must be critically educative; it can not only look at the conditions in which we live, but it must also decide how to change them" (Foster, cited in Marshal & Oliva, 2010, p. 20). Marshal and Oliva (2010) offer a useful model for social justice which has three components:

[1] Leadership for Social Justice [used synonymously with multicultural social justice leadership and equity leadership] interrogates the policies and procedures that shape schools and at the same time perpetuate social inequities and marginalization due to race, class gender and other markers of difference …

[2] [M]oral transformative leadership has three characteristics ... views education and educational leadership from a ... theoretical perspective ... focuses on the use and abuse of power in institutional settings ... deconstructs the work of school administration in order to unearth how leadership practices generate and perpetuate inequities ... [for those] ... outside of the dominant culture ... Moral transformative leadership ... sees schools as sites ... that help create activists to bring about the democratic reconstruction of society.

[3] [S]ocial justice praxis ... activities such as research and scholarship ... that can be used to articulate a broader discourse for social justice and moral transformative leadership. (p. 24)

Multicultural social justice leadership must have a *moral* center, and an explicit social change agenda. And, if we are to achieve justice for all, leadership matters.

Leadership Matters

We Teach Who We Are.

— P. J. Palmer

... there is no basis for education in a democracy except for the belief in the enduring capacity for growth in ordinary people.

—William Ayers

Historically, the concept of a school principal or leader grew out of the idea that a principal was little more than a lead or *principal* teacher. This is a reminder that leaders and principals *are* or *should be* teachers. By extension, Palmer's (1998) prescient statement "[W]e teach who we are" (Palmer, 1998, p. 2) also can be seen as an elegant reminder that *leading* is *teaching*, and that no matter what we do, it reflects the essence of who we are. This idea should be coupled with another powerful one which is attributed to writer Anais Nin: "We don't see things as *they* are, we see things as *we* are." And, we see the world through a cultural lens shaped by the cumulative experiences of a lifetime. No person or group is culture neutral. The assertion of neutrality or objectivity in relation to culture is a myth. It is only by acknowledging the difficulty or improbability of neutrality or objectivity that we can even approach being so. This is an important point, because culture affects everything we say, everything we do, and everything we believe. It affects what we value, how we learn, how we teach, and how we *lead*. Palmer's definition of a leader elaborates on this:

[A] leader is a person who has an unusual degree of power to project on other people his or her shadow, or his or her light. A leader is a person who has an unusual degree of power to create the conditions under which other people must live and move and have their being—conditions that can either be as illuminating as heaven or as shadowy as hell. A leader is a person who must take special responsibility for what's going on inside him or herself, inside his or her consciousness lest the act of leadership create more harm than good. (Palmer, 1998, p. 7)

The impact of acculturation, or the process of internalizing cultural beliefs, and norms, cannot be ignored by educators. Therefore, the successful implementation of equity leadership and social justice pedagogies in schools will be impeded or advanced according to the belief systems of school leaders, not just classroom teachers as the disproportionate focus on teachers and teaching would suggest. Even though there is a growing body of research on diversity, multiculturalism, equity, multicultural education, culturally relevant teaching, social justice education, etc., the current research focuses on students and/or teachers; very little focuses on school administrators or specifically on equity *leadership* models. By focusing on teachers and pedagogy, most of the research and available books propose a *bottom-up* rather than a *top-down* approach to school change, and therefore direct their focus *away* from the engagement of school *leaders*. However, it is counterintuitive to think that any organization can make substantive changes without leaders who are both fully engaged and fully committed to change at every stage of the process.

Professional development consultants regularly report a tendency for leaders to enthusiastically introduce them to the staff, proclaim how important this topic is to the strategic direction of the organization, and then leave the session never to return. Too often, when it comes to leadership in the realm of diversity and multicultural education, the scenario looks like this analogy of a train journey: A leader decides on a destination, and informs his/her organization. The leader then charts a course for this excursion and pays for it, describes the landscape and the expected sights and experiences on the trip, and directs all members of the school organization to board the train. He/she wishes them well, steps off the train, and waves good-bye. I would argue that this kind of disengagement from the process can be costly to students, schools, and, ultimately, to society.

Leading Change

There is widespread agreement that schools need to change dramatically in order to assure success for all students and to end achievement gaps. However, in planning for change, too little attention is given to what is known about managing change. Knowledge of change management theory, a field that is well developed and documented, is crucial to equity-driven leadership. Burke (2008) points out that "... most organization change is not significant or successful" (p. 12). In other words,

> Most efforts by executives, managers, and administrators to significantly change the organizations they lead do not work. By "change significantly," I mean to turn the organization in another direction, to fundamentally modify the "way we do things," to overhaul the structure—the design of the organization for decision-making and accountability—and to provide organizational members with a whole new vision for the future ... Organizational improvements do occur, even frequently, and do work, but large-scale, fundamental organization change that works is rare. (p. 12)

It is important to note the distinction between *improvement* and *fundamental organization change* (transformation). Too often, the goal in schools is simply improvement, not transformation. Although the term transformation is widely used, it is not widely understood. School leaders and staff approach change with much enthusiasm and effort, and very quickly experience frustration because improvement is not enough to deconstruct the deep-rooted structural inequities and deeply held stereotypes and biases that perpetuate the failure of schools to meet the diverse needs of students. Burke points out some reasons that real organizational transformation is so rare:

> There are many reasons. First and foremost, deep organization change, especially attempting the change of the culture of an organization, is very difficult. Second, it is often hard to make the case for change ... Third, our knowledge for how to implement organization change is limited. (Burke, 2008, p. 12)

Change can be characterized as hard, and organizational transformation can be characterized as slow and messy. This may account for why organization change experts report that although organizational improvement is common, organizational transformation is rare. Nader and Tushman (1989) refer to large-scale, long-term organizational reorientation as *frame bending*, and point out that during this process, several kinds of transitions can happen: multiple transitions that may be related or unrelated; incomplete transitions that can be overtaken by, or subsumed under, new events; transitions that are undermined by uncertain future states that are unpredictable and difficult to anticipate; and transitions that unravel over long periods of time (Nader & Tushman, 1989). Moreover, the process is made more complex by *power politics* and *pathology*, two elements which are "tightly intertwined with the implementation of organizational change" (Nadler & Tushman, 1989, p. 202). They make the point that

All organizations are political systems, and changes occur within the context of both individual and group aspirations. Thus, strategic changes become enmeshed in issues that are ideological ... as well as issues that are personal. ... These are not aberrations; they are a normal part of organizational life. However, they will be magnified by and indeed may 'play themselves out' through the change. ... However, the successful change manager works at understanding these dynamics, predicting their impact on the change and vice versa, and shaping the situation to make constructive use of them. (Nader & Tushman, 1989, p. 202)

Schools are organizational structures in need of change, and it is clear that reversing the plight of American schools will require transformation, not just incremental improvement. School leaders, teacher leaders, and policy boards will need knowledge and skill as well as will and persistence, if they hope to be successful.

Understandably, leaders craft plans for changes that are orderly and rational, but when people and systems are actually challenged to make fundamental changes, they are anything but rational. Having a plan is absolutely necessary, but given the capriciousness of human behavior, simply having a plan is insufficient. Fears, emotions, doubts, and conflicts within and between stakeholders will likely erupt and must be managed. Having an awareness of the unconscious cultural stereotypes and biases that can infect thinking processes, and behaviors, is important, and must be confronted with intentionality, vigor, and sensitivity. Any plan must anticipate that various groups will both question and critique one another's motives for any proposed change; some will actively resist it. By confronting subtle underlying problems, a leader can avoid eroding the trust among constituents that is essential to working toward a common goal. Change will have to be skillfully and tenaciously lead, managed, and sustained.

Equity-Driven School Leadership

Highlighting the leadership domain is important not only because it is an often overlooked element of both multicultural education, and social justice education, but also because there is strong evidence that the lack of focus on equity-driven leadership is intimately linked to the miseducation of children of color. Available research continues to underscore the idea that children from racially and ethnically diverse backgrounds are the most vulnerable to school failure. Yet, to a large extent, present educational policy is fixed to maintain and protect current practices which often places educators in the position of doing things the same way and expecting different results which is, at the very least, counterintuitive or, perhaps, insane. Leaders who want to challenge the status quo, transform pedagogy and curricula, and narrow the gaping, racialized disparities in student achievement must begin by examining and critiquing their own belief systems, and engaging in 'courageous conversations' about what perceived 'differences' between individuals mean in educational settings and how this is translated into school policy which is nondiscriminatory.

It can also be argued that the lack of focus on equity-driven leadership is in large part responsible for limiting the success and acceptance of multicultural education and hampering the 'courageous conversations' among educators that must take place *before* social justice can be achieved. It is significant that too often, those who 'lead' have not undergone the same kind of training that they require for others in their organizations; they often invoke their authority to rise above and disengage from the process; this is part of the privilege that comes with power. This is especially meaningful in formal educational settings when, for example, school administrators direct their teachers to undergo training which they themselves ignore. On one level, we can ascribe this to expedience, ignorance, a lack of understanding, or simple political pandering. However, on a deeper level, a leader's unwillingness to acknowledge and change a mindset that helps to sustain unfair policies and practices may point to a pattern of cognitive dissonance that exposes a tension between their actions and their personal belief systems. Research by Argyris and Schön (1974) shows that there is a distinction between what they identify as *espoused beliefs* and *beliefs in use*, or a lack of congruence between *what we think we believe* and *what we actually do*. They point out that

> When someone is asked how he would behave under certain circumstances, the answer he usually gives is his *espoused* [italics mine] theory of action for that situation. This is the theory of action to which he gives allegiance, and which, upon request, he communicates to others. However, the theory that actually governs his actions is this theory-in-use. (Argyris & Schön, 1974, pp. 6–7)

Their findings force us to consider the significance of a lack of congruence between *what we think we believe* and *what we actually do* in the contexts of teaching or leading, and how this could be informed by personal belief systems. This could mean, for example, that what we think we think we're teaching may be vastly different from what students learn. Similarly, a leader's espoused vision for her or his school may be vastly different from how and where that leader is actually leading the school. When looked at in the context of equity-driven teaching and leading, this raises a number of complex questions: Can one demonstrate effective equity-driven leadership without examining and critiquing her or his own belief systems, becoming personally engaged in the sometimes painful and always difficult process of acknowledging and *unlearning* internalized bias, and learning how to acknowledge, respect, and value multiple perspectives? Moreover, as Lisa Delpit points out, this introspection is a necessary precursor to developing skill in cross-cultural communication which is vital. Communicating across cultures, according to Delpit

> ... takes a very special kind of listening, listening that requires not only open eyes and ears, but open hearts and minds. We do not really see through our eyes or hear through our ears, but through our beliefs. To put our beliefs on hold is to cease to exist as ourselves for a moment—and that is not easy. It is painful as well, because it means turning yourself inside out, giving up your own sense of who you are, and being willing to see yourself in the unflattering light of another's angry gaze. It is not easy, but it is the only way to learn what it might feel like to be someone else and the only way to start the dialogue. (Delpit, 1995, p. 46)

* * *

We live in an age that equates technical prowess with social and professional value. Yet effective leadership in diverse settings requires much more than technical expertise; it requires an engagement that goes far beyond physical dexterity or intellectual superiority. Effective leadership requires a profound personal transformation which is a difficult and wrenching process. This process must begin with self-examination that can lead to multicultural literacy, and effective cross-cultural communication, but as Palmer astutely points out, one significant barrier is that the people who rise to leadership in our society have a "tendency towards extroversion, which means a tendency to ignore what is going on inside themselves. [Furthermore, leaders] rise to power in our society by operating very competently and effectively in the external world, sometimes at the cost of internal awareness" (p. 8). Therefore, the challenge for those who profess to be, or for those who want to become, equity leaders is to first look inward; to reenter the *self*; to acknowledge both their own limitations in terms of seeing and understanding diverse perspectives, and the need to undergo a personal, and perhaps painful, transformation of their belief systems. Delpit's image of turning oneself inside out, and giving up one's personal identity in order to learn what it might feel like to be someone else, presents a powerful challenge to those who choose to lead in diverse settings. It is especially difficult to reach a state where you are "willing to see yourself in the unflattering light of another's angry gaze," or to contain the internalized anger that this self-examination can generate. "Now, the question is, why would anybody want to take such a difficult and dangerous journey? Everything in us cries out against it. That's why we externalize everything: It's easier to deal with the external world. It's easier to spend your life manipulating an institution than it is dealing with your own [inner self]" (Palmer, 1990, p. 10). Further complicating this process is the fact that in the United States, a high value is placed on *positive thinking*, which, according to Palmer (1990), may "feed a common delusion among leaders that their efforts are always well-intended, their power always benign ... [Palmer suggests] that the challenge is [for leaders] to examine [their] consciousness for those ways in which [they] project more shadow than light" (p. 7).

The obvious question is when we look at current practices in schools, do we see more evidence of *shadow* or *light*?

It is a form of denial when educators are unable or unwilling to see the cause and effect relationship between leadership, personal belief systems, and academic outcomes. When educators choose to see these as separate and distinct elements, rather than seeing the important ways that they intersect and overlap, they risk under-serving their schools, their students, and their communities. For example, it can be argued that the lack of focus on equity leadership helps to sustain the racialized *achievement gap* because there is a demonstrated connection between systemic inequities, school leadership, and the chronic academic failure experienced by many students of color. Moreover, no matter how well we train teachers to develop multicultural literacy, or practice culturally relevant pedagogies, schools will continue to underserve diverse and nondiverse student bodies until we place an equal focus on developing school leaders who are themselves trained to divest themselves of old ways of thinking, and link leadership to equity.

Joyce King's (1991) research on *dysconsciousness* offers some clarity about the complex process of *unlearning* internalized biases, and *learning* to practice new ways of knowing. She describes dysconsciousness as "an uncritical habit of mind (including perceptions, attitudes, assumptions, and beliefs) that justifies inequity and exploitation by accepting the existing order of things as given" (King, 1991, p. 135). This is in contrast to *critical consciousness*, or the capacity to critique situations and make "ethical" judgments (Heaney, 1984, cited in King, 1991, p. 135) about the social order. Dysconsciousness finds comfort in the *status quo* because it "involves a subjective identification with an ideological viewpoint that admits no fundamentally alternative vision of society" (King, 1991, p. 135). According to King (1991), dysconsciousness is an *"impaired* consciousness or [a] *distorted* way of thinking ..." (p. 135). When we apply the concept of dysconsciousness to school leadership, it becomes easier to understand the difficulty school leaders face when asked to challenge personal belief systems which are complicit in sustaining institutional discrimination, and which undermine progressive changes in schools. Uncritical ways of thinking about racial inequity, for example, permit the acceptance of "culturally sanctioned beliefs which regardless of the intentions involved, defend the advantages whites have because of the subordinated position of racial minorities" (Wellman, 1993, p. xi). Therefore, any "serious challenge to the status quo that calls racial privilege into question inevitably challenges the self-identity of White people who have internalized these ideological justifications" (King, 1991, p. 135). However, Wellman (1993) argues that it is more useful to analyze racial consciousness in terms of the social organization of advantage rather than the structure of personality. According to Wellman

> ... racism continues to be a defense of racial privilege, not a psychological abnormality or the product of ideological manipulation. And the racial consciousness of European Americans is still profitably interpreted as culturally acceptable responses to struggles over scarce resources, not ill will or the deviant expressions of intolerant, unsocialized bigots. (p. 24)

"I Don't Think I'm a Racist, but I Don't Want to Talk About Race!": How Critical Race Theory Reframes Discussions About Race

It is logically inconsistent to assert: *"I don't think I'm a racist, but I don't want to talk about race!"* and yet, whether articulated or not, this represents the prevailing mindset for many who are uncomfortable acknowledging that Americans live in what Toni Morrison (1992) has called *a wholly racialized world.* It is also logically inconsistent to think that we *can* live in a *wholly racialized world* and deny that the omnipresence of race and racism has an enduring, even deepening, deleterious impact on American lives every day. Although it is widely acknowledged that race is a social *construct* rather than a biological reality as was once thought, it also exists as a metaphor for the American experience, a way of referring to and disguising forces, events, classes and expressions of social decay and economic division far more threatening to the body politic than biological "race" ever was ... racism is as healthy today as it was during the Enlightenment. It seems that it has a utility far beyond economy, beyond the sequestering of classes from one another, and has assumed a metaphorical life so completely embedded in daily discourse that it is perhaps more necessary and on display than ever. (Morrison, 1992, p. 63)

If we accept Morrison's premise that racism continues to be *healthy* despite incessant antiracist rhetoric and dust-storms of anti-bias activity, and that racism has assumed a *metaphorical life* that is *completely embedded in daily discourse*, and that it is *more necessary* and *on display* than ever before, we also should be willing to respond appropriately to these chilling realities. One controversial response is CRT which emerged from the field of law in the 1970s. The question is: Can theorizing about race and racism help educators delegitimize discrimination and operationalize democratic values in schools?

Critical Race Theory

The opening epigraph in African-American legal scholar Derrick Bell's (1992) book, *Faces at the Bottom of the Well—The Permanence of Racism*, poignantly expresses several basic assumptions of Critical Race Theory when it asserts that

Black people are the magical faces at the bottom of society's well. Even the poorest whites, those who must live their lives only a few levels above, gain their self-esteem by gazing down on us. Surely, they must know that their deliverance depends on letting down their ropes. Only by working together is escape possible. Over time, many reach out, but most simply watch, mesmerized into maintaining their unspoken commitment to keeping us where we are, at whatever cost to them or to us. (Angelou, cited in Bell, 1992, p. v)

The basic assumption of CRT is that racism, like American slavery "refuses to fade, along with the deeply embedded personal attitudes and public policy assumptions" (Bell, 1992, p. 3) that supported them for so long. Accordingly, racism is "ordinary, not abberational ... [it is] the usual way that society does business, the common everyday experience of most people of color in this country" (Delgado & Stefancic, 2012, p. 7). The evidence for this is striking and incontrovertible. For example, headlines from a 2016 Pew Research Center Report affirm that

- A majority of blacks say they have faced racial discrimination ...
- About half of blacks say someone has acted suspicious of them or has treated them like they weren't smart ...
- Whites more likely than blacks to have college degrees ...
- The black unemployment rate today is double that of whites ...
- Black-white income gap remains large ...
- Blacks more than twice as likely as whites to be poor despite narrowing of the income gap ...
- Blacks significantly less likely than whites to be homeowners ...
- Whites have significantly higher levels of wealth than blacks. ... (from Pew Research Center Report, 2016, p. n.a.)

In other words, in America, poverty "... has a black or brown face" (Delgado & Stefancic, 2012, p. 12). Perhaps even more stunning (and disheartening) than the data points above is the following headline from another 2016 report on the racial wealth-gap by the Institute for Policy Studies and the Corporation for Economic Development: *The Average Black Family Would Need 228 Years to Build the Wealth of a White Family Today* (Holland, 2016, p. 1).

According to critical race theorists these realities exist in part, because whites have been "lulled by comforting racial stereotypes," and have internalized the idea that America presents a level-playing field. Therefore, they believe that any inability of blacks to successfully compete with whites academically or economically or financially is their own fault, rather than because of institutional discrimination, structural inequities, or explicit or implicit racism and bias. The permanence of racism, according to Bell and other theorists (Delgado & Stefancic, 2012; Ladson-Billings, 2010; Ladson-Billings & Tate 1995; Ledesma & Calderon, 2015; Tate, 1997), is largely due to the benefits that accrue to whites from it. For example, whites can generally depend on

- police protection rather than harassment
- option to choose better neighborhoods and better schools
- more attention, respect and status
- higher expectations for white children
- higher earnings
- disproportionately faster and greater accumulations of wealth (Kivel, 2011, pp. 31–32)

However, despite the obvious benefits of racism to Whites, according to CRT, even when *anti-racist social policies* have been put in place ostensibly to benefit Blacks, these policies are really motivated and driven by the underlying benefits that accrue to Whites which may not be evident without deeper study and analysis. Bell (1980) described this as *interest conversion* or *material determinism*. He cited the 1954 Brown decision, and subsequent desegregation policies as evidence of this, and in his article *Brown v. Board of Education and the Interest-Convergence Dilemma* (1980), he developed a strong legal justification for his position which continues to be an essential guiding principle of CRT.

The work of Bell and others launched a movement which brought together a community of activists and scholars who rejected incrementalism and step-by-step social progress. They wanted to study the relationship between *race*, *racism*, and *power*, and create a new paradigm to address civil rights in a broader perspective that was not restricted by discrete academic disciplines. Critical race theorists questioned "the very foundations of the liberal order, including equality theory, legal reasoning, Enlightenment rationalism, and neutral principles of constitutional law" (Delgado & Stefancic, 2012, p. 3). As a result, CRT embraced law and history and economics, and social science, and ultimately education.

Critical race theorists Delgado and Stefancic (2012) point out that concepts which had been taken for granted as helpful, even progressive, like color blindness, court-ordered legal equality, claims of merit-based rewards, school integration, are being "perverted," and actually support, sustain, and perpetuate institutionalized uses of racial power rather than undermine them (Delgado & Stefancic, 2012).

Gloria Ladson-Billings and William F. Tate were among the first scholars to establish a nexus between CRT and education (Ladson-Billings, 1995, 2010; Ladson-Billings & Tate, 1995; Tate, 1997). They lead a community of education scholars and activists who advocated the use of CRT as a lens to analyze and assess existing policies and practices in education. They argued that this required a paradigm shift that deconstructed old ways of thinking about teaching and leading and policymaking. It required educators to rethink and reevaluate their various roles in educating children, and to question the efficacy and *justness* of the overall educational process. CRT required educators to intentionally and explicitly think about race and racism as determinative factors in this process. It required them to set aside preconceived notions of *progress* and *success*, and engage in a critical examination of structural inequities, and conscious and unconscious biases, in an attempt to uncover hidden curricula that perpetuate inequities in school settings especially for students of color. Discussions about multicultural education, culturally relevant teaching, tracking, school discipline, the racialized school-to-prison pipeline, bilingual education, and standardized testing look different through the prism of CRT, and they challenge educators to use their newly acquired insights to disrupt and deconstruct overt or covert racism wherever and whenever it appears in the education pipeline.

The Paradox of Leadership

Among the thousands of books, articles, dissertations, and other forms of research on multicultural education, diversity, and culturally relevant educational practices, comparatively little focuses on equity-driven leadership, and even less of the available research has a focus on the process of challenging belief systems with the goal of bringing about adaptive change in the approach to school leadership. As King's (1991) work suggests, challenging and changing belief systems is difficult. It is like forcing someone to undergo major surgery. Even the thought of *going under the knife* causes people to be afraid and to recoil, because we all fear the uncertainty, the pain, and the loss of conscious control connected to surgery. Similarly, we fear the pain and loss of control connected to "putting our beliefs on hold … ceasing to exist as ourselves … turning [ourselves] inside out … giving up [our] own sense of who [we] are, and being willing to see [ourselves] in the unflattering light of another's angry gaze" (Delpit, 1995, p. 46). Clearly, belief systems are subterranean. Their origins are hard to find and harder to confront. Belief systems are personal, intangible, slippery, and deeply embedded. They are also tied to familial loyalties, socialization patterns, and the acculturation process, and must be seen within sociohistorical and sociopolitical contexts. If, for example, an administrator is asked to overturn, and reject belief systems learned in childhood, this can be perceived as asking that person to reject certain family values and by extension, becomes an implicit critique of one's family. Beyond that, it also can be perceived as a critique of deeply held national values. Further, "[t]he psychological price of loyalty to one's own group can be antipathy toward another, especially when there is a long history of enmity between the groups" (Goleman, 1995, p. 156). This presents both a difficult challenge and an interesting paradox for those who are responsible for *leading* others.

Another fascinating paradox is the connection between leadership, adaptive change, belief systems, and dominant privilege. There is an underlying irony in the fact that those invested with power have the *privilege* to change or not to change themselves and/or the systems for which they are responsible.

Those in power can choose or reject adaptive change; they can choose to *lead* or to *manage* the systems for which they are responsible. Leaders can choose to divest themselves of any responsibility to change themselves, and can instead insist that those in subordinate positions (i.e., teachers) do the hard work of attempting to make adaptive changes to systems over which they have limited control. I contend that this is a major reason that most of the activity surrounding equity education is focused on teachers, not school leaders. This may also be a primary reason that most of the textbooks and articles about diversity and equity education do not delve too deeply into what titled administrators need to *know, do, and become*. Administrators have the power to disengage from the process, while they mandate that others be very engaged. Consider for example, that most workshops and staff development are directed at teachers, and that too often, those who *lead* have not undergone the same kind of training that they require for others in their organizations. They can invoke their authority to rise above and remove themselves from the process, and they can do this with impunity. This is, in part, a result of the privilege that comes with power. On one level, we can ascribe this to expedience, ignorance, a lack of understanding, simple political pandering, or fear of change. However, on a deeper level, a leader's unwillingness to acknowledge and change a mindset that helps to sustain unfair policies and practices may point to a pattern of cognitive dissonance that exposes a tension between their actions and their personal belief systems. The question is: Can one demonstrate effective equity leadership without becoming personally engaged in the sometimes painful and always difficult process of *unlearning* internalized biases, and *learning* to acknowledge new ways of knowing, and to respect, and value multiple perspectives? In addition to raising questions about school leadership on the building and district levels, this also raises questions about the attitudes and belief systems of those above building level leaders such as school board members, as well as those who run state and federal agencies that oversee educational policy.

Adaptive Change

We should take care not to make the intellect our god. It has, of course powerful muscles, but no personality.

—Albert Einstein

The work of Heifetz and Linsky (2002) highlights the rewards and the challenges of enacting adaptive change. Heifetz' framework shows the important connection between *personal and social transformation*. They take the position that adaptation requires giving up an important value or a current way of life, which is compatible with the idea that effective practitioners of equity leadership must shed old ways of thinking, and give up their sense of who they are in order to see the world through the lens of another person. Ultimately, effective leaders must develop policies that address the real, rather than perceived, needs of students who have been traditionally marginalized. Heifetz makes a clear and sharp distinction between leadership that involves the *technical work of routine management* and the *adaptive work of leadership*; not understanding the difference between the two is a dangerous invitation to failure. According to Heifetz and Linsky, adaptive changes

> require experiments, new discoveries, and adjustments from numerous places in the organization or community. Without learning new ways—changing attitudes, values and behaviors—people cannot make the adaptive leap necessary to thrive in the new environment. The sustainability of change depends on having the people with the problem internalize the change itself ... People frequently avoid painful adjustments in their lives if they can postpone them, place the burden on somebody else or call someone to the rescue ... The deeper the change and the greater the amount of new learning required, the more resistance there will be and thus, the greater the danger to those who lead. For this reason, people often try to avoid the dangers, either consciously or subconsciously, by treating an adaptive challenge as if it were a technical one. This is why we see so much more routine management than leadership in our society. (Heifetz & Linsky, 2002, pp. 13–14)

In other words, we must move beyond technical analyses of how the school system does or does not work to discussions of how administrators and teachers make the adaptive changes necessary to serve the needs of children both in schools and in society. This must happen before they can do the hard work of advocating for children, especially those who live on the margins in American society.

Heifetz' excellent work is complemented by the work of Michael Fullan (2001) which deepens and enriches the discussion by linking leadership and change to moral purpose and character, and significantly to social justice pedagogies. However, although Fullan (2001) sees education as the domain which offers the greatest possibility for bringing about change, he points out that until educators are *taught* to see themselves as experts in the *dynamics of change* driven by a moral purpose, they will be ineffective because they themselves will not understand the implications of diversity either globally or locally, or be able to respond appropriately to them in school settings. Importantly, they will also be unable to effectively prepare their students to become global citizens guided by a strong moral sensibility with the capacity to bring about and sustain the social and political changes that are needed in an increasingly diverse and complex world. And, if we as educators are incapable of preparing those who will replace us to be better than we are, are we not little more than intellectual *poseurs* hiding behind a mystifying blend of rhetoric, research, standardized tests, and denial? In the end, it's about authentic leadership, and authentic leadership is an outgrowth of both character and a moral purpose. "Whatever one's style, every leader, to be effective, must have and work on improving his or her moral purpose ... [I]n other words ... [authentic leaders] display character, and character is the defining characteristic of authentic leadership" (Fullan, 2001, p. 4) and I contend that authenticity is a defining characteristic of equity-driven leadership as well.

In *Primal Leadership* (2002), Daniel Goleman reintroduces the concept of emotional intelligence as an important dimension of effective leadership. He argues that "... intellect alone will not make a leader; leaders execute a vision by motivating, guiding, inspiring, listening, persuading—and, most crucially, through creating resonance" (Goleman, Boyatzis, & McKee, 2002, p. 27). According to Goleman et al. (2002), "Great leaders move us. They ignite our passion and inspire the best in us. When we try to explain why they are so effective, we speak of strategy, vision, or powerful ideas. But the reality is much more primal: Great leadership works through the emotions" (p. 3). Accordingly, when a leader is self-aware, emotionally intelligent, and attuned to other people's feelings, and can move people and be moved emotionally by them, they exhibit *resonance*. A resonant leader is an empathetic leader who "leaves people feeling understood and cared for" (Goleman et al., 2002, p. 20). Those who have resonance are also authentic and can speak authentically about their own feelings and values, and by extension invite authenticity from those around them. In contrast, dissonance "refers to a lack of harmony. Dissonant leadership produces groups that feel emotionally discordant, in which people have a sense of being continually off-key" (Goleman et al., 2002, p. 21). Goleman equates dissonant leadership with anger, disharmony, fear, apathy, and emotional toxicity, all of which can infect the workplace, and undermine productivity.

Although this framework comes out of a traditional corporate mindset which equated leadership with domination and a lack of feeling, it is very compatible with the concept of equity leadership, because among other things, it redefines and deconstructs the dynamics of power and dominant privilege as articulated by McIntosh (1988), Tatum (1997), Howard (2006), and many others. For example, a central element of the concept of dominant privilege is that those in a dominant or advantaged group (i.e., school principals) can rationalize that they and a subordinate group (teachers, students, parents, community members, etc.) share the same goals and interests and to some extent, a common experience, even as they remain oblivious to the real experiences and feelings of those group members. The key point is that if you are in the dominant group, you can function, survive, and even prosper without attending to the needs or concerns of those who are beneath you in an organization. In terms of multiculturalism and cross-cultural communication, this can have deleterious consequences by sustaining existing polices or developing new ones, policies which marginalize and underserve some student groups.

Goleman's work on emotional intelligence is useful for understanding leadership in school settings because it allows us to learn something by comparing and contrasting the organizational goals in the corporate domain and the educational domain. There are some clear distinctions as well as some unfortunate parallels. Corporations are essentially driven by their fiduciary responsibilities to shareholders, which sometimes appears to be a bloodless profit orientation which is always striving to improve the *bottom line*. However, more and more, emotional intelligence, a relatively new concept in corporate settings, is being seen as an idea that can have positive effects on productivity and interpersonal relationships as well as improve a company's bottom line. In the 1970s, corporate executives believed that their work demanded that they engage "their heads, but not their hearts" (Goleman, 1995, p. 149). At that time, corporations valued the skills of an executive who was seen as an unemotional take-no-prisoners, *jungle-fighter*. However, a new standard has evolved since then. Now, a corporate executive is expected to be a "virtuoso in interpersonal skills" (Goleman, 1995, p. 149). This means engaging the emotions, and seeing leadership not as domination, but as the art of persuading and motivating people to work collaboratively to achieve the goals of the organization. Although this represents significant positive change, there is a caveat when it comes to dealing with diversity in the increasingly complex workplace. Even as corporations provide training for their employees to improve interpersonal relationships among diverse groups, the *corporatization* of diversity training is noteworthy:

> ... seminars have become a staple of in-house training in companies throughout America, with the growing realization by managers that even if people bring prejudices to work with them, they must *learn to act as though they have none* [italics

mine]. The reasons over and above human decency, are *pragmatic* [italics mine] ... this means the culture of an organization must change to foster tolerance, *even if individual biases remain* [italics mine]. (Goleman, 1995, p. 156)

Clearly, pragmatism and profit subsume other humanistic values like fostering respect and eliminating deeply held prejudices which continue to divide people both in the workplace and in society. In a corporate setting, it is enough for executives and employees to develop a facade of unbiased behavior if this will insure productivity and profitability. "Organizations employ diversity training for reasons ranging from protection against liability to a more liberal notion that 'in diversity there is strength.' The belief that workplace diversity can bring increased productivity, new ideas, and therefore higher profits, appeals particularly to corporations. Although the diversity training may make good business sense, the model falls terribly short of the comprehensive racial justice approach required for progressive social change" (Rogers, 2001, p. 1). The traditional corporate focus on pragmatism, profit, and self-interest is reinforced in Thomas' (1990) analysis of affirmative action and diversity, but he expands the debate to include an examination of the American workplace in sociopolitical, socioeconomic, and sociohistorical contexts to find more effective ways to manage diversity. Debunking assimilationist ideologies centered on the American 'melting pot,' which were thoroughly embraced in corporate settings that valued conformity, Thomas (1990) acknowledges that "the melting pot is the wrong metaphor even in business ... [and] companies are faced with the problem of surviving in a fiercely competitive world with a work force that consists and will continue to consist of unassimilated diversity" (Thomas, 1990, p. 6). Without mentioning social justice per se, Thomas makes it clear that it's imperative to get to the root causes of prejudice and inequality as manifested in the workplace because it blocks some, particularly those in marginalized groups from reaching their full potential and thereby bringing the most benefit to the company. He concludes that "In a country seeking competitive advantage in a global economy, the goal of managing diversity is to develop our capacity to accept, incorporate, and empower the diverse human talents of the most diverse nation on earth. It's our reality. We need to make it our strength" (Thomas, 1990, p. 12).

In contrast to corporations, this type of carefully modulated response to diversity is insufficient in a school setting for many different reasons. For example, schools are not wedded to financial profit, but exist to serve the needs of the general populace. Their goals are informed by the goals of a democratic society in terms of producing students who are "morally literate—possessed of a strong sense of right and wrong, a broad understanding of our culture's values, a foundation for making responsible decisions in the face of moral conflicts, and in general, a firm grasp of the rights and responsibilities of American citizenship" (Heller, 1996, cited in DeRoche & Williams, 2001, p. 137). Therefore, in dealing with diversity, surface behavior that *appears* to be *tolerant* of difference isn't enough. Schools *should have* a different, deeper agenda from corporations, which is tied to a commitment to working toward the achievement of comprehensive social justice and social change. The business model doesn't have to reach these standards, because there's no direct financial profit in it.

Unfortunately, schools can behave like corporations. They can, for example, equate high test scores on standardized tests to a corporate bottom line. They can demonstrate a bloodless pragmatism that devalues other more altruistic goals like working to achieve a more just society. This approach is counter to the goals of multicultural social justice education which, when done well, begins by engaging people on personal and emotional levels. Multicultural education challenges people to engage in self-examination, and thereby see themselves and their relationship to others differently. Moreover, it is committed to *changing the status quo* in schools and society by deconstructing traditional classroom practice, and institutional discrimination. Significantly, it forces people to confront social injustice in the form of racism, sexism, classism, etc., and reconceptualize how children are taught and how schools are led.

Equity Leadership and Race

Central to the meaning of whiteness is a broad, collective American silence. The denial of white as a racial identity, the denial that whiteness has a history, allows the quiet, the blankness to stand as the norm. This erasure enables many to fuse their absence of racial being with the nation, making whiteness their unspoken but deepest sense of what it means to be American.

—Grace Elizabeth Hale

Leadership is dangerous. "To lead is to live dangerously because when leadership counts, when you lead people through difficult change, you challenge what people hold dear—their daily habits, tools, loyalties and ways of thinking—with nothing more to offer perhaps than a possibility ... People push back when you disturb the personal and institutional equilibrium they know" (Heifetz & Linsky, 2002, p. 2). As a consequence, those who lead should approach change with caution because change makes us afraid that our worlds will collide, collapse, implode, be shaken to the core, and that nothing will be the same. And yet, "[p]eople do not resist change per se. People resist loss"

(Heifetz & Linsky, 2002, p. 11). This, of course, is meaningful on multiple levels. In similar ways, the prospect of change will affect both those who lead and those who will be led. Everyone is likely to experience the same cycle of resistance, especially the fear of loss when confronted by change. When, for example, you tell people what they *need* to hear rather than what they *want* to hear, even though you present a clear, passionate vision of future progress, "people will see with equal passion the losses you are asking them to sustain" (Heifetz & Linsky, 2002, p. 12). This becomes a significant challenge for any-one who has assumed the mantle of leadership. However, those who are com-mitted to equity-driven school leadership have a different and deeper level of responsibility and challenge because they must frame their work in broader contexts; a commitment to transforming schools is a commitment to trans-forming society. Among other things, it means a direct confrontation with diversity in all of its manifestations. This means recognizing that although "[d]iversity is not a choice" (Howard, 2006, p. 4) they *can* choose *how*, and *how well* they will respond to it. And how leaders respond to diversity will depend on whether or not they are willing to be risk-takers, and address dif-ficult subjects and problems they've learned to avoid either because of a lack of skill, or because they make people uncomfortable, or both. Clearly, school leaders "… are more comfortable [dealing with, and] talking about *safe* top-ics such as student achievement, standards and quality schools as opposed to more controversial concerns regarding race, gender, gays, lesbians, bisexuals. With an abundance of concerns that can be taken up in the political arena, [administrators and other] policymakers seldom raise troublesome issues that may balkanize [their constituency] … Social justice concerns, however, demand that they enter this contested arena if substantive changes are going to be made to ensure the success of all students" (Marshall & Oliva, 2010, p. 41). For example, transformative leaders must be prepared to challenge insti-tutional discrimination, and interrogate dominance and privilege, especially white privilege.

Consider the difficulty of training administrators to interrogate privi-lege; to interrogate systems of power; the same systems of power from which they receive their livelihood and status, and which they've internalized as the 'norm.' Imagine what it would be like if a new captain came onto the Titanic on its fatal maiden voyage, realized the weakness in the design of the hull of the ship and its vulnerability to impact by the deadly icebergs, informed the passengers, and began to repair the moving ship. Imagine the terror, and anger, and incredulity the captain would incite by announcing that the 'unsinkable' Titanic could sink. Imagine the resistance from people who boarded the Titanic with the fervent belief that 'Even God can't sink this ship.' How do you persuade those people to accept your analysis of the situation and offer their cooperation to save their own lives when they had internalized a contrary set of beliefs?

Schools are in trouble; there is no debate about this. Are they sinking? What does this have to do with multicultural education and equity leadership?

Present and Future Demographics

All of the demographic data collected during the past fifteen years affirms that there is a growing trend toward increasing racial, ethnic, and cultural diversity in the United States, and by extension in U.S. schools. The 2000 census showed that although the percentage of African-Americans and American Indians increased slightly, Asian American and Latino groups showed the greatest increase in the decade from 1990 to 2000. Among other things, these shifts demand that we adopt a more nuanced and informed view of race, ethnicity, and culture, because it has become increasingly clear that ignoring the differences between language, culture, and national origin undermines our ability to either acknowledge or serve the best interests of diverse students. For example, students of Southeast Asian origin—Cambodians, Laotians, and Vietnamese—typically are included in the catchall *Asian* racial category, and this perpetuates unfair stereotypes and cultural misunderstandings which can have a negative impact on academic outcomes. Similarly, *Spanish* is often used as a label to lump together all Spanish speaking groups and cultures, and this has sometimes caused unfortunate outcomes in schools and society at large. This also points to the fact that spoken language is sometimes undervalued as an element of culture when in reality language is a crucial aspect of culture; if you devalue the language, you devalue the culture, and potentially, when you devalue the language and the culture, you devalue the people, and in essence, you devalue the child.

In America, language has always been a contentious and divisive issue as is evidenced by positions that valorized English and English speakers, denounced non-English speakers, and argued that speaking English was a precondition for even staying in the country. For example, *English Only* movements that were organized to make English the official language of the United States can be traced back as far as 1868, and have contemporary iterations. Theodore Roosevelt validated these sentiments in 1919 when he said

We have room for but one language here, and that is the English language; for we intend to see that the crucible turns our people out as Americans, of American nationality, and not as dwellers in a polyglot boardinghouse. (Roosevelt, 1919)

Further complicating these demographic trends is the fact that there was a 16% increase in those who identified themselves as members of more than one race. Conversely, the percentage of Whites decreased in that same period, and it is expected that within a few decades, those of European descent will no longer be the numerical majority in America. The full implications of these expected demographic shifts are yet to be understood.

We know that immigration is increasing, and unlike previous immigrants, who were primarily of European descent, most of the recent immigrants are coming from Latin America and Asia. They all bring with them a rich variety of cultural and linguistic diversity. Paralleling the increasing diversity in schools is a troubling pattern of increasing segregation in schools nationwide which has been documented by Orfield and Yun (1999). This means that children from racially and ethnically diverse backgrounds are more likely to be taught in segregated schools. This pattern shows a reversion to past racist practices and erases many of the gains in school integration made between 1954 and 1990. "For Blacks, the 1990's witnessed the largest backward movement since the Brown v. Board of Education decision, and the trend is continuing. For Latinos, the situation has been equally dramatic: Latinos are now the most segregated of all ethnic groups in terms of race, ethnicity and poverty. Despite this trend, there is growing evidence that schools with diverse student populations are good for students of all backgrounds" (Nieto & Bode, 2012, p. 29). While there is so much flux in the racial and ethnic diversity of student populations, the "… nation's teachers have become more monolithic, mono-cultural, and monolingual. For example, as of 2003, 90 percent of public school teachers were white, 6 percent were African American, and fewer than 5 percent were of other racial /ethnic backgrounds" (Nieto & Bode, 2012, p. 29). Among other things, these trends clearly bring new challenges to educators, and move the discussion of diversity beyond the traditional dichotomy of Black vs. White. "We really have had a biracial mindset in dealing with minority education issues. … This [increasing racial and ethnic diversity] is the new reality. We need to shift to a multiethnic focus in education" (Pachon, cited in Reid, 2001 p. 1).

In view of present and future demographics, Howard's statement, "[d]iversity is not a choice, but our responses to it certainly are" (Howard, 2006, p. 2) should represent something of a clarion call for American schools. The fact is that whether or not schools are ready, willing, or able to address the needs of their increasingly diverse student bodies, the challenges that attend these changes are already at their doors. And yet, "[c]rossing boundaries of race, class and culture is a difficult, disruptive even dangerous, transformative process which requires a long-term commitment to fundamental social change. In schools, this translates to sustained systematic efforts to raise the racial consciousness of educators through [major] overhauls of professional development, specifically in the area of multicultural diversity training" (Holmes & Clarke, 2005, p. 12). Rarely does policy, practice, or financing give teachers access to staff development, which is designed to help white educators look deeply and critically at the necessary changes and growth needed to confront the implications of racial boundaries that must be crossed when white instructors teach black or Hispanic children (Howard, 2006). It is also significant that some educators hold on to their belief systems and consequently the stereotypical racial notions about their students unless they are significantly confronted (Warren, 2002). Administrators and teachers must first acknowledge that increasing diversity demands improved cross-cultural communication, and that crossing boundaries is a two-way process. Educators "must cross their own personal boundaries of race, class and culture. This must begin with a thoughtful examination of their own belief systems, and classroom practices if they are to be efficacious and promote the goals of equal educational access for all of their students. But school administration can mirror and reinforce patterns of dominance and subordination found in society [Bates, 1983]" (Holmes & Clarke, 2005, p. 12).

A major paradigm shift in terms of white racial dominance is underway, and American schools and society will be confronted with an analogous psychic shift because America as a nation is evolving, and for some, this amounts to deconstructing (some will argue, destroying) the unique American identity. For some, the sense of cultural loss or cultural disintegration will be unbearable. This will likely create considerable tension, anger, and resentment because America's *story* will change; the major players in the 'master narrative' will take on new roles; the old heroes will die and new ones will be born. A different America will emerge that looks and sounds different from that which is inscribed in America's dream of itself. In his analysis of leadership, Heifetz (1994) makes a point that implicitly links change and cultural adaptation to diversity as well as provides an underlying warning when he says that

[T]he ability to adapt requires the productive interaction of different values through which each member or faction in a society sees reality and its challenges. Without conflicting frames of reference, the social system scrutinizes only limited features of its problematic environment. It operates at the mercy of its blind spots because it cannot prepare for what it does not see. (Heifetz, 1994, p. 33)

America appears to be (and to have been) operating at the mercy of its *blind spots*. Yet, schools cannot afford to enter this dangerous place; to willingly blind themselves to present and future realities. School leaders can choose to lead us to a different future which deals with injustice and social oppression in direct ways using all the tools and resources available to them, or they can leave us unprepared for the seismic demographic and social changes that await us.

In this context, a number of very important issues and questions immediately present themselves:

- Changing demographics mean that Whites will no longer be the numerical majority in America. Will this result in a loss of power, privilege, and control in schools, and how will this affect present school policies and practices?
- If social justice is not a priority in schools now, what will happen when the numerical balance shifts?
- How will increasing racial and ethnic diversity change the debate about multicultural education and social justice pedagogies?
- Will there be a retrenchment or a hardening of negative attitudes regarding diversity?
- Will those in power be willing to learn how to share power with those who have been traditionally marginalized?
- What impact will the disproportionately high percentage of White teachers have on an increasingly diverse student body?
- What impact does cultural dissonance have on the ability of a white teacher to teach students of color?
- What impact does class differences have on the ability of teachers to effectively teach students labeled as 'poor?'
- What impact do class differences have on the ability of administrators to effectively lead schools comprised of students labeled as 'poor'?

These are important questions because although research provides ample evidence that the causes of the achievement gap are complicated by sociohistorical and economic factors, race and culture continue to be significant issues. "Ferguson, (1998) supports the contention that efforts aimed at closing the achievement gap are likely to be significantly undermined unless there is a fundamental change in the belief systems of educators. Belief systems affect the way teachers [and administrators] interact with students as well as the culture of the classroom and the school at large" (Warren, 2002, cited in Holmes & Clarke, 2005, p. 10). White educators sometimes effectively distance themselves from the underlying causes of the problems created by racial and cultural imbalance in their classrooms and schools. This is consistent with research on white priv-ilege which concludes that whites are not accustomed to seeing themselves as racial beings and can "'exist without ever having to acknowledge that reality'" (Howard, 2006, p. 89). However, in the years ahead no educator will have what Howard calls "the luxury of ignorance" (Howard, 2006, p. 11) about race, racial and cultural identity, and their relationship to student success. Overwhelming research shows that schools are failing many students because "[w]e take the students who have less to begin with and then systematically give them less in school. In fact, we give these students less of everything that we believe makes a difference. We do this in hundreds of different ways" (Haycock, 2001, p. 8). Adrienne Rich dramatizes this in a different way when she says

> When those who have the power to name and to socially construct reality choose not to see you or hear you, whether you are dark-skinned, old, disabled, female or speak in a different accent or dialect than theirs, when someone with the authority of a teacher, say, describes the world and you are not in it, there is a moment of psychic disequilibrium, as if you looked into a mirror and saw nothing. (Rich, cited in Maher & Tetreault, 2001, p. 201)

Rich's description of the psychic disequilibrium which can occur if you "*looked into a mirror and saw nothing*" is chilling, but it represents a daily reality for too many American students, and unless things change, many more students will experience this painful and potentially life-changing disorientation. How-ever, the reality is that significant change will not occur unless those in charge *change themselves* first. School leaders need to be open to becoming teachers and learners as well. But how do you persuade those who have the power to move forward; to face their own assumptions which may support oppressive practices and hidden curricula in their schools? How do you persuade those who have the power to enter the dangerous, often risky waters of transforma-tional leadership? How do you move people beyond suspicion, and fear, and self-interest, to challenge beliefs they've internalized over a lifetime? How do you get people to unlearn old biases, and think new thoughts?

Kumashiro (2000) provides a useful framework for school leaders who are committed to equity, and want to implement social justice pedagogies in their schools. The framework is appropriate for teachers, students, policy boards, and especially for school leaders who understand that the work for social jus-tice must *begin* with them. They must also understand that in a changing world, diversity is not a choice, nor is multicultural social justice education. Kumashiro's four principles are:

1. education of the *other* (focus on improving the experiences of students who are *othered*);
2. education about the *other* (focus on what all students—privileged and marginalized—know and should know about the other);
3. education that is critical of privileging and *othering* (focus on examining not only how some groups and identities are *othered* but also on how some groups are favored);
4. education that changes students and society (focus on how oppression begins in discourses that frame how people think, feel, and interact). (Kumashiro, 2000)

Kumashiro's (2000) framework requires a thoughtful interrogation of attitudes and beliefs, and is an important beginning. In addition to belief systems, research shows that "the *deep structure* [italics mine] of schools can also inhibit change in schools. But the concept of deep structure embraces more than schools. It refers to the larger society's widely accepted beliefs regarding what schools are for, how they should function, and what constitutes success. The pervasiveness and complexity of oppressive practices in schools suggests that school systems must be willing to reinvent themselves" (Holmes et al., 2007, p. 102). This echoes Delpit's image of *turning oneself inside out*, and giving up one's personal identity in order to learn what it might feel like to be someone else; a powerful challenge to those who not only choose to lead in diverse settings, but are committed to social justice, and equity leadership. Being willing *to see yourself in the unflattering light of another's angry gaze* is where learning, social change, and true equity leadership begins.

References

Argyris, C., & Schön, D. A. (1974). *Theory in practice: Increasing professional effectiveness*. San Francisco, CA: Jossey-Bass.

Ayers, W., Hunt, J. A., & Quinn, T. (Eds.). (1998). *Teaching for social justice*. New York, NY: The New Press.

Bell, D. (1980). Brown v. Board of Education and the interest-convergence dilemma. *Harvard Law Review, 93*(3), 518–533.

Bell, D. (1992). *Faces at the bottom of the well—The permanence of racism*. New York, NY: Basic Books.

Blackmore, J. (2002). Leadership for socially just schooling: More substance and less style in high-risk, low-trust times? Cited in Marshall, C., & Oliva, M. (2010). *Leadership for social justice* (p. 23). New York, NY: Allyn & Bacon.

Burke, W. W. (2008). *Organization change: Theory and practice*. Los Angeles, CA: Sage Publications.

Cashin, S. (2004). *The failures of integration—How race and class are undermining the American dream*. New York, NY: Public Affairs.

Cherniss, C., Goleman, D., & Bennis, W. (2001). *The emotionally intelligent workplace*. San Francisco, CA: Jossey-Bass.

Delgado, R., & Stefancic, J. (2012). *Critical race theory—An introduction*. New York, NY: New York University Press.

Delpit, L. (1995). *Other people's children: Cultural conflicts in the classroom*. New York, NY: New Press.

Derman-Sparks, L., & the A. B. C. Task Force. (1989). *Anti-bias curriculum tools for empowering young children*. Washington, DC: National Association for the Education of Young Children.

DeRoche, Edward F., & Williams, M. (2001). *Educating hearts and minds: A comprehensive character education framework*. Thousand Oaks, CA: Corwin Press.

DeRoche, Edward F., & Williams, M. (2001). *Educating hearts and minds: A comprehensive character education framework*. Thousand Oaks: Corwin Press.

Einstein, A. (n.d.). *BrainyQuote.com*. Retrieved May 30, 2015 from BrainyQuote.com https://www.brainyquote.com/quotes/quotes/a/alberteins100659.html

Eliot, T. S. (1949). *Notes toward the definition of culture*. New York, NY: Harcourt Press.

Erickson, F. (2010). Culture in society and educational practice. Cited in Banks, C. A. M., & Banks, J. A. (Eds.). (2010). *Multicultural education issues and perspectives* (7th ed., pp. 33–56). New York, NY: John Wiley & Sons Inc.

Foster, W. (1986). *Paradigms and promises: New approaches to educational administration*. Buffalo, NY: Prometheus Books. Cited in Marshall, C., & Oliva, M. (2010). *Leadership for social justice* (p. 20). New York, NY: Allyn & Bacon.

Fullan, M. (2001). *Leading in a culture of change*. San Francisco, CA: Jossey-Bass.

Goleman, D. (1995). *Emotional intelligence: Why it can matter more than IQ*. New York, NY: Bantam Books.

Goleman, D. (2000). Leadership that Gets Results. *Harvard Business Review*. March-April, 2000, p. 78–90.

Goleman, D., Boyatzis, R., & McKee, A. (2002). *Primal leadership*. Boston, MA: Harvard Business School Press.

Grant, C. A., & Ladson-Billings, G. (1997). *Dictionary of multicultural education*. Phoenix, AZ: Oryx Press.

Grant, C. A., & Sleeter, C. (2007). *Turning on learning—Five approaches for multicultural teaching plans for race, class, gender and disability*. Hoboken, NJ: John Wiley & Sons, Inc.

Hale, G. E. (1998). *Making whiteness—The culture of segregation in the South, 1890–1940*. New York, NY: Pantheon Books.

Haycock, K. (2001). Closing the achievement gap. *Educational Leadership (Helping All Students Achieve Pages)*, 58(6), 6–11.

Heaney, T. (1984). Action, freedom and liberatory education, in Merriam, S. B. (Ed.), *Selected writings on philosophy and education* 113–122. Malabar, FL: Robert E. Krieger.

Heifetz, R., & Linsky, M. (2002). *Leadership on the line staying alive through the dangers of leading*. Boston, MA: Harvard Business School Press.

Heifetz, R. A. (1994). *Leadership without any easy answers*. Boston, MA: Harvard Business School Press.

Holland, J. (2016). The average black family would need 228 years to build the wealth of a white family today. *The Nation*, August 8, 2016. Retrieved from https://www.thenation.com/article/the-average-black-family-would-need-228-years-to-build-the-wealth-of-a-white-family-today/

Holmes, G. G. (2007). Hidden in plain sight: The problem of ageism in public schools, in Kumashiro, K. (Ed.), Six lenses for anti-oppressive education. New York: Peter Lang.

Holmes, G. G., & Clarke, S. (2005). To choose or not to choose: Equity in Connecticut in the wake of Sheff vs. O'Neill. *Equity and Excellence*, 38(1), 3–13.

Holmes, G. G., Davies, Mark R., & Hirsch, J. (2007). Conversation: Unearthing Hidden Curriculums, in Kumashiro, K. & Ngo, B. (Eds.), Six lenses for anti-oppressive education: partial stories, improbable conversations. New York: Peter Lang.

Howard, G. (2006). *We can't teach what we don't know*. New York, NY: Teachers College Press.

Jay, M. (2003). Critical race theory, multicultural education, and the hidden curriculum of hegemony. *Multicultural Perspectives*, 5(4), 3–9.

King, J. E. (1991). Dysconscious racism. *The Journal of Negro Education*, 60(2), 133–146.

Kivel, P. (2011). *Uprooting racism—How white people can work for social justice*. Gabriola Island, BC: New Society Publishers.

Kroeber, A. L., & Kluckhohn, C. (1952). *Culture*. New York, NY: Meridian Books.

Kumashiro, K. K. (2000). Toward a theory of anti-oppressive education. *Review of Educational Research*, 70(1), 25–53.

Ladson-Billings, G. (1995). Toward a theory of culturally relevant pedagogy. *American Educational Research Journal*, 32(3), 465–491.

Ladson-Billings, G. (2010). Just what is critical race theory and what's it doing in a nice field like education? *International Journal of Qualitative Studies in Education*, 11(1), 7–24. Retrieved June 3, 2017 from http://dx.doi.org/10.1080/095183998236863

Ladson-Billings, G., & Tate, W. F. (1995). Toward a critical race theory of education. *Teachers College Record*, 97(1).

Ladson-Billings, G., Tate, W. F. (1995). Toward a Critical Race Theory of Education. *Teachers College Record* 47–68, Volume 97, Number 1, Fall 1995.

Ledesma, M. C., & Dolores Calderón, D. (2015). Critical race theory in education—A review of past literature and a look to the future. *Qualitative Inquiry*, 21(3), 206–222.

Loewen, J. (1995). *Lies my teacher told me, everything your American history teacher got wrong*. New York, NY: Simon and Schuster.

Maher, F. A., & Tetreault, M. K. T. (2001). *The feminist classroom, dynamics of gender, race, and privilege* (p. 201). Oxford: Rowman and Littlefield, Inc.

Marshall, C., & Oliva, M. (2010). *Leadership for social justice*. New York, NY: Allyn & Bacon.

McIntosh, P. (1988). *White privilege and male privilege.* This paper was presented at the Virginia Women's Studies Association conference in Richmond in April 1986 and the American Educational Research Association conference in Boston in October 1986 and discussed with two groups of participants in the Dodge seminars for Secondary School Teachers in New York and Boston in the spring of 1987.

Morrison, T. (1992). *Playing in the dark—Whiteness and the literary imagination*. New York, NY: Vintage Books.

Nader, D. A., & Tushman, M. L. (1989). Organizational frame bending: Principles for managing reorientation. *The Academy of Management Executive, III*(J), 194–204.

Nieto, S., & Bode, P. (2012). *Affirming diversity the sociopolitical context of multicultural education.* Boston, MA: Allyn & Bacon.

Nin, A. (n.a.). Retrieved July 17, 2014 from http://www.quotationspage.com/quote/27655.html

Orfield, G., & Yun, J. T. (1999). *Resegregation in American schools.* Cambridge, MA: The Civil Rights Project Harvard University.

Pachon, H. P. (2001). Cited in Reid, K. S. *U. S. census underscores diversity.* Retrieved April 17, 2014 from http://www.edweek.org/ew/articles/2001/03/21/27census.h20.html?tkn=LWPF2QvVaOSixfYhYO4ATapUcGL6UbfAiryN&print=1

Palmer, P. J. (1990). *Leading from within (this essay is a transcription of an address by Parker J. Palmer given at the Annual Celebration Dinner of the Indiana Office of Campus Ministries in March 1990 with support from Lily Endowment Inc.).* Washington, DC: The Servant Leadership School.

Palmer, P. J. (1998). *The courage to teach.* San Francisco, CA: Jossey-Bass.

Pew Research Center. (2016). On view of race and inequality blacks and whites are worlds apart. *A report by the Pew Research Center,* June 27, 2016. Retrieved from http://www.pewsocialtrends.org/2016/06/27/on-views-of-race-and-inequality-blacks-and-whites-are-worlds-apart/

Reid, K. S. (2001). *U. S. census underscores diversity.* Retrieved April 17, 2014 from http://www.edweek.org/ew/articles/2001/03/21/27census.h20.html?tkn=LWPF2QvVaOSixfYhYO4ATapUcGL6UbfAiryN&print=1

Rich, A. (n.a.). Cited in Maher, F. A., & Tetreault, M. K. T. (2001). *The feminist classroom, dynamics of gender, race and privilege* (p. 201). Oxford: Rowman and Littlefield, Inc. p. 201.

Rogers, D. (2001). *Good for business but insufficient for social change.* Retrieved April 17, 2010 from http://www.foodsecurity.org/race/drvdiversity.pdf

Roosevelt, T. (1919). *Letter from Theodore Roosevelt to Richard Hurd,* January 3, 1919. Retrieved August 31, 2015 from http://www.ushistory.org/betsy/flagquot.html

Salovey, P., & Mayer, J. D. (1990). *Emotional intelligence.* Amityville, NY: Baywood Publishing Co.

Scheurich, J. J., & Skrla, L. (2003). *Leadership for equity and excellence.* Thousand Oaks, CA: Corwin Press.

Sleeter, C. (1996). *Multicultural education as social activism.* Albany, NY: State University of New York Press.

Takaki, R. (1993). *A different mirror, a history of multicultural America.* New York, NY: Back Bay Books/Little Brown and Company.

Tate, W. F. (1997). Critical race theory and education: History, theory, and implications. *Review of Research in Education, 22,* 195–247.

Tatum, B. D. (1997). *Why are all of the black kids sitting together in the cafeteria? And other conversations about race.* New York, NY: Basic Books.

Thomas, R. R. (1990). From affirmative action to affirming diversity. *Harvard Business Review,* 107–117. Retrieved March 21, 2012 from http://www.radford.edu/~kvharring/docs/HRM-Docs/3affirmingdiv.pdf

Warren, S. (2002). African American students in schools: Research and effective instructional practices. *Educational Horizons, 80*(3), 109–116.

Wellman, D. (1993). *Portraits of white racism* (2nd ed.). Cambridge: Cambridge University Press.

· 8 ·

TEACHER LEADERSHIP FOR EQUITY
AND SOCIAL JUSTICE

Teachers' lives are enriched and energized in many ways when they actively pursue leadership opportunities. Rather than remain passive recipients—even victims—of what their institutions deal to them, teachers who lead help to shape their own schools and thereby, their own destinies as educators.

—Roland Barth

"The teacher who leads: gets to sit at the table with grownups as a first-class citizen in the schoolhouse rather than remain the subordinate in a world full of superordinates ..."

—Roland Barth

"Not too long ago, I heard a teacher describe his world as 'rushed, crunched, and isolated'. I'm tempted to add two other adjectives, 'distrusted,' and 'undervalued.'"

—Merrow

"I'm just a teacher. If you want to talk with a leader, he's down the hall in the principal's office."

—Anonymous

There exists a sharp and disturbing contradiction between the public adulation of teachers and the teaching profession, and the self-deprecation implied in the statement, "I'm just a teacher ..." (Barth, 2001, p. 443). "I'm *just* a teacher ..." belittles and undervalues the role, and implies a striking sense of humility and self-abasement about what teachers do, and how valuable, and valued they believe their work is. This teacher's words which "aggravate a very sore spot within our profession" (Barth, 2001, p. 443) and display a hint of cognitive dissonance represent an attitude which is not unique among teachers. This seemingly casual statement reveals a level of tension and confusion between the narrowly defined, formal, content-driven role of *teacher*, and the informal, *de facto* reality of what teachers actually *do* every day for their students, their colleagues, their schools, and, ultimately, for society. It can be argued that it reflects some degree of cognitive dissonance especially when teachers know the significance of the many and varied roles they play in schools every day, and the powerful impact they can and do have on the lives of their students. Ironically, this knowledge of the difficult and important work that they do outside of their formal roles can coexist with attitudes which diminish and delimit their stature in the school structure and in the educative process. Moreover, this tension and confusion between the formal and informal role of *teacher* is further complicated when we introduce the concept of teacher leadership. This is partly because in our society, and in our schools, "we are clearly uncomfortable claiming to be a leader. [And] [w]e are even more uncomfortable with those who claim to be leaders" (Barth, cited in Ackerman & McKenzie, 2007, p. 10). This is true despite the fact that so many of the greatest 'teachers' have also been the greatest 'leaders,' including Gandhi, Socrates, Plato, and Martin Luther King. Yet there appears to be something deeply embedded in school culture that is antithetical, or even hostile, to the idea of teacher leadership. This may be accounted for, in part, by the shallow way teacher leadership has been exploited by some school administrators. In 1993, Troen and Boles argued that when school principals present a façade of teacher leadership only for public consumption, it is "'somewhat like calling a banana republic a democracy if a few of its citizens are allowed to vote'" (Troen and Boles, cited in IEL, 2001, p. 9). The irony is that most research on school reform calls for broader and more well-defined leadership responsibilities for teachers, but "[a]s long as school leadership remains mostly top-down and hierarchical, there is little chance that teachers will ever be more than fringe players—available as a resource when called upon, but seldom directly and continuously involved in decisions of substance" (Troen and Boles, cited in IEL, 2001, p. 9).

There are many conceptions of what a teacher leader is. It could be as simple as "initiatives by teachers which improve schools and learning" (Barth, cited in Ackerman & McKenzie, 2007, p. 10) or as comprehensive as the

Teachers as Leaders Framework developed by Crowther, Kaagan, Ferguson, and Hann (2002), which defines a teacher leader as one who can

Convey convictions about a better world by
- Articulating a positive future for students
- Contributing to an image of teachers as professionals who make a difference

Facilitate communities of learning by
- Encouraging a shared, school-wide approach to core pedagogical processes
- Approaching professional learning as consciousness-raising about complex issues
- Synthesizing new ideas out of colleagues' discourse and reflective activities

Strive for pedagogical excellence by
- Showing genuine interest in students' needs and well-being
- Continuously developing and refining personal teaching gifts and talents
- Seeking deep understanding of significant pedagogical practices

Confront barriers in the school's culture and structures by
- Standing up for children, especially disadvantaged and marginalized individuals and groups
- Working with administrators to find solutions to issues of equity, fairness, and justice
- Encouraging student "voice" in ways that are sensitive to students' developmental stages and circumstances

Translate ideas into sustainable systems of action by
- Working with the principal, administrators, and other teachers to manage projects that heighten alignment between the school's vision, values, pedagogical practices, and professional learning activities
- Building alliances and nurturing external networks of support

Nurture a culture of success by
- Acting on opportunities to emphasize accomplishments and high expectations
- Encouraging collective responsibility in addressing school-wide challenges
- Encouraging self-respect and confidence in students' communities
  - (from Crowther et al., 2002, pp. 4–5)

or, the conception of a teacher leader can be as deceptively simple, and personal as Ginott's:

> I've come to the frightening conclusion that I am the decisive element in the classroom. It's my personal approach that creates the climate. It's my daily mood that makes the weather. As a teacher, I possess tremendous power to make a child's life miserable or joyous. I can be a tool of torture or an instrument of inspiration. I can humiliate, hurt or heal. In all situations, it is my response that decides whether a crisis will be escalated or de-escalated and a child humanized or de-humanized. (Ginott, cited in Barth, 2001, p. 444)

However, all of the conceptions of teacher leader become far more complex and nuanced when we add equity and social justice dimensions to the expectations for effective schools and successful teacher leadership. Adams, Bell, and Griffin offer a useful framework for embedding social justice in schools in *Teaching for Diversity and Social Justice* (1997):

> The goal of social justice education is full and equal participation of all groups in a society that is mutually shaped to meet their needs. Social justice includes a vision of society in which the distribution of resources is equitable and all members are physically and psychologically safe and secure. We envision a society in which individuals are both self-determining (able to develop their full capacities), and interdependent (capable of interacting democratically with others). Social justice involves actors who have a sense of their own agency as well as a sense of social responsibility toward and with others and the society as a whole. (p. 3)

With this as a backdrop, the chapter looks at teacher leaders through a different lens, a lens colored by a focus on social justice, and equity-driven teacher leadership. It interrogates social patterns of power and oppression which affect the belief systems of teachers, and argues that schools and teachers must move beyond a rhetorical embrace of 'diversity' to the development of substantive, action-oriented initiatives that have the capacity to reform and transform schools in ways that reverberate throughout society. Therefore, the chapter explores the efficacy of teacher shared leadership, and school effectiveness, not just in the context of general school improvement, in the form of standardized test scores, grades, or ephemeral allusions to school culture, but by focusing equal attention on how well schools respond to student diversity, promote social justice initiatives, and embody authentic teacher shared leadership. An 'effective' school, I argue, is one that operates from a frame of reference that keeps equity and social justice at the heart of its mission, and allows this value to inform school policy and practice on all levels, especially the leadership level. This means a reconsideration of what we mean when we say 'effective schools.' For example, this means, showing the correlation between institutional discrimination, and inequitable outcomes on standardized tests, the achievement gap, teacher preparation, classroom practice, and teacher leadership. It means taking a careful look at both the special challenges teacher leaders face because they are *teachers*, and not administrators or district policymakers, and the unique opportunities they have to transform school and society in substantive ways. This chapter also challenges the notion that a teacher can be considered 'excellent' without adopting pedagogy that helps develop a critical consciousness, and "empower[s] young people to criticize the emphasis on efficiency and efficacy as primary values—instead of justice and equality ... [and that opens] students to the possibility that there may be more fulfillment to be discovered in living in a just society than in an arrantly inequitable one ..." (Maxine Greene, cited in Ayers, 1998, p. xxxi). Finally, the chapter will examine research on leadership theory, especially distributed leadership theory, the change process and effective leadership practices as they specifically relate to teacher leadership.

In their groundbreaking work, *Awakening the Sleeping Giant: Helping Teachers Develop as Leaders* (2001), Katzenmeyer and Moller introduce an ironic metaphor to dramatize both the power and the dormancy of teacher leadership. Their research revealed an interesting paradox about teachers as leaders: few people acknowledged that teachers *could* be leaders, but when asked, many teachers strongly identified with leadership roles in their schools. They described informal job-related activities in which they functioned as literacy coaches, mentors, staff developers, curriculum designers and more. Katzenmeyer and Moller's research shows that since 1996, a variety of circumstances which go beyond individual schools have created the context for a paradigm shift regarding the role of teacher leadership. Some examples are: consistently dismal report cards on the nation's schools (especially student achievement), new stricter mandates for National Board Certification and state licensure, a plethora of school reform initiatives, the increased impetus toward teacher collaboration facilitated by the availability of on-line resources, and expanded research and data collections on teachers and teaching. As a result of the intersection of these and many other circumstances, teacher leadership has become a centerpiece in most discussions of school reform. Findings from a review of decades of research on teacher leadership conducted by York-Barr and Duke (2004) confirm this.

The potential power of this *sleeping giant* is infinitely magnified when we realize that research by Hampel and others reveals that those identified as teacher leaders usually constitute only about 25% of a school's faculty. It's difficult to imagine the positive impact it could have on school reform if that number were doubled. Borrowing a phrase from Ron Edmonds who challenged the educational establishment in 1978 by declaring that "all children can learn," Roland Barth offers what he calls "an equally revolutionary idea: All teachers can lead" (Barth, 2001, p. 444). Barth contends that "all teachers harbor leadership capabilities waiting to be unlocked and engaged for the good of the school" (Barth, 2001, p. 444). Moreover, good teachers are leaders not only in their classrooms, but their leadership can potentially be felt school-wide and district-wide. In fact, schools could not operate effectively without some level of teacher leadership. In some cases, this is a formal title such as coach, chairperson, lead teacher, etc. But in most cases, teacher leadership is exercised without a formal title or explicit recognition from either their peers or supervisors.

In a testament to the importance and pervasiveness of teacher leadership, there has been an explosion of interest and formal research on it. This is validated by the Interstate School Leaders Licensure Consortium (ISLLC) which published "The Teacher Leader Model Standards" in 2011. The consortium identified seven domains which describe the many dimensions of teacher leadership:

Domain I: Fostering a Collaborative Culture to Support Educator Development and Student Learning
Domain II: Accessing and Using Research to Improve Practice and Student Learning
Domain III: Promoting Professional Learning for Continuous Improvement
Domain IV: Facilitating Improvements in Instruction and Student Learning
Domain V: Promoting the Use of Assessments and Data for School and District Improvement
Domain VI: Improving Outreach and Collaboration with Families and Community
Domain VII: Advocating for Student Learning and the Profession
                        (ISLLC, 2011, The Teacher Leader Model Standards, p. 9)

To some degree, these are skills and behaviors that are an integral part of the daily work of most teachers, but what is often missing is an acknowledgement by either the school establishment, or by individual teachers that what they do constitutes *leadership*, and that this leadership is an essential element in the day-to-day life of a school.

Since the 1980s, although discussions of teacher professionalism, and the teaching profession in general, analyzed the role of teachers with the main goal of attracting and retaining excellent teachers who could improve and revitalize the profession, there were other interesting findings. Patterns of teacher leadership emerged from the research, and there was a growing awareness of the informal leadership roles assumed by teachers which were often unacknowledged or taken for granted. Among other things, York-Barr and Duke found that the alignment of the concepts of *teacher* and *leader* is consistent with the focus on individualism and individual empowerment, which reside in the heart of the *American* identity. "Specifically, the concept of teacher leadership suggests that teachers rightly and importantly hold a central position in the ways schools operate and in the core functions of teaching and learning." Although this is not a new concept, "what is new are increased recognition of teacher leadership, visions of expanded teacher leadership roles, and new hope for the contributions these expanded roles might make in improving schools" (Smylie & Denny, cited in York-Barr & Duke, 2014, p. 255). Moreover, an increasing focus on organizational structures in schools, leadership theory, and teacher efficacy highlighted the different roles of all members of an organization, and has led to more analysis of the many and varied roles teachers play in improving the day-to-day life of schools and more specifically in overall school improvement. However, despite an abundance of evidence of the many ways teachers function in leadership capacities, and the increasing recognition of the importance of teacher leadership in the day-to-day running of schools, as well as in school reform, it is still difficult to state definitively what teacher leadership is. This is due in part to the fact that "teacher leadership research continues to be idiosyncratic in nature, lacking an overarching conceptual framework and common theoretical underpinnings" (York-Barr & Duke, 2014, p. 287). Clearly, the concept of teacher leadership is still being defined, and although this can be seen as a dynamic process that holds promise for the future, the evolving nature of what teacher leadership is and how to harness its power poses particular challenges in regard to school equity.

Teacher Leadership for Equity and American Democracy

"[E]ducation then, is … a unique and essential human endeavor; … [It is a] concern for social justice … and … our nation cannot continue to function as a democracy in the absence of social justice."

—Edmund W. Gordon

Although it often seems to be, the link between equity, social justice, democracy, and public education should *not* be controversial, because equity and social justice are implicit in the basic American values of fairness and equal access. As Maxine Green points out, "Americans are taught to take pride, after all, in being the nation founded on a commitment to 'life, liberty, and the pursuit of happiness' (no longer presumably, for white male property owners alone), a belief in human rights and in conceptions of equity variously articulated by our presidents and the Supreme Court justices" (Greene, cited in Ayers, 1998, pp. xxxi–xxxii). This suggests that most educators enter the field guided by a common, even fixed, idea about their purpose and mission.

This is partly because the beliefs that the main purpose of public education is *to equip our citizens to believe in, and to participate fully in, our democratic system* are deeply inscribed in national, state, and local documents about the purpose of education.

The following excerpts which describe the Civics or Citizenship Education Standards and Curriculum Frameworks from several states in different regions of the country are taken from data collected by the Education Commission of the States. They are connected by a common reverence for democracy and the inculcation of democratic principles in state-mandated curricula:

- **Alabama**—content standards for representative democracy ... evaluating the responsibilities of citizens, including civic responsibilities such as obeying the law, paying taxes, being informed, participating in the political process through such activities as voting ...
- **Arizona**—understand the foundations, principles, and institutional practices of the United States as a representative democracy and constitutional republic ... understand the importance of each person as an individual with human and civil rights and our shared heritage in the United States ... understand politics, government, and the responsibilities of good citizenship.
- **Connecticut**—Students will apply knowledge of the U.S. Constitution, how the U.S. system of government works and how the rule of law and the value of liberty and equality have an impact on individual, local, state and national decisions ... Students will demonstrate knowledge of the rights and responsibilities of citizens to participate in and shape public policy, and contribute to the maintenance of our democratic way of life ...
- **Delaware**— "... preparing young people to become informed and active citizens, who accept their responsibilities, understand their rights, and participate actively in society and government." ... examine the structure and purposes of governments with specific emphasis on constitutional democracy ...
- **Kansas—Mission Statement:** ... enable students to actively participate as informed citizens ... the civic values of the American people, and the rights, privileges, and responsibilities of becoming active participants in our representative democracy.
- **Kentucky** "... equips students to understand the nature of government and the unique characteristics of American representative democracy, including its fundamental principles, structure, and the role of citizens ..." "... understand the democratic principles of justice, equality, responsibility, and freedom and apply them to real-life situations."
- **Louisiana**— "... understanding of the ideals, rights, and responsibilities of active participation in a democratic republic that includes working respectfully and productively together for the benefit of the individual and the community; being accountable for one's choices and actions and understanding their impact on oneself and others; knowing one's civil, constitutional, and statutory rights; and mentoring others to be productive citizens and lifelong learners." ... "Students develop

an understanding of the structure and purposes of government, the foundations of the American democratic system. ..."

- **Maine**— "... learn the constitutional principles and the democratic foundations of national, state, and local systems and institutions ... learn how to exercise the rights and responsibilities of participation in civic life ..." "... understand the historical development and current status of the fundamental concepts and processes of authority, power, and influence, with particular emphasis on democratic skills and attitudes necessary to become responsible citizens."

Clearly, there is a common vocabulary and a consistent theme which links these state standards and shows that implicit in the ideal of democracy is the concept of human rights and a cluster of individual freedoms which are constitutionally guaranteed for every American citizen. Yet, despite the apparent unanimity in the various state standards, there is a great deal of evidence which calls into question whether as a nation we have more than a rhetorical commitment to these principles, and how well we are succeeding in transmitting them to the students in our schools. Despite the national celebration of its unique connection to social justice, rooted in the democratic ideals at the heart of what many call *American exceptionalism*, most initiatives designed to embed equity and social justice in schools are labeled *reform* efforts. The irony is that when we refer to school *reform*, it implies the adoption of ideas, policies, values, or changes that may be considered radical, different, and unfamiliar, and outside of mainstream ideology about the role of schools and teaching. This seems counter to the pledged ideal of *justice for all* unless democracy and justice are non sequiturs.

One important and troubling barometer of our degree of success is evident in recent American voting patterns. Statistics from the Federal Election Commission show that significant percentages of those eligible to vote choose to disregard this democratic privilege/obligation despite the wide range of available courses in history, social studies, and civics to which students are exposed during the course of their education in American schools. For example, research shows that in more than half of the national elections held between 1960 and 2008, less than 50% of those eligible to vote did so (Federal Election Commission). In addition, "between 1972 and 1986, voter turnout in Presidential elections fell by 20%, to just 32%" (Barth, 2001, p. 444). This calls into question how well we have been taught and have learned the lessons of democracy. It also calls into question how well schools are presently teaching these values to our students. According to Roland Barth, part of the reason that "... not many students are graduating from our schools really believing in, let alone practicing democracy" (Barth, cited in Ackerman & McKenzie, 2007, p. 12) is because schools are run by what he calls "benevolent dictators." Students learn daily though a 'hidden curriculum' that "democracy is a fraud" (Barth p. 12 cited in Ackerman). In the end, "the hidden curriculum trumps the overt curriculum" (Barth, 2001, p. 444). Moreover,

> If the primary purpose of public schools is to support democracy, then schools should be structured around a democratic model. This model is important not only for teachers, but also for students, parents and other community members. Shared vision and shared leadership reflect the tenets of democracy by relying on the talents of all members of the school community, rather than just those of an elite group of teacher leaders. (Katzenmeyer & Moller, 2001, p. 26)

However, rather than modeling democratic principles in which individualism and individual effort are valued, and rewarded, schools are systems that thrive on conformity, repetition (of classes, use of textbooks, ritualistic interactions between teachers and students, parents and students, teachers and administrators, etc.), and top-down controls which proscribe what a teacher can and cannot do, and how free a teacher is to learn and grow professionally. This can be seen as a challenge to the primacy of democracy in the minds of students, and teachers as well, and it has implications for how well we are teaching and modeling other important democratic values like equity and social justice. For example, if we can deduce that students are internalizing a shallow commitment to democracy, by extension, they also may have internalized an equally shallow commitment to the basic democratic principles which schools espouse. For teachers, "[t]he enemy of teaching for social justice is 'The Real World', which is characterized as hard, competitive, and unrelenting in its pursuit of personal gain and perpetuation of bias and institutional and economic inequities" (Kohl, cited in Ayers et al., 1998, p. 285). The question is: *Do educators and policymakers mean what they say when they routinely invoke democracy as the foundation for the mission of public schools?* One answer can be found in the history of the American school system.

Spring (2007) and others have pointed out that in America, principles of democracy have always coexisted with social injustice in the form of racism, bigotry, and discrimination. James Baldwin calls it part of an 'illusion,' a 'myth' about America

> to which we are clinging which has nothing to do with the lives we lead ... this collision between one's image of oneself and what one actually is, is always very painful and there are two things you can do about it, you can meet the collision head on

and try to become what you really are or you can retreat and try to remain what you thought you were, which is a fantasy. ... (Baldwin, 1961, p. n.a)

These parallel and conflicting streams of thought are evident in American society and more importantly in the development of the present-day American school system. In other words, for some, democracy and racism are *not* conflicting values, and this is evident in laws and social policies that were exclusionary and racist. For example, in *Civil Ideals* Roger Smith contends that many historians tend to ignore the racist thinking that influenced the formation of many American laws despite the fact that America has a long history of discrimination and bigotry. He concludes that, "for 80% of U.S. history, American laws declared most people in the world legally ineligible to become U.S. citizens solely because of their race, original nationality, or gender ... [and] [f]or at least two-thirds of American history, the majority of the domestic adult population was also ineligible for full citizenship for the same reasons" (Smith, cited in Spring, 2007, p. 9). This is evidence that America simply was not comfortable with the diversity that it uses to define itself as a nation. "In an individual, this disparity would be called cognitive dissonance; in a nation, it becomes a [troubling] psychosis which has broader implications" (Holmes, 2009, p. 134).

Whether we're talking about literal death through hate-filled violence against individuals or groups during racial or cultural conflicts, or the figurative 'death' one experiences when equal access to opportunities for personal and professional growth is aborted in childhood (or even before birth), the cost of this national psychosis is incalculable. Whether looked at through the prism of America's bloody past or through the prism of the present, there is indisputable evidence that American Democracy is fraught with contradictions which challenge many of the lofty ideals and mask a tragic reality. Therefore, "[u]nderstanding how ... democracy and equality are compatible with racism and religious bigotry in some people's minds is key to understanding American violence and the often tragic history of education" (Spring, 2007, p. 9).

Significant contradictions were always evident in the history of American education. For example, Horace Mann, known as the Father of the Common School and a staunch champion of public education in the nineteenth century, may be best known for stating that "Education, then, beyond all other devices of human origin, is the great equalizer of the conditions of men—the balance wheel of the social machinery" (cited in Urban & Wagoner, 2009, p. 123), and yet critics argue that the Common School was never the manifestation of enlightened liberal reform that Mann proffered. In fact, in *The Irony of Early School Reform* (1968), Michael Katz argues that despite Mann's position that the purpose of education was to inculcate moral principles and equalize citizens, "the common school was an institution of social control through which the wealthy of Massachusetts society deliberately sought to control the lower classes while appearing to give them the opportunity for social advancement" (cited in Urban & Wagoner, 2009, p. 130). Nieto and Bode's (2012) cogent analysis of both the sociopolitical and historical factors which have impeded or advanced American education deals with this same contradiction. Using a multicultural education framework, they address the historical inequities in education, and explicitly place the responsibility on schools and teachers for creating the conditions for equitable outcomes for students who have been traditionally marginalized and underserved by the nation's schools:

> Although in the ideal sense, education in the United States is based on the lofty values of democracy, freedom, and equal access for all, these examples point out how this has not been the case in reality. Historically, our educational system proposed to tear down the rigid systems of class and caste on which education in most of the world was (and still is) based and to provide all students with an equal education. (Nieto & Bode, 2012, p. 85)

Rather than being the "great equalizer" that Mann described, Nieto and Bode affirm that historically, American education reinforced inequality, and until John Dewey's influence became widespread in the early twentieth century, schools hardened social class stratifications without much opposition. In Dewey's "utopian view, schools could be the answer to social inequality. Over time, however, schools have become one of the major 'sorting' mechanisms of students of different backgrounds. The contradiction between the Deweyian hope for education as a social equalizer and the actual unequal outcomes of schooling is with us even today" (Nieto & Bode, 2012, p. 85) as evidenced by institutional discrimination, tracking, unequal funding, school segregation, and biased testing practices. Clearly, it is important to reclaim the promise of democracy as both an incentive and justification for developing leadership paradigms which embrace social justice and school change that supports equitable outcomes for all students. Teacher leaders have a unique capacity to bring about these changes because they can ensure that social justice initiatives are "democratic and participatory, inclusive and affirming of human agency and human capacities for working collaboratively to create change" (Adams et al., 1997, p. 4).

When schools are not run democratically, everyone loses. Conversely, when schools are run democratically, everyone benefits. When, for example, schools move away from being what Barth refers to as a 'benevolent' dictatorship to a democracy, and teachers are permitted to expand their leadership capacity, "the more students come to believe in, practice and sustain our democratic government" (Barth, 2001, p. 444). In this setting, "teachers are more involved and influential in establishing discipline, selecting textbooks, designing curriculum, and even choosing their colleagues" (Barth, 2001, p. 444) and this has a correlation with high performance, lower incidences of discipline problems, and healthy school climates.

Teacher Shared Leadership—The Creative Redistribution of Power in Schools: How Does This Affect Equity?

"All animals are equal, but some are more equal than others."
—George Orwell

When teacher leadership is invited, acknowledged, valued, and supported, it can open the door to a creative redistribution of power in schools. Professional Learning Communities (PLCs) and Distributed Leadership frameworks are excellent examples of different conceptions of shared leadership which offer a world of possibilities for school reform, academic improvement, and the implementation of social justice pedagogies. The term *professional learning community* means different things to different people.

Susan Hord's (1997) work, which established a baseline for later research on (PLCs), demonstrates the unlimited possibilities they offer for bringing about positive school change. Although often misunderstood as committee work, grade level teams, or weekly planning meetings, etc. Hord and others point out that a *learning community* cannot be encapsulated as a single model; it represents a *process*, or an *approach* to shared leadership, and provides an amorphous infrastructure within which staff development and strategies for school improvement can be developed. Despite the open-ended nature of the design, PLCs do share important common elements:

- Shared values and vision
- Collaborative culture
- Focus on examining outcomes to improve student learning
- Supportive and shared leadership
- Shared personal practice
  (Center for Comprehensive School Reform and Improvement, 2009, p. n.a.)

It's important to note that the key concepts *collaboration*, *support*, *shared personal practice*, and *shared values and vision* undergird this organizational structure with the ultimate goal of improving student learning and school culture. This structure presupposes that all participants have a common, vested interest in coming together, and therefore invites those from different constituencies, specializations, and perspectives to enter the same arena prepared to work together to engage in problem-solving to achieve their common objective(s).

For faculty and staff, the following results have been observed in schools organized around PLCs:

- reduction of isolation of teachers
- increased commitment to the mission and goals of the school and increased vigor in working to strengthen the mission
- shared responsibility for the total development of students and collective responsibility for students' success
- powerful learning that defines good teaching and classroom practice and that creates new knowledge and beliefs about teaching and learners
- increased meaning and understanding of the content that teachers teach and the roles they play in helping all students achieve expectations
- higher likelihood that teachers will be well informed, professionally renewed, and inspired to inspire students
- more satisfaction, higher morale, and lower rates of absenteeism
- significant advances in adapting teaching to the students, accomplished more quickly than in traditional schools
- commitment to making significant and lasting changes and
- higher likelihood of undertaking fundamental systemic change (Hord, 1997 cited in Southwest Educational Development Laboratory [SEDL], 2012, p. n.a.)

Research shows that "[t]eachers who are leaders lead within and beyond the classroom, identify with and contribute to a community of teacher learners and leaders, and influence others toward improved educational practice" (Katzenmeyer & Moller, 2001, p. 5). Most important, in addition to the improvement of the overall school culture, research shows that students have benefited in demonstrable ways when schools are organized around PLCs:

- decreased dropout rate and fewer classes "skipped"
- lower rates of absenteeism
- increased learning that is distributed more equitably in the smaller high schools
- greater academic gains in math, science, history, and reading than in traditional schools and
- smaller achievement gaps between students from different backgrounds (p. 28). (Hord, 1997 cited in SEDL, 2012, p. n.a.)

Although overuse of the African proverb "It takes a village to raise a child" may seem to have stripped it of its power and meaning, it seems appropriate to offer it here because increasingly schools have begun to remake themselves as smaller *communities*, using the '*village*' model it evokes. The focus on shared leadership responsibility is a leveling process, and creates a fertile environment for the growth and nurturance of teacher leadership because the power dynamics in schools have to change in order to maximize progressive school reform efforts. Shared leadership means that traditional hierarchies collapse a bit, and leadership is *stretched* over many stakeholders in the school community, because "[t]he principal cannot be the only instructional leader in the building. Teacher leadership contributes to moving the leadership role from one individual, to a community of professionals committed to improved student learning" (Katzenmeyer & Moller, 2001, p. 2). Guided by effective teacher leadership, schools are more likely to create and sustain those *learning communities* which are often central to school reform efforts. Not only do learning communities potentially facilitate learning among, and between colleagues, they also allow teachers to become more active learners and model learning for their students. And, as Barth points out, "a powerful relationship exists between learning and leading, and [t]eachers who assume responsibility for something they care desperately about ... stand at the gate of profound learning ... Only when teachers learn will their students learn" (Barth, 2001, p. 445). Only when teachers learn will schools change. Only when teachers learn will society change. Only when teachers learn will social justice prevail.

The concept of Distributed Leadership is informed by basic democratic principles, and like the Professional Learning Community concept, it highlights teacher shared leadership, and challenges the traditional hierarchical organizational structures in schools. Spillane (2003) argues that distributed leadership is about leadership *practice* rather than the official roles which are conferred on individuals who are presumed to have specialized training, credentials, and expertise. Often used interchangeably with 'shared leadership,' 'team leadership,' and 'democratic leadership,' distributed leadership is, in a real sense, synonymous with a PLC. However, researchers have sought to clarify and expand on the differences between them. For example, in an attempt to describe distributed leadership, David Jackson (2003) posits the idea that a major paradigm shift is needed to fully grasp its implications because according to him, we should begin to think of schools not as *organizations*, but as *organisms* (Jackson, cited in Lambert & Harris, 2003, p. xiii). Imagistically, the oppositional pairing of these two conceptions of schools causes us to *see* very different things. The former evokes an image of an inflexible structure, stasis, infertility, lifelessness, and implacability, while the latter evokes an image of life, growth, change, potential, and vibrancy. One seems to suggest petrification, and a somewhat grim predictability, while the other suggests a future orientation, buoyant optimism, surprise, discovery, and perhaps the excitement of the unknown. Jackson offers a series of conceptual differences which are important to discuss here not only because they clarify the distinction between learning communities and distributed leadership, but more importantly, they deepen our understanding of teacher leadership, and leadership in general.

Distributed Leadership, like leadership itself, is abstract and paradoxical. Consider the sequence of paradoxes with which scholars are struggling. Change means that something has to be *different*, or be in the process of becoming different, and by distributing leadership, we're implicitly making a commitment to fundamentally redesigning schools and the way they are run. School redesign needs distributed leadership, and yet, school redesign and the development of distributed leadership patterns usually begin with the vision and goal-setting of a single visionary, charismatic 'leader' which in a sense revalidates the importance of the same traditional leadership hierarchies which distributed leadership is designed to dismantle (Jackson, cited in Harris & Lambert, 2003, p. xiv). This final paradox may present the greatest challenge to distributing leadership because it addresses a human instinct or need which is deeply rooted in us, and is likely connected to our deepest fears and insecurities about survival. Whether we attribute it to our spiritual, or social or political need to be delivered, or saved, this strong human impulse is very difficult to challenge. For example, there's always going to be one person who stands out among the group. The vagaries of circumstance will always create opportunities for those 'special' people with 'special' talents or personalities to step forward, to take risks, to solve problems, to make decisions on behalf of the group, and when they succeed, we laud them for their courage, their daring, their success. This seems like a very natural thing to do. And, as a group, we value them both for who they are, and what they've done. Ultimately, we want to elevate them, to reward them, to separate them from our *commonness* because they've demonstrated *uncommon* talent or skill. Our preoccupation with the 'heroics' of leadership may say as much about our needs (perhaps a deep-seated willingness to be led), as it does about who the 'leaders' are and what leadership means.

In a school setting, the question becomes, how do you challenge these very human impulses and the lofty hierarchical structures we have created and institutionalized to keep these special 'leaders' safely protected in their special roles so they can protect or shape or guide us? Another question is: Are we prepared to take the risks of destabilizing these carefully built structures which have traditionally kept us safe and comfortable? The answers are not simple because even though systemic change seems to cry out for a prime-mover; the one whose vision drives the engine of change, distributing leadership and increasing leadership capacity in an organization cannot be focused on improving the leadership capacity of those who are already officially designated as 'leaders' in a traditional leadership hierarchy. Distributing leadership means moving *beyond* the idea of training or re-training a few subordinates for new leadership roles. "It is about creating the spaces, the contexts and the opportunities for expansion, enhancement and growth among all" (Jackson, cited in Harris & Lambert, 2003, p. xvii) because the old organizational structures have to be dismantled and leadership needs to be shared.

Further complicating this process is the fact that leadership cannot be delegated. The traditional delegation of leadership roles reintroduces a hierarchical power structure which is antithetical to systemic change. "[L]eadership is invitational ... [It] has to be bestowed, denoted willfully by those who are to be led [because we] accept leadership. We allow ourselves to be lead ... It is a reciprocal and dynamic relationship" (Jackson, cited in Harris & Lambert, 2003, p. xvii). Moreover, leadership is an abstraction as we have come to understand it, and it does not exist in a literal sense.

> It is an enacted variable, dependent upon interactions between leader, 'follower' and context. If it did exist, as a trait characteristic, independent of followership and context, then effective leaders would be assumed to be equally successful whatever the situation ... Looked at from this perspective, leadership can be seen to be located in the potential available to be released within an organization. In essence, it is the intellectual capital of the organization residing (sometimes dormant or unexpressed) within its members. The role of the 'leader' in this scenario is to harness, focus, liberate, empower and align that leadership towards common purposes and by so doing, to grow, to release and to focus its capacity. (Jackson, cited in Harris & Lambert, 2003, pp. xvi–xvii)

Finally, Jackson points out that distributed leadership brings about what he calls willful *professional emancipation*, because "distributed leadership patterns not only liberate leadership, they are emancipatory for the person in the professional. ... The release and expression of potential through leadership creates the context for personal as well as professional realization" (Jackson, cited in Harris & Lambert, 2003, p. xviii). This professional self-actualization is intimately linked to the establishment of an interactive, interdependent, *community* of learners.

And yet, to quote Robert Frost, *"Something there is that loves a wall"* which is antithetical to the concept of *community*. Frost's commentary on human nature in his signature poem, "The Mending Wall," can be instructive here on several different levels. Using the central image of a crude stone wall which divides the farms of two country neighbors, Frost makes a powerful comment on the strong competing impulses within humans to commune with each other as well as the countervailing impulse to create blockages to human communication. People consciously withdraw from each other, according to the poem, and erect barriers to feeling, and touching and working together. They find differences where there are none, and when conflicts don't exist, they create them to justify and rationalize the need for the walls they themselves build. This self-imposed separation between people is an offence against nature. The poem implies that something mystical seems to repeatedly attempt to breach the wall, causing stones to tumble out of place opening passages or 'gaps' wide enough for two men to pass through if they chose to do so. Yet the men ritually replace the heavy, rough, skin-tearing boulders annually and carefully re-construct the dividing wall. *Something there is that loves* separation, isolation, exclusion, remoteness, independence, autonomy, self-determination, distance. *Something there is that resists* human contact, collaboration, friendship, intimacy, closeness, human relationships. Frost expresses the idea this way: "... We keep the wall between us as we go" because "... Good fences make good neighbors" (p. 194).

It can be argued that schools institutionalize professional separation, and that the competing impulses to which Frost refers are mirrored in traditional school practices where teachers are literally and figuratively *walled* away from each other physically and professionally. However, there's also something in the human spirit that craves human contact and spiritual communion; in a teacher this would be manifested in collaboration, interdependence, interpersonal relationships, open communication, codependence, and sharing.

Frost's powerful commentary on human nature can also be interpreted more broadly as a critique of social patterns that have the effect of *walling* people away from each other, dividing them, and insulating them from each other's human needs, and pain, and shielding them from our common humanity. These little insular walled 'cells' that people create around themselves are breeding grounds for closed-mindedness, and small ways of seeing the world that are steeped in self-interest, and probably chronic denial. Presumably, these are places that would not embrace diversity of thought or feeling, or culture, or lifestyle, or language, or be sensitive to the injustice that might be rampaging outside of their 'walls' no matter how egregious or inhumane. Adrienne Rich describes what it's like when someone has the power to shut you out; to make you a margin-dweller, and refuses to see or hear you. She says

> When those who have the power to name and to socially construct reality choose not to see you or hear you, whether you are dark-skinned, old, disabled, female or speak in a different accent or dialect than theirs, when someone with the authority of a teacher, say, describes the world and you are not in it, there is a moment of psychic disequilibrium, as if you looked into a mirror and saw nothing. (Rich, cited in Maher & Tetreault, 2001, p. 201)

'*Something there is that doesn't love a wall*,' but something there is that does. Although we keep replacing the 'bricks' and 'stones' that divide us, nurturing the seemingly impenetrable silences that prevent us from seeing our common humanity, teachers must continue to try to "break that silence and bridge some of those differences between us, for it is not difference which immobilizes us, but silence. And there are so many silences to be broken" (Lorde, 1977, p. n. a.). New shared leadership paradigms are trying to break the silences and deconstruct the dividing 'walls' in schools. If they succeed, schools can lead the way to "... full and equal participation of all groups in a society ..." (Bell et al., p. 3) where injustice is intolerable. And it will be a *Teacher* who" [p]ressing past their knowns [will] pull us past ours, too. ... A teacher will be there at the beginning" (Ayers et al., 1998, p. 57).

Teacher, Learner, Leader: A Conceptual Framework for Equity-Driven Teacher Leadership

Much of the rhetoric and research about teacher leadership has an outward focus on external things like systemic and organizational reforms, or a collective reconceptualization of what a teacher is and does. However, if we are to awaken the *sleeping giant* of teacher leadership, and harness the limitless power it promises on behalf of school reform, we have to look inward as well because in order for a teacher to be an effective *leader*, she must be a conscientious and continuous *learner* as well. This does not simply mean learning how to *do* new things. It means much more than learning how to successfully tackle new challenges or develop new kinds of collaborations, or navigate through deeper levels of responsibility. It also means turning inward and being a reflective leader, and "thinking about what we do before, during and after our actions ... [Reflection should be] our cognitive guide for growth and development, [and] a way of thinking that we should engage in continuously" (Lambert, 2003, p. 22). This then becomes the interior landscape of teacher leadership and establishes a vital triangular relationship between teacher – learner – leader. Reflection teaches us to acknowledge and listen to our inner voice, and to develop "the inner voice into the public voice" (Lambert, 2003, p. 61). Lambert points out that reflection is a valid form of self-assessment which applies equally to learning and leading. She also argues that "It is a higher form of learning and an essential dimension of constructivist learning, for it is how we integrate what we're coming to know" (Lambert, 2003, p. 61). Therefore, efficacious teacher leadership begins with this interior examination of one's actions because "[t]eachers cannot presume to lead others before they understand themselves" (Ackerman & McKenzie, 2007, p. 67). And, self-understanding is critical to teacher leadership that is equity driven.

Researchers Zeichner and Liston (1996) point out that there are a variety of tangible benefits of reflective practice. For example, there is a correlation between reflective practice and the level of commitment one has to professional development and lifelong learning. When educators are reflective,

> ... inquiry, questioning, and discovery are norms embedded in their ways of thinking and practice (Bright, 1996; Zeichner & Liston, 1996). Their inquiry focuses not only on the effectiveness of their instruction or leadership but also on the underlying assumptions, biases, and values that they bring to the educational process. (York-Barr et al., 2006, p. 15)

It is also important to note that

> Reflective educators consider issues of justice, equity, and morality as they design and reflect on their practice ... [and] [i]nstead of blindly accepting or rejecting new information or ideas, they carefully examine, analyze, and reframe them in terms of specific context variables, previous experiences, and alignment with desired educational goals (Costa & Garmston, 2000; Zeichner & Liston, 1996). (York-Barr et al., 2006, p. 16)

It is impossible to overstate the importance of the *learner* dimension of the *teacher* – *learner* – *leader* triad especially in the context of an equity-driven frame of reference.

Too often in discussions about teacher leadership, the importance of the learner dimension is understated or the reflective dimension is either absent or unexamined, and the focus is on the more visible and easily identifiable roles that a teacher leader plays. It is easy for example, to point to the work of teacher leaders when they engage in curriculum design and staff development, or function as literacy coaches or mentors. These are activities that can be witnessed, documented, and are usually assessed in traditional ways. They show teacher leaders *doing* something, and they can easily be used by institutions as indicators of changes or improvements in policies and practices. Often, the focus is on *what* they are doing, and *how* they're doing it, but the question of *why* they engage in these activities is often dismissed in superficial ways such as—*these teachers are filling a void in the school leadership structure.* On one level, understanding the *why* can mean an in-depth analysis of the school's organizational structure and how it relates to overall educational progress. However, on another level, understanding the *why* involves a deeper, more personal self-analysis that is reflective, self-aware, and perhaps painful. Palmer (1998) elaborates on this idea saying that

> Teaching, like any truly human activity, emerges from one's inwardness, for better or worse. When talking about teaching, we most often ask the what and how questions, and occasionally the why questions ... but seldom, if ever, do we ask the who questions. ... Who is the self that teaches? How does the quality of my selfhood form—or deform—the way I relate to my students, my subject, my colleagues, my world? (Palmer, 1998, p. 4)

This is an important point when we look at teacher leadership in the domain of social justice and equity because it's not enough for educators to make a superficial commitment to social justice and equity by *doing* things which *appear* to support social change such as engaging in a variety of community service activities. A commitment to equity requires something more, especially for teachers who function in a leadership capacity because "[t]eachers cannot presume to lead others before they understand themselves. When they spend time in self-assessment activities, teachers soon recognize, [among other things], that their colleagues may have different sets of values, beliefs, concerns and philosophies, and behaviors or may be at different stages of development" (Ackerman & McKenzie, 2007, p. 67). And, the realization that their colleagues may have different sets of values, beliefs, concerns, philosophies, and behaviors means that when it comes to equity, they first will have to divest themselves of what Howard (2006) calls the *luxury of ignorance* before taking a leadership role in confronting sensitive issues about race, oppression, privilege and social inequities. These are tough issues which will likely make their colleagues uncomfortable, angry, and perhaps resistant to their efforts in ways that their colleagues don't even understand. Yet, the goals of achieving full and equal participation of all groups, ensuring that all members of the community are empowered, physically and psychologically safe and secure, and receive an equitable distribution of resources, is perhaps the hardest and most important work any educator will ever do, and it is consistent with our national commitment to democratizing our students. It is here that teacher leadership can be transformative because research shows that often school administrators *do not* have an accurate understanding of the types or manifestations of inequity *in their own schools*, and because teachers are the most direct and arguably, the most influential pipeline to students. "Furthermore, some researchers (e.g. McKenzie, 2001, 2002; Pollock, 2001) have also found that in typical school settings teachers and administrators often routinely avoid overt discussions of race as a factor in inequitable school outcomes" (Marshall & Oliva, 2010, p. 265). These circumstances create opportunities for teacher leaders to help change a school's culture in meaningful ways. This is where the work of being purveyors of democratic principles and supporters of social justice initiatives and equity pedagogies coalesce, and it is here that self-awareness and reflection can have the greatest impact on transforming schools.

In *Multicultural Education as Social Activism*, Sleeter (1996) shows how complex this transformation process is. She argues that the typical multicultural training which teachers undergo may in the end be counterproductive because

> Many educators conceptualize this task as helping them "unlearn" negative attitudes about race, develop positive attitudes and a knowledge base about race and various racial groups, and learn multicultural teaching strategies. [However] the task is more complex than that … [T]eachers already have considerable knowledge about social stratification in America, and it tends to be fairly conservative. They integrate information about race provided in multicultural teacher education programs into the knowledge they already have, much more than they reconstruct that knowledge. (p. 65)

And reconstructing knowledge and making adaptive changes to practice is more likely to occur through reflection. That is, "thinking about what we do before, during and after our actions" (Lambert, 2003, p. 22). Kinchloe (2004) describes six types of knowledge that inform educational practice. They are: empirical, experiential, normative, critical, ontological, and reflective-synthetic (p. 60). Although it is counterproductive to rank them, *reflective-synthetic knowledge*, is informed by all of the others because it is achieved when individuals are able to reflect on and synthesize multiple types of knowledge to make appropriate decisions about teaching and student learning. Although he is speaking about teacher education, Kinchloe's concept of *reflective-synthetic knowledge* expands our general understanding of reflective practice and is appropriate here. He explains that

> Since our purpose is not to indoctrinate practitioners to operate in a particular manner but to think about practice in more sophisticated ways, a central dimension of teacher education involves reflecting on and examining all of these knowledges in relation to one another. A reflective-synthetic knowledge of education involves developing a way of thinking about the professional role in light of a body of knowledges, principles, purposes, and experiences. In this process, educators work to devise ways of using these various knowledges to perform our jobs in more informed, practical, ethical, democratic, politically just, self-aware, and purposeful ways. At the same time, they work to expose the assumptions about knowledge embedded in various conceptions of practice and in the officially approved educational information they encounter. (p. 62)

Moreover, "[i]n the reflective-synthetic domain practitioners learn they cannot separate their knowledges from the context in which they are generated" (Kinchloe, p. 62) and are therefore likely to subject their various forms of knowledge to more critical scrutiny. This is a difficult and perhaps painful process for both the leaders and those who choose to take this journey because "[s]ignificant learning generally involves fluctuating episodes of anxiety-producing self-scrutiny ... [At the same time, this scrutiny can result in] 'energy-inducing leaps forward in ability and understanding'" (Brookfield, 1992 cited in York-Barr, p. 18). It then becomes more likely that teachers and teacher leaders will develop the capacity to reconstruct knowledge, think new thoughts, challenge internalized biases that they might have preferred to leave unaddressed and unacknowledged, especially feelings about race and personal privilege. Most important, this kind of reflective practice makes it more likely that teachers can lead the way to the development of new pedagogies that support school reforms to bring about equity and social justice.

References

Ackerman, R. H., & McKenzie, S. V. (Eds.). (2007). *Uncovering teacher leadership—Essays and voices from the field.* Thousand Oaks, CA: Corwin Press.

Adams, M., Bell, L. A., & Griffin, P. (Eds.). (1997). *Teaching for diversity and social justice.* New York, NY: Routledge.

Ayers, W. (1998). Foreword—Popular education—Teaching for social justice. In William Ayers, Jean Ann Hunt, & Therese Quinn (Eds.), *Teaching for social justice* (pp. xviii–xxv). New York, NY: The New Press.

Ayers, W., Hunt, J. A., & Quinn, T. (Eds.). (1998). *Teaching for social justice.* New York, NY: The New Press.

Baldwin, J. (1961). *Nobody knows my name.* Retrieved August 31, 2010 from http://www.goodreads.com/quotes/show/316685

Barth, R. (2001). Teacher leader. *Phi Delta Kappan, 82*(6), 443–449.

Bell, L. A. (1997). Theoretical foundations of social justice education. In Adams, M., Bell, L.A., & Griffin, P. (Eds.), *Teaching for Diversity and Social Justice.* New York: Routledge.

Brookfield, S. D. (1995). *Becoming a critically reflective teacher.* San Francisco: Jossey-Bass.

Center for Comprehensive School Reform and Improvement. (2009). *Professional learning communities.* Retrieved January 6, 2012 from http://www.centerforcsri.org/plc/elements.html

Crowther, F., Kaagan, S. S., Ferguson, M., & Hann, L. (2002). *Developing teacher leaders—How teacher leadership enhances school success.* Thousand Oaks, CA: Corwin Press.

Costa, A.L., & Garmston, R. J. (2002). *Cognitive coaching: A foundation for renaissance schools.* Norwood, MA: Christopher-Gordon.

———. *An introduction to the philosophy of education.* New York, NY: The McMillan Company.

Frost, R. (1973). The mending wall. In Richard Ellman & Robert O'Clair (Eds.), *The Norton anthology of modern poetry.* New York, NY: W. W. Norton & Company.

Ginott, H. (1972). *Teacher and child; a book for teachers and parents.* New York, NY: MacMillan.

Gordon, E. W. (1999). *Education & justice a view from the back of the bus.* New York, NY: Teachers College Press.

Greene, M. (1998). Introduction—Teaching for social justice. In William Ayers, Jean Ann Hunt, & Therese Quinn (Eds.), *Teaching for social justice* (pp. xxviii–xlvi). New York, NY: The New Press.

Harris, A., & Lambert, L. (2003). *Building leadership capacity for school improvement.* Maidenhead, PA: Open University Press.

Holmes, G. G. (2009). "Power concedes nothing without demand" educating future teachers about the value of dissent in a democratic society. In M. Gordon (Ed.), *Reclaiming dissent civics education for the 21st century.* Rotterdam: Sense Publishers.

Hord, S. M. (1997). Professional learning communities: What are they and why are they important? *Issues About Change, 6*(1). In Southwest Educational Development Laboratory (2012). Retrieved January 29, 2012 from http://www.sedl.org/change/issues/issues61/outcomes.html

Howard, G. (2006). *We can't teach what we don't know.* New York, NY: Teachers College Press.

Institute for Educational Leadership (IEL). (2001). *Leadership for student learning: Redefining the teacher as leader: School leadership for the 21st century initiative.* A Report of the Task Force on Teacher Leadership April 2001. Retrieved February 22, 2011 from http://www.iel.org/programs/21st/reports/teachlearn.pdf

Interstate School Leaders Licensure Consortium (ISLLC). (2011) *Teacher leader model standards teacher leadership exploratory consortium.* Retrieved March 17, 2012 from http://www.teacherleaderstandards.org/downloads/TLS_Brochure.pdf

Jackson, D. (2000). School improvement and the planned growth of leadership capacity. Paper presented at BERA Conference, Cardiff, September in Alma Harris and Linda Lambert (2003). *Building leadership capacity for school improvement.* Maidenhead, PA: Open University Press.

Katzenmeyer, M., & Moller, G. (2001). *Awakening the sleeping giant helping teachers develop as leaders.* Thousand Oaks, CA: Corwin Press.

Kincheloe, J. L. (2004). The knowledges of teacher education: Developing a critical complex epistemology. *Teacher Education Quarterly*.

Kohl, H. (1999). Social justice and leadership in education: Commentary. *International Journal of Leadership in Education: Theory & Practice—1464–5092, 2*(3), 307–311.

Lambert, L. (2003). *Leadership capacity for lasting school improvement*. Alexandria, VA: Association for Supervision and Curricular Development.

Lorde, A. (1977). *The transformation of silence into language and action*. A speech by Audre Lorde originally delivered at the Lesbian and Literature panel of the Modern Language Association's December 28, 1977. Retrieved February 15, 2012 from http://shrinkingphallus. wordpress.com/the-transformation-of-silence-into-language-and-action-by-audre-lorde/

Marshall, C., & Oliva, M. (2010). *Leadership for social justice*. New York, NY: Allyn & Bacon.

McKenzie, K. B. (2001). White teachers' perceptions about their students of color and themselves as white educators. Doctoral dissertation, University of Texas at Austin.

McKenzie, K. B. (2002). Equity traps. Paper presented at the annual convention of the University Council for Educational Administration, Pittsburgh, PA.

Merrow, J. (2001). *Choosing excellence*. Lanham, MD: Scarecrow Press.

Nieto, S., & Bode, P. (2012). *Affirming diversity the sociopolitical context of multicultural education*. Boston, MA: Allyn & Bacon.

Orwell, G. (1946). *Animal farm* (p. 123). New York, NY: The New American Library.

Palmer, P. J. (1998). *The courage to teach: Exploring the inner landscape of a teacher's life*. San Francisco, CA: Jossey-Bass.

Pollock, M. (2001). How the question we ask most about race in education is the very question we most suppress. *Educational Researcher, 30*(9), 2–12.

Rich, A. (n.a.). Cited in Maher, F. A., & Tetreault, M. K. T. (2001). *The feminist classroom, dynamics of gender, race and privilege* (p. 201). Oxford: Rowman and Littlefield, Inc.

Sleeter, C. (1996). *Multicultural education as social activism*. Albany, NY: State University of New York Press.

Southwest Educational Development Laboratory. (2012). Professional learning communities: What are they and why are they important? *Issues About Change, 6*(1). Retrieved January 29, 2012 from http://www.sedl.org/change/issues/issues61/outcomes.html

Spillane, J. P. (2003). Educational leadership. *Educational Evaluation and Policy Analysis, 25*(4), 343–346.

Spring, J. (2007). *Deculturalization and the struggle for equality*. Boston, MA: McGraw-Hill.

Urban, W. J., & Wagoner, Jr., J. L. (2009). *American education a history*. New York, NY: Routledge. Retrieved July 23, 2012 from http://chronicle.com/temp/email2.php?id=h25rbnmq6fQGX fpzCgFBcwvFnKhvvh82

York-Barr, J., & Duke, K. (2004). What do we know about teacher leadership? Findings from two decades if scholarship. *Review of Educational Research, 74*(3), 255–316.

York-Barr, J., Sommers, W., Ghere, G., & Montie, J. (2006). Reflective practice for continuous learning. In J. York-Barr, W. Sommers, G. Ghere, & J. Montie (Eds.), *Reflective practice to improve schools. An action guide for educators*. CA, Corwin: Thousand Oaks.

Zeichner, K., & Liston, D. P. (1996). *Reflective teaching: An introduction*. New York, NY: Routledge.

· 9 ·

ALL TEACHERS CAN LEAD—
ALL LEADERS CAN LEARN

Making the Case for Social Justice in Teacher and Leader Preparation

The chapter examines the evolution of the image of 'teacher' as a powerless female underling in the educative process, which is being replaced by a more progressive view of teachers as empowered, efficacious *actors* who affect policy and school governance. Complementing this change is the evolving image of school principal as 'monarch.' The chapter shows how these role changes have been spurred by school reform initiatives, changing demographics, and the complex social challenges that face schools. The evolving roles and expectations for teachers and school leaders are promising because this can create a climate that embraces constructive change in terms of teacher and leader preparation. Using a teacher preparation program as a case study, the chapter concludes with a consideration of how teacher and leader preparation programs can integrate equity and social justice into the programs of study for preservice professionals.

Keywords: teachers, school leaders, teacher preparation, NCATE, social justice pedagogy, equity, social justice, in-service teaching, teacher leadership

> *"The idea that you have to advocate teaching for social justice is a sad statement about the moral sensibility in our schools and society."*
>
> —Herbert Kohl

> *"We teach who we are."*
>
> —P. J. Palmer

Roland Barth was channeling educator Ron Edmonds when he offered what he called a 'revolutionary' idea that 'all teachers can lead.' I would like to offer another 'revolutionary' idea that 'all leaders can learn.' That these concepts are deemed 'revolutionary' speaks volumes for how deeply the old, outdated ideas that diminish and delimit the role of 'teacher' and 'leader' are inscribed in our cultural mythology. The image of 'teacher' as a powerless female underling who is fixed, isolated, content driven, and a mere functionary in the educative process is passing into history. This image is being replaced by an enhanced view of teachers as engaged, empowered, efficacious actors who affect school governance, and have "a sense of instrumentality, investment, and membership in the school community. ... These teachers [have] become owners and investors in the school, rather than mere tenants" (Barth, 2001, p. 449). Also passing into history is the idea of a school principal as a veritable 'monarch,' who is comfortably omnipotent, and able to singlehandedly 'save' the school community. Both images are evolving, and moving on parallel and intersecting trajectories. Both images deconstruct old modalities and point the way to new ones. These role changes, spurred by school reform initiatives, changing demographics, complex social challenges, and new areas of school research, provide fertile ground for the development of equity driven pedagogies and social justice initiatives in schools. Among other things, the evolving roles and expectations for teachers and school leaders are promising because of the infinite possibilities they offer for learning to understand and embrace the sociopolitical contexts in which schools are forced to operate, and for leading the way to social change. And yet, these roles and expectations for teachers and school leaders are evolving within a heated sociopolitical climate in which even the term social justice as a goal in teacher preparation is being contested as a form of thought control that is "ideologically freighted" and "necessarily ambiguous" (cited in Wasley, 2006, p. 1) by national organizations like the National Association of Scholars, and the Foundation for Individual Rights in Education. Among some segments of the intellectual community justice has virtually become a 'dirty' word which is evidenced by the 2006 decision by NCATE, a nationally recognized accrediting body for teacher preparation, to alter their guidelines by dropping the term social justice as a dispositional standard for teacher candidates. Prior to this decision, NCATE's target standards urged teacher preparation programs to produce candidates who could "demonstrate the content, pedagogical, and professional knowledge, skills, and dispositions necessary to help all students learn" [with dispositions] "guided by beliefs and attitudes such as caring, fairness, honesty and responsibility, and social justice" (cited in Wasley, 2006, p. 1). This is evidence that the concept of *social justice* has been politicized, and has landed in the middle of a larger philosophical debate which challenges some deeply held democratic ideals. Among other things, the NCATE decision exposes a schism between schools of education which are increasing their commitment to *social justice* as a guiding principle for practitioners, and the accrediting body which establishes the standards to which they adhere.

The primary focus of this chapter is on teacher and leader preparation. Using a research-based framework developed by Capper, Theoharis, and Sebastian (2006) outlined in their article *"Toward a Framework for Preparing Leaders for Social Justice,"* the chapter will take a careful look at the teacher preparation program at Quinnipiac University in Hamden, CT, and present an analysis of how it conceptualizes 'leader,' what this means in terms of leadership for social justice, and to what degree the program appears to incorporate equity and social justice as integral parts of its overall mission.

Although the Capper et al. (2006) framework is specifically directed toward the preparation of school leaders, it is an equally useful instrument to examine a teacher preparation program because of its focus on diversity, and social justice pedagogy and advocacy. Moreover, there is an obvious overlap between teacher and leader preparation since most, if not all, administrator candidates are required to earn a teaching certificate, and have teaching experience before admission to most leadership programs.

The choice of the Master of Arts in Teaching program at Quinnipiac as a case study is strategic. First, I am a former professor of education at Quinnipiac University, I and taught and helped to develop, the diversity class offered to preservice teachers, and I will incorporate excerpts from anonymous student journals to provide a more personal context for the analysis. Additionally, the Master of Arts in Teaching program, is inspired by the *teacher – learner – leader* model, and is of particular interest not only because of its stated commitment to social justice, or because it embraces the *teacher, learner, leader* model, but also because this model highlights the *leader* domain. This allows me to align it with the Capper et al. (2006) framework in discernible ways. Guided by Quinnipiac's Conceptual Framework, the analysis will not attempt a comprehensive review of the entire program since that would entail an evaluation of the overall curricular structure including the scope and sequence of all coursework in the different programs. Instead, this analysis is limited to whether or not the Conceptual Framework articulates a viable commitment to equity and social justice that can be translated to in-service practice as it relates to teacher leadership and social justice pedagogies.

The chapter begins with a detailed description of the Capper et al. (CTS) framework because it is being used as a lens to evaluate whether or not the program can be considered a viable model for preparing teacher candidates to be effective *teachers, learners,* and *leaders* for social justice. Finally, the chapter considers how well the Quinnipiac program is aligned with the general goals for social justice education and social justice leadership as articulated by various scholars and advocates for equity-driven school leadership.

The guiding questions for the analyses are: Does Quinnipiac's Conceptual Framework have most of the elements needed to move social justice, and equity from a pro forma, rhetorical commitment to explicit advocacy for positive changes in schools and society? and, Does the teacher preparation program promote and develop assessable leadership capacity in its candidates, and if so, how?

Because social justice means different things to different people, this evaluation process becomes infinitely more complex because social justice can mean:

- ... full and equal participation of all groups in a society ... [an equitable] distribution of resources ... and [a condition in which] all members are physically and psychologically safe and secure. (Bell, 1997, p. 3)

and

- ... reaching the deep roots of injustice emanating from competitive market forces, economic policies, political practices, and traditions that maintain elite privilege. (Marshall & Oliva, 2010, p. 6)

or

- ... it [is] *a philosophy, an approach, and actions that embody treating all people with fairness, respect, dignity and generosity.* (Nieto & Bode, 2012, p. 12)

These complex, intersecting definitions of social justice provide a context for this analysis.

Toward a Framework for Preparing Leaders for Social Justice: The Capper, Theoharis, Sebastian Framework for Social Justice Leadership Preparation

The *Capper, Theoharis, Sebastian* (CTS) framework which aims to serve as a guide for the evaluation, development, and assessment of leadership preparation programs committed to social justice, is informed by research on critical consciousness and critical pedagogy, and is aligned with the educational theories of Freire and other proponents of critical consciousness and critical pedagogy. Capper et al. (2006) used the following questions to guide their research: "What are the common themes in the literature and research on preparing leaders for social justice?; How can this framework serve as a guide for developing a course, set of courses, or an entire program for preparing leaders to lead socially just schools?; and How can this literature and conceptualization inform future scholarship on administrator preparation?" (Capper et al., 2006, p. 209).

Using available research as a guide, the CTS framework posits the idea that programs preparing educators to be leaders for social justice should be focused on the development of three things: *critical consciousness, knowledge,* and *practical skills.* To achieve these goals, three vital components are necessary. They are: (1) curriculum, (2) pedagogy, and (3) assessment. According to this framework, these are the vehicles that can deliver effective, sustained social justice leadership in schools, and needed school reform. And there needs to be a synergy which enables all of these elements to work together to enhance, reinforce, and support each other in the service of preparing leaders to promote, practice, and institutionalize social justice principles in their school communities. The authors' belief is that a programmatic commitment to social justice should infuse everything, and should represent a world view and shared vision that shapes every aspect of the program design.

This framework posits the idea that social justice needs to be omnipresent; part of the 'DNA' that is deeply encoded in all aspects of any leadership preparation program. Social justice needs to be the connective tissue that not only links the various areas and ideas, but also one that strengthens and nurtures each element of the preparation program individually and collectively. The work of Young and Laible (2000, cited in Capper et al., 2006, p. 211) reinforces this idea, and points out that addressing one categorical area (e.g. knowledge) will likely inform another categorical area (e.g., consciousness). When, for example, "students learn about racial identity development, then write critical papers on their own identity development, [they] gain knowledge about an area (white or racial identity development) and then, engage in critical reflection that raises their consciousness (writing a paper about their own identity development)" (Capper et al., 2006, p. 211).

Critical consciousness, the first, and I would argue, most pivotal component in this paradigm because it lays a foundation for everything else, is sometimes used synonymously with belief systems or dispositions, but here the concept is driven by a social justice perspective. In this Freireian construct, critical consciousness means that leaders need to "possess a deep understanding of power relations and social construction including white privilege, heterosexism, poverty, misogyny and ethnocentrism" (Capper et al., 2006, p. 213).

Knowledge in this model refers to content related to leadership preparation, but more specifically leadership preparation for social justice. "School leaders for social justice need to know about evidence-based practices that can create an equitable school. For example, this knowledge would include understanding the positive and equitable effects of de-tracking and eliminating pull-out programs. It would include developing [a] specific knowledge base around language acquisition, disability, and current research on reading and mathematics curriculum and instruction" (Capper et al., 2006, p. 213).

Skills are the third element in the overarching design. However, for the purpose of this framework, *skills* are not simply interpreted as the performances, or processes, or activities that an administrator will either facilitate, or engage in, but as the "specific skills that leaders require to enact justice. These skills allow them to put their knowledge and consciousness into practice. For example, they need to be able to … use data to lead conversations about equity and school improvement, and hire and supervise staff to carry out these socially just ideas" (Capper et al., 2006, p. 213). The goal is to produce candidates for leadership positions who possess the specific skills necessary to institutionalize social justice policies and practices that challenge systemic inequities.

Table 9.1 outlines the CTS schema for a social justice leadership preparation program:

Table 9.1: Capper, Theoharis, Sebastian: Schema for Social Justice Leadership Preparation.

	Curriculum	Pedagogy	Assessment
Critical Consciousness (i.e., belief systems and dispositions)	**Curriculum** on critical consciousness, social justice, and/or social justice leadership	**Pedagogy** related to critical consciousness related to social justice and/or social justice leadership	**Assessment** related to critical consciousness in regard to social justice and/or social justice leadership

	Curriculum	Pedagogy	Assessment
Knowledge (i.e., knowledge of evidence-based practices that can create an equitable school)	Curriculum about knowledge related to social justice and/or social justice leadership	Pedagogy related to knowledge of social justice and/or social justice leadership	Assessment related to knowledge in regard to social justice and/or social justice leadership
Skills (i.e., skills needed to enact justice; translate knowledge and consciousness into practice)	Curriculum focused on skills related to social justice and/or social justice leadership	Pedagogy related to development of skills connected enacting social justice and/or social justice leadership	Assessment related to knowledge in regard to social justice and/or social justice leadership

Capper et al. (2006), are careful to define the major terms in their framework to avoid confusion, and to avoid trivializing or compromising the outcomes they expect their framework to achieve. Accordingly, every aspect of a leadership preparation program should be designed to prepare leadership candidates to enact change, not to nurture and maintain the status quo and existing power relations in schools and society. The clarifying terminology also distinguishes it from other models that have a social justice orientation, but without a persistent and explicit focus on giving prospective school leaders the tools to become change agents in their schools and by extension in society at large. For example, Capper et al. conceive of leadership and the leadership development process, as transformative on several different levels. This framework hopes to transform the way leadership candidates, think about themselves, first as individuals, and then as social beings who must define their existence in relation to others. This also means redefining the role of leader by seeing it through the prism of social justice. From this vantage point, leadership looks different. School excellence looks different. For example, schools that are well managed, and boasting high scores on standardized tests, and a highly trained professional teaching staff could not be considered excellent if they simultaneously engaged in unfair practices which systematically marginalized or disenfranchised some of their students. For example, a school could not be considered *excellent* if it facilitated the school-to-prison pipeline for some students of color through racialized disciplinary policies that made school what Senator Dick Durbin called a 'gateway' to the criminal justice system. In the CTS framework, this would never happen because, leaders, would have developed a critical consciousness that transformed their perceptions of what justice is and is not, and they would have developed the insight to see inequities in their schools and would respond to them appropriately. These leaders would have internalized a perspective like the following one:

> Students who are at the bottom, so far down they have very few real choices, only have us who make this commitment. They don't get to quit being at the bottom; they don't have this choice. Children don't get to choose to no longer experience inequity. For example, if there is racism toward children of color, they don't get to quit being children of color experiencing that racism. If you understand what racism is about and how critically important it is, if you have a core commitment to equity and excellence, if you believe that you can make a difference, you just don't get to quit. You do not allow yourself to quit. You understand that to quit is to betray the children who do not get the choice or the chance to quit. Instead, you are persistent, relentless, unstoppable in your continuing work to increase equity and excellence. (Scheurich & Skrla, 2003, pp. 103–104)

Every process has to begin somewhere, and the process of developing a critical consciousness, and equity driven leaders and teachers must begin with a candidate's self-examination of his or her beliefs. Although this may seem self-evident, it can neither be taken for granted, nor should its importance be understated. Delpit's (1995) affirmation of this is a powerful reminder. She says: "We do not really see through our eyes or hear through our ears, but through our beliefs ..." (p. 46). Our beliefs drive not only what we 'see' and 'hear,' they drive what we learn, how we learn, what we care about, and what we advocate for or against. Moreover, a candidate's belief system determines how they define equity and how they position themselves in relation to it. And how educators position themselves in relation to equity and social justice is determined in large part by 'race', class, ethnicity, social conditioning, and whether or not they are perceived to be members of a dominant or subordinated group in society. These factors are powerfully linked to teacher and leader attitudes, behavior, and pedagogy, and this cannot be ignored or trivialized especially when we realize that of the four million teachers in America, approximately 83.5% of them are classified as White while only 14% of them are classified as either Black or Hispanic collectively. In contrast, statistical data shows that American students are becoming more and more ethnically diverse, and within twenty or thirty years, Caucasians will no longer be the numerical majority. In the United States, 'race' matters, and the term 'race' which is already ambiguous and controversial will become more so as biracialism increases. Regardless of one's color, culture, or ethnicity, Americans are surrounded by racist ideologies because American racism is endemic, contagious and deeply embedded in the American psyche, and everyone is damaged by these ideologies and the *de facto* social policies to which they are linked. Schools can and have been a large part of the problem by perpetrating and reinforcing these mindsets, but the good news is that schools offer the greatest hope for changing these deleterious mindsets.

Self-examination is an important metacognitive process that requires educators to consciously think about how they make sense of the world, and especially about how humans tend to define *difference* through oppositional paradigms. Ignoring this process can undermine our attempts to foreground social justice, and mediate human difference because as Schultz et al. (2007) point out,

> The human mind has a powerful and limiting tendency to create binary, oppositional categories as it attempts to understand group identity. As educators, "when we teach about gender, race, and sexual orientation, we warn students about the artificial ways in which Americans dichotomize these characteristics." People tend to define "women" in opposition to "men," "people of color" in opposition to "white people," "youth" in opposition to "age" (Shultz, 2006, p. n.a.). We warn our students that language can reinforce divides between people when words fail to fully express the continuous nature of identity. This dichotomous language can vastly complicate our attempts to work for social justice. (Shultz, Skilton-Sylvester, & Shultz, 2007, p. n.a.)

Dichotomous language and thinking reinforces the need to address the implicit or unconscious racial bias that may underlie our thinking patterns. Gary Howard (2006) addresses this point when he says "We cannot help our students overcome the negative repercussions of past and present racial dominance if we have not unraveled the remnants of dominance that still lingers in our minds hearts, and habits" (p. 4).

It is important that teacher and leader candidates see this self-examination as the manifestation of two foundational principles of teaching: (a) learning is a process that *never ends*, and (b) teachers should see themselves as always being in the process of *becoming*. Freire (2008) refers to this as *our incompleteness*, and says that "[w]omen and [men] are capable of being educated only to the extent that they can recognize themselves as unfinished." He goes on to say that "[e]ducation does not make us educable. It is our awareness of being unfinished that makes us educable" (p. 58). This is a crucial point for preservice teachers and leaders because the increasingly complex diversity in American classrooms demands that we see the world through ever-changing prisms; it also demands that we be willing to be transformed by this new knowledge. By training teachers and leaders to see society as interconnected, interdependent as well as inequitable, they will also begin to understand that assuming the role of *teacher* or *leader* is an obligation to challenge the "social reality in which discrimination and oppression are 'natural'..." (Greene cited in Ayers, 2001, p. xxx). Moreover, they must be helped to internalize the idea that they must be active in creating a better, more equitable world though their teaching and leading. Curricular design drives this process.

Capper et al. (2006) clearly outline what they mean by curriculum, in their leadership framework. Although their framework is directed at those enrolled in formal leadership programs, and whose future positions will place them in charge of schools as administrators, this analysis will often refer to teachers and leaders interchangeably for several reasons: First, as has been argued, school leadership roles often overlap as teacher leadership becomes more pervasive, and is more widely acknowledged; Second, most school administrators are recruited from the ranks of practicing teachers; Third, the *teacher, learner, leader* paradigm merges the three roles in ways that are difficult and even counterproductive to separate. Therefore, the references to curriculum and the specific content areas related to leader preparation, especially as it relates to critical consciousness that can "deepen the knowledge, and build skills of future leaders to carry out their work" (Capper et al., 2006, p. 213) are equally relevant to teachers and leaders.

For all educators, there needs to be curricula explicitly focused on critical consciousness in ways that directly address school structures that perpetuate inequities. This includes giving teacher and leadership candidates a clear understanding of the history, sociology and philosophy of education as they relate to systemic inequities and institutional discrimination in both schools and society, as well as learning "to leave the comforts and confines of professional codes and state mandates for the riskier waters of high moral callings" (Rapp cited in Capper et al., 2006, p. 214). Additionally, there should be curriculum centered on knowledge about relevant theories, and subject areas "such as special education, law, and knowledge about evidence-based practices such as reallocating resources, second language acquisition, reading, and math curriculums" (Capper et al., 2006, p. 214) especially when they can be linked to inequitable learning outcomes for children.

Case Study: In Search of a Model of Teacher Preparation for Equity and Leadership: An Examination of the *Conceptual Framework* of the School of Education at Quinnipiac University

The research synthesized by Capper et al. (2006) presents several ideas for how social justice curricula can be designed and presented. For example, Brown (2004) suggests an 'integration of social justice and equity issues throughout a range of courses …,' (Brown cited in Capper et al., 2006, p. 214), while Young and Laible (2000) rely on the addition of new courses, and argue that more than one professor should be responsible for addressing social justice issues and that at least one course should be completely dedicated to this subject. Young and Laible (2000) also insist that social justice be an integral part of all curricula that is offered in a leadership program, and that it should be 'nurtured' for the entire time candidates are in the program. Additionally, they argue that social justice themes and ideas should be woven into any ancillary activities which involve leadership candidates, including advising and general department activities. The teacher preparation program at Quinnipiac University addresses several of these targeted goals in various ways: there is one multicultural education course dedicated to discussions of 'diversity' as opposed to 'social justice,' and although there is currently no evaluation or assessment of this, there is an explicit commitment to streaming content about diversity and social justice throughout the entire program. In addition, teacher candidates are encouraged to engage in consciousness-raising extracurricular service activities which are socially responsible.

The *Conceptual Framework*

The Conceptual Framework is organized in sections that address the *teacher*, *learner*, and *leader* domains separately. The *Teacher* domain is divided into five sections: Teacher Beliefs, Content Knowledge, Pedagogical Techniques and Methodologies, Reflection/ Mindfulness, and Teaching that Values Diversity. These are followed by sections on the *Leader* and the *Learner*.

Metaphorically, it is significant that the *Conceptual Framework* begins with *Teacher Beliefs* which has been equated with critical consciousness, a key component of the CTS framework. In the CTS construct, critical consciousness means that leaders need to "possess a deep understanding of power relations and social construction including white privilege, heterosexism, poverty, misogyny and ethnocentrism" (Capper et al., 2006, p. 213). Implicitly, this means understanding that schools, teachers, and the students they teach don't exist in as vacuum; they are actors in the same play.

Teacher Beliefs

From the **Conceptual Framework**
The Teacher Domain

Teacher Beliefs

At the basis of all else is the teacher's belief system about his/her role as a teacher. What an individual believes about the learner, the content, and her/his own ability to effect learning ultimately determines the degree to which learning occurs in the classroom …

Excellent teachers believe that education is transformative. They believe they can make a difference and are relentless in their expectations for themselves and their students …

Excellent teachers believe that ensuring that all children learn means that the teacher is responsible for creating a classroom and school environment that is conducive to learning for all students. These teachers believe that … they must have … the knowledge, skills and dispositions to engage in teaching that is multicultural, and … a commitment to reflective, mindful practice. (2007, p. 2)

Although an equity-driven frame of reference is implicit in the above statements, they stop short of clearly articulating the idea that teaching, learning, social justice and excellence itself, are (or should be) part of the same continuum. Instead, they offer a circumscribed, even parochial, sense of teacher beliefs which are detached from sociopolitical contexts, and perhaps detached from debilitating cycles of human suffering and oppression that make social justice pedagogies necessary. There are, however, code words and phrases which can be equated to, and are compatible with, social justice pedagogies. For example, note the synergy between the excerpts from the various definitions of social justice, and the statements from the *Conceptual Framework* which follow them:

Definitions of Social Justice

- ... full and equal participation of all groups in a society ... [an equitable] distribution of resources ... (Bell, cited in Adams et al., 1997, p. 3).
- Equity goes beyond equality. It means that all students must be given the *real possibility of an equality of outcomes*. (Nieto & Bode, 2012, p. 11)
- ... it [is] *a philosophy, an approach, and actions that embody treating all people with fairness, respect, dignity and generosity.* (Nieto & Bode, 2012, p. 11)

From *Conceptual Framework*

- *education is transformative,*
- Excellent teachers believe they can *make a difference,*
- Excellent teachers ensure *that all children learn,*
- Excellent teachers *must have ... the knowledge, skills and dispositions to engage in teaching that is multicultural ...*

Clearly, as both the *Conceptual Framework* and these selected definitions of social justice imply, excellence in teaching and leading is far more than skillful pedagogy; it means a commitment to equity and equitable outcomes for all students, fairness, and individual and social transformation.

Excellence in teaching and leading also means that every teacher must begin by reentering the 'self' through "deeply reflective, mindful practice." As Palmer has pointed out, "[t]eaching ... emerges from one's inwardness ... [and it's important to ask] ... Who is the self that teaches? [and] How does the quality of my selfhood form—or deform—the way I relate to my students, my subject, my colleagues, my world?" (Palmer, 1998, p. 4). Without this self-knowledge as a foundation for teaching, it is likely that the goals of "... full and equal participation of all groups ... [and an equitable] distribution of resources ..." (Bell et al., p. 3) will never be fully achieved, and the desired social transformation will be superficial if it occurs at all.

Although the stated goal is to embed a social justice focus in the entire teacher preparation program at the Quinnipiac University School of Education, only one course, *Diversity in the Classroom*, is completely dedicated to discussions of diversity, multiculturalism and social justice.

The course description is below:

Consistent with the goal of the Division of Education to produce practitioners who function successfully in multiple domains, this course aims to prepare educators to be *teachers, learners* and *leaders* who are prepared to enter the teaching profession with a heightened awareness of the importance of social justice and a commitment to improving our profession. This course is designed to help students understand that teaching is essentially a social enterprise invested with moral responsibility and that, as teachers, they will be called to act as agents for social justice in their classrooms and in their schools. Through readings, activities, and class discussions, prospective teachers will examine attitudes and behaviors, which prevent classrooms, schools and society from being fair and equitable for all students, and will commit to a personal plan of action for providing meaningful and equitable educational opportunities for all of their students. This course will help students acquire the dispositions, cultural knowledge, and competencies to adapt their curriculum and instructional skills for culturally responsive classroom practice.

(Excerpted from Syllabus for ED 325/ED 525)

Consistent with the CTS framework, the course is designed to develop critical consciousness, knowledge, and skills related to social justice and/or social justice leadership, but the description is vague regarding the specific knowledge, and skills candidates will acquire, and how this will be assessed. However, this class is clearly designed to help students confront rather than conceal their identities, belief systems, socialization patterns, cultural traditions and family values. They learn that they must first see and understand themselves before they can see and understand others. They learn that they must develop the skill to see the world through different cultural lenses in order to begin the process of communicating with and understanding the 'other.' This is a difficult and disruptive process

because it means turning yourself inside out, giving up your own sense of who you are, and being willing to see yourself in the unflattering light of another's angry gaze. It is not easy, but it is the only way to learn what it might feel like to be someone else and the only way to start the dialogue. (Delpit, 1995, p. 46)

How do you get people to turn themselves "inside out, giving up [their] own sense of who [they] are," when this can be seen as a form of self-annihilation? "What will it take to get someone to submit to this deep self-examination when he or she is a member of the dominant group, and has been socialized to see the racialized dynamics of power and privilege as the social norm? How do you get people to open their hearts and minds to new ways of *seeing* especially when the old ways of seeing gives them comfort and pride?" (Holmes, 2009, p. 144). How do you get people to *put their beliefs on hold* especially when they have been carefully taught to accept the power dynamics of race?

The work of Tatum (1997), Heuberger (2002), and countless others shows that it is necessary for educators to deconstruct the dynamics of dominant privilege, especially racial dominance, given the present and future demographic makeup of American classrooms. They point out that if you are in a dominant group, privilege is rarely mentioned and usually is taken for granted. This is important in a social justice framework because the dominant group controls the quality of life for those nondominant 'others' by establishing the limits and/or the constraints for them in terms of who gets the *best* or *worst* jobs, and significantly, who gets the *best* or *worst* education among other things. Further, the dominant group has the power to label the 'others' *defective* or substandard. When the dominant group is largely comprised of white teachers, and the 'others' are students of color, the effects can have a catastrophic impact on student learning. Tatum's work shows that privilege protects and sustains itself. For example, those with dominant privilege can rationalize that they share common interests, experiences and needs with those in subordinated groups. This can make social *injustice* invisible, and allow those in the dominant group to preserve a comfortable illusion of shared equality, even in the face of institutionalized discrimination and systemic inequities. They can therefore acquit themselves of any responsibility for social change which both contradicts and undermines social justice pedagogies (Tatum, 1997, pp. 23–28).

As a professor, teaching *Diversity in the Classroom* to both graduate and undergraduate teacher candidates, my goal has been to help preservice teachers learn that before they can begin a dialogue with others about social justice, they must engage in an internal dialogue in order to confront their own implicit biases as well as sensitive issues like social dominance, institutional discrimination, race, power, and privilege. They are helped to understand how they can be complicit in maintaining structures of inequality. They also learn that a commitment to social justice means that they must become agents of social change.

In this class, journals are used as a primary assessment tool because they allow the teacher candidates to engage in an internal dialogue even as they share their development of a critical consciousness with the professor, and sometimes with their colleagues. In addition, at least on the secondary level, some discipline courses (English, for example) can choose content designed to deepen their critical consciousness by continuing the conversations about diversity, equity and social justice in new contexts. The goal is to give students a deep understanding of power relations and socially constructed inequities including white privilege, heterosexism, poverty, and other marginalizing conditions, as well as an understanding of how they benefit from these conditions, and the ways in which they are complicit in maintaining the status quo in society and in schools.

The following passages, excerpted from random, anonymous, final journal entries of undergraduate and graduate preservice teachers in *Diversity in the Classroom* course shows how difficult it is to confront and change belief systems.

The general student profile is white, female, middle class and suburban. Most have stated openly that they were brought up in racially segregated schools in the northeast, and most never had a teacher of color. The student comments reveal a great deal about the process of challenging belief systems, and the value that one fourteen-week diversity class can have in the development of preservice teachers. It is significant that common themes and patterns emerge describing their ignorance about themselves and the 'other,' the pain and discomfort of self-revelation, and a passage through a variety of emotions including anger, shame and guilt to a respect for *difference*. These teacher candidates acknowledge that for the most part *they did not think about diversity of thinking, feeling or being, because they didn't have to think about these things*, and it is significant that they've accepted that this is part of their privilege as members of a racially dominant group. Moreover, the reflections show the transformation to a deeper level of commitment to personal and professional growth as well as a commitment to moving from passivity to advocacy for social change.

Anonymous Reflections from Pre-Service Teacher Candidates

This first journal entry expresses the common sentiment, that there is a lack of awareness about the inequities that exist in society, and the need to 'open one's eyes' about social inequities. This raises the question of whether or not blindness is ever an excuse for navigating around another's distress. In the general public, this is unfortunate; in a teacher, self-imposed blindness can be tragic because equity-driven teachers cannot afford what Howard (2006) calls the 'luxury of ignorance.'

> ... the class opened up my eyes to issues that I hadn't thought about before: White privilege, tracking in schools, and many other issues that deal with race and equality, but we don't discuss because it would effect (sic.) our day to day lives. I felt that I was doing my share by just not being as racist. What this class did for me was show me that I'm still part of a society that has been set-up and run and mostly by white guys

… Throughout the semester I felt angry at times that somebody was accusing me of this bigotry. I even at times rejected the very notion. However, the discussion with myself and others has begun and that is the first step to living in a more equitable situation.

One of the most hopeful things about this entry is that the student admits to having a conversation with himself/herself which is a crucial first step to personal transformation. This teacher candidate acknowledges that during the course he/she has become more open-minded, and developed the ability to think new thoughts, and see things differently. In addition, the student admits to being complicit in the process of self-delusion by refusing to face the sad, painful, or embarrassing truths about the impact of dominant privilege, especially how it confers unearned benefits on some. This student also acknowledges a previous unwillingness to relinquish privilege or disrupt the comforts of his/her day-to-day life while embracing silence and denial.

Recognizing the difficulty of the process, the student below accepts the various stages of growth including a period of defensiveness and anger.

- I think this course has helped me realize how important it is to share my beliefs about accepting diversity rather than just avoiding people that do not have the same point of view as me. Coming into this course, I recognized that racism, sexism and various other—isms—were unacceptable, yet I do not think I felt as compelled to do something about them. Previously, I would react internally with disgust at what others were saying, but I wasn't aware of the ways in which my silence made me complacent in what they were saying … this class has helped me recognize that stating that you accept diversity is meaningless if your actions do not support your statement. Finally, this class has made me much more aware of the way in which dominant and subordinate groups experience this country in entirely different ways.

This student has embraced diversity, has learned to move beyond the silence surrounding difficult subjects, and has developed the ability to talk about them openly and honestly. Importantly, this student has linked silence to complacency, and has also learned that he/she has to be active rather than passive in the face of injustice. This teacher candidate now understands the dynamics of dominance, and how it causes members of different groups to experience the world differently.

The statement by the student below is striking because of the strong sense of entitlement to the privileges that he/she enjoys. Also, there is a defensiveness that permeated this student's attitude at the beginning of the class which has all but dissipated by the end of the semester.

- At first I was reluctant to see these differences because I did not want to feel as if I did not deserve what I had gotten in my life. I believed that I had earned every single thing I was given, such as my college education, my awards in high school, and my abilities to play sports both in high school and college. This idea slowly changed during this class once I realized that it was not an attack on what I had done, but an acknowledgement that others have not been given the same privileges that I have. Rather than disheartening me as it did before, it creates a desire in me to change the situation, at least where I have an influential sphere. That would be my classroom ... After learning so much from this class, I feel much more comfortable in thinking about dealing with underprivileged students. More importantly, I now have more of a desire to help where there does not exist help, and go where most choose not to go.

Consistent with the general dynamics of dominant privilege, this teacher candidate above also showed a reluctance to see difference, or to acknowledge that difference means something in the context of privileged group membership. Preferring self-delusion and evasion, this student had rationalized that all of his/her privileges were fairly earned, but has learned that society structures disadvantage for those in marginalized groups to the same degree that it structures privilege for others. Now the student has an understanding of the relationship between dominant privilege and inequitable social relations in society, and has developed a sense of responsibility to those who have less. It is interesting to note that this teacher candidate is not only more self-aware, but feels a greater sense of empowerment as a future teacher who can make a difference in the classroom.

This final entry summarizes the potential of one education class to help a teacher candidate see himself/herself through new lenses:

I can be the first to tell you that there were many times in my life where I took my privilege for granted ... I never thought twice about it. I never thought about less fortunate subordinate groups, or the people of color who faced a different lifestyle every day. I always thought about me, and that's pretty much it. I now feel embarrassed to admit to that, I was so one-sided and never really let myself open up to the world around me. As a wannabe teacher there was no way I could go into a classroom with a mindset as a 'privileged white dominant teacher.' There would be no way I would make any connections with my students or craft an environment where those students would be comfortable. In just 14 weeks ... I have changed. ...

As the student reflections demonstrate, challenging belief systems and developing a critical consciousness is a wrenching process, which will likely move people out of their comfort zones into unknown territory because it means crossing boundaries of race, class, and culture which is difficult and disruptive, and places one at risk of what Adrienne Rich (1986) calls *psychic disequilibrium*. Yet, this critical self-examination is essential for developing teachers and teacher leaders who are committed to equity driven pedagogies, and equate excellence in teaching with advocacy for '*an equality of outcomes*' for all of their students. According to Maxine Greene, teaching for social justice is "teaching what we believe ought to be" (cited in Ayers, 2001, p. xxix) and unless teacher candidates have confronted their deeply held beliefs, they will be unprepared to fully understand or challenge structures of power and privilege that normalize social injustice and inequity in schools and society.

Challenging belief systems and implicit biases, and being willing to replace old beliefs with new ones requires nothing less than a paradigm *shift*. And we should not underestimate the difficulty and the importance of this process and the potential it has to affect student learning and engagement, school climate, and equitable outcomes for underserved students both in and outside of schools. It is therefore important to understand both what we mean by *paradigm*, and how affective it is. The following perspectives are helpful

A paradigm is a world view, a general perspective, a way of breaking down the complexity of the real world. As such paradigms are deeply embedded in the socialization of adherents and practitioners, telling them what is important, what is reasonable. (Patton, cited in Ladson-Billings, 1995, p. 470)

… the adherence to one paradigm as opposed to another predisposes one to view the world and the events within it in profoundly differing ways. (Rist, cited in Ladson-Billings, 1995, p. 470)

The power and pull of a paradigm is … a means by which to grasp reality and give it meaning and predictability. (Rist, cited in Ladson-Billings, 1995b, p. 470)

These perspectives help us to understand how deeply transformational this change process is. It is so much more than making a verbal commitment to *justice*, mouthing the words in a rote, formulaic way as many do when they pledge allegiance to the flag of the United States, and recite the words "with liberty and justice for all."

Reflection/Mindfulness

From the *Conceptual Framework*
The Teacher Domain

Reflection/Mindfulness

… Reflection is certainly a powerful tool, and when done well and often, it improves the quality of any teacher's instruction. The capacity of teachers to see the 'whys' of their teaching (e.g. why a particular strategy was/wasn't effective), and to adjust their teaching accordingly, is critical to their overall capacity to be effective …

… In order to make sound decisions while in the act of teaching, excellent teachers are mindful, meaning that they are fully present in the classroom …

… Mindfulness refers to the full, complete, and nonjudgmental awareness of the present moment; it involves cultivating a sustained, steady, clear awareness of what is occurring in each and every moment. (Kabat-Zinn, 1994; Hanh, 1998) …

Interestingly, reflection and mindfulness are not specifically mentioned in the CTS framework, even though they are part of a critical consciousness continuum which links them to belief systems and deeper ways of knowing in general. However, it is significant that even though reflection and mindfulness *are* highlighted in Quinnipiac's teacher preparation program as essential dimensions of effective teaching, learning and leading, they are not explicitly or implicitly linked to social justice or equity in their Conceptual Framework which seems counterintuitive in light of current research.

Mindfulness, as we know it, is a kind of consciousness-raising based on Buddhist practices that have been used for over 2000 years. This process is designed to increase self-awareness by forcing individuals to be present in the moment to whatever they are experiencing without filters; without judgment, and without self-recrimination. Recent research on implicit bias have shown that mindfulness has the potential to help mitigate unconscious bias and improve intergroup harmony (Staats et al., 2016). Crowder (2010) argues that mindfulness supports social justice by creating possibilities for personal, professional, and social transformation. According to her, it helps us internalize a new way of seeing the world, and a new way of listening to the people in it. Accordingly, mindful listeners can:

1. Sustain their attention over time
2. Hear and see the whole message
3. Make the speaker feel valued and respected
4. Listen to themselves.
   (Crowder, 2010, p. n.a.)

Hick and Furlotte (2009) also connect mindfulness and social justice, by identifying the links between mindfulness and antioppressive professional practice, and they too point out that mindfulness forces us to listen differently, and listening to others' stories is an important first step to validating their life experiences. In The Zen of Listening: Mindful Communication in the Age of Distraction, Shafir (2003) offers that "… mindful listening is a gift not only to yourself, but to others" (p. 13). It can be argued that it is a gift to society as well.

Mindfulness is different from reflection, and the distinction is important for teachers to understand, but the Conceptual Framework confuses the issue by making it appear that the two processes are synonymous. Mindfulness is a quality of the mind while reflection is a quality of the brain. The mind and the brain are actually two different systems. The mind is involved with consciousness while the brain is involved with cognition. We know that there is consciousness, but we don't know precisely where it resides. We know that there is cognition and we are quite certain that it is a function of the brain. The two—consciousness and cognition—are so intertwined that they are often referred to as though they are synonymous, but they are not. Medical and metaphysical experts have done thorough studies on each that can help us to understand how they are unique, and why it's important to understand the differences.

When author Ambrose Gwinnett Bierce quipped that "The brain is the organ by which we think that we think" (p. n.a.), he captured the dilemma that underlies brain/mind discussions. For the purposes of this study, there is no need to probe deeply into it the various theories about the distinctions between the mind and brain. It is only necessary to clarify how reflection and mindfulness are different and how understanding this distinction can support more effective teaching and equity driven leadership.

It's enough to remember that the brain, as the key organ of the body, is the control center of our nervous system and all of our actions and responses. The brain is material and we can see it, touch it and examine it directly. This is not true of the mind. The mind is not material and its functions cannot be examined directly. The mind refers to a person's understanding of things, the consciousness; the conscience and the thought process that drive the mechanistic functions of the brain.

In Wherever You Go, There You Are (1994), Kabat-Zinn offers an important lesson for educators: understanding the powers of the mind is a complex eclectic process. When, for example, educators, Roland Barth (2001), Parker Palmer (1998), William Ayers and Terrance Deal (2009) offer insights into the art, heart, and soul aspects of teaching, they invoke what we think of as the mind:

The connections made by good teachers are held not in their methods, but in their hearts—meaning heart in its ancient sense, as the place where intellect and emotion and spirit and will converge in the human self. ... (Palmer, 1998, p. 11)

A teacher needs a brain to break through the cotton wool smothering the mind, to see beyond the blizzard of labels to this special child ... A teacher needs a heart to fully grasp the importance of that gesture, to recognize in the deepest core of your being that every child is precious. ... (Ayers, 2001, p. 135)

However, the *heart* and the *very core* that these authors reference, are in the domain of the mind from which mindfulness emanates. Kabat-Zinn explains that mindfulness:

has to do with examining who we are, with questioning our view of the world and our place in it, and with cultivating some appreciation for the fullness of each moment we are alive. Most of all it has to do with being in touch. (Kabat-Zinn cited in Nugent, Moss, Barnes, & Wilks, 2011, p. 1)

By extension, *examining who we are*, and *questioning our view of the world and our place in it*, has implications for social justice because it also means examining the lives of those around us, and examining how we respond to their life circumstances. In a study that explores the meeting of eastern and western thought, author Anodea Judith describes mindfulness as:

... paying attention, noticing the subtle flavors and textures of each moment and appreciating their many interwoven levels of meaning without getting attached to any particular one ... mindfulness doesn't have to do anything—it is instead a state of observation ... It does not judge, value, negate, or applaud. It simply witnesses. (Judith, 1996, pp. 441–442)

In the classroom, and in school leadership, mindfulness is a highly valued tool of veteran teachers and administrators. In a chapter entitled "Reconfirming the Soul of Teaching," Terrence Deal (2009), puts it this way:

Knowledge and tradition are passed on through teaching and learning prances and twirls. But even more important, in the rhythmic frolic the soul of the teacher touches the soul of the student. This intangible intermingling of passion, with fond recollection, the occasional chuckle or tear, and a glimmer of direction is tattooed permanently onto the student's heart to be called on when happenstance presents a need. (Deal, 2009, p. 19)

This is another reference to the subtle mind-based interactions and transactions that are at the core of teaching, learning, and leading that touch and stir the emotions and the *soul* of the teacher, the leader, and the student.

Black (2011) offers research that complicates and deepens our understanding of mindfulness, and reminds us that what he calls *mindfulness science* is still in its '*adolescence.*' However, he points out the common thread that links all of the various definitions: "a general receptivity and full engagement with the present moment [in contrast to experiences of *mindlessness* which can] occur when attention and awareness capacities are scattered due to preoccupation with past memories" (Black, 2011, p. 1) or beliefs or experiences. The article offers one definition of *mindlessness* which has implications for social justice teaching and school leadership: "waking up from a life lived on automatic pilot and based in habitual responding" (Black, 2011, p. 1).

Developing a social justice frame of reference also can be seen as '*waking up from a life lived on automatic pilot and based in habitual responding*' to socially marginalized groups, and the social oppression to which they are often subjected. Since teaching and learning are so focused on the acquisition and mastery of content knowledge aimed at the brain, we run the risk of neglecting the amelioration of the mind, and *mindfulness science.* The absence of tasks and processes that nurture mindfulness ignores a vital aspect of our nature, as well as a powerful tool that can help educators build more equitable schools and classrooms. Finally, education that fails to address the mind and mindfulness may demotivate many of our students whose cultures (consciously or sub-consciously) are more attuned to the centrality of the mind and mindfulness.

Content Knowledge

From the *Conceptual Framework*
The Teacher Domain

Content Knowledge

One cannot teach well that which one does not know well. Therefore, a depth and breadth of content knowledge is an important prerequisite to excellent teaching. Such knowledge includes knowledge of facts, concepts and procedures that define a given field as well as an understanding of how those pieces fit together ...

Content-specific pedagogical knowledge defines another area of expertise as defined by Shulman: the knowledge of how to teach specific concepts to specific students. Content-specific pedagogical knowledge ... must be present for one to become an effective teacher in that subject ...

The *Content Knowledge* section of the teacher domain begins with "One cannot teach well that which one does not know well," and defines 'content' in traditional ways as knowledge that includes the "facts, concepts and proce-dures that define a given field as well as an understanding of how those pieces fit together" (Conceptual Framework, 2014, p. 2). Teachers are typically seen as content specialists, and purveyors of a specific knowledge base, but researchers have refined this to include content-specific pedagogical knowl-edge defined by Shulman (1992) as "the knowledge of how to teach specific concepts to specific students." Moreover, according to Shulman, teacher effi-cacy is linked to mastery of this complex body of knowledge because it gives a teacher "... a deep understanding of the essential concepts and questions in their discipline, knowledge that is indispensable to direct student learn-ing in a meaningful way" (Shulman cited in Conceptual Framework, 2014, p. 4). The point here is that *knowing* something, and knowing *how to teach it*, are two distinct things. We typically think of this in terms of the major disciplines, science, math, English, and history, but if we also consider con-tent knowledge, and teacher efficacy in terms of equity and social justice, it means a major paradigm shift. It means, for example, that one's mastery of history and the social sciences, even when aligned with content-specific pedagogical knowledge, is not enough to prepare one to enter the classroom and be *excellent*. One is still *unfinished*, to use Freire's term, and lacking what he calls *conscientization*, the heightened social consciousness that would make injustice unendurable. When teachers foreground equity and social justice, it means to

> ... teach for enhanced perception and imaginative explorations, for the recognition of social wrongs, of sufferings, of pestilences wherever and whenever they arise. It is to find models in literature and history of the indignant ones, the ones forever ill at ease, and the loving ones who have taken the side of the victims of pestilences, whatever their names or places of origin. It is to teach so that the young may be awakened to the joy of working for transformation in the smallest places, so that they may become healers and change their worlds. (Greene, cited in Ayers, Hunt, & Quinn, 1998, p. xiv)

And this is how teachers can transform society; this is how teachers can pre-serve and sustain democracy; this is how teachers can help to change the world. And there is danger here because change frightens people; it forces them to see and confront things they don't want to see or confront; it shakes them out of the comfort zones to which they cling, and people have a ten-dency to *not like* those people and things that make them uncomfortable. As Herbert Kohl points out, a teacher can be fired for stirring up ideas and "provoking conversations that challenge privilege and try to make issues of democracy and equity work in the everyday life of the classroom. The problem is that many people [including colleagues, administrators, students, parents and board members] do not believe that justice is a value worth fighting for ... One cannot simply assume that because an action or sentiment is just, fair or compassionate that it will be embraced" (Kohl, cited in Ayers, 2001, p. 285). Nor can one assume that *teachers* who practice and advocate for social justice and equity pedagogies will be celebrated in the school community especially when they are interrogating privilege.

Adopting an equity pedagogy can place a teacher *at risk* because it can, and should, be interpreted as a critique of the status quo, especially school practices that fossilize underachievement for those who live in the margins. Adopting an equity pedagogy is a commitment to change; it means a glacial paradigm shift. According to J. A. Banks (2008), an equity pedagogy can exist only when "teachers modify their teaching in ways that will facilitate the academic achievement of students from diverse racial, cultural, and social-class groups (C. A. Banks & J. A. Banks, 2007). This includes using a variety of teaching styles and approaches that are consistent with the wide range of learning styles within various cultural and ethnic groups ..." (Banks & Banks, 2007, p. 21). Yet it is important to remember that these modifications must be preceded by a Palmerian self-examination which poses the questions: *"Who is the self that teaches? ... How does the quality of my selfhood form—or deform—the way I relate to my students, my subject, my colleagues, my world?"* (Palmer, 1998, p. 4).

Although Martin Luther King was speaking out in opposition to the Vietnam War when he said, "Our only hope today lies in our ability to recapture the revolutionary spirit and go out into a sometimes hostile world declaring eternal hostility to poverty, racism, and militarism," (King, n.a.) his strident advocacy for change and his passion for justice is as relevant today as it was fifty years ago. King's words can strengthen the resolve of social justice educators, and provide a foundation for social justice pedagogies today, because social justice educators are now fighting a different kind of *war*, and they already know who the *losers* are. The *losers* are among the burgeoning numbers of hopelessly poor, undereducated, disenfranchised citizens who subsist among us as a permanent underclass. Most of them are products of an American public education that masquerades as "the great equalizer." These *losers* are a sad, contemporary reincarnation of Hemingway's 'lost generation.'

The *Conceptual Framework* offers a generic, traditional definition of *content knowledge*. Although silent on the subject of social justice, it does contain a separate section, entitled, *Teaching that Values Diversity* which is unambiguously committed to social justice and equity pedagogies, and heavily influenced by James Banks (2008), considered by many the 'father of multicultural education.'

Teaching that Values Diversity

From the *Conceptual Framework*
The Teacher Domain

Teaching that Values Diversity

Excellent teachers have the knowledge, skills, and dispositions to design and implement lessons that reflect an equity pedagogy …

Excellent teachers continually examine their own beliefs and behaviors for biases that have the potential to deny some students an opportunity to be successful learners …

Excellent teachers continually strive to understand the way in which race, ethnicity, gender, sexual orientation, and socio-economic status influence students' perspective on the world. These teachers continually work to acquire the pedagogical skills and methodologies that will enable them to provide students with equitable learning and assessment activities (Gay, 2000; Nieto, 2000) …

Excellent teachers recognize the need to help students develop an understanding of and an appreciation for other cultures …

Excellent teachers provide opportunities for students of diverse backgrounds and experiences to work together in meaningful ways for the common good. This is the essence of good citizenship and civic responsibility that is important for the survival of a democratic society.

This section, *Teaching that Values Diversity*, incorporates references to both the requisite knowledge base and pedagogy for teachers who *value* diversity, but more importantly, it equates teacher excellence with equity. This is significant because as Maxine Greene argues, teaching for social justice moves far beyond discipline-specific content knowledge, it means, to paraphrase Shulman, having "… a deep understanding" of the essential concepts of justice and injustice, and the ability to use this deep understanding "to direct student learning in a meaningful way" (Conceptual Framework, 2014, p. 2). However, it is interesting to note that it is presented as a separate, stand-alone section in the Framework rather than be directly linked to *Content Knowledge*. The question is: does this mean something, and if so, what?

Visually and symbolically this design segregates diversity/multiculturalism/ social justice from content knowledge and pedagogy and, in a sense, replicates the marginalization to which diversity, multiculturalism, and social justice are subjected in schools and society at large. Organizationally, at least, the Conceptual Framework does not equate mastery of discipline-specific content knowledge and pedagogy with social justice content knowledge and pedagogy, but sees them as distinct entities, which runs counter to the CTS framework which calls for the wholesale integration of curriculum, pedagogy, and assessment so that they work together to support social justice teaching and leadership. Segmenting *content knowledge*, and *teaching that values diversity* also runs counter to many standard approaches to multicultural education, culturally relevant teaching, or teaching that is responsive to diversity, and is akin to the problem that many social justice educators see in traditional Eurocentric approaches to teaching and learning (Banks, 1994; Gollnick & Chinn, 2006; Howard, 2006; Nieto & Bode, 2012). Their critique is that many educators who practice or express support for equity pedagogies, multicultural education and culturally relevant teaching often compartmentalize, marginalize, sideline or completely ignore the implications of racism, and the dynamics of power and privilege, and disconnect their teaching from sociopolitical contexts. "To put it another way, multicultural education, or any kind of education for that matter, cannot be understood in a vacuum. Yet in many schools, multicultural education is approached as if it is divorced from the policies and practices of schools and from the structures and ideologies of society. This kind of thinking results in a one-dimensional, focus on cultural artifacts, such as food and dress, or on ethnic celebrations. It can become a 'fairyland' multicultural education, disassociated from the lives of teachers, students, and communities. This is multicultural education without a sociopolitical context" (Nieto & Bode, 2012, p. 4). For some, this 'fairyland' multicultural education is synonymous with a superficial 'heroes and holidays' response to diversity.

Although Nieto and Bode's (2012) critique is essentially directed at in-service teachers, their comments are equally relevant to preservice teacher candidates, as well as those in schools of education who teach them because a 'fairyland' approach to multicultural education, diversity training, and social justice pedagogies, is not limited to what goes on in public schools. The myriad reasons for this have already been discussed, including acculturation and socialization patterns, and the history of racism in America. But, there may be something else at work here; something more subtle, and perhaps more pernicious, because of its subtlety.

Many educators internalize the idea that a stated belief in social justice is enough, and they don't need to put this social justice work on the same plane as content specific pedagogy. If, for example, they believe that they are 'good people,' have 'good intentions,' and are committed to *truth, justice* and the *American way*, they can do no harm, and will do no harm because their practice will automatically reflect these democratic values and beliefs, *because* they are good, well-intentioned people. This facile thinking is equally true for in-service teachers, preservice teacher candidates and, those who teach them in schools of education, because as one young woman once said, 'you can be a nice person and be a racist too.' We live in an age where we have been carefully conditioned to behave in politically correct ways, and in general, people are less likely to delve deeply into sensitive subject matter that causes discomfort, anger, shame, guilt, or fear. And this is especially true if they are members of a privileged racial group or class. However, it's important to remember that

> Teachers [and teacher educators] also are the products of educational systems that have a history of racism, exclusion and debilitating pedagogy. As a consequence, their practices may reflect their experiences, and they may unwittingly perpetuate policies and approaches that are harmful to many of their students. We cannot separate schools from the communities they serve or from the context of society in general. Oppressive forces that limit opportunities in the schools reflect such forces in the society at large. (Nieto & Bode, 2012, p. 6)

If we acknowledge that we are all products of *"educational systems that have a history of racism, exclusion and debilitating pedagogy"* we realize that the effects of this indoctrination are evident everywhere, even in the vocabulary we choose to describe our best efforts to achieve social justice. A subtle, but provocative example of this is evident in the title of the section, *Teaching that Values Diversity*. By definition, to *value* means to cherish, to treasure, to prize, to appreciate. But what does this actually mean in the context of teaching for social justice? What does it mean to *value* diversity? For example, most Americans *value* justice, and if that were enough, then social justice pedagogies would be superfluous because most Americans would then display what Freire called *conscientization*, that heightened social consciousness that would make injustice unendurable. Therefore, looked at more critically, the phrase, '*Teaching that Values Diversity*' implies a troubling, but subtle subtext, and may be evidence of how even those who work to achieve equity may have themselves been damaged by *debilitating pedagogy* in ways that they may not be able to see or critique. Moreover, they may be 'blind' to how this thinking could undermine their best efforts to promote equity, and make them complicit in perpetuating the *debilitating pedagogies* which helped *form* or *(de)form* their own thinking. It's important to remember that "... we take in the ideologies and beliefs in our society, and we act on them *whether we actively believe them or not*" (Nieto & Bode, 2012, p. 8).

In summary, when we pair *Content Knowledge* with the goals articulated in *Teaching that Values Diversity*, it becomes clear that the pairing is a powerfully productive one that foregrounds equity and social justice in ways that could transform *what* we teach and *how* we teach, and move us closer to the articulated goal of equal access and full participation of all members of our society. Teachers have unique opportunities to make social justice an integral part of their teaching, (and leading) and it becomes clear that teacher educators have a responsibility to reframe their conceptualization of content and pedagogy accordingly. As content specialists, teacher candidates understand academic rigor, and they need to be taught to apply the same academic rigor that they apply to their individual disciplines to social justice content and pedagogies. This takes work, lots of work. But, if you are being honest with yourself, it means that when you begin to see differently, you have an obligation to act differently. For teachers, this involves internalizing new ideas, being a perpetual learner, and moving out of their comfort zones.

Educator as Learner

From the *Conceptual Framework*
The Learner Domain

Learner

We believe that

... teaching and learning are mutually supportive, and that a professional has the responsibility to continue to learn as she/he continues to teach and lead.

... educators must remain students of teaching and leading throughout their careers ...

... Good teachers and school leaders constantly ask themselves not only "what do students know and what can they do" but also, "what do my students need me to know and be able to do so that they might learn?..."

Just as it is necessary to be a reflective teacher, it is essential to be reflective as a learner, to be a mindful learner. Excellent educators understand that the quality of the work they do as teachers is inextricably linked to who they are as people ...

... Excellent teachers and school leaders accept the challenge to examine on an ongoing basis who they are and who they want to become, which in turn will influence the work they do as educators.

More often than not, when those in the educational arena refer to *learning*, it is understood by most of us that *learning* is the desired outcome for *students* who are in an educational environment controlled by someone designated as a *teacher* and invested with specialized knowledge and authority for that position. Similarly, when we hear the phrase *teaching and learning*, we are conditioned to think of it in terms of two distinct entities and processes, a *teacher*, and a *learner* who fit traditionally prescribed roles. However, it requires a bit of a paradigm shift when we introduce the idea of *teacher as learner* which supersedes the idea that teachers arrive in the classroom with a fixed set of skills and a fully developed knowledge base rather than as *continuous learners*. It's commonplace to hear phrases like *learning never ends* or *lifelong learning* in the context of teacher preparation or staff development for in-service teachers. Yet the idea that teaching and learning are mutually supportive and must coexist also requires us to think of teachers in Freireian terms as being 'unfinished,' and 'incomplete,' and always in the process of *becoming*. Conceptually, this is hopeful and full of promise because it allows us to imagine teachers as constantly renewing themselves, their teaching, and by extension, being catalysts for the renewal of the schools in which they teach. Further, the idea of *teacher as learner* implies an openness to new ways of seeing and knowing, and importantly, new ways of teaching. This offers the possibility of making *excellence* the norm especially when learning is cultivated by reflection and mindfulness. And, according to this model, ongoing reflection will lead teachers to understand that the choices they make and the quality of the work they do as teachers is inextricably linked to who they are as people because as Palmer reminds us, "[t]eaching, like any truly human activity, emerges from one's inwardness, for better or worse" (Palmer, 1998, p. 4). The *'for better or worse'* is Palmer's way of waving a red flag in front of us; a reminder that teachers have the potential to do as much damage as they have to do good. Moreover, this level of self-critique is a necessary prelude to acknowledging that we live in a society which continues to embrace inequality, and we teach in school systems which have institutionalized racism, classism, sexism, linguicism, homophobia and other pernicious forms of bias which directly target some of our students in destructively life-changing ways. It also means understanding that when society damages some of us, it damages all of us. Reflection predisposes teachers to "consider issues of justice, equity, and morality as they design and reflect on their practice ... [and] [i]nstead of blindly accepting or rejecting new information or ideas, they carefully examine, analyze, and reframe them in terms of specific context variables, previous experiences, and alignment with desired educational goals (Costa & Garmston, 2000; Zeichner & Liston, 1996)" (York-Barr et al., 2006a, p. 16).

The *teacher as learner* model equates excellence with personal transformation and a willingness to shed old ways of thinking which undermine the ability to adapt teaching to the needs of all students. Increasingly, the complex pattern of diversity in American classrooms insures that satisfying the needs of students will present new and different challenges for teachers. This is a different and changing world, and teachers need to see the world differently and be willing to be transformed by these new realities. This demands that teachers develop the capacity to dream a world in which discrimination and oppression are *unnatural* and therefore *intolerable*. When teachers are able to internalize the idea that they can create a better, more equitable, world though their teaching, integrating equity pedagogies will be a natural response to perceived social injustice. Further, teachers need to take responsibility for their own learning and professional growth. In the same way that good teachers urge their students to be proactively engaged in their own learning, teachers must model these same behaviors. It means a day-to-day, week-to-week commitment to professional growth that goes beyond simple engagement in officially sanctioned professional development activities organized by their school districts. This is one vital way in which they can create classrooms that affirm all students, and help them create an affirming society "in which racism, sexism, social class, discrimination, heterosexism, and other biases are no longer acceptable" (Nieto & Bode, 2012, p. 9).

Educator as Leader

The *Leader* dimension of the *teacher* → *learner* → *leader* construct completes the model that has been adopted by Quinnipiac's School of Education, and it appears to fit seamlessly to form what Lambert (2003) calls a 'sacred alliance' between *teaching*, *learning* and *leading*. Lambert, a constructivist, argues that this complex idea is deeply embedded in our basic humanity, pointing out that "everyone is born to lead in the same way everyone is born to learn" and goes on to say that

> Learning and leading are understood as intertwined since these conceptions arise from our understandings of what it is to be human. To be human is to learn, and to learn is to construct meaning and knowledge about the world that enables us to act purposefully. (Lambert, 2003, p. 423)

Despite differences in their vocabularies and designs, both the Conceptual Framework and the CTS model affirm these fundamental positions by underscoring the idea that leading is a vital part of the learning process, and that teachers have both the capacity and the responsibility to lead themselves, their colleagues and their schools with the ultimate goal of improving student learning. However, although the Conceptual Framework and the CTS model have common goals, they have distinct differences which should be noted: the Conceptual Framework is more theoretical and vague in terms of how teacher candidates develop the *critical consciousness, knowledge,* and *practical skills* which are at the core of the CTS model. This vagueness is apparent in the **Leader** section below, and raises questions about whether or not the Quinnipiac program has most of the proposed elements needed to move its teacher candidates from passivity to advocacy, and from being rhetorically committed to social justice, and equity, to being skilled, efficacious leaders committed to school and social change in demonstrable ways. Further, it is not clear that this teacher preparation program promotes and develops assessable leadership capacity in its candidates which Capper et al. (2006) imply is a program's biggest challenge because in spite of their exhaustive research, they "could not locate any literature that assessed leadership knowledge and skills related to social justice" (Capper et al., 2006, p. 217).

**From the *Conceptual Framework*
The Leader Domain**

Leader

Whereas only a few educators will hold formal positions of leadership in their schools and school districts, each educator has the responsibility for exercising leadership through other channels ...

The leader dimension of a teacher's role implies assuming responsibility for what happens both in the classroom and beyond the classroom walls. All educators have an obligation to influence the culture of the school and the profession in ways that support best practices in teaching and learning.

Excellent teachers continue to learn as they continue to teach and lead, and they contribute to the growth of colleagues and to the knowledge base of the profession through sharing what they have learned.

... leaders demonstrate professional leadership by engaging colleagues in building and sustaining professional learning communities.

'Easily identified in any school are teacher leaders ... who show initiative, willingly experiment with new ideas, and then share their experiences with others.' (Katzenmeyer & Moller, 1996, p. 71)

... These teachers help establish and contribute to a community of learners dedicated to ongoing study of the teaching-learning process.

Still other leaders help shape and sustain a school culture that fosters the growth of all who are part of that culture

... As leaders, teachers draw on this broad knowledge of the community and the social context of schools to develop a curriculum that is multicultural. And always, excellent leaders find the courage to speak up and challenge behaviors and practices that are harmful to one or more children.

According to the outline above, teachers are leading when they: *exercise leadership, influence the culture of the school and the profession, continue to learn as they continue to teach, demonstrate professional leadership by engaging colleagues in building and sustaining professional learning communities, [help] to shape and sustain a school culture that fosters the growth of all, draw on the broad knowledge of the community and the social context of schools develop a curriculum that is multicultural, and find the courage to speak up and challenge behaviors and practices that are harmful to one or more children.* Unfortunately, despite these ambitious goals, and an implied commitment to equity and social justice, it can be argued that the Conceptual Framework doesn't go quite far enough to take a convincing stand on behalf of social justice pedagogies, social justice advocacy, or social justice leadership. It's notable, for example, that the terms *social justice* and *equity* don't appear in the outline at all. Furthermore, there appears to be a lack of articulation between the *teacher, learner, leader*, domains which essentially undermines the strength and coherence of the entire theoretical framework.

Two pivotal statements from the *Leader* section of the Conceptual Framework are evidence of this weakness: they are vague, lack specificity, and offer only muted support for teacher leadership that is equity driven.

The first statement says teachers are leading when they:

> ... *draw on the broad knowledge of the community and the social context of schools to develop a curriculum that is multicultural* ...

Taking a leadership role in 'developing a curriculum that is multicultural' sounds good to the uninitiated, but to those in the multicultural community, who are guided by a basic understanding of the work of Banks (2008), Banks and Banks (2007), Sleeter (1996), Grant and Ladson-Billings (1997), Grant and Sleeter (2007), Howard (2006), and countless other scholars who have shaped the conversation about diversity, ethnic studies, and multicultural education, realize that whether they are teaching or leading, educators must make a distinction between 'multicultural education,' and 'education that is multicultural.' The former is an approach that envisions multicultural education as a cosmetic or veneer used to tinge existing curricula and could be a mile wide and an inch deep. Many with this shallow orientation develop multicultural curricula and related school activities in response to social and political pressures and the curriculum becomes a concession made to accommodate what they perceive to be a *culturally diverse* environment. In contrast, 'Education that is multicultural' is dedicated to whole school reform and explicitly identifies, and challenges racism and other forms of bias. It is not an accommodation, or an *approach* but a fundamental way of defining education and teaching, and a way of defining oneself as an educator. Beyond that, it is a world view; a way of defining the world in which we coexist with others. It is neither adopted nor abandoned because of the particular times or the particular clientele in the school and surrounding community. 'Education that is multicultural' is all-encompassing because it understands and acknowledges that 'diversity' is a fundamental reality in *all* contexts, and not limited to the obvious, superficial, and often politically charged ways some think of it as 'race,' ethnicity and culture. Banks (2009) argues that multicultural teaching should

> ... help students expand their conceptions of what it means to be human, to accept the fact that ethnic minority cultures are functional and valid, and to realize that a culture can be evaluated only within a particular cultural context. Because cultures are made by people, there are many ways of being human. (Banks, 2008, pp. 26–27)

Tiedt and Tiedt (2002) are even more specific saying that

> ... multicultural education is fundamental to all learning. It is an integral aspect of the discussions about fair behavior on the playground ... It underlies the dialogue of middle school youngsters as they respond to Maniac McGee's efforts to get along in a hostile society. Multicultural education belongs in science, history, mathematics, language arts, and the fine arts. To be effective, multicultural education must be infused throughout any well-designed curriculum. It requires the efforts of committed teachers at all levels of education. (Tiedt & Tiedt, 2002, p. 17)

The second statement from the Conceptual Framework is surprisingly anemic. It says teachers are leading when they:

> ... find the courage to speak up and challenge behaviors and practices that are harmful to one or more children.

No one can argue with the generic commitment to protect all children from 'harm.' However, this statement seems like a missed opportunity to express strong advocacy for teacher leadership on behalf of the thousands of children who are underserved, undervalued, and assaulted daily by inequitable policies and practices both in and outside of schools. The statement could have been extended to interpret 'harm' more broadly, to include the 'harm' done by deeper social ills and systemic injustices which have been linked to depressed learning outcomes.

The *Leader* section is also weakened because it does not mention the word *equity* as is does in the earlier section, *Teaching That Values Diversity*. Among other things, this points to the need for a common vocabulary that links the key ideas in the *teacher, learner, leader* domains; this would present a consistent position, throughout, and strengthen the entire document.

Conceptually, there is a natural integration of the three domains, *teaching, learning,* and *leading,* creating a symbiotic relationship in which each area has the potential to sustain, strengthen, and enrich the other. The obverse is also true. Presumably, if one or more of the three domains is weak or absent, the other domains would then be weakened, and either atrophy, or be severely undermined or neglected. Unlike the tendency in the human body to compensate for some areas of weakness or loss (i.e. that blindness can cause increased tactile sensitivity or improved hearing), there is no similar outcome here. If, for example, there is little or no reflection, teaching will be undermined, and learning (for students and teachers) will be compromised. Similarly, the absence of a strong pattern of teacher leadership can reinforce teacher isolation, and cripple attempts to create the vibrant learning communities that can actualize school reform. By understating or muting its commitment to equity and social justice, the Conceptual Framework marginalizes the role of teacher leadership in all three domains. This is an especially significant omission because it is the *Leader* section, and because research firmly fixes teacher leadership at the heart of the school reform efforts designed to transform school culture, classroom practice, and academic outcomes. Moreover, it can be argued that advocacy for social justice is where leadership finds one of its greatest failures because leadership for social justice is least demonstrated in schools where it is most needed.

Lambert (2003) addresses the failure of leadership in schools, and the implications it has for us domestically and globally. She says that our failure

> ... to address the confounding questions of ... poverty, illiteracy, conflict and war, inequity, are failures of leadership ... We have not educated children to be broadly literate, to access their places in the [national and the] world economy, to mediate conflict, and to value and practice equity ... (Lambert, 2003, p. 423)

A social justice focus can easily be incorporated into the *Leader* section of the Conceptual Framework by conflating the goals from the earlier section, *Teaching that Values Diversity* with the teacher leadership goals. Below, are suggested revisions; insertions have been italicized and highlighted:

Leadership That Values Diversity
(suggested revisions)

Excellent *teacher leaders* have the knowledge, skills, and dispositions to design and implement lessons that reflect an equity pedagogy, and *they work to develop these same skills in their colleagues* ...

Excellent *teacher leaders* continually examine their own beliefs and behaviors for biases and *encourage their colleagues to do so as well. They recognize that personal beliefs* have the potential to deny some students an opportunity to be successful learners ...

Excellent *teacher leaders* continually strive to understand the way in which race, ethnicity, gender, sexual orientation, and socio-economic status influence students' perspective on the world. These *teacher leaders* continually work to *acquire for themselves and their colleagues* the pedagogical skills and methodologies that will enable them to provide students with equitable learning and assessment activities (Gay, 2000; Nieto, 2000) ...

Excellent *teacher leaders* recognize the need to help students develop an understanding of and an appreciation for other cultures ...

Excellent *teacher leaders* provide opportunities for students of diverse backgrounds and experiences to work together in meaningful ways for the common good, and *they provide instructional leadership to bring this knowledge to their colleagues. Teacher leaders realize that* this is the essence of good citizenship and civic responsibility that is important for the survival of a democratic society.

This appears to be a simple fix that involves shifting and inserting a few words into this section. However, words like *excellence, tolerance, equity, justice, respect, diversity, democracy,* are simply vocabulary words, "words walking without masters" (Hurston, 1978, p. 10) unless their inherent power, meaning, and possibilities are harnessed and actualized in educational practice. Too often, educators spend an inordinate amount of time *wordsmithing,* skillfully manipulating words to make them say the *right* things for political rather than substantive reasons. Wordsmithing is easy, seductive, even game-like, but potentially dangerous, because we can make words provide false positives that mask imprecision and ineffectiveness, encourage self-delusion, and hinder progress. We can use words to insulate us from harsh realities that we choose not to face. This is serious and potentially harmful especially when those in leadership are in the position to make weighty decisions which impact the lives of others under their control and care. Perhaps the danger is greatest when those in leadership positions lead through a misguided or misunderstood sense of what social justice leadership *is* or *means.*

Scheurich and Skrla (2003) offer a definition of *leader* which is helpful; it is an unambiguous characterization of what a leader is, and significantly, it is grounded in sociopolitical and historical contexts:

The most important characteristic of a leader—whether a principal, teacher leader, counselor or custodian—who is creating or who is going to create an equitable and excellent school is that this person has developed a strong ethical or moral core focused on equity and excellence as the only right choice for schools in a democracy. For this person, this is an indomitable belief, an indomitable commitment.

A leader for equity and excellence understands that the most important issue in public education is creating schools that are both equitable and excellent. This leader understands that it is our responsibility—our ethical and moral responsibility; even our sacred or spiritual responsibility—to create such schools. The leader understands that this responsibility is central to our country's long history of dedication to equity for all people—for working people, the poor, women, people of color, people with disabilities, for any people who have been excluded. This leader, whatever her or his position within the school, understands that this mission for equity and excellence in our nation's schools is part of a 200 year old civil rights movement that is central to what is truly valuable about our country. (Scheurich & Skrla, 2003, pp. 100–101)

Scheurich and Skrla reinforce the idea that leadership for social justice is not defined by a formally conferred title or limited by a job description; the charge of leadership is much deeper and broader than that; one must be fully invested. "[S]chool leaders need to understand how racism works as a system of oppression, that anti-racism moves beyond multiculturalism ... [and] school leaders need to learn how their own racial identity development impacts their leadership practice" (Capper et al., 2006, p. 215).

Among other things, this analysis of the Quinnipiac program highlights this and other dilemmas educators must confront when preparing teachers and leaders to make equity-based changes in their schools. Clearly, it's possible to see the difference between theory and practice in this program's teacher leadership preparation, and what this means in the context of social justice and equity-driven leadership. For example, Quinnipiac's adoption of a *teacher, learner, leader* model thematically linked to social justice offers a useful theoretical framework which is an excellent starting point. However, when held up to scrutiny using the schema designed by Capper et al. (2006) it becomes even more clear that there is still a great deal of work to be done especially in terms of linking social justice and leadership and making sure that they inform every element of the program's design. This examination also shows that the program design needs more clarity, and focus, and more intentionality in terms of social justice and leadership outcomes. Fortunately, the Capper et al. (2006) framework provides a way forward.

Using the Capper, Theoharis and Sebastian Framework: Implications for Social Justice Teacher Leadership Preparation

Although Capper et al.'s work is based on a thorough analysis of existing research on leadership preparation programs designed around equity-based school leadership, and presents a detailed process for program designers to follow, the authors concede that a great deal of work still needs to be done in this area. However, their cogent analysis is helpful in clarifying a program's goals and objectives, and curricular content. Moreover, they underscore the absence of and the need for, an assessment process, which is virtually unaddressed in the existing research on school leadership programs. Despite this, the CTS framework can be used by faculty in leadership preparation programs as a way to conduct what the designers call a 'hypersensitive' assessment of their programs.

Clearly, there is much work to be done in all areas. For example, one would not expect critical consciousness or belief systems to be controversial in a leadership preparation program; however, it can be a problem when it is narrowly defined. Capper et al.'s review of available research shows that most current leadership preparation programs committed to social justice conceive of critical consciousness as a way to sharpen their focus on white racism and white privilege, but pay significantly less attention to raising consciousness about the social construction of other forms of bias like disability, homophobia, heterosexism, and linguicism. Similarly, according to the authors, preparation programs find it difficult to prepare leaders to acquire the actual skills needed to make equity-based changes in schools, and they provide a series of questions that can be used for program assessment:

- To what extent are we addressing critical consciousness?
- To what extent are we addressing knowledge related to social justice?
- Do we have a stand-alone course?
- To what extent is this knowledge integrated throughout all the courses?
- To what extent do our courses and field experiences teach prospective school leaders actually how to take action and engage in skills to make equity oriented changes? (Capper et al., 2006, p. 218)

Faculty can perform their own-self-assessment by asking similar questions to assess their own practice; the following questions are a guide

- To what extent is my course addressing critical consciousness, knowledge about equity issues, and skill development?

- Where are my strengths and areas for improvement in each of these areas? What areas of difference do I address and which areas of difference do I need to further develop in my teaching capacity? (Capper et al., 2006, p. 218)

Pedagogy is an essential element in the Capper et al. (2006) framework especially as it relates to critical consciousness, knowledge acquisition, and skills, and they highlight the importance of a program promoting innovative teaching. According to their analysis, this is one way to ensure that prospective leaders acquire the knowledge and develop the skills they will need to introduce equity-based changes in their schools. The following questions are offered for this assessment

- Are the instructional methods that faculty are using aimed more toward consciousness, knowledge, or skill development?
- Where are our strengths and weaknesses in this regard?
- To what extent are the program's pedagogy "in-house" that is, activities that take place in the classroom (e.g. case studies, debates, videos, diversity panels), as compared to teaching strategies where students are required to engage in their communities and schools (e.g. equity audits, spending time in low income or diverse communities visiting neighborhood homes, working in a food pantry).
- What pedagogy seem to be most effective and efficient for achieving student learning goals and what data do we have to show this? (Capper et al., 2006, p. 218)

Although Capper et al.'s (2006) system offers a great deal of promise for future teacher and leadership program design and evaluation, they acknowledge that it is incomplete because "research on assessing leadership preparation programs, their content, delivery, and outcomes, is virtually non-existent" (Capper et al., 2006, p. 219). They argue that "[p]reparation programs aimed toward social justice are languishing in hypocrisy when faculty expect equity-oriented leaders to maintain high standards of accountability, supported by federal legislation, when these programs themselves engage in no systematic, empirical studies or equity audits of their own" (Capper et al., 2006, p. 219). However, as Capper et al. (2006) go on to point out, authentic assessment, acknowledged as one of the most effective ways for educators to measure learning outcomes, is a mainstay in K–12 settings, and can provide an important model for teacher and leadership preparation programs. Specifically, preparation programs need to ask "what assessments will help us to know if our students are social justice leaders?" (Capper et al., 2006, pp. 219–220). But more importantly, these programs must use the assessments to design frameworks that prepare strong teachers and leaders with a highly developed critical consciousness and moral sensibility who understand that "equity and excellence

[are] the only right choice for schools in a democracy" (Scheurich & Skrla, 2003, pp. 100–101). American students deserve nothing less.

Conclusion

"If you are neutral in a situation of injustice, you have taken the side of the oppressor.
—Desmond Tutu

The most important characteristic of a leader—whether a principal, teacher leader, counselor or custodian ... is that this person has developed a strong ethical or moral core focused on equity and excellence as the only right choice for schools in a democracy.

—Scheurich and Skrla

Herbert Kohl reminds us that we cannot afford to take for granted that teacher preparation programs, as they are presently designed and structured, function in the best interests of all children, or that we can rely on social justice and equity to be primary values in schools and society. When he says that *"The idea that you have to advocate teaching for social justice is a sad statement about the moral sensibility in our schools and society"* (Kohl, cited in Ayers et al., 1998, p. 285), it's a warning that many educational institutions have either lost or perhaps never had more than a rhetorical commitment to social justice and equity. What we do know is that every day, in thousands of American schools, children ritualistically recite words that pledge fealty to a democratic country and its high ideals of *'liberty and justice for all'* while educators and policymakers on all levels simultaneously *say* they use these same principles to guide curricular decisions and program goals in public schools and in higher education. And yet, the fact that we have to become vigorous advocates for teaching and leading for social justice, and often face significant resistance while doing so, is not simply *"a sad statement about the moral sensibility in our schools and society"* (Kohl, cited in Ayers et al., 1998, p. 285), it also raises questions about whether or not our core focus as a country has devolved into ritualized, statements and pledges that no longer have real meaning for us. The Capper, Theoharis, and Sebastian framework offers a way to elevate teacher and leadership preparation, by ensuring that social justice and equity don't become footnotes in the discussion of school reform, or that democracy itself becomes nothing more than a convenient shield for a specious commitment to true social change.

References

Ayers, W. (2001). *To teach: The journey of a teacher*. New York, NY: Teachers College Press.

Ayers, W., Hunt, J. A., & Quinn, T. (Eds.). (1998). *Teaching for social justice*. New York, NY: The New Press.

Banks, C. A., & Banks, J. A. (2007). *Multicultural education issues and perspectives*. Hoboken, NJ: Wiley.

Banks, J. A. (2008). *An introduction to multicultural education*. Boston, MA: Pearson Education.

Banks, J. A. (1994). *Multiethnic education: Theory and practice* (3rd ed.). Boston: Allyn and Bacon.

Barth, R. (2001). Teacher leader. *Phi Delta Kappan, 82*(6), 443–449.

Bell, L. A. (1997). Theoretical foundations for social justice education. In Maurianne Adams, Lee Ann Bell, & Pat Griffin (Eds.), *Teaching for diversity and social justice*. New York, NY: Routledge.

Black, D. (2011). A brief definition of mindfulness. *Mindfulness Research Guide*. Retrieved May 8, 2012 from http://www.mindfulexperience.org/resources/brief_definition.pdf

Brown, K. M. (2004). Leadership for social justice and equity: Weaving a transformative framework and pedagogy. *Educational Administrative Quarterly*, Vol. 40, No. 1, pp. 79–110.

Capper, C. A., Theoharis, G., & Sebastian, J. (2006). Toward a framework for preparing leaders for social justice. *Journal of Educational Administration, 44*(3), 209–224. Retrieved February 22, 2012 from http://www.centerx.gseis.ucla.edu/principal-leadership/documents/Capper%20Theoharis%20-%20Sebastian%20Framework%20for%20Prprng%20Ldrs%20for%20social%20justice.pdf

Costa, A. L., & Garmston, R. J. 2002. *Cognitive coaching: A foundation for renaissance schools*. Norwood, MA: Christopher-Gordon.

Crowder, R. (2010). *Introduction to mindfulness: An interactive workshop*. Presented at The Fifth North American Conference on Spirituality and Social Work held from June 17–19, 2010, in Calgary, AB, at the University of Calgary. Retrieved from http://www.stu.ca/~spirituality/pdfs/Crowder.pdf

Deal, T. (2009). *Reviving the soul of teaching: Balancing metrics and magic*. Thousand Oaks, CA: Corwin Press.

Delpit, L. (1995). *Other people's children*. New York, NY: New Press.

Freire, P. (2008). *Critical consciousness*. London: Sheed & Ward Ltd.

Gay, G. (2000). *Culturally responsive teaching: Theory, research and practice*. New York: Teachers College Press.

Gollnick, D., & Chinn, P. C. (2006). *Multicultural education in a pluralistic society*. Upper Saddle River, NJ: Pearson Merrill Prentice Hall.

Grant, C. A., & Ladson-Billings, G. (1997). *Dictionary of multicultural education*. Phoenix, AZ: Oryx Press.

Grant, C. A., & Sleeter, C. (2007). *Turning on learning—Five approaches for multicultural teaching plans for race, class, gender and disability*. Hoboken, NJ: John Wiley & Sons, Inc.

Greene, M. (1976). Challenging mystification: Educational foundations in dark times. *Educational Studies*, 7(1), 9–29.

Hanh, T. N. (1998). *For a future to be possible*. Berkeley, CA: Parallax Press.

Heuberger, B. (2002). *Cultural diversity building skills for awareness, understanding and application*. Dubuque, IA: Kendall/Hunt Publishers.

Hick, S. F., & Furlotte, C. (2009). Mindfulness and social justice approaches: Bridging the mind and society in social work practice. *Canadian Social Work Review*, 26(1), 5–24.

Holmes, G. G. (2009). "Power concedes nothing without demand" educating future teachers about the value of dissent in a democratic society. In M. Gordon (Ed.), *Reclaiming dissent civics education for the 21st century*. Rotterdam: Sense Publishers.

Howard, G. (2006). *We can't teach what we don't know*. New York, NY: Teachers College Press.

Hurston, Z. N. (1978). *Their eyes were watching god*. Urbana, IL: University of Illinois Press.

Judith, A. (1996). *Eastern body, western mind, psychology and the chakra system as a path to the self*. Berkeley, CA: Celestial Arts Publishing.

Kabat-Zinn, J. (1994). *Wherever you go, there you are*. New York, NY: Hyperian.

Kabat-Zinn, J. (2011). Cited in Nugent, P., Moss, D., Barnes, R., & Wilks, J. (2011). *Clear(ing) space: mindfulness-based reflective practice*. Published online: 25 January 2011. Retrieved December 17, 2016 from http://dx.doi.org/10.1080/14623943.2011.541088

Katzenmeyer, M., & Moller, G. (1996). *Awakening the sleeping giant. Leadership development for teachers*. Thousand Oaks, CA: Corwin Press, Inc.

King, M. L. (1967). *Why I am opposed to the war in Vietnam*. Sermon delivered at the Ebenezer Baptist Church on April 30, 1967.

Kohl, H. (1999). Social justice and leadership in education: Commentary. *International Journal of Leadership in Education: Theory & Practice—1464–5092*, 2(3), 307–311.

Ladson-Billings, G. (1995). Toward a theory of culturally relevant pedagogy. *American Educational Research Journal*, 32(3), 465–491.

Lambert, L. (2003). Leadership redefined: An evocative context for teacher leadership. *School Leadership & Management*, 23(4), 421–430.

Marshall, C., & Oliva, M. (2010). *Leadership for social justice*. New York, NY: Allyn & Bacon.

Nieto, S., & Bode, P. (2012). *Affirming diversity the sociopolitical context of multicultural education*. Boston, MA: Allyn & Bacon.

Nieto, S. (2000). *Affirming Diversity*. New York: Addison Wesley Longman.

Nugent, P., Moss, D., Barnes, R., & Wilks, J. (2011). *Clear(ing) space: Mindfulness-based reflective practice*. Published online: 25 January 2011. Retrieved December 17, 2016 from http://dx.doi.org/10.1080/14623943.2011.541088

Palmer, P. J. (1998). *The courage to teach: Exploring the inner landscape of a teacher's life*. San Francisco, CA: Jossey-Bass.

Quinnipiac University School of Education. (2007). Conceptual Framework. Unpublished document.

Quinnipiac University School of Education. (2014). Conceptual Framework. Unpublished document.

Rapp, D. (2002). Social justice and the importance of rebellious imaginations. *Journal of School Leadership*, 12(3), 226–245. Cited in Capper, C., Theoharis, G., & Sebastian, J. (2006).

Toward a framework for preparing leaders for social justice. *Journal of Educational Administration, 44*(3), 209–224. Retrieved February 22, 2012 from http://www.centerx.gseis. ucla.edu/principal-leadership/documents/Capper%20Theoharis%20-%20Sebastian%20 Framework%20for%20Prprng%20Ldrs%20for%20social%20justice.pdf

Rich, A. (n.a.). Cited in Maher, F. A., & Tetreault, M. K. T. (2001). The feminist classroom, dynamics of gender, race and privilege (p. 201). Oxford: Rowman and Littlefield, Inc.

Scheurich, J. J., & Skrla, L. (2003). *Leadership for equity and excellence.* Thousand Oaks, CA: Corwin Press.

Shafir, R. Z. (2003). *The Zen of listening: Mindful communication in the age of distraction.* Wheaton, IL: Quest Books.

Shulman, L. S. (1992). Merging content knowledge and pedagogy: An interview with Lee Shulman (Interviewer: Denis Sparks). *Journal of Staff Development* 13.1: 14–17.

Shultz, J., Skilton-Sylvester, E., & Shultz, N. P. (2007). Exploring global connections: Dismantling the international/multicultural divide. *Diversity and Democracy, 10*(3). On-line publication of the American Association of Colleges and Universities. Retrieved July 19, 2008 from http://www.diversityweb.org/DiversityDemocracy/vol10no3/shultz.cfm

Shultz, J., Skilton-Sylvester, E., Shultz, N. P. (2007). Exploring global connections: Dismantling the international/multicultural divide. *Diversity and Democracy,* Vol. 10, No. 3. On-line publication of the American Association of Colleges and Universities. Retrieved July 19, 2008 from http://www.diversityweb.org/DiversityDemocracy/vol10no3/shultz.cfm

Sleeter, C. (1996). *Multicultural education as social activism.* Albany: State University of New York Press.

Staats, C., Capatosto, K., Wright, R. A., Jackson, V. W. (2016). *State of the Science: Implicit Bias Review, 2016 Edition.* Kirwan Institute. Retrieved August 2, 2016 from http://kirwaninstitute. osu.edu/wp-content/uploads/2016/07/implicit-bias-2016.pdf

Tatum, B. D. (1997). *Why are all of the black kids sitting together in the cafeteria? And other conversations about race.* New York, NY: Basic Books.

Tiedt, P. L., & Tiedt, I. M. (2002). *Multicultural teaching—A handbook of activities, information and resources.* Boston, MA: Allyn and Bacon.

Wasley, P. (2006). *Accreditor of education schools drops controversial "social justice" standard for teacher candidates.* Retrieved from http://chronicle.com/temp/email2.php?id=h25rbnmq6f QGXfpzCgFBcwvFnKhvvh82

York-Barr, J., Sommers, W., Ghere, G., & Montie, J. (2006). Reflective practice for continuous learning. In J. York-Barr, W. Sommers, G. Ghere, & J. Montie (Eds.), *Reflective practice to improve schools. An action guide for educators.* CA, Corwin: Thousand Oaks.

Young, M. D., & Laible, J. (2000). White racism, anti-racism, and school leadership preparation. *Journal of School Leadership, 10*(5), 374–415. Cited in Capper, C., Theoharis, G., & Sebastian, J. (2006). Toward a framework for preparing leaders for social justice. *Journal of Educational Administration, 44*(3), 209–224. Retrieved February 22, 2012 from http://www. centerx.gseis.ucla.edu/principal-leadership/documents/Capper%20Theoharis%20-%20 Sebastian%20Framework%20for%20Prprng%20Ldrs%20for%20social%20justice.pdf

Zeichner, K., & Liston, D. P. (1996). *Reflective teaching: An introduction.* New York: Routledge

·10·

CONCLUSION

An Empowering Vision: Harnessing Bias and the Possibility for Change

This chapter provides an overview of several themes that connect social justice to teaching and school leadership. It argues that *courageous conversations* about diversity and race, and prejudice, and bias, focused on social justice and school leadership, are a necessary part of personal transformation and school reform. Building on the premise that talking about racism and bias is a first step toward eliminating them, the chapter provides a number of methodologies including multicultural education, culturally responsive education, and anti-bias education which help undermine personal biases. Although the chapter underscores the importance of confronting biases, it also acknowledges the difficulty of assessing and deconstructing them. This is because racial identity development, and the way humans are socialized to *believe* what they *believe* and *do* what they *do*, is inherently imprecise, and cannot easily be captured by statistics. Finally, the chapter invites a reconsideration of the intersection of social justice, ethical behavior, and moral transformative teaching, and school leadership, and it argues that transformation is possible when confronting bias is the first step.

Keywords: implicit bias, prejudice, double-consciousness, diversity, culturally responsive education, social justice, dysconsciousness, privilege, (de)biasing, multicultural education

"Our continuing existence depends on a diversity of life that surrounds and quite literally inhabits us. And still we have an innate distrust of diversity. It is fear that makes talking about diversity so difficult. Fear that I will say something that will offend you or reveal my ignorance or prejudices. Fear that you will think less of me after I speak. ... We need to be and feel heard, to be willing to listen without feeling that we must change to conform to another's way of thinking and being. Until we can create a place for such conversations to occur, I doubt we will be able to create new ways of being together that honor us all."

—Linda Ellinor and Glenna Gerard

"I am an invisible man. No, I am not a spook like those who haunted Edgar Allen Poe; nor am I one of your Hollywood movie ectoplasms. I am a man of substance, of flesh and bone, fiber and liquids—and I might even be said to possess a mind. I am invisible, understand, simply because people refuse to see me. Like the bodiless heads you see sometimes in circus sideshows, it is as though I have been surrounded by mirrors of hard, distorting glass. When they approach me, they see only my surroundings, themselves, or figments of their imagination—indeed, everything and anything except me."

—Ralph Ellison, Invisible Man

When Ralph Ellison published Invisible Man in 1952, it was long before the debates about the *implicit* nature of bias and prejudice against Black men. In 1952, the focus was on explicit manifestations of racism and social injustice in America like cross burnings, Jim Crow laws, and lynching; 1952 was two years before school integration was legalized. Brown vs. the Board of Education had not yet become law, which means that the nation was still operating under the guidelines of Plessy vs. Ferguson's segregationist policies that established clear demarcations between how different races should coexist in American society. And yet, Ellison's vision of the 'race' problem in America is consistent with Dubois' idea of *double consciousness* described in 1903 as a psychic split in Black racial identity, and Woodson's 1933 charge that 'Negroes' were living in a country where schools were teaching Black men to despise their own skin. However, Ellison moves the conversation into a different existential realm by seeing the Black Man as *invisible* within a fiercely democratic country that valorized individual rights and freedoms, and promised equality and justice for all. By implication, Ellison was saying that an *invisible* man has *invisible* freedoms because if *he* has does not exist in the consciousness of the White establishment, his *rights* can have no substance.

    And yet, even in the context of what Toni Morrison (1992) has called a 'wholly racialized' society, democracy demands more than this. It places a heavy burden on Americans of all colors, shapes, and sizes to *do the right thing*, and to stand up for *justice*. The schooled and the unschooled, the rich and the poor, the young and the old all know that democracy is demanding. It imposes a deep, and abiding responsibility on its citizens to be fair and just, and it demands that all Americans profess, and live up to, those values (*that's why we're expected to restate our pledge again and again in public settings*). This makes some Americans simultaneously love and take pride in the *idea* of America, while secretly resenting the unrelenting pressure to be 'American' in the purest and truest Constitutional sense of what that actually means. As a result, most Americans simultaneously flaunt and cower under the words *freedom*, and *justice*, and *equality for all*, because they make Americans proud to be American, but they also shame or anger them when they are accused of falling short of achieving their own professed ideals.

Yes. Democracy weighs heavily on Americans. And, it should weigh most heavily on Americans who are responsible for educating American children to know, believe in, and embody the values all Americans instinctively pledge to uphold. Nowhere in the lexicon of American values is there a place for bias and prejudice and injustice and racism, and if we know about injustice, ignore it, and simply move on, we become accomplices in undermining American values and trivializing the principles that supposedly make America that *exceptional* embodiment of the Biblical *city on a hill*.

Over fifty years ago, the fictive protagonist in *The Invisible Man* said "I am invisible, understand, simply because people refuse to see me." The tragic reality is that the average Black male in an urban school today can utter the same words, express the same psychic terror, and expect to be subjected to a frightening array of abuses from society at large, as well as in many of their own schools. The irony is that schools function *in loco parentis*; legally, they are surrogate parents for *all* of the children in their care. This means that they are charged with educating, protecting, and acting in the best interests of *all* children regardless of race, class, ethnicity, religion, gender, sexual orientation, etc. However, data disaggregated by race overwhelmingly confirms that American schools are increasingly segregated by race and class, and that students of color, especially Black males, are the most stigmatized and marginalized, and the most at-risk for academic failure, high drop-out rates, and antisocial behavior. The data confirms and reconfirms that "[w]e take the students who have less to begin with and then systematically give them less in school. In fact, we give these students less of everything that we believe makes a difference" (Haycock, 2001, p. n.a.).

The data also confirms and reconfirms that America is a highly racialized and sometimes racist country. Institutional discrimination and individual acts of bias are strong indicators of the problems that continue to plague the country. To understand the problem of bias better, we can look at it like a chronic disease, because even though we now know that we cannot eradicate it like polio or the measles, we can inoculate ourselves against it. However, we must first acknowledge that it exists, and that it lives in all of us. The research suggests that all humans are hosts, and are subject to implicit and explicit biases. The question is, is the relationship a parasitic or symbiotic one? If parasitic, biases will weaken and destroy us over time; if symbiotic, we can control and use bias as the motivation to become better than we are as individuals, and to become the nation we say we want to be.

Bias Cannot Be Eradicated, But It Can Be Harnessed

The good news is that although there are significant challenges, prejudice and bias are not insurmountable, and social justice is not simply an ephemeral ideal; it can be achieved in schools. However, it requires committed equity-driven, anti-bias school leadership, not just from formal 'leaders' like principals, school superintendents, department chairs, and such. Leadership happens in large and small ways, and in formal and informal settings. It happens in classrooms, and department meetings, at extracurricular events, at school board meetings, staff development workshops, at basketball games, etc. etc. Teachers should be *leaders*, and school leaders should be *teachers*, and both have an obligation to teach their students to be advocates for justice.

Each of the chapters in this book provided a background for *courageous conversations* about diversity and race, and prejudice, and bias, in the context of social justice and school leadership. Social justice and school leadership are the unifying principles that lay at the core of the chapters, all of which are designed to examine the issues from a variety of perspectives including classroom teaching, building and district level leadership, as well as teacher and leadership preparation. Building on the premise that talking about racism and bias is a first step toward eliminating them, the book argues that discrimination and democracy should not coexist in a democratic society but especially not in the educative process. Beginning with an exploration of the resistance to confronting 'race' in educational settings, and the response to this resistance through aggressive anti-bias curricular approaches that valorize multiculturalism, the book described a number of methodologies including multicultural education, culturally responsive education, and anti-bias education. The implication is that in a democracy, good teaching and leading are synonymous with social justice advocacy. The question should not be *if* teachers and leaders should be advocates, but *how*, and their highest goal should be to help *create a society in which injustice is intolerable*.

Significantly, the research presented showed that there is a countervailing process underway in the sense that as America's population is becoming more ethnically, linguistically, and culturally diverse, *diversity* as a concept is more contested and more controversial. As a result, culturally responsive practices are being, if not lost, increasingly considered superfluous, or approached in superficial ways that do not address deep-seated issues of discrimination and the cluster of *isms* that allow injustice to thrive and flourish even among well-meaning people. And yet, if asked, most Americans would concede that *in-justice* is *un-American*, and opposed to everything America traditionally stands for. The problem is trying to reconcile America's core values, and the persistent, even violent way injustice is manifested in society and schools. The existence of a permanent racialized underclass overpopulated by black, brown, undereducated people who are often hopeless and poor tarnishes us as a nation. And, the research shows that it's not enough to hide behind the racialized 'achievement gap' data and ignore the fact that 'achievement gaps' are symptomatic of other racialized gaps in housing, health care, political access, policing, and criminal justice. Moreover, discussions about the 'achievement gap' are implicitly or explicitly about justice or the lack thereof, and in America, they always implicitly or explicitly involve race.

Although a significant amount of data is presented in the book, the underlying theme is that data should not be *the tail that wags the dog*, so to speak. In other words, data has significant limitations when it comes to understanding personal attitudes and belief systems that inform the *human* behaviors, decisions, and policymaking that may or may not conform to one's espoused values and ideals. This is because racial identity development, and the way humans are socialized to *believe* what they *believe*, and *do* what they *do*, is inherently imprecise and cannot easily be captured by statistics. "Everything that can be counted does not necessarily count [and] everything that counts cannot necessarily be counted" (Einstein, p. n.a.), which means that the causes and motivations for man-made social inequities, and the presence or absence of personal and/or institutional bias require introspection not necessarily more data collection. This is especially true when it comes to racial identity development, and how this factors into teaching, leadership, and policymaking because data-driven, fact-based approaches to education, although important, can mask other issues because they run counter to the way humans develop racial identities. They run counter to the way humans form judgments about abstract *human* issues like *justice* and *fairness*, and ignoring this is not only self-defeating, it stymies progress, and helps sustain racialized achievement gaps and other inequities.

In one way or another, the chapters have challenged educators to *see* themselves, their social contexts, and their students differently, and to reconceptualize their role as educators, because the problem of bias is persistent, highly politicized, and appears to be worsening. In part, this is because explicit bias is either ignored, or those who want to address it lack the skills to do so, or are reluctant to risk being ostracized by their colleagues. In part, bias continues to contaminate the educative process because implicit bias is *implicit*. In a sense, it is *invisible*, which allows some educators to actually *believe* that they believe in justice and change while clinging to practices like zero-tolerance, or racialized tracking policies that continue to harm members of traditionally marginalized groups.

These issues are complicated by the fact that the concept of 'diversity' is somewhat amorphous because society is becoming more aware of, and more sensitive to, all of the ways that one can be *diverse*. And, this expanded sense of 'diversity' is forcing society to move its definition beyond the limiting and limited confines of 'race.' This suggests that as we begin to rethink 'race' and 'diversity,' we also need to rethink bias and how we *can* respond to it with a mindset that moves past the discredited ideas of *color blindness* and *color muteness* because talking about bias *does not* create it any more than talking about racism makes you a racist.

Much of the theoretical basis of the book is informed by the wisdom and work of Maxine Greene who wrote about what she called the *mystification* of social justice by pre- and in-service educators. Mystification, according to Greene, is a surreptitious uncritical acceptance of social inequities and the status quo. Conceptually, this is similar to what Joyce King calls *dysconsciousness*, an "... uncritical habit of mind (including perceptions, attitudes, assumptions, and beliefs) that justifies inequity and exploitation by accepting the existing order of things as given" (King, 1991, p. 135).

Greene argues that some preservice teachers are being programmed to embrace rather than deconstruct institutional discrimination through an uncritical acceptance of what she calls an *unexamined surface reality* that is presented as *"natural,"* and *"fundamentally unquestionable"* (Greene, 1976, p. 10). In other words, according to Greene and King, teachers are being taught to overlook the constructed character of social reality, and this is connected to an inherent, socially sanctioned resistance to being reflectively self-critical and self-analytical, as well as a resistance to questioning whether or not the decisions they make are intrinsically *right*, and *just*, and *bias-free*. In surreptitious ways, *mystification* and *dysconsciousness* can inform classroom practice, as well as policy decisions on the leadership level.

For example, in a school setting, *mystification* and *dysconsciousness* can account for a number of things some choose to ignore or normalize such as an erroneous belief in social hierarchies that privilege some groups because of color, class ethnicity, religion, or sexual orientation. *Mystification* and *dysconsciousness* can cause some educators to *not see* the causes and consequences of social ills like poverty, homelessness, the school-to-prison pipeline, racialized gaps in academic achievement, and economic opportunity that can hide behind statistical data. *Mystification* and *dysconsciousness* can cause some educators to *not see* their own privilege, or their own biases, and how privilege and bias shape self-perception, professional relationships, and the decisions that they make every day on behalf of, or against, the best interests of their students.

Dysconsciousness is the result of a racial socialization process that begins in childhood as dramatized by Bartoli et al. (2014), and by adulthood, these complex ways of thinking, speaking, and behaving have taken deep root, and *mystification* can become normalized. According to Allport (1979), society condones a kind of *double-dealing* and *double-talking* that segments personal biases and public positions. It's not difficult to imagine what this could look like on an individual or interpersonal level. One example would be that a white male could *worship* a black sports figure, but simultaneously resist the idea of welcoming him into the family as a son-in-law, into the social circle as a friend, or into the community as a neighbor. Another example would be social studies teachers teaching about American government and the Constitution, who simultaneously support punitive zero-tolerance policies that disproportionately target, and perhaps criminalize, students of color *in their own classes* without seeing a conflict with the fundamental democratic value *of justice for all*.

Psychologists and social scientists have probed deeply into these seemingly contradictory attitudes and behaviors, and have produced some answers. Among other things they have identified what some are calling *modern* forms of racism which are subtle, multifaceted, and more difficult to detect and address. Researchers have categorized them as follows: symbolic racism (indirect expressions of racism sometimes expressed as opposition to policies rather than to people), ambivalent racism (characterized by conflicting feelings about racial/ethnic minorities, etc.), aversive racism (belief in concept of social equality but experience a personal aversion toward racial minorities), and modern racism (seeing racism as wrong, but considers equalizing resources among diverse groups unfair). These subtle forms of racism and bias make *(de)biasing* more complex, and more necessary. However, these subtle forms of racism and bias also make *(de)biasing* more challenging because they are more difficult to detect, identify, and disrupt through exposure to counter-stereotypes and counter-stereotypical individuals, or through anti-bias training. And yet, as several chapters make clear, *(de)biasing* needs careful facilitation, and equity-driven leadership because bias does not simply go away over time like a bad cold.

Some educational researchers have proposed multicultural education as a panacea to address discrimination and bias, and although this is an important step in the right direction, it is important to be aware that multicultural education is amorphous, and it is unhelpful to treat multicultural education as though it were monolithic, "static and homogeneous rather than dynamic and growing with its own internal debates" (Sleeter, 1996, p. 4). Different approaches to multicultural education have different outcomes and different degrees of success, and it is important not to approach it as a *cure* for discrimination and injustice, etc.; it should be approached as a vital part of transformative school reform.

Although most forms of multicultural education generate controversy from one degree to another, multicultural social justice education is one of the most aggressive and comprehensive approaches designed to interrupt bias, and institutionalize justice in the overall educative process. It is infused with the concepts of social dominance, and race, and privilege, and implicit bias, and prejudice, and it seeks to uncover and disrupt unfair school practices that privilege some students and (dis)privilege others. This means that effective multicultural education is explicitly about school reform, and experience tells us that reform is synonymous with *change*, and *change* is usually accompanied by resistance and fear. And yet, "[p]eople do not resist change per se. People resist loss" (Heifetz & Linsky, 2002, p. 11).

Strong equity-driven leadership is not only imperative, it is also dangerous. "To lead is to live dangerously because when leadership counts, when you lead people through difficult change, you challenge what people hold dear—their daily habits, tools, loyalties and ways of thinking—with nothing more to offer perhaps than a possibility … People push back when you disturb the personal and institutional equilibrium they know" (Heifetz & Linsky, 2002, p. 2). With this in mind, equity-driven leaders should approach (de)biasing with sensitivity, because confronting personal biases is akin to a loss of self. It means *turning yourself inside out*, which is scary; it takes courage, and a commitment to *doing the right thing*. For equity-driven leaders, it also means framing personal transformation in much broader contexts because in a sense, they are also responsible for transforming schools, and by extension they are responsible for transforming society.

Without strong, committed equity-driven leadership, we embrace stasis and reject social progress; instead of moving forward, we will be moving backward, and we will be taking the students with us. And yet, what constitutes equity-driven leadership is problematic. Several chapters raise the issue of what amounts to a kind of *divine right* of leaders to believe that as 'leaders,' they are endowed with special knowledge and special privileges that absolve them from the need to be trained, self-reflective, or even questioned about their own biases. This perspective literally gives them the power to rise above, and ignore, the process of (de)biasing themselves, even though they may publicly espouse a commitment to eliminating inequities and bias in their schools. Whether they believe what they say or not can be murky and unclear because implicit biases operate far beneath the surface of human consciousness. The irony is that anti-bias training may even be going on in their schools because school leaders have the *power* to require it for their own teachers and staff even though they may be personally disengaged from the process.

A leader's unwillingness to be engaged in personal (de)biasing, and acknowledge a mindset that may help to sustain unfair policies and practices may point to a pattern of cognitive dissonance that exposes a tension between their actions and their personal belief systems. Although much of this is speculation, and subject to interpretation, what is crystal clear is that a disproportionately high percentage of students of color continue to be marginalized in schools and continue to languish at the bottom of the academic and social hierarchy. There is no dispute about this.

Again, and again, the book returns to the idea that as a democratic nation, Americans place a very high value on equality, fairness, and fair play, and misguidedly assume that these outcomes naturally emerge if one is a good, fair-minded, moral person. This, some believe, ensures that you will make decisions that are unbiased, and fair, and naturally serve the best interests of all students. Yet we know that this is not always true. For example, many ardent American slaveholders were considered 'good' church-going Christians. Clearly racism and a strong sense of morality not only can coexist, but also can nurture each other, even in a democracy. However, as Maxine Green has pointed out, "democracy is, and has been, an open possibility not a possession."

Although it is clear that these are very complex questions with no simple answers, it is equally clear that these questions pose particular challenges for educators, especially school leaders, because, among other things, they invite a reconsideration of the implications of ethical behavior and moral transformative leadership. Although Palmer's prescient statement, "we teach who we are" (Palmer, 1998, p. 2) is undeniably true, it is also true that we lead where we want to go. And, where we want to go is informed by everything that shapes our thinking and our being. Despite what may appear to be insurmountable challenges, change, even transformation, is possible because we do have some control over who we are, what we believe, and the attitudes and beliefs that guide the decisions we make in both our personal and professional lives. This change can be the gift we leave for our children.

***

In the end, democracy is what we have to guide us; its core values provide the template for how we should live, how we should interact socially, and how we should design our schools. Democracy is implacable and demanding. It imposes a deep, and abiding responsibility on its leaders to show us what justice is and is not, and to show us how to be fair and just as a nation. And, if we believe that change is an important part of progress, and if we want our children to actually believe the words they are encouraged to pledge daily, and if we ever want to actualize those lofty ideals of individual freedom and justice for all, we have to listen differently, and learn deeply, and stretch ourselves, unless, in the end, democracy is no more than an abstract ideal forever beyond our reach. I hope not.

References

Allport, G. (1979). *The nature of prejudice.* Cambridge, MA: Perseus Books.

Bartoli, E., Michael, A., Bentley-Edwards, K. L., Stevenson, H. C., Shor, R. F., & McClain, S. E. (2014). *Chasing colorblindness: White family racial socialization.* Manuscript submitted for publication. 2014.

Einstein, A. (n.d.). Retrieved May 16, 2016 from https://www.thoughtco.com/quotes-by-albert-einstein-1779801

Ellinor, L., & Gerard, G. (1998). *Dialogue: Rediscover the transforming power of conversation.* New York, NY: John Wiley & Sons.

Ellison, R. (1992). *Invisible man* (p. 3). New York, NY: Random House.

Greene, M. (1976). Challenging mystification: Educational foundations in dark times. *Educational Studies, 7*(1), 9–29.

Haycock, K. (2001). Closing the achievement gap. *Educational Leadership, 58*(6), 6–11.

Heifetz, R., & Linsky, M. (2002). *Leadership on the line staying alive through the dangers of leading.* Boston, MA: Harvard Business School Press.

King, J. E. (1991). Dysconscious racism. *The Journal of Negro Education, 60*(2), 133–146.

Morrison, T. (1992). *Playing in the dark.* New York, NY: Vintage Books.

Palmer, P. J. (1998). *The courage to teach: Exploring the inner landscape of a teacher's life.* San Francisco, CA: Jossey-Bass.

Sleeter, C. (1996). *Multicultural education as social activism.* Albany, NY: State University of New York Press.

APPENDICES

APPENDIX A

A CONVERSATION WITH AN IMPLICIT BIAS SKEPTIC[1]

While conversations about implicit bias are flourishing in some arenas such as the social justice field, the reality is that many people remain unfamiliar with the concept and its dynamics. This section provides a model to help guide conversations with those who have not yet been informed about this phenomenon. The tone used here mirrors that of a normal conversation in an effort to illustrate how this academic and scientific concept can be made accessible to a broader audience. Since these conversations often originate in the context of doubt or confusion from one party, the dialogue is structured to be intentionally persuasive in an effort to help counter and rebut skeptics.

I'm sorry, but I'm not familiar with that term you just mentioned—implicit bias. What are you talking about?

Oh, implicit bias? It's a fascinating concept! Implicit biases are attitudes or stereotypes that we carry around with us unconsciously. These mental associations influence our perceptions, actions, and decisions, yet because implicit biases are unconscious and involuntarily activated, we are not even aware that they exist.

So you're saying that all of this occurs in my head without my knowledge? I'm a pretty self-aware person. I even meditate and engage in reflection exercises regularly. I seriously doubt there is much going on in my mind that I do not already know.

Research indicates that even the most self-aware people only have insights into a mere fraction of their brains because so much of our cognition is unconscious. Some studies suggest that the brain is capable of processing approximately 11 million bits of information every second, but our conscious mind can handle only 40–50 of those bits. Other research estimates that our conscious mind may only be capable of handling a mere 16 bits each second. That leaves the bulk of the mental processing to the unconscious.

You may be familiar with the iceberg analogy used often in psychology when discussing Freud. The visible part of the iceberg that exists above the surface of the water is a meager fraction of the structure's overall size when you account for the bulk of it that is located underwater. In this analogy, the conscious mind is represented by the part of the iceberg that exists above the surface of the water, while the unconscious mind corresponds to the much larger portion of the iceberg. This analogy applies to conscious/unconscious processing. In fact, given that we consciously process such a tiny portion of our mental processes, it could almost be said that relative to the iceberg as a whole, we only are consciously aware of a portion of our cognition equivalent to a snowball on the top of the iceberg!

Where do these biases you're talking about come from?

Everyone has implicit biases. The implicit associations we harbor in our subconscious cause us to have feelings and attitudes about other people based on characteristics such as race, ethnicity, age, and appearance. Research suggests that these associations begin to develop very early in life as we're exposed to both direct and indirect messages. Some studies have documented implicit biases in children as young as six years old. Beyond early life experiences, the media and news programming are often regarded as influencing individuals' implicit biases. Keep in mind, though, that not all of the messages we're talking about are blatant; many are quite subtle.

Wait a minute, everyone is biased? Oh no, that can't be right. After all, I know I'm not biased. I have friends of all races and live in a very diverse community. I treat everyone equally.

Well, the reality is that everyone is susceptible to implicit biases. It's important to keep in mind that there are lots of different types of implicit bias. It is possible that while you may not have a bias with respect to certain attributes, such as perhaps gender, you may hold biases related to age, race, or other characteristics. No one is completely free of implicit biases. Even the most egalitarian people, such as judges who devote their professional careers to fairness, possess these biases.

But, come on now. It's completely obvious that biases and discrimination are considered unacceptable in modern society.

True, we have come a long way with respect to explicit bias, discrimination, and prejudice in our society. However, the reality remains that even though overt, explicit biases are less common, implicit biases remain incredibly pervasive. You have to realize that the implicit biases we've been discussing are different from explicit biases. The main difference is that explicit biases are the ones that are consciously acknowledged, while implicit biases are those that we hold without introspective awareness of their existence. While these two concepts are related, they are very distinct.

What's really fascinating—and may be helpful for you as you consider these ideas—is that our implicit associations do not necessarily align with our explicitly held beliefs. For example, consider the stereotype that males are better at math than females. As a woman, I may consciously disagree with this stereotype; however, implicitly—in my unconscious—it's perfectly possible that I may actually implicitly associate mathematic superiority with men rather than women. This goes to show that you can actually hold biases against your own ingroup; in this case my bias would be against my ingroup of females. I may have internalized that implicit association, even though consciously I would strongly disagree with the notion that women are inferior to men with respect to mathematic abilities in any way.

I don't know. It still all sounds like a bunch of psychological hokum to me. If I believe what you're telling me about how even I'm unaware of associations I'm carrying around in my own head, how is anyone else able to prove they exist?

Psychologists have been working on instruments to assess implicit associations for many years. One of the most popular and sophisticated techniques that has emerged for assessing implicit biases is the Implicit Association Test, often called the IAT. This computerized test measures the relative strength of associations between pairs of concepts. The IAT is designed as a sorting task in which individuals are asked to sort images or words that appear on a computer screen into one of two categories. The basic premise is that when two concepts are highly correlated, people are able to pair those concepts more quickly than two concepts that are not well associated. So, for example, if I told you that every time the IAT prompted you with the word 'thunder' you should place it in the same category as 'lightning,' you probably wouldn't have any problems with that task. It would come easily to you because, like most people, you associate lightning and thunder together without having to even think about it. But what if I then switched the categories and told you that every time you saw 'lightning,' you needed to place it in the same category as 'milk.' This would likely be much more difficult to do. It would probably take you longer, and you'd almost certainly make more mistakes because lightning and milk are not concepts that you typically associate easily. The IAT measures the time differentials between how long it takes participants to pair concepts in different ways. The test's categorizing tasks are completed quite quickly, and without having time to consciously think about the pairings, the test therefore is measuring the unconscious associations people hold.

This example was pretty rudimentary, but the real IAT has much more insightful tests. One popular one assesses how long it takes participants to categorize black and white faces, respectively, with 'good words' (e.g., happiness, joy, etc.) versus 'bad words' (e.g., terrible, angry, etc.). The racial group that individuals most quickly associate with the positive terms reflects a positive implicit bias toward that group. Extensive research has uncovered an implicit pro-White/anti-Black bias in most Americans.

I'm still not entirely sure why exactly I should care about implicit bias, especially if they're just hidden away in the depths of our brains anyways. Does this mean anything for people's everyday lives in the real world?

Of course! There are so many real-world effects of implicit biases across a range of domains—employment, criminal justice, health care, etc. Hundreds of scientific studies have been done to explore this phenomenon, and many of the findings are very compelling. Consider these examples: In a video game that simulates what police officers experience, research subjects were instructed to 'shoot' when an armed individual appeared on the screen and refrain from doing so when the target was instead holding an innocuous object such as a camera or wallet. Time constraints were built into the study so that participants were forced to make nearly instantaneous decisions, much like police officers often must do in real life. Findings indicated that participants tended to 'shoot' armed targets more quickly when they were African American as opposed to White, and when participants refrained from 'shooting' an armed target, these characters in the simulation tended to be White rather than African American. Research such as this highlights how implicit racial biases can influence decisions that have life or death consequences. Or, consider the health care field. A 2012 study used identical case vignettes to examine how pediatricians' implicit racial attitudes affect treatment recommendations for four common conditions that affect kids. Results indicated that as pediatricians' pro-White implicit biases increased, they were more likely to prescribe painkillers for vignette subjects who were White as opposed to Black patients. This is just one example of how understanding implicit racial biases may help explain differential health care treatment, even for youth. Because these biases are activated on an unconscious level, it's not a matter of individuals knowingly acting in discriminatory ways. Implicit bias research tells us that you don't have to have negative intent in order to have discriminatory outcomes.

That's a pretty huge statement, if you think about it. I have to admit, this is all kind of fascinating. How can I learn more?

I would encourage you to go online and take the IAT. You'll find it at http://implicit.harvard.edu. There are so many different versions available, including ones that address race, age, sexuality, religion, skin tone, and a couple related to gender, among others. The tests are very straightforward, do not take very long to finish, and are incredibly insightful.

Thanks for the info! I'll look into this further.

Note

1. Kirwan Institute for the Study of Race and Ethnicity (2013). Implicit Bias Review, 71–72.

APPENDIX B

EXAMPLES OF MICROAGGRESSIONS IN THE CLASSROOM

Definitions of Microaggressions

Microaggressions are defined as "brief and commonplace daily verbal, behavioral and environmental indignities, whether intentional or unintentional, that communicate hostile, derogatory or negative racial slights and insults that potentially have harmful or unpleasant psychological impact on the target person or group" (Solorzano, Ceja, & Yosso, 2000).

Microinsults are behaviors, actions, or verbal remarks that convey rudeness, insensitivity, or demean a person's group or social identity or heritage (Sue et al., 2007).

Microinvalidations are actions that exclude, negate, or nullify the psychological thoughts, feelings, or experiential reality of people who represent different groups (Sue et al., 2007).

Microaggressions cut across all social identities including race, ethnicity, religion, nationality, sexual orientation, gender identity, gender expression, age, disability status, socioeconomic class, and other important social dimensions. At the University of Denver, these insults and invalidations also occur across all majors, departments, and colleges.

Examples of Microaggressions

- Continuing to mispronounce the names of students after they have corrected you time and time again. "Is Jose Cuinantila here?" "I am here, but my name is Jesús Quintanilla."
- Scheduling tests and project due dates on religious or cultural holidays. "It has just been pointed out to me that I scheduled the mid-term during Rosh HaShanah, but we are OK because I don't see any Jewish students in the class."
- Setting low expectations for students from particular groups or high schools in Denver. "Oh, so Robert, you're from Montbello High School? You are going to need lots of academic help in my class!"
- Calling on and validating men and ignoring women students during class discussions. "Let's call on John again. He seems to have lots of great responses to some of these problems."
- Using inappropriate humor in class that degrades students from different groups. "Anyone want to hear a good joke? Ok, well there was a Jew, a Mexican, and a Black. The Mexican says to the. ..."
- Expressing racially charged political opinions in class assuming that the targets of those opinions do not exist in class. "I think illegal aliens are criminals because they are breaking the law and need to be rounded up and sent back to Mexico."
- Hosting debates in class that place students from groups who may represent the minority opinion in class in a difficult position. "Today we are going to have a debate on immigration. I expect the three Latino students and a few of you to argue in favor of immigration. The rest of you will provide arguments against immigration."
- Denying the experiences of students by questioning the credibility and validity of their stories. "I've eaten and shopped plenty of times in West Denver and it's nothing like you describe it. How long have you lived there and who are you hanging out with?"
- Assigning class projects that are heterosexist, sexist, racist, or promote other oppressions. "For the class project, I want you to think about a romantic relationship that you have had with a member of the opposite sex. Think and write about your observations."
- Using heterosexist examples or sexist language in class. "Atoms sometimes attract each other like this male and female here. At the same time, atoms sometimes repel each other like these two males here."

- Assigning projects that ignore differences in socioeconomic class status. "For this class, you are required to visit four art galleries located in the downtown area. The entrance fees vary but I am sure you can afford it."
- Singling students out in class because of their backgrounds. "You're Asian! Can you tell us what the Japanese think about our trade policies?"
- Assuming that all students are from the United States and fully understand the English language and culture (i.e., be aware that there may be International students in the class). "What do you mean you have never heard of *The Cosby Show*? Where have you been hiding?"
- Discouraging students from working on projects that explore their own social identities. "If you are Native American, I don't want you to write your paper on Native Americans. You already know everything about that group and besides you will be biased in your writing."
- Asking people with hidden disabilities to identify themselves in class. "This is the last time that I am going to ask. Anybody with a disability who needs extra help, raise your hand!"
- Ignoring student-to-student microaggressions, even when the interaction is not course-related. "Don't be retarded! That party this weekend was so gay."

Making Assumptions About Students and Their Backgrounds

- Assuming that all Latino students speak Spanish. "You're Latino and you don't speak Spanish? You should be ashamed of yourself!"
- Assuming that all Asians are good at math. "I know who I'm calling on a lot to work some of the math problems in this class—Mr. Nguyen!"
- Assuming that all African-Americans know about poverty and the "Ghetto." "Mr. Summers! We just read about poverty among Blacks in America. Does this fit your experience and can you tell us about it?"
- Assuming that all Native Americans are knowledgeable about the 500 plus diverse tribes that exist in the United States. "Many Native American tribes are in favor of using casinos to increase revenues and many others are against it. Mr. Begay, as a Navajo what are your thoughts?"
- Assuming that all Jewish students are well versed in the Israeli–Palestinian conflict and history and that they all have the same opinions about that complex situation. "Oh, your Jewish! Can you tell us about what the Israelis think about Jewish settlements in the West Bank?"

- Assuming the gender of any student. Moreover, continuing to mis-use pronouns even after a student, transgender or not, indicates their preferred gender pronoun to you. "I would like for Mike to share her stories related to her life as a young woman growing up in New York City."
- Assuming all students fit the traditional student profile and are profi-cient in the use of computers. "All you millennials are on Facebook. I will post the evite for the class project on the site."
- Disregarding religious traditions or their details. For example, Rama-dan involves fasting from sunrise to sundown, so pressuring observant students to attend a food-focused event is disrespectful. "I am invit-ing you all over to my house for dinner after class next week to dis-cuss your projects. Ali, I know its Ramadan, but hope you'll join us anyway."
- Forcing students with nonobvious disabilities to "out" themselves or discuss them publically. "If anyone has a disability, raise your hand right now so that we can make special accommodations for you."

Suggestions for Addressing Microaggressions in the Classroom

1. Do not expect students to be experts on any experiences beyond their own and do not make them speak for their entire group (or others). For example, just because a student is Latino does not mean that they have an academic background in the study of Latinos. The same can be said about African-Americans, members of the GLBTIQ commu-nity, Jewish students, Students with Disabilities, etc. (See 'Singled Out' document on the Office of Teaching & Learning website, under teaching resources.)

2. Do not assume that the groups that you are talking about are not represented in the classroom. A professor who states "Illegal aliens are criminals because they have broken the law in coming to the U.S." may be assuming that there are no undocumented students in the classroom. Moreover, they are not aware of how unsafe those stu-dents feel after hearing those comments. The same goes for making pejorative statements about people from different areas of the region, United States, or the world (e.g., "People from Aurora, CO are on welfare and lazy," "People from Boulder are left-wing nuts").

3. Set high expectations for all students. For example: "You are all very bright and talented. I know that you will do well in my class. I have high expectations for everyone of you." In contrast, do not say: "Those of you from West High School will probably need a lot of help in my class."

4. Do not assume that all students in your class have good command of the English language or have intimate knowledge of U.S. culture. Many International students are not familiar with U.S. slang words or other language idiosyncrasies. Often, many of these students are using electronic translators in class as you lecture and present information.

5. When you are studying and discussing in class different group identities or issues related to specific groups (immigration, same-sex marriage, affirmative action), do not lock eyes with a student whom you think represents one of those groups. Your action assumes the identities and opinions of the students, potentially 'outs' that student, and puts the individual on the spot. In addition, all the other students in your class will also notice what you are doing.

6. Work to create a safe environment for all identities in the classroom by establishing ground rules and expectations regarding discussions about and presentations on issues of diversity. (See the 'Diversity in the Classroom' section on the Office of Teaching & Learning website, under teaching resources.)

7. Debates are one technique that instructors often use in class to explore and get students engaged in issues. However, it is important to distinguish between debates and dialogues. Debates are about people discussing issues and competing to see who has the 'best' response. They have the explicit assumption that someone will win and someone will lose. Dialogues, on the other hand, are about achieving greater levels of understanding by listening to each other as we delve deeper into issues. In the end, whichever technique you use, make sure that you establish ground rules and set the context for the activity.

8. If you are going to express your political opinions in the classroom, understand that there is a risk of silencing students who do not agree with your views. As a faculty member, when you express your views to students you are doing so out of a position of power. That is, students may be afraid to express themselves given that they know your position on an issue and that their grade may be on the line. Similarly, be aware of how balanced you are in challenging student opinions that do or do not agree with your own.

9. If you are going to bring in guest speakers, make sure that your objectives are clear in bringing those individuals to class—clear to you, the class, and the guest. If the reason is to introduce a particular perspective, try to balance the discussion by inviting different guest speakers with other perspectives.

10. It is ok to use humor in class. However, make sure that it is appropriate humor that does not target or degrade any student in the class or group of people overall. Classrooms are for engaging issues and learning concepts and new ideas; not having students, faculty, or guests mock or denigrate people.

11. Be cognizant that microaggressions are also directed by students against other students. Be prepared to interrupt those incidents, too. Even if you are not sure how to address the climate issue in the moment, it is appropriate classroom management to stop problematic behavior immediately. You can follow up with individual students or the entire class later, after reflecting and/or consulting with colleagues on how best to do so.

12. In those cases where students do have the courage to contact you and point out that they were offended by a remark that you made or an action that you undertook, listen to them. As indicated above, given that you are in a position of power it probably took a lot of courage for them to raise the issue with you. ...
(Portman, J., Bui, T. T., Ogaz, J., & Treviño, J. (n.a.). *Microaggressions in the classroom*. A report for the University of Denver, Center for Multicultural Excellence, Denver, CO. http://otl.du.edu/teaching-resources/creating-an-inclusive-classroom)

INDEX

R

S

W

Studies in Criticality

General Editor
Shirley R. Steinberg

Counterpoints publishes the most compelling and imaginative books being written in education today. Grounded on the theoretical advances in criticalism, feminism, and postmodernism in the last two decades of the twentieth century, Counterpoints engages the meaning of these innovations in various forms of educational expression. Committed to the proposition that theoretical literature should be accessible to a variety of audiences, the series insists that its authors avoid esoteric and jargonistic languages that transform educational scholarship into an elite discourse for the initiated. Scholarly work matters only to the degree it affects consciousness and practice at multiple sites. Counterpoints' editorial policy is based on these principles and the ability of scholars to break new ground, to open new conversations, to go where educators have never gone before.

For additional information about this series or for the submission of manuscripts, please contact:

Shirley R. Steinberg
c/o Peter Lang Publishing, Inc.
29 Broadway, 18th floor
New York, New York 10006

To order other books in this series, please contact our Customer Service Department:

(800) 770-LANG (within the U.S.)
(212) 647-7706 (outside the U.S.)
(212) 647-7707 FAX

Or browse online by series:
www.peterlang.com